Leila Christenbury • Ken Lindblom

FOURTH EDITION

MAKING THE JOURNEY

Being and Becoming
a Teacher of English
Language Arts

Heinemann

DEDICATED TO TEACHERS™

Heinemann
361 Hanover Street
Portsmouth, NH 03801–3912
www.heinemann.com

Offices and agents throughout the world

> *The authors have dedicated a great deal of time and effort to writing the content of this book, and their written expression is protected by copyright law. We respectfully ask that you do not adapt, reuse, or copy anything on third-party (whether for-profit or not-for-profit) lesson-sharing websites. As always, we're happy to answer any questions you may have.*
>
> **—Heinemann Publishers**

The authors and publisher wish to thank those who have generously given permission to reprint borrowed material:

Excerpts from the Common Core State Standards © Copyright 2010. National Governors Association Center for Best Practices and Council of Chief State School Officers. All rights reserved.

Acknowledgments for borrowed material continue on page 392.

Library of Congress Cataloging-in-Publication Data
Names: Christenbury, Leila. | Lindblom, Ken.
Title: Making the journey : being and becoming a teacher of English language
    arts / Leila Christenbury, Ken Lindblom.
Description: Fourth edition. | Portsmouth, NH : Heinemann, [2016] | Includes
    bibliographical references and index.
Identifiers: LCCN 2016029351 | ISBN 9780325078212
Subjects: LCSH: Language arts (Secondary)—United States. | Teaching. |
    English philology—Study and teaching—United States—Vocational guidance. |
    English language—Study and teaching—United States. | Classroom
    management—United States. | English teachers—Training of.
Classification: LCC LB1631 .C4486 2016 | DDC 428.0071/2—dc23

LC record available at https://lccn.loc.gov/2016029351

Illustrations of the authors are based on author photographs, for which we'd like to thank Jean-Philippe Cyprès–Photographer (Leila) and Jeanne Neville (Ken).

Editor: *Sue Paro*
Production: *Vicki Kasabian*
Illustrations of authors: *Jim Roldan*
Cover and text designs: *Suzanne Heiser*
Typesetter: *Kim Arney*
Manufacturing: *Steve Bernier*

Printed in the United States of America on acid-free paper
20 19 18 17 16   PAH   1 2 3 4 5

to Paul and Leila,
my first teachers
—LC

to Patty
—KL

IF IT IS DARK
WHEN THIS IS GIVEN TO YOU,
HAVE CARE FOR ITS CONTENT
WHEN THE MOON SHINES.

—Robert Creeley,
"A Form of Women" (*For Love*)

CONTENTS

ACKNOWLEDGMENTS

The idea of *Making the Journey* was born around 1992, it was written over the next two years, and it was first published in 1994. Since then, it has had an interesting life, moving through three decades and four editions. The book has acquired, along the way, readers, adopters, contributors, and now, in 2016, an invaluable coauthor. Begun as a book in which Leila Christenbury told stories about her classroom teaching and offered both research findings and practical advice, it has, with the addition of Ken Lindblom, become richer and wider with different stories, ideas, resources, a stronger sense of humor, and a new perspective.

What has not changed is the heart of this book. Both of us, Leila and Ken, use the lessons from our own years of high school and middle school teaching. Both of us, Ken and Leila, also use our work as English educators at our respective universities and our work as editors and officers in our professional organizations, notably the National Council of Teachers of English.

In this fourth edition of *Making the Journey*, in some cases it has been appropriate not to use our students' actual names; therefore, when a student's first name only is cited, it is a pseudonym. Many of the stories, however, do not call for anonymity, and when first *and* last names are mentioned they are real names of students who, at one time, were in our classrooms. For whatever errors of memory or detail in these stories, we take full responsibility. Throughout this book we also quote from the papers, journals, and notes of our students both at Virginia Commonwealth University and Stony Brook University (SUNY), all of whom we have taught in English Education and most of whom are now teaching in their first years in an English language arts classroom. For their permission to use their words and insights, we are very grateful: we think their voices are part of the strength of this book.

In Chapter 4, Leila cites the work of her friend and teaching colleague Nancy Rosenbaum of Patrick Henry High School, Roanoke (Virginia) City Schools; she is grateful for Nancy's practical and useful ideas. Chapter 5 details a research study Leila conducted; to the gifted teachers who allowed Leila to record their classrooms—Ellen Seay Young, then of Midlothian High School, Chesterfield County (Virginia) Public Schools, and Mil Norman-Risch, of The Collegiate Schools, Richmond, Virginia—she once again thanks them and their students. Chapter 5 includes the story of an intrepid book-challenge survivor, Nicole Galante, Ken's former graduate student and now cherished colleague; Ken is grateful for her exceptional skills and quick wit.

Students, what they taught us and continue to teach us, are the heart and soul of this book, and it would be hard to overstate our indebtedness to the thousands of people with whom we have shared the classroom through the years. Again, we thank our students, each and every one of them, and gratefully acknowledge their powerful and ongoing influence on our lives. Ken also wishes to thank Leila, who has been a hero he knew only from her writing, then a trusted mentor and friend, and now an honored coauthor. That his path has merged with Leila's journey is testament to the wonders of the teaching profession.

The making of a book, even a revised edition, is a complicated process. We thank our Heinemann partners: our brilliant editor, Sue Paro, whose meticulous and insightful work helped shape this book, and our inestimable production editor Vicki Kasabian for her care and attention to detail. The folks at home also mean the world in this writing business. Leila thanks Tucker for his constancy and faith and for being there, as always, on the journey. Ken thanks Patty for her formidable intelligence, her quiet strength, and her legendary, well-tested tolerance.

Working on this revision has given us a renewed appreciation of the tremendous courage it takes to begin the journey of teaching. It has never been easy to make a life in the classroom, and today it is as challenging as ever to be an effective teacher. To those of you just entering the classroom, we send you our best as you embark upon this daunting but crucially important venture. May you find strength, grace—and also some laughter—on the journey.

1 | THE TEACHER, THE STUDENT, THE SCHOOL

When we listen to the stories of language learners over time, we appreciate the enormous responsibilities that fall to English teachers—the potential for what we teach and how we teach it to reverberate in relations between parents and children; to affect decisions at the levels of individual conscience and institutional power; to condition identity; or to cultivate the resources, individual and collective; to sustain tradition and adapt to change . . . While there is an overwhelming immediacy to what teachers teach and learners learn, this work leaves residues, unintended legacies that can make things easier or harder later on future teachers and future learners. In short, we operate in fraught circumstances.

—Deborah Brandt, "Foreword," *Reading the Past, Writing the Future: A Century of American Literacy Education and the National Council of Teachers of English*

Beginnings

Leila's Story: How I Became a Teacher

I never planned to be a middle school or high school English teacher. It was very much a second choice. What I really wanted to be, a college professor specializing in medieval literature, got lost in the now almost legendary English teacher glut of the 1970s and a complete lack of funds. There were few jobs, and I, who had been on scholarship, faced the inescapable fact that time *is* money. I had completed my undergraduate degree in three and a half years and my master's in a record nine months; at the end of this dubious achievement I couldn't afford any more education—financially or psychologically.

So I filled out about two dozen applications, interviewed at every commutable school system, and, after this grueling job search, gratefully accepted my first job as an English teacher, grades 8 through 12, in a tiny high school.

But because teaching high school had not been in my plans, I was not prepared. I had had no student teaching and had taken no courses that gave me the slightest indication of what I was getting ready to do. I came to the high school classroom with a Phi Beta Kappa key, a bachelor's and a master's in English, an appreciation for fourteenth-century alliterative poetry and the origins of English biography—and not a clue as to how to connect what I knew to the 120 teenagers I would be teaching. Fortunately, as any teacher will tell you, students taught me. During my first semester they endured my unscoreable exams, my lame directions, my changes of curriculum, my indecipherable comments on their essays, my wavering concept of discipline. Directly and indirectly, sometimes tactfully, sometimes sharply, they gave me advice about what I could do to improve over those first few months; when they found me fairly receptive, our relationship stabilized.

And, for my part, I was too overwhelmed at first to feel awfully upset about teaching "just" high school. In fact, it quickly became my guilty secret: I found my students interesting—no, that's not accurate—I found them consuming. I found myself talking a great deal about them and what they said and what I said, often to the exasperation of friends and family. My classroom blunders became fuel for thought, and I began to plot and plan each day, each period, with a new sense of adventure. I began to watch my students' reactions and body language and expressions, convinced that actually the key to what to do was right there in the class, right in front of me—if only I could clear my eyes and just *see* it. I was experiencing something very intense, and I was struggling to make sense of it.

And then, as in a scene from a bad movie, I had my epiphany. One wintry morning somebody in the back row—somebody whose name I no longer remember and, tellingly, from whom I *do* remember I hadn't expected that much—made an observation about the short story we were reading. I heard his comment. And then I really *heard* it. The comment was so original, so insightful, so full of possibilities, that I was stunned. It was the proverbial standing still of time; if it *had* been a movie, the heavens would have opened, a shaft of sunlight would have flooded the classroom, and music would have swelled. But real life is usually nothing at all like the movies. My recollection is that I halted and, for a moment at least, just froze. The comment was one that with all my knowledge and education and insight—and class preparation—I had not anticipated. Further, the observation blew the top off our—the class' and my—assumptions about that particular short story.

My next reaction was one of almost overwhelming excitement, an excitement that was infectious as the class began to discuss this wonderful possibility about this story.

Well, what about that? Is it true? Why do you think so? If that's right, what else can we assume? I was excited, exhilarated, and the students were, too. I know now that I saw that day what could happen in a class and how, if I was lucky, I could spend my life. It was a central and almost searing experience: I turned, really saw that student, that classroom, really heard that comment, and, essentially, in that class, on that day, fell in love with teaching. It was, for me, the experience that Rainer Maria Rilke describes in "Archaic Torso of Apollo" when, after viewing a powerful piece of sculpture, he is overwhelmed and realizes, simply, awfully, "You must change your life" (1962, 181). After that experience I had, actually, to change my life. And I did.

My vision of being a medievalist yielded, replaced by the reality and guts and fascination of the classroom and my students. I had found my home, almost by accident, and my blood seemed to run quicker than it ever had in the library looking up the etymology of words in the *Oxford English Dictionary* (1971) or while studying alliterative devices in the fourteenth-century poem "Pearl" (Gordon 1966).

I would never recommend that anyone come into teaching as I did; it was unnecessarily hard on me and, more to the point, it was demonstrably not fair to my students for me to learn at their expense. Certainly, after my first fairly isolated semester, I began to seek—and find—other sources of help; I talked with other teachers, took courses, and began reading professional journals and books. Fellow and sister teachers gave advice and shared techniques; organizations such as the National Council of Teachers of English (NCTE) and my own state English-teaching organization published journals and held conferences. I tried to catch up as quickly as I could and become a teaching professional. It was, however, an uneven learning process, some of which had to do with the inevitable difficulty of learning to teach and a great deal of which had to do with my complete lack of professional preparation.

Hit-and-miss is a difficult and dangerous way to enter this business, and I was often highly self-conscious about my shortcomings. Even in the midst of progress, I almost aborted my teaching career after one crisis too many; and, truth be told, I have always suspected that if some of my instructional stumbling and lurching had been regularly observed by those in charge, I might have, charitably, been invited to leave.

But, as is the case in many school settings, I was largely left alone, and because I was self-conscious about my teaching, I was glad to be left alone. I hung in, made what I felt were some breathtaking mistakes, and learned some vivid and painful lessons. During my biggest crisis, when I had left the security of a small school for a larger and more challenging one and was finding the transition overwhelming, I felt I was taking my personality apart and putting it back together so that I could succeed in the classroom. It was a daunting task, and I do not encourage anyone to follow my example.

My interest in helping others become teachers is therefore part of my own experience as a far less prepared beginner than most. There is knowledge and theoretical basis in our field, and you can come into the classroom with a far more comprehensive view than I had. I also trust you will find what I found: that teaching can be a marriage of soul and mind, that the classroom can be a place of discovery, passion, and very real joy. Although not every class is wonderful every day—for there is occasional bitterness and pain and disappointment in this business—teaching is, for me, a consuming and deeply satisfying profession. Once I emerged on the other side and realized that I was a teacher, had *become* a teacher, I realized that I had also found, in essence, my calling, my life's work.

Ken's Story: How I Became a Teacher

By most official measures, I was a well-trained teacher with a traditional preservice teacher education. About halfway through my undergraduate English major, I decided that if my plans of becoming a journalist didn't work out, I should have a backup plan. So I added a secondary education minor. I attended a very small college and all my education courses, including methods of teaching, included preservice teachers in all subjects and at all grade levels. The courses were fun, practical, and interesting, but it was student teaching that did it for me.

On the morning of day one, my cooperating teacher (better known as my CT) explained that I would just observe for a week and then take on one course, and then another each week, until I had his full schedule. It sounded logical. At the end of the first day he said, "You know, you seem like a smart man. I'd like you to pick up my first class tomorrow morning." I did, and it was fine, though certainly not easy and not, even in that single class, without the myriad anxieties, problems, and mistakes all new teachers make. Regardless, at the end of that class he said, "You did great. Tomorrow you take *all* my classes." So on day three, I was teaching his entire schedule. My CT was a really helpful mentor, and in hindsight I realized he determined quickly that just throwing me right in and letting me work my way through was actually an excellent method for me. It was not, of course, how it was "supposed to be" in my teacher training program but, for me, it worked. Like Leila, I made a lot of mistakes. I also got very little sleep, and I put on quite a bit of weight (I eat when I'm anxious—or excited or relaxed). But I loved it.

In a school district on the East End of Long Island populated with the super-rich, the service workers who attended to them, and lots of people in between, I student taught a range of students from what was then called "vocational" level to "school" level to "Regents" level (aka "college-bound"). I found them equally funny, challenging, unnerving, fascinating, frustrating, and rewarding. I was hooked, and journalism was reduced to a hobby—though it did help me get my first teaching job, which included advising the school newspaper. One of my favorite classes was when I taught a lesson on being a critical consumer with the senior vocational English class. I have a very silly sense of humor (sometimes to my colleagues' chagrin), and I decided we would use purchasing vacuums as our topic because it would allow me to tell this joke: "What does a good vacuum do? It sucks!" Silly as it was, the students got a kick out of it. They were so good that most of them refused to say it themselves, and they turned red when I said it. But the silly joke was also a great way to establish community with this well-intended but significantly challenged group of students nervous about a new teacher (who was secretly more nervous than they were).

I also remember a very difficult and scary situation a few weeks later in another class. The only two students who failed a speech assignment were also the only two African American students in my Regents-level English class. One of their fathers, a local minister, called my CT to find out if my grading was discriminatory, or to put a finer point on it, racist. To his credit, my CT put me right on the phone with the parent and helped me respectfully and clearly explain my position. With the CT's help, this appropriately concerned father politely accepted my explanation, and things went smoothly from there. I also learned a valuable lesson about always making sure grading is fair, accurate, and explainable. And I learned to treat parents with respect and consideration, rather than fear and defensiveness.

In my school-level course, I learned an important lesson as a young man about how and when to phrase questions to some students. "Must you take your purse with you to the bathroom?" I said to a young woman who reeked of cigarette smoke every time she came back from the bathroom. On her way out of the room and in front of the whole class, she yelled back, "Of course I do. Don't you know I have my period!? Am I supposed to show my tampons to the whole class?!" Yikes. Lesson learned. A day later—following advice from my CT—I spoke with this student in private about my concern about her smoking, and I apologized for embarrassing her. I also asked her to apologize for embarrassing me. We never became quite friendly in class, but things worked out well enough.

Of course, the most exciting thing about student teaching was getting to teach English. The poems, novels, and plays we read. The nonfiction texts and essay writing. The in-class speeches and discussions on varied and engaging topics. They were all richly fulfilling, and I was fascinated with the challenge of finding ways to engage and cajole very different kinds of students into serious work across the English language arts.

In the late 1980s, it was easier to secure a teaching position than when Leila was first looking, but after a summer of searching locally, I had to move about four hours away from home to upstate New York. I found a full-time high school English teaching position at a district in a suburb of Albany, where I also taught seventh- and eighth-grade English in the summers. I earned my master's in English at night and in summer sessions. I got so excited about learning more about teaching—especially teaching writing—that after four years I left full-time teaching for four years to earn a doctorate in Rhetoric and Composition.

I've now been a teacher for over twenty-five years, and I've taught English from grade 7 through doctoral students. I'm most honored in the position I have now, directing an English teacher education program, in which I get to prepare others for the profession that has defined me and that I have helped to define for myself for over half my life.

Although, unlike Leila, I had a traditional teacher education background, it wasn't until I began teaching full-time that I discovered organizations like NCTE and its state affiliates. In my teacher education program, I learned a great deal about English and about education, but I didn't learn much specifically about English education. I learned about *English Journal* when I saw it lying on a table in the English department office. By reading this and books in English education (from presses such as Heinemann, NCTE, Teachers College, Corwin, and many others), I learned a great deal about teaching writing, responding to students' writing, creating effective assignments, using rubrics to give formative feedback, encouraging meaningful reading practices, and developing productive student discussion around literary and informational texts. I had a solid and valuable education background, but coupling that with my engagement with the field of English education really sent my learning skyward. And here I am retired as editor of *English Journal* and coauthoring a book with one of my professional heroes. And the hilarious stories I can tell about my own mess-ups and unexpected responses from students! What other profession gives us memories that so quickly evoke tears from laughter or poignancy?

How lucky we English teachers are to get to teach the best content to the most interesting students with the support of a vast network of professional colleagues. It makes those tough days all teachers face much easier to get through. And, as you read this book, you'll hear plenty more about my tough days and the many mistakes I've made and learned from.

Your Story: Becoming a Teacher

You are, right now, writing your own story of becoming a teacher, and one emphasis of this book, besides imparting technical and professional information, is to encourage you to look at yourself and your experiences. It is dangerous to generalize from yourself to each and every one of your students, yet it is also terribly shortsighted not to use your own insights and discoveries when you think about teaching and being and becoming a teacher. Being self-conscious and self-aware can be a powerful tool as you begin this great adventure. Our belief in that power is the major reason we start this book with our own stories—some of which are less than flattering—of how we became teachers.

Throughout this book we will tell more of our stories and let some of our students—who, like you, are embarking on their first years as English language arts teachers—tell theirs. Their words, coming as they do from the journal entries and papers of "experts" at this being and becoming, may help you puzzle out some of the great issues facing middle and secondary language arts teachers.

Finally, this book outlines existing research and knowledge about classrooms and students and teachers, patterns and techniques and concepts.

The Limitation of Any One Person's Point of View

We are, as are many in this business of teaching, conscious of the limitations of one person's perspective. Leila can tell you that she has been a teacher for almost thirty years, that she has two degrees in English and one in education, that she has publications and editorships, and that she has been elected to professional offices. She can tell you she has taught in private and public schools; has taught remedial classes and classes for the gifted; has taught experimental courses, summer enrichment programs, and even classes for adults in a city jail. She can tell you that just recently she went back to high school teaching for a semester and learned a lot about schools and young people today.

Ken can tell you that he has been teaching for just over twenty-five years, that he has three degrees in English (including a specialty in Rhetoric and Composition), that he has published on his own and with colleagues—and, like Leila, he has been editor of *English Journal*. He has taught in two public high schools, two public universities, and one private university. He has taught students grade 7 through graduate school; he's taught both struggling and academically talented students, but he has never taught an honors class. He has also consulted with many English teachers and administrators to address and improve schoolwide literacy.

Yet we also need to remind you that we each come from a background, a culture, and that we bring with us a specific perspective and a point of view. To a certain extent we both have earned the right to talk to you in this book, to function as experts. Our experiences, though, are not universal, and everything we feel about teaching and learning may not echo the feelings of others—may not, in fact, echo yours.

The books and articles we cite are ones we like and have read. The activities and games and procedures we propose are ones we used as high school teachers and suggest our students use in their own English classes. We do not want to imply that we have read everything in the field or that we have experienced every conceivable teaching approach. We offer what we know with the acknowledgment that it is—as is all knowledge—undeniably partial.

Finally, the two of us are greatly aware of the many people—pioneers in this business of English teaching, great thinkers, gifted theorists—who have written and practiced at levels we can only dream of. Neither of us assumes that we are their equals. We take heart, however, from a section of *The Four Quartets* and add our slices of teaching experience, largely because of what T. S. Eliot reminds us:

> There is only the fight to recover what has been lost
> And found and lost again and again: and now, under conditions

That seem unpropitious. But perhaps neither gain nor loss.
For us, there is only the trying. The rest is not our business. (1952, 128)

Making the Journey

So, what about this *trying* that Eliot talks about? Actually, it goes to the heart of teaching and is the reason for the title of this book. Regardless of how prepared or unprepared for English teaching you may be, you are from day one a teacher making a journey. But the paradox is that from day one you will continue to become, evolve, and change as a teacher. It is, oddly enough, happily enough, a simultaneous process of both *being* a teacher and *becoming* a teacher. The two events are not separable and, actually, are not mutually exclusive.

Right now you are probably a lot more interested in arriving at your destination than in making the journey. You are more concerned about *being* a teacher: looking like the real thing, acting like a person who can take charge of a class, negotiating a school day gracefully. But as you will see or have perhaps already glimpsed, *becoming*, the ongoing process of changing and shifting and redefining, is also part of this business of teaching.

And that is what makes teaching so exciting: it is never the same. Not only, of course, are the students different each year, each class, but, necessarily, so are you. Unless you lose your curiosity and passion and interest—in which case it's time to find another career—teaching will continue to evolve and change, *become* more and more, as you continue in the profession.

Teaching Today

These are tough times in which to be a teacher. Issue~~...~~ ...ricular mandate, high-stakes testing and reporting, school violence, v~~...~~ed student learning, community involvement, and control swirl everywh~~...~~ threaten to overwhelm even the most dedicated. Numerous media reports focu~~...~~chers as the major cause of American educational woes, and controversy over ~~...~~mon Core State Standards (CCSS) and mandated tests are often centered aro~~...~~chers. When there are school shootings or student crises, some believe it ~~...~~achers who should have anticipated, should have known, should have interven~~...~~ teachers are often—sometimes unreasonably and unfairly—held strictly accountable.

For English language arts teachers, constant battles over which literature is of most value, how much writing can be squeezed into a crowded schedule, and how the teaching of skills can be balanced with the excitement of reading and talking about texts complicate the picture. Despite these issues, you have decided to make the journey, to *be* (and to continue to *become*) an English language arts teacher. For that decision, you have our respect, and all of us in the classroom welcome you into the profession. It is exhausting and exhilarating and important work, work that is as enduring as it is difficult.

Teaching is the central defining truth of our lives, the core and heart of our identity. For you, too, teaching may become that important and that sustaining. Not for the complacent nor for the fainthearted, making the journey toward being and becoming a teacher is an adventure of the first order.

For Your Journal

Journals are a good way to keep track of your thoughts and ideas. Many times, after reading a section of this book, you will be invited to write a response to the issues and ideas raised. If you wonder how those responses should "look," you might pay close attention to the passages we provide. We quote students who, like you, are entering teaching and who, in our classes, use a journal or blog to record ideas and questions and responses.

Journals can be handwritten or typed, and an entry should be two or three pages long; they are informal and should be concerned more with ideas and content than with correctness or spelling or even neatness. The point is to address a subject or issue and to *write your way into* ideas and answers. This last phrase is crucial: these journal entries are not meant to *record* what you have concluded but to help you *find out* what you know and believe. Writing can be a means for learning what you think.

So, in this first journal entry, think of how people get started in a profession and how that may or may not relate to your choosing to be a teacher. One way to start might be to do some quick field research on how people choose professions: interview two or three people about how they entered their job field; informally poll relatives, friends, or coworkers.

Use the following questions as idea starters; you don't have to answer all of them, but they may help you focus this journal entry about people and choosing professions.

Questions to consider for your interviews: How did you choose your profession? What attracted you to that type of work? How long did you stay/have you stayed in the field? Why did you/didn't you leave? What do you consider to be the greatest rewards of your profession? The greatest drawbacks?

Now, think about you. Very briefly, in a paragraph or two, write about what has attracted you to English teaching. Was it an actual experience with a teacher? A film or a book about teaching? Some other "trigger" (such as reading—and being moved by—a literary work)? Are your feelings about teaching similar to or different from the feelings of those you interviewed about their careers? How?

Teacher, Student, School: The Dance of the Three

The quotation at the beginning of this chapter, written by Deborah Brandt as the foreword to one of the most comprehensive histories of English teaching in the United States, is relatively sobering. Although it may not be the first thing you wish to contemplate as you think about being and becoming a teacher, the nature of the task and the many factors involved do indeed make our work nothing less than highly complex. Brandt writes about "operat[ing] in fraught circumstances" (2010, x), and she is both accurate and a bit daunting. The irony is, however, that most of us beginning language arts teachers give scant attention to context—that is, to the community and to the schools and to our teaching as part of a wider vision. Instead, many of us center our thoughts on something closer to home when we begin teaching. We think of ourselves, the instructor, and what *we* are going to instruct—that novel or play we loved so much, that poem that changed our lives, that writing experience that was powerful, that insight about language that seems to stay in our mind. Yes, we know there will be students—some bright, some quiet, some not so bright, some motivated, some unhappy to be there—but students are students, right? We are going into the classroom to bring to the students and to share with them what we have learned and learned to love. We're not exactly missionaries, but it's somewhere in the territory.

And, of course, as a beginning teacher, we know that we will be teaching in a setting, a physical classroom, a school with a website and a mailing address and a staff and other teachers and a principal. And we know that there will be bells and schedules and corridors. But school is a place in which we teach, right? It is, essentially, despite pressures to teach and test state standards, a setting that will mostly allow us to exercise our craft. For some of us, school is a place that will operate as a "safe harbor" where we can continue our delight in our content, the written word.

Right?

No. Very wrong.

Most experienced teachers know very well that the vision of teaching just described is not true at all. In fact, these descriptions of students and school are well meaning—but seriously naïve—concepts that not only are shared by the majority of beginning teachers but also can engender misunderstanding, difficulty, and failure in beginning teachers. Over recent years, the statistics reported from numerous studies may vary by a few points, but the general conclusion is consistent. Anywhere from a third to a half of all teachers leave after their first five years in the classroom (Alliance for Excellent Education 2014). The questions for us, then, are crucial: What have these teachers failed to see, and how have they failed to adjust? And, where will you be five years after you begin teaching?

Three Truths About Teaching

What is the truth about this business of teaching English language arts? Among others, there are three:

1. Teaching is far more than sharing what we learned to love as students in our own English classes.
2. Students and who they are shape what and how we instruct.
3. School as an institution is a real a factor in teaching. Far from being a neutral setting, it limits and influences what we can and cannot do in our classrooms.

Whether we come prepared for it or not, we as teachers are only one part of a triad that also features a bewildering array of students, all of whom have fierce needs and aspirations and brilliance and weaknesses and problems and cultural expectations, and a setting, an institutional context, which we soon find can more often than not keep us from teaching and keep our students from learning.

It's a difficult dance, with the three partners moving and shifting and leading and taking turns. Although we might want to, we don't (can't) teach in the relative isolation or even protection of ourselves and our ideas about William Shakespeare's plays or Emily Dickinson's poetry or the novels of John Green and Jane Austen. Because we are teachers, we must move among all those loud and messy and frequently challenging and restless people, our students, and we must move through a linoleum-tiled, bell-ringing, rule-driven place: school. And, if this is true, does it change how we think about ourselves as English language arts teachers and what we can do in a classroom? Yes. And no.

So Just How Much Can One Teacher Do?

Few teachers are pessimists. During (and because of) their years of teaching, they are necessary optimists, workers with lights in their eyes. But what has informed and even protected those teachers is the knowledge of what they are up against. It also took them a while to learn it. So although we as teachers can't give you 101 nifty activities that work with any group of students in any school setting—we can't because we know they won't work with all students all the time—we want you to know about students, generally and specifically, and to recognize your formidable and sometimes difficult partner in this business—the school. Knowledge of these two elements will help you as you begin to teach. And then you can look more critically at activities and resources and techniques that you can adapt to your own teaching life. It is worth it? *Absolutely.* Teaching is some of the most important work in the world; it transcends the concept of job or even career or profession into the sphere of *vocation*—as that word is used in a sense of being called, being chosen for a life role. In fact, if you would like to pursue this idea a bit farther, read Sonia Nieto's (2003) *What Keeps Teachers Going?* in which she explores the beliefs and practices of dozens of passionate, committed teachers. Personal fulfillment is a large part of teaching and, of course, there are other rewards. Shamelessly put, teaching is also a chance at a bit of immortality. This is serious stuff, and although no one will insist that it be true for you or for all teachers, it's true for many teachers; it's why we stay in this business, and it's why we want you to be aware of what we know. Knowledge is not only empowering, it will keep you in the classroom and tell you what is going on in that incredibly demanding—but terribly exciting— place: school.

But now let's turn to you, the becoming teacher.

The Teacher/Learner

Why Do You Want to Be an English Teacher?

From our experience working with those who wish to be teachers, most people at the elementary level go into teaching because they like children and can see themselves working with the very young for a living. This, we think, is different from those of us who become middle or secondary school language arts teachers—we do so because we love our subject, especially literature.

It is rare to want to teach language arts, at least initially, because of the lure of writing or linguistics; for many, we were drawn to it by a piece of literature. Each one of us has a story to tell: the first novel that seemed to be written just about us and our lives; that night we stayed up reading until dawn; the poem—some of whose lines we can still recite—that changed our lives. These students would agree:

> When I was twelve I literally vanished from the real world into the world of literature. My older brother handed me *The Hobbit*, and suddenly everything else in my world was thrown aside.
>
> —Werner Doerwaldt

> In a single, pristine moment of understanding, *The Catcher in the Rye* made me realize that books weren't just escapism. They weren't just entertainments—thrills. It made me see that books could have a real effect on people's lives as it had done on mine.
>
> The book put me in a stupor for days. Holden Caulfield was me. His words were mine. Every attitude, every action we shared—or so it seemed. After reading *The Catcher in the Rye*, somehow I didn't feel quite so ugly. Holden had come down from the mountain carrying their sacred tablets and had shattered them at my feet. I was free to unashamedly be myself. I didn't have to go along—I could be different—an individual.
>
> —M. Kevin O'Farrell

> My teachers . . . used literature as a means of communicating "deeper lessons" about ourselves. I pondered the American Dream through Jay Gatsby, uncovered the harsh

realities of murder and guilt through Lady Macbeth, and found strength of human spirit in Hester Prynne. Nearly every piece of literature held an important message about [my] life.

—JANE HUNTER

Another student, Holly O'Donnell, wrote just before her student teaching that "literature is personal, not just art for art's sake" and she wanted to use that power in the English classroom. Holly is right; literature is the power that propelled most of us into teaching in the first place.

Teachers We Loved

And although literature propelled most of us into this field, a person may have also had a strong effect. Perhaps it was a teacher whose praise or encouragement led us to believe we could understand literature or even write it ourselves. One such student, Paul Fanney, remembers a teacher who was so powerful that in her class "sometimes I even forgot to feel so self-conscious about being a teenager, which is hard to do in high school." English class allowed Paul to come "to a closer awareness of the powerful rush in articulating what it's like to be a part of the human experience."

Here, also, are a few recollections from students about to begin their student teaching:

I remember being excited about eighth-grade English and the writing assignments given to me. To help the class understand the concept of interpreting poetry, our teacher had us write about the songs of [a popular rock group]. We listened to [an album], discussed several songs and then wrote our personal responses and interpretations of each. We then moved on to the poetry of William Carlos Williams and e. e. cummings. The teacher was successful in tapping into the enthusiasm and imagination of the students by tying what they valued into what he was trying to teach. Because the lyrics of the rock album and the poetry of Williams and cummings were given equal validity, the students were better able to accept and understand the skills and techniques of critical interpretation.

—BARBARA POPE

Senior year was a very interesting year in English for me. . . . The first day of class [the teacher] brought in a Kitaro (New Age music) tape, and he told us to free write. I wrote several short stories, including one about a sheik and a British Lady having a romance in America. He loved my writing, found ways to help me improve individually, and boosted my confidence in general. He also had us do a multimedia project connecting words, music, pictures, and ideas to create a philosophical statement of some belief we held (it could be deep, humorous, or fluff as long as it was well done). . . . [He] allowed us to be ourselves, ask questions, discuss things with other students, and do a lot of work independently—which motivated most of us to do our best. He also took the time and energy to help us by doing some individualized instruction, and he's one of the main reasons I chose to teach high school English.

—ELIZABETH MILNE

Coach, the Minister of Doom, the Grand Enunciator, these all were the names of my eleventh grade English instructor. He was a slender man with a wit for words, always energetic and articulate. As we walked into his class at the blurry hour of 7:45 A.M. his words could be heard filling the class, "My little lemmings, prepare yourselves to enter into a vast panorama of pleasure as we immerse ourselves into the world of Stephen Crane." Words became musical notes and stories became songs, and *Red Badge of Courage* wanted me to keep reading on.

—DAVID SMALL

[My English teacher] looked like a koala bear, hence his nickname, Mr. K. Mr. K. was a short, stocky man who was gentle natured and smiled all of the time. He seemed to love all of the students including the trouble makers. I believe that is why all the students loved him. He had a way of never actually answering a question. Instead, he would turn things around and make you answer your own question. It was an art that he had refined so well that the technique rubbed off on his students. We would stop asking questions and evaluate the situation or problem in our own mind and come up with a solution. Independent thinking was Mr. K.'s motto. No thought was ever wrong, it was always correct as long as there was some basis for the thought.

[My other English teacher] was a throwback from the 1960s. He wore raggedy pants and his hair was always messed up. He looked like he just rolled out of bed. But he had a great mind and he treated all the students with the respect that he wanted. He . . . had a way to open discussions up and to make everyone feel special. We wrote all the time and some of the stories that the "bad" kids wrote were incredible. These are the same kids that [the other teachers] had thrown out of class for bad behavior.

—MELISSA CAMPBELL

One of my best memories of [my English teacher's] class was when we were doing some seat work, reading in groups or something, and she hung up a large white sheet of paper in front of the class. Casually, she told us if we liked we could come up and write or draw our ideas about "Life" on this sheet with the colorful markers she provided. Throughout the class period, students meandered to the front, wrote poems, drew rainbows or angry faces, made a statement. I wrote "Whoops." Near the end of class, she scanned the filled sheet smiling at a few things, nodding her head.

Then she stopped, turned around and said, "Who wrote 'Whoops'?" I raised my hand.

"What did you mean?" she asked.

"You know, like slipping on a banana peel," I said.

She laughed and nodded at me . . . That smile and nod she gave me meant more to me than any grade I ever received. It was her way of saying that what I thought was important, even clever, that I had something to contribute. She is what high school English should be.

—LARRY GOLDMAN

Whatever the specific impetus, for most of us it was not so much a love of *who* we would be teaching but *what* we would teach (the literature) or *how* we would teach and emulate our model of a great teacher.

Leila's Story

My impetus was finding *me* in an unlikely place—in a 1900s North Carolina town in Thomas Wolfe's *Look Homeward, Angel*. It was seventh grade in Linkhorn Park Elementary School, and I *could not* put the book down: I was so taken with it I brought it to and from school for three days. I read at home; I read in class. Wolfe spoke of passion and loss and the difficulty of knowing the world—and one another. He sang of longing and sadness and all the things I could not articulate (but so keenly felt) at thirteen. I concealed the novel on my lap and read it, virtually straight through, during work time in Mrs. Pendleton's room. I am certain Mrs. Pendleton saw me reading during class and—to her credit—left me alone. The novel has no more charms for me—looking at it now, I find it dated and long-winded, not to mention sexist and self-indulgent—but it was my introduction to the power of literature. And I have loved Mrs. Pendleton ever since.

The teacher who inspired me was Larry Duncan, who in eleventh-grade English at Norfolk Catholic High School was both exotic and demanding. He put Ezra Pound's (1973) "In a Station of the Metro" on the board and asked us what we thought. He showed how close analysis of the opening lines of Shakespeare's *Richard III* could reveal level upon level of meaning, and then he asked us to try. He told us about the Harlem Renaissance and asked us to consider what *explode* really meant, then in 1967, in Langston Hughes' (1959) "Harlem." He chose pieces for the spring play like Eugene O'Neill's (1972) *The Hairy Ape* and actually expected us not only to learn but to understand the lines. In general, Mr. Duncan treated his students like intellectual peers. He asked us real questions as if he was interested in our giving him real answers. We didn't always respond, and often our class "discussions" consisted of a lot of puzzled silence on our part and a lot of frustration on his.

We thought he was weird (and I still think that assessment was not only accurate but complimentary), but Mr. Duncan set an example and a tone you had to hear, if not accept.

Ken's Story

My most profound English teacher memories come from my earliest years in St. Helena's Grammar School in the Bronx. In this small school—about 500 students in grades K–8—I had the same teacher, Mrs. Ronald, twice. In second grade, a momentarily overburdened Mrs. Ronald once responded to one of my essays by telling me it was "abominable." That night, I was so enthusiastic in telling my mother about the "compliment" that she was genuinely confused. Then she taught me a valuable vocabulary lesson: the next day, I asked Mrs. Ronald more about her evaluation of the assignment. Later, in sixth grade, Mrs. Ronald gave an assignment that has stuck with me ever since. It was a simple writing assignment, but she offered several possibilities, including writing a story about the class, and she created a contest in which the two best essays would be read aloud by the authors. I took an unusual amount of time, really working hard on the essay—which is not something Ken the Abominable generally did in grammar school—and I ended up one of the contest winners. I read my story aloud, which told a funny but not mean-spirited story about the members of the class, and the class laughed uproariously. Mrs. Ronald may have created a monster that day, but she also taught me an important lesson about the powerful effect real writing could have on real audiences. Although Mrs. Ronald probably didn't have today's concept of "authentic assessment" underpinning her lesson, she did an excellent job of tapping into my inner ham to fuel my work in class. To this day, I try to immerse students in writing for real audiences to tap into their interests and passions, whether it's making people laugh, informing them, changing their minds, hiring them, or whatever else the students want.

You have a story, too, and a reason for wanting to do this business of English teaching. That reason, that passion will be part of your strength as a teacher and, further, conveying that story to your students may be appropriate at some time. It's valid; it's part of why you're here, and its power will carry you through the very dailiness and the occasional discouragement of teaching English.

But your love of your subject or a very good experience in English class is only part of the story.

Not Everyone Loved Literature, Their English Teachers, or Even School

Not all our students like English, love English, will willingly take English classes if they further their education, or will continue to read literature or write poetry or essays after they leave—or escape—us. Many of our students have had very bad experiences with English (the subject and those who teach it) and feel that they and their language are not good enough, are not correct, are not acceptable. They may text and tweet fluently, but many of our students are uninterested in extensive writing, feel they don't have anything to say, or, if they did, probably couldn't say it right anyway. Some of our students don't read frequently or easily or with a whole lot of understanding. Many of them have encountered few books that seem to have any connection to their lives. For a significant number, English language arts is the primo arena of the majority—white, Anglo, Western, male, and financially comfortable—and they rarely see themselves reflected there. Many of our students in English language arts classes are asked questions that seem hardly worth answering about people and life choices and issues that seem to exist solely in books and solely for English teachers' tests. Listen to a few of these stories, written by people who are planning on entering the classroom:

I know I had an English teacher in every grade from eighth to twelfth. I know that each year someone attempted to teach me high school English because that is what English teachers were instructed to do by the school board. The school board asked teachers to teach literature, reading, and grammar. However, the school board failed to make it a rule that English teachers make high school English interesting, enlightening, and entertaining enough that students be able to recall classroom experiences and teachers' names.

—JAN BUTTERWORTH

Freshman English was conducted by [my teacher], a kindly aging spinster. I say conducted, but in actuality she was both the conductor and the chorus. The classroom was her stage, and any interruption by a student was a wrong note. We were there for her audience as she read to us some of the great works of literature. She read *The Merchant of Venice* from beginning to end, and a very effective Shylock she was, I might add!

—KATHERINE SULLIVAN

[My eleventh-grade teacher] sat in her desk at the front of the evenly aligned rows of gleaming metal, orange desks. She rested the textbook on her chest which rested on top of the desk and drilled us. She was very predictable. She asked the questions from the back of the book. Her eyes saw everything. There was no talking, laughing, or writing. Of course she didn't react to you sleeping in class as long as it was quiet. Most of the time we had to do busy work, worksheets, crossword puzzles. . . . She would give us any assignment as long as it kept us quiet, so that she had time to read the book on top of her heaving chest and to rub hand lotion on her hands.

—MELISSA CAMPBELL

I once had a friend tell me, "English class ruined every good book I ever read."

—RALPH B. HOLMES JR.

But because this, by and large, is not the experience of every person who takes English, why dwell on it? We dwell on it, we linger over it, because if we are to improve education, if we are to make the classroom an alive, languaging kind of place, such events must become even rarer in our classrooms.

If you have talked to anyone recently about being or planning to be an English teacher, have you noticed his or her reaction? First, you might hear something about the CCSS controversy or about the recent downturn in the teacher job market, which now appears to be fueling a teacher shortage and may result in a much better job market for teachers. But once you get past those responses, you'll likely hear what English teachers have heard for decades: "Uh-oh, I'd better watch my grammar" or "I never did well in English." Many times people will tell you that you seem to be too bright or too talented to "waste" your life in the classroom. In particular, many women are counseled against teaching because it is considered too safe, too traditional; many men are reminded of the financial sacrifices that teachers make. Rarely do you meet someone whose eyes light up at the prospect of talking with you, an English teacher—for many people English teachers represent something negative and almost fearful, and for many people becoming an English teacher seems a futile way to spend a life.

Why is this? We wonder at times if it is because a number of individuals have had bad experiences with English teachers and in English classes and bad memories of school. Those bad experiences, we hope, will stop with you. And although Leila can write with energy and pride about Mrs. Pendleton and Mr. Duncan, there is also her nameless eighth-grade English teacher at Blair Junior High School. Red pen in hand, she took the poem Leila had written about mountains (a poem that meant so much to her she not only showed it privately after class but had also painstakingly recopied it in peacock ink on her best paper), read it, first circled the spelling errors, and then marked the punctuation with "UNNECESSARY" in large letters. Leila was fourteen and about as morbidly sensitive as they come. She nearly stopped writing poetry, and she never showed that teacher anything that meant anything to her ever again.

For some students, there will be little chance that they will show a teacher their poetry. Some of our students are fearful about their abilities, their vocabulary, their accent. They feel they have no place, no voice, in our classrooms, and come by compulsion, with no illusions about learning or even having a relatively pleasant experience. For these students, unsatisfactory incidents in English class will be far more serious than one marked-up poem.

What you are planning to do would not be such a challenge if the students with whom you worked saw immediately the reasons for the literature on the agenda Wednesday afternoon and if they fell with zest and comprehension to whatever tasks you assign. The bulk of our job, however, is not to ratify understanding and gracefully preside over the honing and polishing of skills. It is to do what our title dictates—teach. And sometimes that is terribly difficult to do.

We teach under a big tent. In that tent are Anglos, Latinos, Native Americans, Asian Americans, African Americans; students with learning disabilities or with emotional challenges; recent immigrants; students who are straight and gay, trans and bi, male and female. Our preparation for the classroom may not give us a deep background with all these learners, but make no mistake about it: they are, once they walk into our classrooms, ours. Ours to teach.

Teacher Ego: Having It/Losing It

And thus we come to the subject of ego. You've got to have a special confidence even to think of being a teacher, of being in charge of and accountable for a class, of organizing what 150 or so people will be doing five hours a day, five days a week in school. You have to be able to see yourself helping large groups negotiate subjects and facts and concepts. Somewhere along the line you have decided you can be the equal or superior of the teachers—good and not so good—you had in your own background. In short, you have a healthy ego if you can seriously contemplate being a teacher.

But one of the things you may not realize is that very early on, especially if you want to be successful in this teaching business—in other words, if you want your students to learn—you will need to lose a lot of that ego. You will, rapid-fire, need to do the following:

1. Put into perspective what appears to be the occasional indifference or insensitivity of your students.
2. Care more about your students' learning than about your dominance.
3. Talk less and listen more.
4. Answer less and question more.

You will, actually, have to become the quintessential, archetypal adult, one who sublimates personal needs for others, who steps aside so that others can step in, who is silent so that others can learn to speak. If you are used to being the smartest kid in the class, now, as a teacher, you will have to modify if not totally relinquish that role. Can you do it? Maybe not immediately, maybe not even in the first couple of years, but sooner or later the ego will have to soften. And in the space that is left, your students will flourish.

In his methods classes, Ken calls this "the teacher shift," preservice teachers moving from focusing on themselves to focusing on their future (and then current) students. At first, you might be more concerned that students respect you or that they like you, and this is understandable for a very new teacher. Quickly, though, successful teachers will prioritize their students' perspectives. A student who acts out may not be intending to disrespect you but may be trying to get your attention about something: that she had a bad experience at home the night before or in the hallway earlier that day, or that he doesn't understand the lesson and feels stupid. As teachers we must learn not to take student behavior personally, so we can objectively assess situations and learn quickly how to best meet our students' needs. Coincidentally, and perhaps ironically, this is also the best way to earn our students' respect.

Some of our students who are preparing to teach English already understand this, understand it long before we ever did. Jane Dowrick writes that she realizes the importance of making "oneself empty in order to be ready to receive—that in our efforts to be smart, and ready, and on top of things, we cannot hear what we need to hear" in the classroom. For Jane, the whole process of getting ready to teach is a round of "filling myself up with information, advice, and now I need to make some room" for the emptiness and silence that can be necessary for an effective teacher.

As Sheryl Gibson, a teacher in the early stage of her career, notes,

> I now realize that it is not impossible to be a teacher who does not indoctrinate. Kids need to think on their own and develop their own interpretations. . . . Once I realized that teaching is not being the knowledge factory but the knowledge filter, my desire to teach was rekindled.

Sandra Greer sums it up well. And if all teachers were more like Sandra, the future would be in good hands:

> I know that when it is *me* standing in front of those high school students I want to put on a smiling face because I feel that way, and let those kids "express" to their hearts' content and write till doomsday if that's what they want to do. I don't want to change the world, I just want to encourage them to do what they're capable of and hopefully open up their minds to the exciting and wonderful (I won't get out the thesaurus for any more synonyms!) world of Literature. Yeah! I know . . . it sounds kind of sickening doesn't it. I guess it does sound like I want to change the world. Maybe I do. Maybe I do like to think that because of my effort I'll really help out some kid. But, you see, I want to. I really want to. Even if it's only one student, that's better than none at all. I want to be a good teacher. People ask me all the time, "What do you want to be a teacher for? You won't make much money." You know what I say? Who gives a *#@!?! about money, these kids need an education because that's about the only thing going for them these days. They are our future. And I'd hate to see our future go to waste.

For Your Journal

Choose one or two of the following. Make a list of three things you would like to do as a teacher. Write about a memorable teacher who was great. Write about a memorable teacher who was awful. Write about one of the first "English" successes you had: in class; tutoring you did with another student; something you read that made a real difference in your life.

The Student/Learner

What Is This Thing Called Adolescence?

In the world of social and cultural history, the concept of *adolescence* is a relatively new one, related to Western ideals of childhood, concerns about child labor, and beliefs about the need for education. It is "the unique space between childhood and full adulthood" (Christenbury, Bomer, and Smagorinsky 2009, 4) and is characterized by much "myth and fiction" regarding its roles, responsibilities, expectations, and duration (4). And it has changed with the times: adolescents mature physically far earlier than previous generations, are bombarded with more adult content sooner, face an economic future that is more uncertain, and, in school, remain the most tested and, in many middle class homes, the most "regulated and scheduled" of all groups of young people. One serious aspect that teachers and adults miss, however, is that adolescents are not "individuals in crisis, and not in deficit" (5) but do have a great deal to offer socially, emotionally, and intellectually. Far from being "adults-in-training who have not quite mastered their roles" (5), adolescents can bring much to the classroom and to school.

That said, it is amazing how once we pass our own adolescence, many of us tend to forget what it was really like. With the best of intentions, but certainly inaccurately, we often cloak adolescence with veils of what it should have been, not what it was. It is tough being young. It was tough years ago, and it hasn't changed. Adults, even fairly young adults, tend to become nostalgic or just amnesiac; as teachers, we really can't indulge ourselves so. To be successful, we need to look at the wily, fascinating, exhausting, exhilarating adolescent and who he or she is. We also need to make some distinctions about age groups.

Intellectual changes At this point in your career, you probably have some developmental psychology background, and you are aware of learning stages and cycles. You know about the work of Swiss psychologist Jean Piaget and his division of cognitive development into four stages: sensorimotor thought, preoperational thought, concrete operational thought, and formal operational thought. These last two stages particularly concern us. To briefly review: Piaget (1959) defined the stage of concrete operations as taking place from about ages seven to eleven. This is followed by a transitional formal operations stage from about eleven to fourteen and a permanent formal operations stage from about age fourteen on. Broadly speaking, concrete operations involve real, observable situations; formal operations deal with abstract, speculative thought.

The work of Piaget is a landmark in education, but you also need to know that it has not gone unchallenged. For many educators, Piaget's belief that the concrete and formal operations stages are truly definable by age is misleading; further, many young people do not enter a permanent formal operations stage until much later than fourteen years of age. In fact, the entire designation of adolescence is seen by some as quite problematic. Researcher Donna Alvermann calls much of what we assume about adolescents "fictions" and quotes William Ayers in *Re/constructing "The Adolescent"*: "Puberty is a fact; everything surrounding that fact is fiction" (2009, 20). Regardless of the mythology and the fictions, the movement of your students from one stage to another is a very real phenomenon but is often not readily perceivable to you, the teacher. It is helpful for you to know that some of your students will be struggling with a change in thinking abilities and patterns, but that will not give you as much information as you might need. Today there is convincing research that demonstrates that brain activity in young people is markedly different from that of adults (Casey, Jones, and Hare 2008) and also occurs at a pace that is equaled only by the brain growth/activity of young babies (Strauch 2003). Again, however, this knowledge will not, unfortunately, give you a precise guide for dealing with the questions you may have about your students and their response to language arts tasks. You can accept with some surety that some of your students will be moving through the stages; it is a fallacy, though, to believe that the stages will be exact or readily demonstrable.

Psychological changes As argued before, the mythic "crisis" of adolescence may be just a myth. It is not common to every culture that all adolescents go through the Sturm und Drang of alienation and rebellion. You may not have experienced such huge upheavals nor may many of your friends. In fact, when Leila went back to teach high school she found that the majority of her eleventh-grade students had very positive and close relations with their parents. On the other hand, there may be people in your own life or young people in your class for whom growing up is painful and difficult, characterized by a number of issues, including emotional challenges, a quest for sexual identity, and early physical maturation. All of these are serious and can often derail adolescents as they struggle not only to achieve but find balance in their lives.

Adolescence: Early and beyond The middle school concept was born out of a concern for what is termed the *early adolescent*, aged roughly ten to fourteen. In the mid-1970s there was a renewed and widespread interest not so much to segregate those students as to try to make their educational experience more appropriate for their development. The idea of a middle school is to offer a more distinctive education than the literal "junior" high school, which had been in place since the 1920s as the educational setting after elementary school and a training ground of sorts for secondary school (Muth and Alvermann 1999, 2–4). Although the middle school concept has a very wide variance in this country (and is periodically reassessed as perhaps not the best way to provide for transition), the middle school as an entity is based on the fact that early adolescence is a special time and requires a different sort of educational setting.

What Are Some of the Factors of Early Adolescence, of the Middle Schooler?

First, the years before puberty are characterized by more profound physical change than any other time of life—with the exception, of course, of infancy. Second, early adolescence is when cognitive development changes, in Piagetian terms, from concrete operations to formal operations. As previously sketched, the latter is when students begin to think in the abstract, not in the purely observable, and that expanded capability in thinking has serious implications for what we do in our classrooms. Indeed, a "wide range of cognitive ability" is probably most demonstrable at the early adolescent stage (Muth and Alvermann 1999, 31). Third, in the area of reading, early adolescents can encounter serious difficulties moving to a higher level of comprehension as reading takes a more academic turn, causing a decline in interest and, as many teachers will attest, an unwillingness to read widely and extensively. Fourth, in the area of writing, early adolescents may have serious difficulty moving to prescriptive, academic, argumentative writing and away from narrative. Surely middle-level students are capable in their own ways of bringing to their reading and writing not only "social capital" but different kinds of literacies based on their up-to-the-minute experiences with social media and new electronic formats. Yet school and the English curriculum do not always make room for this competence. This can also be a time when young people begin to explore their power and may begin to exhibit, or suffer from, bullying behaviors. (For more on bullying, see Chapter 10.)

What About Middle and Later Adolescence?

In middle and later adolescence, students will show more social awareness, more orientation toward peer and away from parent, and some will begin to master skills, especially of academic vocabulary and academic norms. Others will fall more seriously behind in writing and reading tasks. They will also (some more gracefully than others) continue to master the tasks of maturation. Most will fall in between these poles, and it's important that adults remember that maturation is not a consistently progressive journey. There are setbacks and regressions as well as sudden leaps forward. It can be a time of tremendous excitement, anxiety, impatience, and stress.

So What Do Adolescents Want?

More than anything, young people want a part of the action, a piece of the control, as one of Leila's students expresses in this lament about her high school English classes:

> Being a prospective educator myself I know exactly what was lacking in my own high school education. I should have been given the chance to question anything that I was learning; I should have been able to feel comfortable saying I didn't understand something. I should have been challenged to come up with my own ideas instead of my mind remaining dormant. I should have been in an environment where the student's word was equally important as the teacher's. I should have been given not only the opportunity but the instruction . . . to express myself in written work.
>
> —SANDRA GREER

A number of educational researchers have looked at what they call "locus of control" and have found that passive students who exhibit "learned helplessness" just don't learn efficiently (Furhmann 1990, 167). Such passive students are also, as you can readily observe, relatively unhappy in their classrooms. Most will cooperate, at least to the outside observer. It may be more accurate to say these students are merely *compliant* rather than truly cooperative. For these students, school is a place where they have to be, but their real lives are often outside its walls.

And Another Story

Listen to this student's description of herself as a teenager in English class; she is representative of the large number of young people who aren't challenged in our classrooms. This young person, who, by the way, is now in her first years of English teaching, was neither gifted nor remedial; she is, however, a voice for the majority of students, and we may learn something from her story:

> I majored in English in college because in high school I thought that I was naturally and amazingly gifted in the subject. For instance, in [my] ninth-grade English class, we had a test, and one of the questions was "Why did Sherlock Holmes beat the sidewalk with his walking stick before entering the building?" I had no clue. As usual, I hadn't even bothered to read the story, let alone study for the test. But I must have been pretty clever,

because I took a wild guess and replied, "To see whether or not the ground was hollow—whether or not there was a room beneath." I was right! I got an A! I couldn't tell you what the name of the story was now; I've never even read a story by Sir Arthur Conan Doyle. I just know how to get through high school English without cheating or studying.

I think [my English teacher] used to get frustrated with me and some of my friends, because she was usually pretty crabby when we were around. As hard as she tried, she couldn't nail us for our disrespect. She would stand at the front of the class talking about gerunds or Sherlock Holmes while we carried on our own conversations. Eventually, she would glare in our direction and ask one of us to read aloud. We either had no idea what page she was on or we couldn't control our laughing well enough to oblige her. To add insult to her injury, no matter how disrespectful we were in class, we always did well on her tests. I don't really know exactly how the others got around her, but my secret was that I knew grammar rules intuitively, and I paid just enough attention in class to know what was in the reading that I was supposed to do but rarely did. She was serious about teaching English, but she just didn't challenge me enough for me to show her any respect.

Getting away with murder became a sick little game to make fourth period go by more quickly. [In other English classes with other teachers] I repeated her gerund exercises. . . . Bewilderingly enough to me, the mathematically inclined kids struggled with gerunds. . . . I, on the other hand, completed the exercises in a matter of minutes, which was nice because that left me with plenty of time to talk and pass notes. Thus I added another year of unearned As in English to my high school transcript.

High school English; what a pathetic experience! I get a little angry now when I think of how much I could have learned but didn't. Maybe it was my fault. I could have read the assignments and behaved better in class. But, why bother? I was doing well as I was. I was secretly quite interested in learning—especially reading and writing—but it wasn't cool to admit it then, and I had no reason to embarrass myself.

I always secretly felt a little sorry for [my English teacher] because, deep down inside, I always got the feeling that she was trying to teach me something—that she wanted to challenge me more than harass me. I'm not sure why she failed. Why did she make her tests so easy? Perhaps she was too confined by the curriculum. Maybe her teaching abilities were stifled. . . . I often wonder what she would think if she knew that I want to be an English teacher. Would she curse me? "Someday, I hope you have students who are just like you were." Or would she secretly feel sorry for me?

—Patty Duffy

Patty Duffy expresses well the sort of mind-numbing contact some students and teachers can engage in in our schools. No one is a particularly bad actor here, no great dramatic events occur, but learning is not the outcome. Further, for both teacher and student, contact is a trial. Patty, as an adult, now understands what her English teacher was doing, but at the time the two did not connect. Why is that?

Some of it is because teachers fail to take into account the adolescent and why he or she really comes to school and sits in our classes. Some of it is because our students, in their development cycle, are often difficult to entice into the intellectual life—particularly as it is represented by school. These same students may well have vivid lives online and with their friends—but school as school is not part of the excitement. Much of it, of course, is no one's direct fault at all, but we must make the best effort possible with the classes we have and with all the students in them.

A Few Observations About Your Students and Their Behavior

Students don't, by and large, want to be in school for the reasons teachers want them to be there. The action, the heart, is often outside the class in the halls and in the faces and lives of their classmates, not in their teachers. Many of them have already internalized what society judges them to be and are trying to mirror that expectation. Many feel that the game is biased from the start, and they see you, the teacher, as another of the game masters. Some students "play" school classes as if they are the world's most boring first-person adventure games; students push the right buttons and move their joysticks to get to the next class. But, are they truly present?

The point is that our students are different from us as adults. Holly O'Donnell, a student teacher, trying to make sense of adolescents and her own perceptions, wrote in her journal:

> I'm not surprised by the kids—well, I was at first. But I wasn't surprised about what they talk about—it's *how* they talk about stuff. Maybe I've just got good ears, but I hear more swearing! And I was initially surprised at how belligerent they were. I'm not really so sure it's belligerence, now, as it is adolescence. They are so vocal, so verbal—at first it's scary because adults aren't like this. Adults get up every morning w/o asking why (or w/o asking it very loudly) and do what the capitalistic, bipartisan democracy expects; kids get up and they want to know *why*—and they're not scared to ask, why? and, who died and left you boss? I mean, they *look* like us, but then they open their mouths and "everything's changed!"

The following observations regarding young people, teens, and preteens may give more specific insight:

- Adolescents can feel misunderstood and often misjudged. They suspect adults don't listen to them. Many times they are quite correct. When teachers only expect students to accept and agree, we are contributing to their sense that no one listens.

- Emotions run high in these years; an hour can be an eternity, and a trivial incident can be a major disaster. Just because an adult's perspective "proves" this to be untrue, the young person's feelings to the contrary are not trivial or discountable.

- The culture of the young person and the culture of the adult are often at odds. It's often the adults, however, who try to impose their culture on the teens, not vice versa.

- Teens look at adults in a highly critical way. At no other time in life is the detection of what teenage Holden Caulfield (in J. D. Salinger's *The Catcher in the Rye*) called the "bullshit factor" more acute. Unfortunately, however, as most adults are well aware, that detection of bullshit is usually other-centered.

- It's all new for adolescents, which is not always that exciting or reassuring. Uncharted territory is scary—as the ancient map of the "edge" of the world indicated, "beyond this place here lie monsters."

- The power of social media and the lure of a presence online are irresistible to many young people. Many find access is easy even though the risk can be serious. It is wonderful to find like minds on the Internet, but cyberbullying is real, and many young people wither under its pressure. Some, as we know from the daily press, commit suicide.

- A great many males, especially Caucasian males, begin to find strength in these years; a male-defined culture is ready to receive them. A great many females begin to suspect—and become depressed by—the outline of their future lives and their place in the world. Young women suspect that their lives are changing profoundly: being smart and outspoken in tenth grade carries different implications than it did in fifth grade.

- Being different, not having a sure command of a second language, being one of the few in a group can be uncomfortable and limiting, and often teachers and other students do not reach out. Students who are a racial or ethnic minority in school feel even more keenly the alienation of adolescence. For those who are questioning their sexual identity, the difficulties are compounded.

- Adolescents don't come to school to see you or to go to class; they come to experience the real action: one another. In some ways, you and your class are merely the backdrop of the play.

- In English class, students want to read something that speaks to them and their experience; they want to write about what they know; they want to talk about issues of importance. This does not mean that they can't or won't read about different cultures and different ages, but it must, somehow, relate to now. If you can't give this to them or don't think this is important, you may have problems in your classroom.

- Our young students are not children, and don't want to be termed as such. They usually know more and have experienced more than we give them credit for. Patronize them, let them know that they're just kids, and they'll dislike you for it. First, it's demeaning, and second, it's just not true. One student remembers that "I had always believed that adults didn't expect adolescents to have any worthwhile ideas." That's not what we want to be known for.

- Most of your students are participating to some extent in sexual activities, and many are using or experimenting with drugs, both hard and soft, including alcohol. Some of this is growing up and learning; some of it is highly dangerous. But, despite the earnest work of groups such as Promise Keepers, scare tactics or a shallow approach to moralizing doesn't help here. Some of this behavior is what you and your friends did, too, and just saying no doesn't make the problem—or even the complexity of the issues—go away.

- Many of your students will have jobs outside of school, which, frankly, mean more to them than your class because, unlike your class, those jobs pay them money. Given a chance, some students will tell you this, too.

- Despite how untouched they may appear, your students want you to care about them and to be concerned about them. They do not, however, want you to invade their personal lives or their privacy. It's a fine line they ask you—that they expect you—to walk.

- Despite how indifferent they may appear, your students want to respect you as a teacher and as a person. In fact, despite all disclaimers to the contrary, they look to you for some sort of clue as to how they should live their lives and what choices they should make.

- Despite how broad-minded or sophisticated they may appear, adolescents do not want you to do drugs with them, drink with them, or use risqué language or obscenities around them. They want you to be a responsible role model who sets appropriate boundaries. They want you to show them what a responsible, caring adult looks like.

- Don't be surprised if students who like you lash out at you in unexpected anger. Sometimes, students who trust their teachers will lash out at them because they are feeling hurt about something (perhaps totally unrelated to the teacher's class), and they know a trusted teacher will ask them what's wrong and help them—not just yell at them and move on.

- Despite how infatuated they may become with you—or you with them—adolescents do not want you as a boyfriend or a girlfriend or as a sexual partner. You are an adult, a teacher, in a trusted role, and intimate contact is a flat violation of that trust. Fall in love with someone your own age; put your students' feelings of affection or just experiments with flirtation in perspective. In this area, you have limited rights; you are a teacher first and foremost. To violate that trust is a profound betrayal. If you find yourself attracted to your students, you should consider another profession. Feelings do not make you a bad person, but acting on them might.

- Remember always that youth is a territory all its own: adults may visit but are guests only on temporary visa.

- Adolescents can act quite differently in front of their peers than in a one-on-one setting. Be sensitive that students may not want their peers to think you like them or that they like you. And never deliberately embarrass students in front of anyone. That's very hard for them to forgive. If you embarrass them accidentally, be sure to apologize swiftly and sincerely.

- Remember also that youth is necessarily, inescapably, self-centered: young people really don't think your life or your problems are anywhere near as important as theirs and, anyway, it's your job to be there because you're the teacher. Furthermore, you get paid for this stuff.

- Remember, finally, that adolescents are the toughest audience in the world—and one of the most rewarding. They may never tell you thanks or write or phone or come back to school to let you know how they are doing, but don't worry; if you did your job, they'll remember, and they just might be better people for it. And you, necessarily, are much the better for having known them. Many of your students will, in fact, stay in your mind and your heart for the rest of your life. And that's a job benefit few professions can offer you.

For Your Journal

Try to remember who you were during adolescence. *Questions to consider:* What is one thing you loved? Hated? Who were your best friends? What was the major challenge you had during this time? What do you recall about your relationship with your parents? With your teachers? If you worked during the year or during the summer, what did you do? What did you read? What was your life online? If none of these questions seem appealing, find a young person between the ages of thirteen and eighteen and informally interview him or her. *Possible questions for the interview:* What does the person think are the biggest hurdles to being that age? The deepest satisfactions? If there was one thing he or she would like teachers to understand, what would it be? What about for parents? For adults in general? What does the person think being an adult will be like? Finally, if you hate these questions and the interview, think about another avenue. One of the characters in Richard Peck's young adult novel *Unfinished Portrait of Jessica* remarks, "There were only three ages: *now*, *high school*, and *grown up*. All adults were the same age" (1991, 63–64). If this is true, if this is what most young people really assume, what is your responsibility, obligation, problem as a teacher? What, essentially, are the implications of such a statement?

The School

A Little Bit of Selected History

If you become interested in the history of teaching English in the United States, you will want to read Arthur N. Applebee's (1974) *Tradition and Reform in the Teaching of English* as well as Erika Lindemann's (2010) edited work, *Reading the Past, Writing the Future: A Century of American Literacy Education and the National Council of Teacher of English.*

Both are comprehensive texts, and if you are interested in the various movements and trends in our profession—all of which are greatly influenced by culture, economics, and history—they are worth your time. And, in a very self-serving way, it is to your advantage to know your educational history, if for no other reason than to appreciate that the latest outcry and call for change has probably been made, with just as much energy and intelligence, sometime in the past. Many of the issues in language arts teaching are perennial, and much of what American education debated at the beginning of the twentieth century is with us now in the twenty-first. (As a side note, if you wish to delve into the issue of literacy per se, Deborah Brandt's [2001] *Literacy in American Lives* is a great read and traces, using the stories of individual lives, how literacy has changed in this country over the decades.)

You may well not have time for these books or—at this point in your life—the interest. So, to give you a quick tour, there are a few historical landmarks and a few issues worth reviewing, a number of which follow.

Education for life versus education for college   *So just what is a school for? Should it be geared to prepare a student for the world—that is, work—or for college?*

Does this question sound familiar? It was a raging debate in 1892 when the Commission on the Reorganization of Secondary Education of the National Education Association sponsored what came to be known as the Report of the Committee of Ten. The group was concerned that high school courses were taught differently depending on whether the students were going to college or not. The Committee of Ten also found that English language arts courses were not being geared to two basic needs: developing communication skills and cultivating a taste for reading. A few years later, in 1918, the significantly more influential *Cardinal Principles of Secondary Education* report said much the same as the Committee of Ten, but it also added that English should include "studies of direct value" and that theory and student experience should be related.

The student's interest as the basis for all learning   The *Cardinal Principles* was influential, and the interest in preparing students for life became a major tenet of an encompassing concept called the Progressive Movement. The movement's most influential proponent was the legendary writer and educational theorist John Dewey, and the movement started formally in 1919 with the founding of the Progressive Education Association and didn't really fade until the 1950s.

For the Progressive Movement, the real needs of students were of great import, and in language arts, the 1935 publication of *An Experience Curriculum in English* tried to meet student interests in a realistic course of studies. The curriculum seemed successful, and research involving 240 schools and 3,600 students, called the Eight-Year Study (Aikin 1942), confirmed the fact. According to the Eight-Year Study's results, students prepared around problems and issues that concerned them did as well in college as their more traditionally educated counterparts. The compelling nature of the Progressive Movement's ideas is enduring, even today, and you will find echoes of its tenets in many contemporary books about American education.

The academic model and the romantic revolt Carried to its extreme, the Progressive Movement, especially through an early 1950s manifestation called "life adjustment education," lost the faith of the American public. Meeting the real needs of students was carried to the limit, actually went over the edge, and when units in English class on housing the family, choosing a mate, and even how to answer the telephone were brought to public attention—and ridicule—the bloom was off the Progressive rose. Especially with the fears of international competition, embodied by the former Soviet Union's bold launching in 1957 of the first orbiting space capsule, *Sputnik*, the English language arts curriculum drew back into what Arthur Applebee terms the "academic model."

It was the early 1960s, and rigor and the concept of English as a discipline held sway. Drawing on the influential writing of Jerome Bruner (1963) in the seminal *The Process of Education* and rejecting the "soft" idea of student interest as being the basis of education, the English curriculum in particular became serious, structured, and rigorously tested. Although some gains may have been made, the result was an alienation of certain students and teachers although, admittedly, many thrived in the classroom. English language arts in the early 1960s was not about adjusting to society. Instead, there was the academic formalism of studying structural linguistics and the close analysis of the New Criticism.

Nothing, of course, stays in place, and the academic orientation of the previous years was transformed in the mid-1960s. Education was not untouched by the upheavals of the age: the civil rights movement, the women's movement, and a general call for societal change. In the schools, a number of educators demanded that the English classroom open up and be more for all students of all persuasions; its intellectual rigor was seen as an impediment to learning, not an enhancement, especially for racial minorities and those not admitted into the prestigious, exclusive, and Advanced Placement classes sponsored by the College Entrance Examination Board.

In the mid and late 1960s, it was a time of educational experiment. Students were invited to choose their courses in elective programs, schedule their classes in variable time slots, take courses pass/fail, and take classes with people younger and older than themselves and in spaces without walls or without rows or sometimes without desks. As Neil Postman and Charles Weingartner happily wrote in 1969, teaching could be viewed as a "subversive" activity. According to many 1960s reformers, the classroom could, appropriately, undermine and challenge the omnipresent and scorned "establishment."

Accountability: Let's go back to the basics Well, of course it didn't last. By the mid-1970s the public temperature indicated that it was time to worry that standards were slipping, that teachers slaphappy with freedom and students talking much too expressively were taking over the English classes and not doing or learning a darned thing. A fear emerged that was somewhat akin to that of the late 1950s: Where were the testable skills? Where was the practice development? So the wind shifted to going "back" to the basics of English and testing, testing, testing, under the umbrella term *accountability*. Competency tests were in vogue, and the idea of making materials or texts "teacher-proof" resurged.

The "sea of mediocrity" and the standards and testing movements   In 1983 the United States Department of Education issued *A Nation at Risk*, a scathing and at the time influential report that concluded that education was currently drowning in "a sea of mediocrity." It was alarming language, it was widely believed as true, and it set off a national conversation where many concluded that the schools were not doing enough to foster excellence. What seemed to be the solution? Because policy makers, not necessarily the public, suspected that little worthwhile was going on in classrooms, it seemed appropriate to institute more state control over school curriculum.

Additionally, as undisputed evidence of achievement, it also seemed important to test students far more extensively and to report the results of those tests to a broad constituency. Thus more control of the curriculum, more testing, and more reporting and analysis of those tests combined as a three-punch whammy. The need for this change was reinforced by widely publicized—and often misinterpreted—comparisons of American students' test scores in math and science to those of young people from other countries. Certainly many felt that the unfavorable conclusions about American schools and comparisons to students from other countries were unfairly reported, but the avalanche had started to snowball. For the first time, there was statewide consensus that something unified should be enacted. That something was the crafting of curricular benchmarks and skills standards for every state, accompanied by the testing of those standards. (For a discussion of the standards crafted by our professional organization, the National Council of Teachers of English, and for all teachers and students in English language arts, see Chapter 3.)

With few exceptions, most states fell into line, and the testing and standards juggernaut has done little but escalate, resulting in high school diplomas tied to the passing of state tests. Today students and teachers face more testing than ever in the history of American education. Further, the results of those tests are regularly publicized and, through the 2002 enactment of the federal No Child Left Behind (NCLB) legislation, where students in grades 3 through 8 are tested every year and in one year of high school, there are sanctions for schools and school districts that did not meet requirements of Adequate Yearly Progress (AYP). Today, despite significant changes regarding the details of federal oversight of public education, massive testing is still a characteristic of all grade levels in all schools. This kind of oversight of student achievement, almost completely determined by standardized test scores, is without precedent in American education. It has also not been without controversy: scores of educators and educational associations have raised questions about these tests and about the punitive provisions, and parents, teachers, and students have regularly protested, occasionally refused to sit for the mandated tests, and, in some cases, taken their concerns to court. Some states have rescinded their participation in CCSS, largely based on the testing provisions but also in concern over a national curricular standardization. The wider concern is, also, that such tests dictate the scope of the content taught, meaning that only what can be testable is what is taught. (For more information, you may want to consult studies by Au [2007], Tierney [2009], and the *English Journal* themed issue "The Standards Movement: A Recent History" [Gorlewski and Gorlewski 2014].) It is a quickly moving target, and by the time you enter your first classroom, what is written here may be out of date.

In a related development, tax-funded alternatives to public education—charter schools—are now developing side by side with traditional public schools although the debate about student achievement in those schools remains fierce on both sides. In addition, the more widespread use of Advanced Placement courses (and the attendant Advanced Placement tests, which can result in college credit) and the International Baccalaureate curriculum are attempts to put more rigor into high school courses. Further, many schools in this country offer "dual" enrollment, where high school seniors can take college-level courses in either their home school setting or on a college campus for which they receive college credit. With college tuition on the increase and student debt a real factor for many young people, the appeal of entering college with earned college credits from Advancement Placement and dual enrollment is strong.

Right now, we continue to deal with these issues, and we can add to them a few ongoing others. There is, in general, a continual concern about the teaching of the "classics" in English, and one change has been that many works in the canon, once taught in senior high schools, are now taught in middle schools, driving literature from middle schools down to the elementary level. Suggested CCSS reading lists for grade levels reinforce this practice, positing that, for instance, students in as low as grade 6 be able to read and comprehend eighteenth-century texts (such as John Adams' "Letter on Thomas Jefferson"). The authors of the CCSS believe that "text complexity" hasn't been taken seriously enough in younger grades, but many educators are concerned that texts with significantly advanced emotional content have been moved to younger students without concern about whether younger students are intellectually or emotionally prepared for this content. Whether most students are capable of reading these more complex works at the time they are taught is not clear, but, for instance, plays by Shakespeare and nineteenth-century novels, once reserved for the last years of school, are now introduced to students far earlier. And the debate goes on.

School as Repository of Hopes and Dreams—and Traditions

There is ongoing discussion—as always—of the institution of school and how it is not serving education or young people. More specifically, we continue to hear today that American business is not receiving qualified workers and that the national economy is falling and our country is in second—or third—place because of the failure of school, especially as it is now structured. And despite the consistent comments of reform-minded individuals, it is clear that even today of all the American institutions with which we are familiar, school is the one—virtually the only one other than some organized religions—where a person deep-frozen in the mid-twentieth century could return to our age and be comfortable and feel a sense of familiarity. In high schools particularly, the same curriculum patterns, much of the same subject matter (including the very same pieces of literature taught in English classes), the same general organization of the school day, have survived from mid-twentieth-century American public education. And, ironically, the calls we hear now for school reform are many of the same calls that have been issued for almost 100 years, and some of the "new" proposals for flexible/modular scheduling days, for year-round school, and for school on patterns that do not automatically include a summer (maybe a winter?) vacation are ideas we have heard for the last fifty years. The perennial concern about school being preparation for college or preparation for life is a debate from the early 1900s.

America changed its eating habits from home to restaurant to fast-food drive-through in less than a decade, shifted from cars to sport utility vehicles in the same time, and adjusted to the computer and then laptop and then tablets in about twenty years. We embraced the smartphone, email, texting, and social media in fewer years than that, and we absorbed massive social change regarding women, people of color, second language speakers, gay marriage, and gender identity in a decade and a half. So, why the foot-dragging with school?

As a teaching friend of Leila's notes, "school keeps." We may face tremendous changes around us, but school, with its familiar structure and content, is a reassuring touchstone of sorts for many Americans. It's also, maddeningly enough, a repository for many of our hopes and dreams about our future and what our youth, our young people, represent to us. It may seem to be just a graduation speech cliché, but for many Americans youth is indeed the future, and school is where many of us hope that youth will be formed and shaped.

School is where we try to preserve, transmit, carry on, and it's a sensitive issue for the majority of taxpaying, child-rearing adults. When it looks like what we experienced, many of us feel comforted. School is the "universal environment" for adolescents, a "vast, standardized, relatively homogeneous experience" that all students in this country share (Furhmann 1990, 144). When some parents hear of practices they did not experience—such as the "new" CCSS math or texts such as graphic novels or YouTube videos—there is often dislocation and confusion. As one research article notes, there are "artifacts of social practices . . . used fluently by early adolescents but . . . [that are] a foreign language to some adults" including "blogging, emailing, podcasting, instant messaging, texting, wikis, tweeting, threaded discussion groups, Kindles, Facebook, MySpace, and YouTube" (Many, Ariail, and Fox 2011, 55). All of these may, in one way or another, wander into your classroom, if not into your own students' lives. Not every parent or taxpayer will like it, and they will let you know it.

As you may well understand—we are back to Brandt's observation at the beginning of the chapter regarding teaching in "fraught circumstances"—school can be a controversial and touchy place to teach and to learn, especially when a society feels that its sense of order and values are threatened by any combination of social shifting. For example, debates over the place of grammar in the curriculum, which piece of literature to study, or how to teach English to those for whom it is a second language are often a product of politics in the very broad sense of the term and not just questions that well-meaning English departments can rationally solve in some sort of vacuum or isolation. Today, schools are also indicators of what educational critic Jonathan Kozol calls "apartheid schooling" (2005) where the student population is as segregated as the neighborhoods from which students come. School can be a political minefield, and it is certainly an accurate reflection of the anxieties of the culture.

It is important for you to know about school, the institution, how it is organized, and how that affects you and your classes. There may, in the coming few years, be real changes in the shape of schools—some reforms often talked about may really come to pass—but in the meantime you will experience, at least for the first part of your teaching life, a high school or middle school structured not very differently from the way it was organized when your great-grandparents walked the halls.

And although that continuity may be comforting on one level, it also is not serving young people efficiently, as one educator grimly notes:

> The comprehensive high school, designed to meet the needs of everyone, is criticized for having become an assembly-line system that denies adolescents access to adults, breeds frustration, creates failure, and is concerned only with conformity and order rather than intellectual curiosity and love of learning. (Furhmann 1990, 148–49)

Further, and this is a reality of the business, the structure of school often gets in the way of teaching and learning. You will find yourself in your classroom wondering if there isn't a better way to set up this contract among learners, and your speculation will be appropriate. Unfortunately, however—and this has been true of educational history in this country for over a century—you, as the teacher, will probably be one of the last people seriously consulted about institutional change. It will be up to you at times to make the best of what can be a difficult situation, at times to make changes as you can in your own school community, and possibly at times to really get a piece of the teacher empowerment that is often touted. But that's another story. Let's look at what the issues are.

Five Aspects of School That May Not Serve You or Your Students

The compulsory nature of school and your English class First, you need to remember that your wonderful students, your clientele as it were, even in charter, private, or independent schools, are there by compulsion. School is required, it is not optional, and by the time you get ready to meet your English classes, your students have been doing this compulsory stuff for many years. They may, by fourteen or seventeen, even be a little jaded. They often come, as Richard Hawley (1979) remarks in his article "Teaching as Failing," like an audience with little anticipation of being pleased. You may, indeed, pleasantly surprise them, but do not expect huzzahs as you enter the classroom. You may know you are different, but to many of your students you look a lot like every other teacher they have ever had. And that, by the way, is not necessarily a compliment. As a result, you may be rather surprised at the absentee rate in your school and the practical effects of that rate on your classroom. Student teacher Debbie Martin wrote this in her journal:

> These kids never come to school or, when they do, they come late or leave early. I had one student out of 120 who didn't miss a day last semester. By the same token there were 19 students who missed a total of 750 days out of the teaching days of the semester, and 212 students who were tardy over a total of *1,100* times in the same period of time. Trying to keep track of late work is an administrative nightmare.

Second, you need to recall that English is also not optional. School itself is compulsory, and with very few exceptions, everyone must take English every year. Get the picture? You are not the instructional purveyor of the creative, like art or drama; what you offer in the classroom is not associated with excessive brilliance or arcane knowledge, like physics or calculus; you will not preside over classes where folks can learn about sex or can sweat and yell and play a game, like health and physical education. You don't help people learn about different cultures and languages, such as Japanese or Spanish, or calculate angles or predict trends like geometry or statistics. It's the most common, most broadly required, most repeated game in town: it's English language arts, and you're the teacher.

Grouping students into grade levels It seems ridiculous to think that the one-room schoolhouse was actually a great educational idea. But, as we'll see, we could do worse than to go back to some of its principles. But that's getting ahead of the story—a little history first. In the nineteenth century in this country, the one-room schoolhouse was rather grudgingly supported by the community through taxes and levies. It was predominately rural, undersupplied, and often badly heated, ventilated, and lit. It was in session in direct relation to the local crops and economy and to the weather. There was often no continuity of instruction—the turnover in teachers and students was startlingly high. The one-room schoolhouse was presided over by one very young, unmarried, and undereducated teacher (most in the late nineteenth and early twentieth century had not the equivalent of a high school diploma), usually female (and if so, required to be unmarried), for whom the job meant low pay, severe community scrutiny, and a great deal of work. That teacher taught and supervised as many young people as the single room could hold, and students often ranged in age from six years old to fourteen or fifteen—and with very few books, if any, to work with.

Just for a minute imagine the distance intellectually between a six-year-old and, say, a thirteen-year-old, between first graders and seventh graders. What they can read and comprehend is wildly different, and when you go back in your mind and imagine our turn-of-the-twentieth-century schoolteacher trying, day after day, to structure learning experiences for such a widely disparate group, you can understand why educators thought it would be a great advance to group students by age, to put all of the six-year-olds together and all of the fourteen-year-olds together somewhere else. It was seen as an advance and a sensible way to deal with the differences between young people at varying stages of development. As researcher Larry Cuban observes, "teaching [an] entire class together is an efficient and convenient use of the teacher's time—a valuable and scarce resource—to cover the mandated content and maintain control" (1993, 253).

What happened over the years, however, is that many of us in education lost sight of how nebulous and changeable some of those age differentials are. In fact, there will be more variation intellectually *among* your students in your third-period, ninth-grade English class than *between all of the ninth graders and all of the tenth graders* in your entire school. The segregation by age also seems to imply a few things that we need to examine carefully. Let's imagine we're talking about those tenth graders. If we accept grade levels by age, then these propositions ought to be true:

✗ There is something all tenth graders should either be ready to learn or should already know, based on their chronological age.

✗ All tenth graders should be taught pretty much alike because they are at the same stage of development.

✗ Tenth graders will not benefit from intellectual contact with students either older or younger than themselves.

None of these three propositions is true. Indeed, we know something about how and when people learn, but we don't know enough to be able to say with any certainty what a single year of school should offer intellectually. Further, the kind of crossover that occurred in the one-room schoolhouse—despite its many other manifest drawbacks—is something we could do well to return to. *Each one teach one*, *collaborative learning*, and *cooperative learning* are concepts that share one idea: when we teach someone else, we not only help that person but, by helping them, we solidify our own skills.

So, when our overworked schoolteacher had to give a geography lesson to the older students, she would, possibly, ask one of the older students to listen to and help two or three of the very young students with their reading. It was a cross-age endeavor. Further, this older student was probably more adept in reading than were those older kids getting the geography lesson; that student would not be kept in a group level but would be allowed to proceed at his or her own pace.

When you begin to teach, or when you teach this week, you may be puzzled at the disparity *among* your eleventh graders. Curricular plans that feature nongrouping—in other words, putting tenth and eleventh and twelfth graders together in a given class—militate against this sort of "Now you're fifteen; that means . . ." kind of mentality.

Tracking Again, it seems a good idea at first glance; put the adept kids together, let them go on, and put the less adept kids together so they can receive extra attention and help. It sounds sensible, but it is based on a few things that we're not sure actually operate in the schools. Although tracking has undergone a recent dip in American classrooms, it remains "pervasive," and it is something about which you need to know (Strauss 2013). For tracking to be *successful*, it must be based on the following principles:

1. **Neither teachers nor students should indulge in a "self-fulfilling prophecy" type of behavior;** that is, the kids tracked in the higher brackets cannot always be assumed to be smarter, and the kids tracked in the lower brackets cannot always be assumed to be struggling. Lower-tracked students will often assume they aren't smart and therefore won't try. Higher-tracked students may just fail to exert the effort. Also, teachers often internalize these attitudes and deal differently with students in different tracks. And, by the way, disguising tracking designations is virtually impossible. Students and teachers *know*.

2. **Students must be mobile between the tracks;** once in a lower track, they must be allowed to achieve their way to a higher track and vice versa.

3. **The placement of students into tracks must be based on real evidence,** not on

   - ability gauged by single-measure tests or even standardized tests

   - race or economic background

   - personal characteristics such as appearance, ability to interact positively with school authorities, ability to adhere to school rules.

The sad fact is that these three conditions are rarely met in schools; students are placed into tracks for reasons other than out-and-out ability and intelligence (Oakes 2005, 9–14); students, once placed, are rarely moved between tracks; and the "smart" ones know they are in that track and can act accordingly, as do those designated less able. There is no strong research evidence that tracking is doing what we want it to do, especially for those who are not at the top of the academic spectrum. (For a thorough look at the subject, see Jeannie Oakes' [2005] *Keeping Track*.) In fact, an article in the *Atlantic* notes that "The US Department of Education has called tracking a 'modern system of segregation' that favors white students and keeps students of color, many of them black, from long-term equal achievement" (Kohli 2014). To compound the problem, we know that students in higher tracks, simply put, receive a better education (Furhmann 1990, 158). Although her remarks are over twenty-five years old, Helen Featherstone's (1991) discussion of a study of 108 eighth- and ninth-grade classrooms is still pertinent. In that study, researchers found that

> teachers in high-track classes ask more "authentic" questions, ones that have no predetermined answers, "but instead call for student opinions or for information the student must uncover independently of the teacher." They all follow up on student responses more often . . . All this makes it sound as though schools conspire against low-track students, but that isn't true . . . Almost all high school teachers would agree with researchers

that students in low-track classes are less engaged than those in high-track classes, but things get more complex when we begin to speculate about the reasons for that disengagement . . . Placed together in one classroom, without the leaven of more enthusiastic and academically successful classmates, disengaged adolescents create a culture unfriendly to effort. Teachers respond with teaching that asks less of students, perhaps reinforcing the students' disengagement. Before long neither teacher nor students have much heart for academic work. (7)

In addition, there is some evidence that lower-level students benefit strongly from the influence of other, more adept students. The cognitive psychologist Lev Vygotsky found that what students "can do with the assistance of others might be in some sense even more indicative of their mental development than what they can do alone" (1978, 85). Vygotsky called this a "zone of proximal development," and clearly students stronger in language arts skills can benefit those less strong, especially when a talented teacher creates assignments and an atmosphere that encourages a community of students that achieves together. When this zone is closed, all students suffer. Indeed, "is tracking one of the culprits for the persistent and terrifying achievement gap between white and Asian and black and Latino students?" (Kohli 2014).

Jane Hunter learned more than she expected in an advanced poetry class:

For many years, I thought that all of the various "tracks" were taught the same things, in the same manner, and that they just varied in pace from one another. I couldn't have been farther from the truth! During my first semester of my senior year, I ran face-to-face into this prejudice after signing up for an advanced poetry class. The first sign that I was out of my territory came from a fellow student on the first day of class. "Andrew," one of the school's most promising students, walked over to my desk that morning and snarled, "Jane, what are you doing in this class?" I responded with a few choice words and wrote him off as being a stuck-up geek. As time went on, however, I began to realize where these kids' attitudes were coming from—the instructors! Students in these advanced English sections were handed a multitude of privileges by the instructors and the administration. These AP classes were run totally different from the "average" tracks—they all sat in a circle and held open discussions/debates amongst each other and with the instructor. They were also permitted to publish a class journal each month that was then distributed school wide. And worst of all, they were given first dibs in the computer room!

Finally, as Paul Fanney, a former student of Leila's, writes, it can be a depressing experience to be placed in the "wrong" track:

In tenth grade I discovered firsthand the horror of being placed [not in an honors class but] in a "regular" level class. Tenth-grade English had to be one of the most boring, irritating, and desultory experiences I have ever had. The teacher I remember did her best to keep it boring, too. The reason I got into trouble so much with her was because of how she taught and what she taught; like math classes I constantly asked myself "What's the point?" or "So what?" I got the impression that somehow we weren't to be trusted with books, novels I mean, based on the "probability" that we wouldn't know what to do with them once we got them. I actually remember feeling as if I was being intellectually insulted, if you know what I mean. I never forgave my advisor for putting me in that class, or the teacher for making me so restless. Instead of an interesting learning environment, we got worksheets; instead of stimulating talks on relevant and meaningful issues good English classes raise, we were given homework in monotone.

Ken taught for several years in a tracked environment, and he had some successes within it by deliberately flouting the idea that a track somehow indicates your future achievement level. First, Ken frequently moved students from his tenth-grade school-level English class to his tenth-grade Regents-level class, always with the student's permission and with a promise that they could return if it didn't work out. Some students, who enjoyed the school level because they liked not having to work too hard, had to be convinced to try a higher level—sometimes by their parents, with whom Ken also communicated when they were receptive. Most of the students who switched stayed with the new class, but a few moved back.

Also, Ken tried to get the students in both levels to do the same work, but he approached it differently. Students in the school-level classes did a lot more hands-on, concrete work with texts: more moving around, working with images and sketches, writing shorter but still meaningful texts. And Ken was vocal with these students about why they were doing what they were doing and how it would help them in the future. Regents-level classes were asked to abstract more readily and read and write longer texts, but weren't given as much explanation about why. It's not so much that school-level students weren't as smart or interested as the Regents-level students; it's that what engaged them and how they learned were different. An observant teacher with an open mind can help almost any student expand his or her efforts, and once students achieve something they didn't think they could, they are often transformed.

Ken owes a great deal of his thinking about nontraditional ways of engaging students in high-level English language arts work to Patricia A. Dunn (2001), whose *Talking, Sketching, Moving: Multiple Literacies in the Teaching of Writing* explores ways of using multiple channels of communication to improve students' writing (and reading).

What does all this mean to you? It means that you will encounter students who, at fifteen, know that it is too late; the school has judged them "slower" or "less able" or, as Paul writes, not to be trusted with books or creative projects or open-ended questions. That's a heavy burden for an adult—it's insupportable when you're young.

You will also have classes where the "smart" kids are on the fast track and no longer feel the need to work. They have, by the system's designation, succeeded, so why break a sweat? They have a perennial case of "senioritis" as sophomores or juniors. Finally, you will see a ghettoization of the student body with young people permanently marked and sorted into designations of being smart, not so smart, and so on. Tracking just doesn't do a thing for real teaching and real learning.

A final reason tracking doesn't enhance teaching or learning is that despite your effort to be open-minded, once you enter a classroom you know has been designated as a certain track, your expectations will be subtly and not so subtly affected. This kind of thinking has a name—*phenomenology*—and, to put it in overly simple but useful terms, it's when one sees what one expects to see regardless of what's objectively there. You will have assumptions about the low-level class that are hard to shake. Paul's teacher, for example, did not see him as a bright person. It would be unfortunate, indeed, if you allowed yourself to fall victim to what President George W. Bush once memorably called "the soft bigotry of low expectations." You will also have assumptions about higher tracks, some of which will help your students (you'll have high expectations for them) and some won't (you may assume their writing is good enough because it's pretty good but maybe not at the level they can achieve if pushed). You will also become accustomed to hearing other teachers discuss students and classes solely in relation to their tracking designation. In this game of tracking, then, the students have roles and designations that they are not allowed to change. And you, as their teacher, will also be affected.

Instructional time When T. S. Eliot's character J. Alfred Prufrock complained about measuring his life out in coffee spoons ("The Love Song of J. Alfred Prufrock," 1952), he might have been discussing the life of a middle school or high school teacher who must deal with short periods of instructional time. With the best intentions of organizing the school day intelligently, educators first divided the seven or so hours into short periods, in some schools from forty-five- to fifty-five-minute periods. In English language arts particularly, that's a tight block of time to manage every day, every week, every month. Discussions can last longer, reading a piece of literature and then reacting to it often fails to fit into such a slice of the clock, and beginning a piece of writing can proceed in fits and starts much broader than the time allotted. Yet, as beginning teacher Clary Washington laments, "It often seems that the schedule is more important than the learning. This makes me crazy." For high school and middle school students, the class period can be difficult to negotiate, and, for their teachers, it can inspire a mild form of insanity.

In recognition of this fact, many school districts moved to block scheduling where students and teachers meet on alternate days for longer periods (or "blocks") of time, such as ninety minutes every other day. In block scheduling there is more freedom to explore longer projects without the interruption of the bell. Expanded class periods provide time for extensive activities in literature, writing, and technology.

On the other hand, block scheduling itself is not always the magic solution to timing of classroom instruction: for some students, ninety minutes of instruction in the same room with the same teacher can yield less than optimum results and, further, the alternate-day scheduling can be confusing. For a teacher intimidated by such a long period of instructional time, a block class can be, at least initially, unwieldy to organize.

In general, however, block scheduling militates against the hectic nature of previously ubiquitous daily fifty-minute periods of instruction. Certainly most teachers find that they and their students accomplish more extended projects in class. And, with judicious use of stretch breaks (*no one* can work unbroken for ninety minutes without some sort of break) and shifts in activities, block classes are highly productive.

In the meantime, understand that both you and your students are responsible to the clock. You must adjust to working within a specific, timed instructional unit. No matter how dull or how exhilarating the class, it comes to an end in a certain amount of minutes, every day, every week, every month of the teaching year. It limits what you can do, and it is a recipe, of and by itself, for routine. You will need to fight that routine so that it becomes not the boredom of utter predictability but the comfort or outline of order. And unlike the other "constraints" mentioned so far in this section, there are a few things you can do to improve the situation.

How do you do that? You mix it up and shake it up; you keep track of how many days in a row the students had a discussion, worked in small groups, did silent work at their desk, made presentations, or served on panels. You make sure that each week features a variety of large-group, small-group, and individual work and that class time is alternated appropriately with computer work, short videos, silent reading, and talk. Again, if you are teaching on a block schedule, you give your students a stretch break somewhere within the ninety minutes. Although you do not want to have a class where students really don't know what to expect every day—that can get scary after a while— we flourish, all of us, on variety. One way to beat the boredom trap is to build change into your class. And, as an additional complication, a block schedule requires that you pace your instruction so that students are provided a sense of continuity: seeing them every other day can mean that you, the teacher, need to spend time reviewing on Wednesday what you did on Monday, questioning students so that they can recall on Thursday what they concluded on Tuesday.

Finally, remember that school business may give you much less than the allotted instructional time you expect. Announcements, school pictures, field trips, and tardy slips will cut into that period of time. In addition, you may have school-scheduled events suspend your class during the week. After all, how do you think the whole school gets to see the play during the day or hear the special speech imported for their edification? It may be, and with little notice to you, that your Tuesday, fourth-period class doesn't meet nor does your Wednesday, first-period class. You are responsible for adjusting and planning appropriately. And sometimes, we repeat, it's on short notice. So you remain flexible as you try to teach in this place called school.

Grades, testing, and curriculum We are a nation of competitors, who's in, who's out, the ten best, the twenty worst, a list and ranking society. We want to know the average, the top, the worst, the mean, the median, and most of us measure ourselves pitilessly against the standard, however we define it. Our students, and our schools, are no different. While we are concentrating on leading an exploration of the power of Martin Luther King's prose, the students—not unexpectedly—want to know whether it will be on the test. We are so pleased with the beginnings of a revision of a student's essay; she wants to know what her grade will be if she keeps on revising. We feel our sixth-bell class has made much progress during their year with us, but all the school district wants to know is whether the sixth-bell students can score a specified percentage on the state standardized test.

It's the serpent in the garden, but we can't duck it. We are in the business of teaching, for credit and grade, which in turn lead to an official recognition of achievement—a diploma. What we do is required by law, and we are paid for it. Not only are we expected to keep good records—and in many school districts those records are often required to be posted online in real time and viewable by students and their parents—we are also expected to know, for almost every assignment we give, what we are expecting students to learn (objectives), how we will tell if they learned it (evaluation), and how we will rank students' learning (grading).

Issues of grading and evaluation have always been part of teaching, as noted in this chapter, and one inevitable result is the intense emphasis on testing, largely due to public perception that schools are not performing up to standards and that testing will ensure more accountability. On the other hand, educational critics, such as the late Gerald W. Bracey, stubbornly contend that schools *are* doing a good job and certainly better than many members of the public believe. Bracey (2004) spent his professional life arguing this point, and, periodically there are press reports of students—with the backing of their families—sitting out annual testing. For example, an influential group of parents and teachers in New York have formed an "opt out" movement intended to resist the testing tidal wave. In 2015 and in 2016, more than 200,000 students opted out of standardized tests. They and others of like mind are, to date, however, in the minority. At least for now, the present educational mantra is one of test, test, test.

Further, if you are skeptical about the relationship between learning and testing, you are probably correct. With drilling and repetition, with daily practice on test items and test time management and test tricks and shortcuts, with total concentration on the test and testing, young people can learn to pass the test and even to improve test scores. Most teachers know this, but they also worry: What do their students really know about the material? Could, in fact, students do as well on a different kind of assessment, a different kind of test? Will they pass that particular test but not know much else? Would a more authentic assessment be better than an easily measured but not very informative standardized exam? How many of the complex skills of literacy and critical reading, writing, speaking, and listening can really be objectively measured anyway? What essential literacy skills are we leaving out?

Many educators don't share uncritical faith in standardized tests. In a perfect world, passing or scoring well on a test would absolutely indicate mastery of the material: Isn't that the point? But when one kind of test and test score become the focus of all instruction and result in intensive practice drilling for that particular test—as is done now in school districts all over the country—then mastering the material can become truly secondary. It's not about learning; it's about learning to take the test.

As a beginning teacher, you will work in an environment of large-scale, state-administered standardized testing in which students are expected to perform at a specified level. In some states, this yearly, mostly multiple-choice testing is tied to state curriculum standards, and the results of the testing can determine school accreditation as well as student progress through the grade levels. This is, as a frequently used phrase accurately describes it, "high-stakes" testing, and, in some regions, it has seriously affected classroom instruction and classroom climate.

The expectation to test and measure at all levels—school, school district, and state— is not very good news for us as English teachers, especially when so much of what we do is, frankly, difficult to quantify or fit into an hour-long, fifty-item multiple-choice test. How, for example, in the instance of a specific classroom period, do you assign a letter grade to each of the twenty-seven students who for two solid days discussed the meaning of Nathaniel Hawthorne's "Young Goodman Brown"? What constitutes an A or a C in that situation—or do you just give up and give everyone who participated a reasonably good grade? Do you ignore letter grades entirely and move to pass/fail or to check, check-plus, check-minus? If you decline to evaluate individually each student on an activity such as two days of class discussion, aren't you avoiding accountability?

Well, the point is you *can* justify such discussion; you can give students credit—and response—for that discussion, but you can't, unlike other areas of academic endeavor, truly grade everything you do in English language arts. Nor should you.

Much of what we do is cumulative and builds on long periods of time. We are rarely given to know if a student's facility with language or a highly complex idea makes a grade-level change in our classroom. Thus we are kidding ourselves if we believe that progress during any given academic year will always show in the results of a state-administered standardized test. So what do we do?

We can justify such activities if we can't precisely grade them; we can spend time on classroom exercises even if we know with some certainty that it will not appear on the state-mandated test. We evaluate what we can, and we simply leave the rest to a few instruments: tests, writing assignments, notations of participation and completion. We also do not hijack our own curriculum in total service of the standardized test. To do so abrogates not only our role but our obligation as a teacher.

Patti Smith, writing about preparing our students for the future, presents two aspects of literature, only one of which can be easily graded:

> Everyone agrees that education is supposed to prepare one for the future. The best way to do this is to prepare [students] intellectually, not with the ability to supply the names of the main characters of *Hamlet*, but with the ability to make the connection between *Hamlet* and modern problems. Critical thinking, that's what kids should learn in English class.

And although, certainly, one can grade aspects of a student's critical thinking about *Hamlet* (there has to be some external evidence that a student has connected the play with modern problems), it is a lot easier to grade his or her knowledge of the play's main characters and plot.

Our job, ladies and gentlemen, is not an easy one.

We also want to avoid the following scene (even though we may admire the teacher's temporary solution and even though in this case the students responded positively):

> There was one incident that occurred in [my English teacher's] class that stands out in my mind and describes him and his philosophy of teaching perfectly. Since I was in an Advanced Placement class, the class was small (15 students). Most of my classmates were ambitious, competitive, goal-oriented kids. This is good . . . to a point. All they cared about were grades. They wanted to know at all times what was needed for a grade, and essays and subjective tests drove them crazy. The teacher hated this attitude. He wanted to have discussions and to make these kids think for themselves, not memorize for a grade.
>
> One day the grade-oriented students were really anxious. They kept asking how they were going to be graded on some assignments. They were wasting a great deal of time and we could not get back to the topic being discussed. Something triggered him; he went off! One of the students told him that he had to know how he was going to be graded because of college entrance requirements. Then the student went on to say he wanted to be taught what he needed to know for college and what he needed to know to score high on the SATs. [The teacher] looked at us and said that he wasn't training us for a few crummy classes in college. . . . The next day he came in and tore up the grade book and said that from here on out it would be pass or fail. The only requirements for an A would be real discussions and participation. . . . After that day, class was great. The pressure was gone, and we could really discuss topics.
>
> —MELISSA CAMPBELL

Yet, as a student in the middle of her student teaching writes, the pressure to give and get grades is powerful:

> [Teaching] is frustrating because I want so much for all of my kids to do well. I have had to veer away from taking their success (or failure) as my success (or failure). To a certain extent, I must look at the whole class and evaluate if my teaching is soaking in. This can be gathered from looking at them, listening to them, and checking performance. But I realize now that not everyone is going to get an A. It took me a long time to accept this.
>
> —JULIE LEPARD

And it may take you some time to sort out your feelings about grades and their pressures and realities. Regardless, they are a feature of school and the teaching life, and until things change markedly in public education, you will need to make your own compromise with grades and quantification, a subject that will run through almost all the chapters of this book. Certainly in the case of your own state's standardized testing of students—testing that is now almost universal across the country—you will need to balance, as much as any single teacher can, what you see as your students' needs and what is a responsible approach to the state-mandated test.

Along with grades and testing, there's also the question of how much control you will have over your classroom curriculum. Some districts have adopted scripted curricula that essentially tie the hands of individual teachers, and Ken and Leila have even heard talk of administrators walking through halls listening to ensure teachers are following the scripts. The New York State Education Department even outsourced the writing of such curricula (called "modules") and offered them to school for adoption or adaptation. As examples or guides, such modules are fine, but when professional educators are required to follow someone else's script, something is wrong. What will the situation be in the school at which you're employed? How effectively will you be able to advocate for what you think are the best methods and content for your students?

Teacher, student, school. The three intertwine perhaps more intimately than you had first imagined. Our job is to find a balanced configuration that truly serves learning and teaching and that does not kill the mind and extinguish the spirit. It is an ongoing issue, an ongoing struggle of school, and no teacher, veteran or novice, has a quick or even permanent answer as to the exact dimensions of the balance. It is, actually, a daily endeavor, depending upon context and myriad other factors, and it is one of the most important jobs facing a teacher.

For Your Journal

Look back at the five "constraints" you will face in the public school setting. Choose any two of them and make *your* list of options/alternatives/practices that *you* think could lessen the impact of these potentially negative forces.

Think about your own schooling or what you have observed in school visits; what constraints do you remember experiencing or seeing? Imagine an ideal school: How would it avoid the problems discussed? What would the teachers be like? What attitudes/expectations would students have? How would an ideal community support an ideal school?

References

Aikin, Wilford M. 1942. *The Story of the Eight-Year Study*. New York: Harper & Brothers.

Alliance for Excellent Education. 2014. "Teacher Attrition Costs United States Up to $2.2 Billion Annually, Says New Alliance Report." *Straight A's Newsletter* 14 (14). http://all4ed.org/wp-content/uploads/2014/07/Volume14No14.pdf.

Alvermann, Donna E. 2009. "Sociocultural Constructions of Adolescence and Young People's Literacies." In *Handbook on Adolescent Literacy Research,* edited by Leila Christenbury, Randy Bomer, and Peter Smagorinsky, 14–28. New York: Guilford.

Applebee, Arthur N. 1974. *Tradition and Reform in the Teaching of English*. Urbana, IL: NCTE.

Au, W. 2007. "High-Stakes Testing and Curricular Control: A Qualitative Metasynthesis." *Educational Researcher* 36: 258–67.

Ayers, William. 2005. Introduction to *Re/constructing "The Adolescent,"* edited by J. A. Vandeboncoeur and L. P. Stevens, ix–xi. New York: Peter Lang.

Bracey, Gerald W. 2004. *Setting the Record Straight: Responses to Misconceptions About Public Education in the U.S.* 2nd ed. Portsmouth, NH: Heinemann.

Brandt, Deborah. 2001. *Literacy in American Lives*. New York: Cambridge University Press.

———. 2010. Foreword to *Reading the Past, Writing the Future: A Century of American Literacy Education and the National Council of Teachers of English*, edited by Erika Lindemann, ix–xiii. Urbana, IL: NCTE.

Bruner, Jerome S. 1963. *The Process of Education*. New York: Random House.

Casey, B. J., Rebecca M. Jones, and Todd A. Hare. 2008. "The Adolescent Brain." In *Annals of the New York Academy of Sciences*. Vol. 1124, The Year in Cognitive Neuroscience. doi:10.1196/annals.144.010.

Christenbury, Leila, Randy Bomer, and Peter Smagorinsky. 2009. Introduction to *Handbook on Adolescent Literacy Research*, edited by Leila Christenbury, Randy Bomer, and Peter Smagorinsky, 1–13. New York: Guilford.

Commission on the Reorganization of Secondary Education of the NEA. 1918. *Cardinal Principles of Secondary Education*. Washington, DC: U.S. Government Printing Office.

Creely, Robert. 1971. "A Form of Women." In *Contemporary American Poetry*, edited by A. Poulin Jr., 57. Boston: Houghton Mifflin.

Cuban, Larry. 1993. *How Teachers Taught: Constancy and Change in American Classrooms 1880–1990*. 2nd ed. New York: Teachers College Press.

Dewey, John. (1916) 1961. *Democracy and Education*. New York: Macmillan.

Dunn, Patricia A. 2001. *Talking, Sketching, Moving: Multiple Literacies in the Teaching of Writing*. Portsmouth, NH: Boynton/Cook.

Eliot, T. S. 1952. *The Complete Poems and Plays 1909–1950*. New York: Harcourt Brace & World.

An Experience Curriculum in English. 1935. A Report of the Curriculum Committee of the National Council of Teachers of English (Wilbur W. Hatfield, Chairman). New York: D. Appleton-Century Company.

Featherstone, Helen. 1991. "Making Diversity Educational: Alternatives to Ability Grouping." *Changing Minds*. Michigan Educational Extension Service, Bulletin 4 (Fall). East Lansing, MI.

Furhmann, Barbara Schneider. 1990. *Adolescence, Adolescents*. 2nd ed. Glenview, IL: Scott Foresman/Little, Brown.

Gordon, E. V., ed. 1966. *Pearl*. New York: Oxford University Press.

Gorlewski, Julie, and David Gorlewski, eds. 2014. "The Standards Movement: A Recent History." *English Journal* 104 (2).

Hawley, Richard A. 1979. "Teaching as Failing." *Phi Delta Kappan* 60 (April): 597–600.

Hawthorne, Nathaniel. 1970. "Young Goodman Brown." In *Hawthorne: Selected Tales and Sketches*. 3rd ed. San Francisco: Rinehart Press.

Hughes, Langston. 1959. "Harlem." In *Selected Poems of Langston Hughes*, 268. New York: Vintage.

Kohli, Sonali. 2014. "Modern-Day Segregation in Public Schools." *The Atlantic* (November 18). www.theatlantic.com/education/archive/2014/11/modern-day-segregation-in-public-schools/382846/.

Kozol, Jonathan. 2005. *The Shame of the Nation: The Restoration of Apartheid Schooling in America*. New York: Crown.

Lindemann, Erika, ed. 2010. *Reading the Past, Writing the Future: A Century of American Literacy Education and the National Council of Teachers of English*. Urbana, IL: NCTE.

Many, Joyce E., Mary Ariail, and Dana L. Fox. 2011. "Language Arts Learning in the Middle Grades." In *Handbook of Research on Teaching the English Language Arts*, 3rd ed., edited by Diane Lapp and Douglas Fisher, 53–59. New York: Routledge.

Muth, K. Denise, and Donna E. Alvermann. 1999. *Teaching and Learning in the Middle Grades*. 2nd ed. Boston: Allyn & Bacon.

National Governors Association Center for Best Practices, Council of Chief State School Officers. 2010. *Common Core State Standards for English Language Arts & Literacy in History/Social and Technical Subjects*. Washington, DC: National Governors Association Center for Best Practices, Council of Chief State School.

Nieto, Sonia. 2003. *What Keeps Teachers Going?* New York: Teachers College Press.

Oakes, Jeannie. 2005. *Keeping Track: How Schools Structure Inequality*. 2nd ed. New Haven, CT: Yale University Press.

O'Neill, Eugene. 1972. *Selections: The Emperor Jones. Anna Christie. The Hairy Ape*. New York: Vintage.

Oxford English Dictionary. 1971. New York: Oxford University Press.

Peck, Richard. 1991. *Unfinished Portrait of Jessica*. New York: Delacorte.

Piaget, Jean. 1959. *The Language and Thought of the Child*. 3rd ed. London: Routledge & Kegan Paul.

Postman, Neil, and Charles Weingartner. 1969. *Teaching as a Subversive Activity*. New York: Delacorte.

Pound, Ezra. 1973. "In a Station of the Metro." In *Lustra of Ezra Pound*, 45. New York: Haskell House.

Rilke, Rainer Maria. 1962. "Archaic Torso of Apollo." In *Translations from the Poetry of Rainer Maria Rilke*, translated by M. D. Herter Norton, 181. New York: Norton.

Salinger, J. D. 1991. *The Catcher in the Rye*. Boston: Little, Brown.

Strauch, B. 2003. *The Primal Teen: What the New Discoveries About the Teenage Brain Tell Us About Our Kids*. New York: Doubleday.

Strauss, Valerie. 2013. "The Bottom Line on Student Tracking." *Washington Post*, June 10.

Tierney, Rob J. 2009. "Literacy Education 2.0: Looking Through the Rear Vision Mirror as We Move Ahead." In *Changing Literacies for Changing Times*, edited by J. V. Hoffman and Y. M. Goodman, 282–303. New York: Routledge.

United States Department of Education. 1983. *A Nation at Risk*. Washington, DC: General Printing Office.

Vygotsky, Lev. 1978. *Mind in Society: The Development of Higher Mental Processes*. Cambridge, MA: Harvard University Press.

Wolfe, Thomas. 1952. *Look Homeward, Angel*. New York: Scribner.

2 | WHAT IT'S LIKE TO BE A TEACHER

In order to arrive at what you are not
You must go through the way in which you are not.
And what you do not know is the only thing you know
And what you own is what you do not own
And where you are is where you are not.

—T. S. Eliot, "East Coker" (*The Four Quartets*)

From Expert Learner to Novice Teacher

Leila's Story: Being and Becoming a Teacher

It was a late afternoon in the fall of my first year of teaching. The students had all gone home, the buses had lumbered off, most of the other teachers had packed up for the day, but I was still mopping up details from the day and working in my classroom. I took a break and stepped for a minute into the long corridor of the first floor. I looked down the hall and saw the row of closed classrooms and a few locker doors left ajar. Some stray student books littered the corridor; a few papers had fallen out of notebooks and had not been swept up. I smelled the rubber stuff the janitor sprinkled on the floors to help with the cleaning and polishing and heard the distant voices of the few teachers and students left in the building.

This was school at the end of the day, and I was a new teacher. But standing alone in the quiet corridor, something made me recall, for a strong pulse, a view of school I had repressed for many years. Right then, I felt and remembered how school had for a brief but important period in my life often scared me, terrified me. School had been a place not of success but of failure and disapproval. I felt my stomach tighten as I remembered three specific, chaotic years.

It was when my family was in crisis: my parents were divorced, and my mother was gone. I came to my elementary school, more often than not, with clothes askew, hair uncombed, and, more to the point, homework incomplete and tests not studied for. My teachers made their disapproval clear, my grades fell, and no one at home was available to help. I managed as best I could, but for most of those three years, I feared and hated school.

I looked around me, down the hall, in the building where I was now teaching—it was, yes, that same place, that familiar, alien, scary place: school. What in the world, I wondered in a sick rush, was I doing *as a teacher in a school*? Was I going to be one of those people who had succeeded in so frightening me for those three years? Was I going to spend five hours a day, five days a week doing to others what had been done to me?

It was a jarring, dislocating moment in my early teaching career. Because I could not deal directly with it or make sense of it in my new context as a teacher, I chose to set that bitter but accurate memory aside and literally move on. I went back into the classroom and got to work on a stack of papers. For years I could not think the incident through because I could not really understand it, and I did not want to consider what its implications might be. It was only much later I recognized what was happening: I was shifting, and it wasn't easy or pleasant, from student to teacher. I knew in that moment that school, which had not always been a wonderful place for me, was now my place of employment and teachers, who at one point in my life had terrified me, were now my professional colleagues. I had to make a new vision, which I did, that school was my home and I was a teacher. I also realized later that I could call upon my memories of being a frightened child to help me understand my students for whom school was also hostile and disapproving. The dislocation became actually a positive force, and I accepted my memory—school-as-scary-place—as an asset in understanding.

Ken's Story: Being and Becoming a Teacher

I remember distinctly being a bad good student, a bad student, and finally a good student. I attended a small Catholic grammar school and a very large, specialized public high school. I was a bright, cooperative youngster, eager to please, but also quite able to stay near the top of my class without much effort. I was a bad good student because there were few assignments that got as much of my attention as they should, and I have few memories of going to class with all my homework done. We were taught in large classes by well-meaning but low-paid teachers, many of whom were devoted nuns, and it seemed rule compliance was at least as important as content learning.

Moving from that sheltered community school environment to a public high school with about 1,000 students in the freshman class alone from all over New York City, all of whom had passed a rigorous test to get in, was utter culture shock! Competition among students was fierce, and each student was smarter than the next. I could bore you with a litany of famous graduates of this school, but I won't. Suffice it to say, I went quickly from floating at the top of the class to sinking to the bottom. I graduated, barely, relieved the school was philosophically opposed to reporting students' class rank.

Like most, I had effective and ineffective teachers—teachers who cared, teachers who knew their stuff, teachers who tried to engage the students, and teachers who did not care, were not well prepared, and were not engaged in their classrooms. My primary memory of my high school days, however, is falling between the cracks, feeling left out, and checking out of school without much consequence. Like Leila, at this time I was dealing with significant family strife—divorcing parents and an actively alcoholic father—and I coped with these problems by fading to the background in my classes, working in after-school jobs, immersing myself in TV reruns, and learning how to cut class and get away with it.

It wasn't until years later, when I attended a wonderful, small, not especially distinguished college that I was able to get the distance, maturity, and support from teachers and staff mentors to allow me to become the truly good student I could be. Seduced by too many Jacques Cousteau shark documentaries, I entered as a misplaced marine biology major and nearly flunked out of college in my first year. A dose of tough love from a biology professor helped me realize that my one good grade (in English) and my chosen after-school activities (the school newspaper and literary magazine) might just be clues as to my true calling. Duh. At that point, as a sophomore in college, I switched my major to writing and literature and finally started to study and to work for more than just grades. I began to appreciate the knowledge I was building, and I learned the satisfaction of truly earning an academic record I could be proud of.

My personal experiences have clearly had an impact on the kind of teacher I am. Even as teacher education program director, I gravitate to the first course our new preservice English teachers take. I enjoy helping motivate uncertain or even ambivalent students and getting them excited about their work. I don't assume they have a great deal of support beyond our classroom walls, and I enjoy helping students understand how they can enrich themselves with serious study. I understand when students have issues, but I don't allow that to prevent them from having to reach the required bar—and a high bar it is—to become an English teacher. Overall, I think that the experience of being a good student and a not-so-good student has really enhanced my ability to teach others.

You may have no such mixed memories in your history, but regardless, there is no way to soft-pedal the fact: the shift from student learner to teacher learner is a tough one. It is no small exaggeration that the world looks very different on the other side of the desk, and for some novices it is almost a loss of innocence to confront the classroom with the board *behind* you. Making that transition is a difficult one under the best of circumstances; you have had some success in school or you would not envision becoming a teacher, but the shift from a member of the class to the principal organizer of the class is not automatic or, as in our cases in particular, a graceful event.

Teaching is also, as you suspect, a tough profession. Although some teachers stay in the classroom for many years, others dream of new professions and many, if asked, will tell you they would not enter the profession again.

So why do teachers stay in the classroom?

Schoolteacher gives somewhat of an answer. It is a classic and one of the widest studies of the profession. Dan C. Lortie's study, involving almost 6,000 teachers, found that teachers' overwhelmingly greatest satisfaction is the interaction with students; other "rewards" such as salary, community status, security, summer vacation time, and freedom from competition are much lower on the scale (1975, 105). Lortie calls what teachers cited as the interaction with students a "psychic" reward (103 ff.), and it is true for many veteran teachers and is the reason they continue to meet first period every morning.

But *becoming* a teacher is a different matter, and often the psychic rewards are not as apparent early in the game. Becoming a teacher sometimes involves unlearning what you know or think you know—and possibly involves recognizing that what you may assume about teaching is, as T. S. Eliot writes, precisely what you do not know.

Lee Shulman, a professor at Stanford and a respected figure in the study of how people become teachers, writes this:

> [One of the reasons] it is so difficult to learn to teach is that, unlike many other professions, people who learn to teach learn it after having completed, in Dan Lortie's phrase, a seventeen year "apprenticeship of observation." They have spent seventeen years, more or less, and nearly 20,000 hours as observers of teaching and they've learned an enormous amount about it. . . . Another reason learning to teach is difficult is that much of learning to teach depends on learning from experience. . . . The whole idea of learning from experience is: I do something, it doesn't work, so I try something else until I finally find something that does work. It's a kind of thoughtful trial and error, but it's predicated on two assumptions: one, we have reasonably accurate access to what we do, and two, we are reasonably accurate in identifying the consequences of what we do. But it is very difficult to establish those two assumptions. (1987)

Thus we come into the classroom with our own history as students—and a relatively successful history at that—and we assume that what we see in our own classes is not only what is happening there but that we can figure out the effects of what is happening. Sometimes we are very wrong.

Characteristics of Good Teachers

There are a number of studies about personality traits that teachers need to be successful, and some education or certification programs even tie tests to their students to ensure that students are psychologically equipped for the profession. Most teachers know, however, that successful teachers have a formidable range of personalities and that the classroom atmospheres those teachers foster can be remarkably varied. Beyond that range, however, there are a few generalizations we can make. Successful teachers:

- **Like people (young people in particular):** Some folks even rather humorously advocate being "arrested in development" in order to be a successful teacher, but it is true that you must almost have an appetite for the age group you teach. Those who thrive in middle school, for example, express a certain affinity for persons that age and the characteristics of their developmental level. There's an energy and vitality that young people exude. If you're mostly invigorated by it, great. If not, this could be one very long, exhausting career.

- **Are flexible:** You may have the whole day planned only to find that an assembly has been scheduled—with little advance warning—for all of your second-period and part of your third-period classes. You may find that your lesson plan that worked well for the morning section of a course is a bomb with the afternoon section. The two students whose reports were going to take up half the period need all the period; one of your students is upset by something and is quietly crying. Successful teachers adjust and adjust quickly.

- **Draw appropriate conclusions from classroom observation:** Students are bored or disaffected; the small-group arrangements in third period were especially successful; over half the class did not understand the homework reading assignment. A number of factors may explain these observations, and the successful teacher makes a judgment regarding subsequent planning. Such teachers use real data to make these judgments, and they don't blame the students.

- **Listen actively and attentively to students:** Students often tell teachers nearly all they need to know if indeed the teachers have, as the biblical aphorism tells us, the ears to hear and the eyes to see. Students also will share more in class if they have the impression their comments are being really listened to. It is important to recognize the overt *text* of what our students say and the covert *subtext* of what they are saying. Successful teachers make appropriate eye contact, don't interrupt, listen, and through body language get students to feel their remarks are worth attending to.

- **Have a sense of humor:** Laughter, in its best manifestation, is emotional warmth, and both students and teachers can make significant personal contact through lighthearted exchanges. Some of us—let's not mention Ken specifically, but yeah, people like him—have deeply silly senses of humor that often work better with young people than with their peers. Others aren't as amused by corny stories and bathroom humor, but they still enjoy the atmosphere that adolescents create.

You do not need to have the skill of a stand-up comic, but you do need to have a sense of play and liveliness. This, of course, does not embrace the extremes of humor, which are often best left to one's peers. The use of mocking remarks, sarcasm, or jokes at students' expense is unpleasant and often scarring, but the happiness of a more gentle humor can permeate a successful teacher's classroom.

- **Have a sense of intellectual curiosity—and encourage one in their students:** Truly exciting things happen in the classroom, especially when the parties involved are somewhat prepared to be surprised and pleased and intrigued. "Why is that so? If it is true, what else could be true? Does anyone know about, has anyone heard of _____?" are all questions that can open doors of exploration. Try to ask your students questions that you truly don't know the answers to. Good teachers ask these questions frequently. Give students room to explore the world around them in ways that encourage their curiosity and align with English language arts outcomes.

For Your Journal

Think about your personality and who you are. How would you describe yourself to others? Don't be modest; list six or so of your best traits. Then look at those traits and pick two or three that you think will *help* you be a good teacher. Why do you think those traits are important? How do you think they will function in your interaction in the classroom?

What a Teacher Needs to Do

Despite your enthusiasm and preparation, you may experience what Leila's student Brian Durrett described in his student teaching journal. Brian raises important questions:

I think the thing that bugs me . . . is . . . the whole teacher–student battle for the classroom. I have heard many a lecture about how it is important to have students experience the curriculum in a way that applies to their lives. Is it possible to do that with a student whose mind is closed? The students who are rude are the ones that are not into the material and have nothing better to do. I know that it is my job to teach every student and it is my responsibility to make my lessons interesting enough that they engage the students. I know that if there is a student that is not learning and he or she is being rude, I need to do what is necessary to make sure that the student learns. Period. But the important piece of that puzzle is that there is only so much I can do. I had been the idealist and thought that I would do everything in my power to touch every student. I thought that might be possible. Now that I have spent time [student teaching], I am not sure if that is possible. . . . There are a number of students [in my classes] who genuinely do not want to be at school, have failed for the year by the end of the first semester, and could care less. There are other students who are bright and at most times do what is necessary to get by, but do not apply themselves. And there are very bright students who for whatever reason just play and don't do their work. . . . So how far do you go?

How far do you go? For us, there are some answers in one of our favorite books about teaching, *After the Lesson Plan: Realities of High School Teaching* by veteran teacher Amy Puett Emmers. Her book is both hard-nosed and compassionate. Emmers believes a teacher has four major tasks:

1. A teacher must gain students' attention.
2. A teacher must insist that students perform at the level of their ability.
3. A teacher must provide consequences for learning.
4. A teacher must recognize and insist. (1981, xiv, xv, 60)

Gaining Students' Attention

We all remember classes where the students were having a great time carrying on their own conversations while the teacher futilely tried to either quiet them or just talk above them. During her student teaching, Debbie Martin recalls one class:

> Third period—GAWD!!!! When I asked them to pleeease quiet down for the video [we were seeing], it was as if I wasn't in the room—there was a total disregard for anything & everyone except what they were interested in. I repeated my request several times by standing in the middle of the room saying, "Excuse me, excuse me, please. Let's get quiet. Let's not be rude to those who wish to watch the video." One student shouted, "Hey! Show some respect." I thanked her and started the video.

On a longer-term basis, we also can remember semesters where we just endured a course (and a teacher), resigned that we were not going to learn or do much of anything interesting. Sometimes we wondered if the teacher noticed what we certainly knew. Sometimes we made the best of the class by daydreaming, passing notes, or surreptitiously talking with friends.

Actually this activity has been studied and researched. It is occasionally called the "underlife" of a classroom, a sociological term that refers to all the things that students can—and do—do in class instead of what they are expected to do. If you have spent any time in a field experience just observing students—possibly from the back of the room—you have seen these behaviors. Certainly much of this is normal classroom behavior and can be completely neutral, if not wholly innocent. When carried to an extreme, however, it can be highly disruptive and demoralizing to class order. And when it happens in your classroom, it can be a real problem.

Emmers suggests a number of principles to help us gain—and keep—our students' attention:

- Interest students in the subject matter and relate it to their lives.
- Build on what the students know.
- Discuss, don't lecture.
- Answer student questions.
- Provide an element of excitement through reasonable competition. (1981, 23–47)

As you will see later in this chapter, the discovery model of teaching may be closest to what Emmers suggests. Certainly, when we care about our students' learning, it is rather automatic that we will adopt many of Emmers' suggestions in our teaching.

Insisting Students Perform at the Level of Their Ability

This may seem so obvious that it is simpleminded, but the difficulty is that we are often clueless about where our students truly are in their level of ability. Test scores and grades are not the reliable indicators you may have been led to believe. People also, we know from cognitive psychology, can "plateau" in their development—stay at the same level for long periods—and then make remarkable gains in relatively rapid periods of time. How do we know where they are? Surely some students need special help and those who are unwilling need prodding, but Emmers is most concerned about our setting limits on the other students:

> We still know very little about what actually occurs in the brain when people learn. Moreover, teachers cannot possibly be aware of all of the many factors that contribute to their students' motivation to learn. Is it really the function of teachers ever to discourage a student from attempting something he wants to do? If he can't do it, he'll discover that soon enough for himself. He certainly won't thank anybody for advance information about his shortcomings.
>
> When asked whether he knows how to do any specific task, whatever it is, a friend of mine usually replies, "Maybe I do; I haven't tried." Most people smile at his whimsy, which they do not regard as a very realistic appraisal of ability. Perhaps, though, students would benefit if teachers could be just this optimistic. Teachers would not be requiring anyone to do what he can't. They would not be forcing anyone to do what he really doesn't wish. Rather they would be trying to extend a student's possibilities. After all, maybe he can! (1981, 87)

And perhaps the tragedy of many classrooms is not that we ask too much of our students—but that we ask too little. Certainly when we assume that a "less able" or "slower" group cannot handle classroom tasks above the level of filling in worksheets, we are not trying to get our students to perform at the level of their ability. Nor are we giving them the chance to move to a higher level.

Providing Consequences for Learning

There are many ways to reward learning: with praise, class privileges, posting of work on bulletin boards or online or publishing it in anthologies, positive emails sent home, grades, awards. Once students are motivated and capable of the work level, they will perform. What about students, however, who are not motivated or not capable? Although teachers need to make their best effort and attempt, rather unceasingly, to capture students' attention and motivation, there is a limit. This kind of response may surprise or even offend you, but here's what Emmers writes:

> For teachers to blame themselves unnecessarily when students are inattentive or unmotivated is a waste of time and emotion, for it is, after all, an individual student who must change these conditions. Teachers can't do it for him. All they can do is try to conduct the kind of class in which uninterested students will at least be tempted to reverse their feelings about the subject. (1981, 57–58)

Beginning teachers especially feel the sting of students who refuse to engage in class. Where are the limits of our attempts to overcome this? Although we have had different teaching experiences, we are agreed here: yes, we have an ethical obligation to do our best in a class, but we also must acknowledge that teachers cannot learn *for* the students, cannot study for them, and cannot be motivated for them. We can create the classroom atmosphere that emphasizes all students should—and can—do their best, but we cannot absolutely ensure that everyone is engaged all the time. For students who, despite our best efforts, despite our demonstration of care, resist working in our classes, often we have no choice but to give them the grades they have earned.

It is a teacher's job to support students. Sometimes support is assistance on an activity, more time to work on something, or an empathetic ear. But sometimes support looks more like insisting students get their work done, holding firm to deadlines, and ensuring that students accept the consequences of their actions, or lack thereof, such as low grades or appropriate disciplinary measures. We can and should be kind as we show all these forms of support, but we cannot allow students to choose not to succeed and appear to succeed nonetheless.

Recognizing and Insisting

Besides the three tasks just listed, Emmers also articulates a teaching principle that is worth lingering over: *recognizing and insisting*. She explains it this way:

> At the opposite extreme from those students who for whatever reason can't do the work are those who are capable but won't do it. While there are various causes for students' not working, or at least not working as much as they should, most . . . think they can get by without doing the assignments. They are also convinced that what they neglect won't make much difference in their lives. (1981, 68)

Again, our students come largely by compulsion—which can make the relationship in the class a difficult one. On the other hand, a student's very presence in a class can imply that she or he is there to learn; as teachers we recognize that. We can also insist that we be allowed to teach the reluctant students as well as the others. Class is for learning; participation, in some form, is a way toward that learning. What we have to recognize and, at the end, resist, is what Lauren Dean describes in one of her classes during student teaching:

> Today I called my first parent. Three weeks ago I had to make a seating chart for my fifth period class. . . . Many of the students are extroverted, sarcastic, and hyper (just after lunch). Six of these students are on the basketball team, and they are all friends. Needless to say, they like to push my buttons, so I developed a seating chart in an effort to increase student focus and decrease the chatty distractions. Since that day, one student refuses to sit in his appropriate seat. Each day he comes in and sits in the wrong seat until I notice, and then have to tell him to move. Each day this disrupts the first few moments of class, unless of course I catch him before the bell rings. At first it was kind of funny. Now it is just disrespectful and frustrating.
>
> So today when I noticed this student was again in the wrong seat, I asked him to step out in the hall. First I asked him why he thought the new seating chart rule did not apply to him and it did for the other students. He shrugged. I then told him his behavior was disrespectful and disruptive. He shrugged. I asked him if he understood why this was dis-respectful and disruptive. He shrugged. I asked him if his mother would be upset to hear about his behavior. He shrugged. I asked him if I should call his mother. He shrugged. So I did. That very afternoon I called her.

Perhaps one of the worst things we can do with our students is ignore them, min-imize them. We need to let students know we know them and that they are in our classes; while they are there, we need to insist upon their participation. Indifference is, ultimately, killing. We have an obligation to see and recognize our charges and to demand from them as much as we can—we must insist on their learning. To do less is to turn our backs on them and, ultimately, on ourselves. We'd be willing to bet that at least on some level Lauren's student was relieved that she called his parents. She showed him that she cared enough about him to make an effort to ensure his coop-eration. And, it's possible, the student and his mom had a good conversation that will build their relationship as well.

Beginning Your Life in the Classroom

On your journey of being and becoming a teacher, you will live a significant portion of your waking hours among young people and in a classroom setting. If you have worked in any kind of a business office or corporate complex, either for the summer or full time, you may find some of the aspects of living and working in school challenging as there are real obstacles. Although there is no single book that can anticipate all of your questions and issues during your first few years of teaching, this section is an attempt to outline some things that might get lost otherwise. There is, actually, much to your life in the classroom that is serious—such as dealing with the politics of school and discipline—and a lot that is pretty mundane—such as where to scrounge supplies for your room or what to do about eating lunch. Both the serious and the mundane, however, are important to your early success in the classroom.

The journey begins.

The Politics of School

Every school is different, a city with its own laws and rules and culture and climate and, yes, its politics. It would be wonderful to think that you will truly understand the climate and politics of your first school before you sign that contract, but the character of a school community is often not clear until you are actually on staff and teaching. You would be well advised, in your first few months in your new school, to observe closely as to what you can tell about what is important in this school and, essentially, what are the mores and values. For instance, some schools and staff are very warm and personal; others are more formal and expect the same from you. In some schools, teachers talk freely among themselves about their lives, their personal and even religious convictions, and their families. In other schools, such conversation is more limited to close friends. As with other issues, there is wide variance in schools regarding forms of address within the staff (do you call everyone by their first name?), chain of command (when do you go to your team leader, lead teacher, department chair, an assistant principal?), and regulations regarding dealing with parents (how often are you to email or possibly call parents and on what issues?). You will undoubtedly make mistakes and have misinterpretations, but if you approach your teaching setting as if it were neutral, you are being naïve. There is a distinct climate of sorts in every school, and the sooner you scope it out and learn how to manage it—if not adjust to it, because after a year or so you may want to transfer schools—the less stressful your beginning career will be. Things to consider for your early successful career:

- What kinds of topics are discussed in the teachers' lounge? What seems to be off limits? To what extent should you add your comments?

- How much of your personal life do you—should you—share with members of the staff, especially in the beginning?

- How do you deal with teachers who may be negative about their careers and their students? To what extent do you spend time with these teachers and listen to their advice—or complaints? Are these conversations serious, or are some really just colleagues blowing off steam?

- Who are the teachers who have a reputation for success in the classroom? How can you get to know them and learn from them?

- How do you feel about having lunch with certain groups or even socializing with them after school? To what extent are you expected to attend weekend and night school events (such as football or basketball games, plays, concerts)?

- What are the requirements for dealing with parents, a group that can be a potent ally and also a potent adversary? What kinds of communication strategies and regulations are in place? How much notification to parents is expected regarding their children's final and interim grades, regarding your projects, deadlines, and your class?

- What are the staff rules or deadlines that are nonnegotiable? What should you be sure that you do on time and very well? What appears to be less crucial?

- What is the role of your team leader or department chair? What are the functions of the assistant principal or the principal? Are there subject matter specialists, aides, members of the counseling staff to consider? Who is approachable and who is not? To what extent do you—can you—talk with these individuals and ask them for help?

Although the answers to these questions may not be clear to you, especially in the beginning, it is important to know that your school community has distinct characteristics and ways of doing things. The sooner you assess these, the better you can make choices and negotiate successfully the politics of school.

Discipline

Most people getting ready to enter a classroom for the first time, especially after having completed courses on teaching and having read books on students and classroom management, expect that they will be able to quickly establish an orderly atmosphere and run a classroom fairly smoothly. This expectation, however, is rarely fulfilled, and some novices are bitterly disappointed that they were not "taught" what to do or how to react in real classroom situations.

The fact of the matter is that no class or book can teach an early career teacher what to do and how to do it in every specific instructional situation. Even a very successful student teaching experience is no guarantee that the first year in the classroom will go smoothly in the discipline arena.

Discipline seems a simple concept, but it is actually very complex and is the sum of a number of variables, not the least of which is the beginning teacher's rather nascent perception of what is acceptable behavior and what is not. School context is important here, as are school rules. In certain schools there is a surprising level of informality that is expected and acceptable; in other schools, the opposite may be true. What you assume to be polite or respectful behavior between teachers and students and students and students may not, indeed, be what your students assume. The only way to determine this is to watch and learn, ask and adjust your own expectations—and, yes, you have the right to have those expectations—to the reality of your school context. And, of course, if for whatever reason you find the school context antithetical to your beliefs, you need to change schools or school systems.

In addition, in the beginning of anyone's teaching, the fit between what a teacher thinks is happening in a classroom and what is actually occurring is often not exact. Thus a beginning teacher may honestly feel that the entire class is out of control when actually two or three students are being disruptive. A novice may think that her tone of voice was sufficiently commanding when, in actuality, it barely could be heard. The teacher may be frustrated that students, although instructed to raise their hands to be called upon, simply call out answers and unaware that he routinely accepts answers from students who do not raise their hands and thus reinforces the behavior.

Having someone observe your classes, watching other teachers' classes, and trying to become more self-perceptive are three ways to establish a clearer view of what you are doing in your own classroom. Videoing yourself is also helpful. In fact, video is quickly becoming recognized as a powerful means of professional development for teachers who want to learn more about their teaching and its impact. If you are in a state that requires the edTPA for certification, you will have to submit two ten-minute clips from your student teaching along with in-depth commentaries on them. The Teacher Channel is an online organization that has created hundreds of videos from real classrooms, along with commentaries from the teachers and experts. Because the videos are short (many fewer than five minutes), you can watch a quick video rather than update your Facebook page, when you could use a quick break. Even better, Teacher Channel resources are free!

Further, although they are as general as anything you will read in any similar book, the following principles may help you establish and maintain good discipline. They are not magic, and implementing all of them will not automatically ensure a well-managed class, but they are sensible and common sense.

Keep These Principles in Mind

Be firm; be fair   Once you decide on a procedure or a consequence for behavior, stick to it. Of course, be sure the procedure or consequence does not favor or punish in an inequitable manner. Thus if something goes for one student, it must go for the other, and, unless it is an unusual circumstance (a judgment call you must make in and of itself), you should not be talked out of or into anything different for different students.

Be consistent   If it's a rule on Monday, it should be a rule on Wednesday. Constant change confuses students and confuses you. Although there are often real and compelling reasons for altering classroom procedures or consequences, don't do it willy-nilly.

Use "I" messages As much as you would like to tell a student that he or she is the problem, phrasing statements such as "*I* can't accept this behavior in class" or "*I* would appreciate/ prefer that you sit down" helps students see the issue as an issue, not as a direct attack on them personally.

Single out students but don't humiliate them Often, talking with or disciplining individual students—not the entire class—is sufficient to change a disorderly atmosphere into an orderly one. Be aware, however, that such attention to individual students needs to be done thoughtfully. If you wish to talk to one student, whisper a few words quietly to him or her, go out in the hall, or meet before or after school; don't discuss students' behavior in the presence and hearing of their peers and their class. And, we suggest always starting with "Is there something wrong I can help with?" to begin such a conversation. If the student says yes, you might find out something important that you can quickly address. If the student says no, then you can explain to the student why you are troubled by his or her behavior.

Use praise and rewards Students enjoy praise for working well or for working better than before. Students are people, too, and they often appreciate positive attention from you. Students also respond to rewards, which can include pencils or pens or a copy of a paperback book. Offering praise and rewards to students if they achieve or continue to achieve can be helpful. Although certainly we would all like to think that students come to class to study and work without the need for reward, that is often not true. Judiciously used, praise and rewards can help students stay on track and stay out of trouble. But remember that praise and rewards may improve extrinsic motivation, but they don't do much to help students become truly motivated about learning and building their own future.

Do not ignore bullying One of the lessons to emerge from the past decades' melancholy list of school shootings is that students who are consistently bullied become enormously frustrated with teachers, school, and the students who harass them. This frustration, as we have seen from news coverage of tragic events at numerous schools across this country, can erupt into deadly violence. Whether the bullying is subtle or obvious, whether it is physical (involving hitting or shoving or touching or groping) or verbal (such as name-calling, shunning, or shaming), your class should never be a place where such harassment is tolerated. In addition, you may learn from other students regarding individuals being bullied outside school or online. Whether outside of school or in your class, you may be tempted to ignore it and hope it goes away, but when students see that you will allow bullying in your presence, it is likely to escalate. You have an obligation to intervene and squelch all such behavior. In addition, if you have evidence that one of your students is being harassed by others online, you need to make that fact known to the counseling staff.

Many excellent resources on bullying are available. See the July 2012 *English Journal*, "Preventing Bullying Behavior," guest-edited by Nancy Mack, which includes articles that tie bullying prevention directly to ELA lessons. See also *Generation Bullied 2.0: Prevention and Intervention Strategies for Our Most Vulnerable Students* (Miller, Burns, and Johnson 2013) and Chapter 10 in this volume. Many prevention programs focus not only on bullies and victims but also on the role of bystanders.

Make your students too busy to misbehave A class that starts on time and in which much happens is a class where a student will have to work to get in trouble. You do not want to assume that students might have misbehaved just because the class was not sufficiently organized or rigorous—some incidents will occur regardless—but you can head off a lot of trouble by establishing a productive, busy atmosphere. It has been attributed to numerous sages, but the comment, "Make the work interesting, and the discipline will take care of itself" is good advice for all of us.

Reflect on the sources of student misbehavior One of the reasons it's so important for teachers to put their egos aside is so they are able to pinpoint why a student is misbehaving. If a teacher doesn't take the behavior personally, she or he is much better able to answer these questions, which may help identify a problem: Is there something wrong with this lesson? Is there something I am doing that is causing this problem? Is this student experiencing a problem in this class (is the lesson too hard?) or outside of class (is this content touching a nerve)? Does this student simply want me to notice that something is wrong so that I ask him or her about it later? Or, is this student simply opting out of classwork and choosing to misbehave instead? As you learn to run an orderly and engaged classroom, you'll find student misbehavior usually only occurs when there's a reason. The sooner you get to that reason, the better for everyone.

Involve parents As noted in the Politics of School section in this chapter, parents can be potent allies. Use whatever communication channels your school suggests (your class website, emails, phone calls, written notes) and inform parents when you need their help—or even when things are going well. Harmony between teacher and parent is not always assured, but you might be pleasantly surprised to find that you and your students' parents agree more often than you think. As a checklist, you might consider these five questions from the U.S. Department of Education (2014), all of which relate clearly to what we do in our classes and what parents might want to know:

- Quality: Is my child getting a great education?
- Ready for Success: Will my child be prepared to succeed in whatever comes next?
- Safe and Healthy: Is my child safe and cared for at school?
- Great Teachers: Is my child engaged and learning every day?
- Equity and Fairness: Does my child, and every child at my child's school or program, have the opportunity to succeed and be treated fairly?

The questions may not strike you as terribly inventive and/or creative, but as the website notes, the underlying theme is not just finding the answer but looking for indicators (i.e., how will I know?). When we can answer that for our parents, we have gone a long way toward enlisting them as our partners in teaching and learning.

For Your Journal

Discipline is a large issue for most beginning teachers. Which of the principles just described seem to you to be the easiest to enforce or adopt? Which seems to be the hardest? Why? What do you assume will have to happen in your classes before you have what you feel is an acceptable and orderly environment?

Classroom Environment, Room Arrangement, Creature Comforts, Food

Shortly into our teaching careers, we realized that the schedule of school was our schedule, too. Somehow we both had assumed that although students were responsible for being in a specific place at a specific time on a daily basis, teachers' schedules just had to be somewhat different. Not so. We soon realized that, just like our students, we too were in a classroom for hours every day, and we too could not leave. Students had to be strictly on time for the beginning of every class; so did we. Students had five minutes to change class; we had five minutes to set up for the next class. Students had twenty minutes for lunch; we had the same. Students could not leave the school when they wished or use their cell phones when they wanted; neither could we. Students turned in assignments, which meant that very soon after we had to grade those assignments. Students met deadlines, which, in turn, meant we met deadlines, too. In fact, we soon learned there is a profound reciprocity to this business of living and working in school that is more exacting than we at first realized.

You may already be aware of this, but it was news to us as beginning teachers. Bluntly put, teachers have the same schedule restrictions as students—in fact, in some ways it is more demanding because, unlike our students, we can't routinely go to our locker or be excused to go to the bathroom during class. What this means for you is that the freedom to pursue your own daily schedule and rhythms during class is forever changed. For some of you, this will not be much of an issue. For others, however, adjusting to living life in a classroom may take some time.

Classroom Environment

Practically speaking, you need to know that you will be logging many hours inside a classroom and that if that environment is not a friendly or pleasant place for you, it probably will not be for your students, either. No one is suggesting that you spend a great deal of money or consult an interior decorator for your teaching space—if indeed at the beginning of your teaching career you have your "own" room and teach there all day or even for part of the day. On the other hand, there are some things you need to think about.

Despite the appeal of many recently built schools—which often have courtyards, atriums, skylights, and extensive landscaping—most school buildings are functional, relatively bare, even antiseptic institutions, and the heart of those schools, the class-rooms, are rarely better. Unless you are teaching in one of the new educational Taj Mahals, think of bringing color and light and, yes, beauty, into what may at first appear a sterile space. Without spending a huge amount of money, you can purchase or scrounge (yard sales are great sources) some of the following for your classroom:

- **Posters:** There are many inexpensive, colorful, and thought-provoking posters, which range from inspirational (with art, photography, and famous quotations) to the informational (offering facts about authors, literary works, components of language, historical events). We are particularly fond of the posters from ALA, the American Library Association (write ALA at 50 E. Huron Street, Chicago, IL 60611, or go to alastore.ala.org). ALA sells all kinds of posters, many in a series, advocating literacy (such as the celebrity READ posters), supporting intellectual freedom, and even marking monthly celebrations such as GLBT Book Month. Other educational organizations and commercial teacher outlets also sell posters; check their catalogs. Your local bookstore, either of the small or of the mega vari-ety, often will give away dated posters touting new authors or books. *Practical tip:* If you get some posters for your classroom, do change them every marking period or so: even the most attractive posters get stale after months and months.

- **Bulletin boards:** A great place to put those posters is on your bulletin board (most school classrooms have at least one, sometimes more, attached to the classroom wall), but you can also use this space to display student work and to put reminder announcements. At times we as teachers reserved part of the bulletin board and made it a student comment/graffiti area where students were encouraged to write. Students could leave quotations that they have found, ask thought-provoking questions, or just write something that they want expressed publicly (you may have to provide a few etiquette guidelines here, but it shouldn't be that difficult). Watching students wander over to that section of your bulletin board to check for what's new is, by the way, gratifying. Covering the board with bright paper as a background is helpful and, again, you want to think of changing the paper and the look of the bulletin board about every marking period. Do not be intimidated by a bulletin board! Even those of us who are artistically chal-lenged can staple paper on the board, slap up a poster, and leave space for other items of interest to the class—the effort is worth it.

- **Books and bookcases:** You will need a modest classroom library for that day when the schedule is shot and students need something to read or for when those three students finish the test early and turn it in, telling you, in all earnestness, they now have nothing to do or read. (In a later chapter we will also talk about free reading and, if you provide time for that in your teaching, you will definitely need a classroom library.)

For your class library, get old magazines from your friends and relatives, scrounge old paperbacks (remember those yard sales again), throw in some crossword puzzle books, and, if you have a player, audio books and CDs; use anything that is readable (or hearable) and appropriate for the age level of your students. If you can find an old bookcase (some classrooms come equipped with these already, some do not), put the magazines and books there. For us, the classroom library, the books and bookcase, were indispensable additions to our teaching areas, and before class and even when the room was empty at lunch, we would find students going to the bookcase to check for what might be new or interesting. Without explicit instructions from us, students can get into the habit of browsing through what may have been brought in. *Practical tip:* Post nearby a sign-up sheet for when students want to borrow something from the library. On the sheet students can write their names and the dates they removed materials. This record will help you keep some track of what goes in and out of the bookcase—you don't want the bookcase bare by the end of the first month of school. You can, of course, decide that nothing goes out of the classroom on loan; that is up to you, but if you do let students take things home, keep a record. Certainly, though, you need to think of your collection as "disposable": even with teacher vigilance, a sign-up sheet, and conscientious students, some of your materials will naturally leave your room and never return. In fact, you'll want to keep some young adult books on topics that students might need to know about but might be embarrassed to ask about: LGBTQ issues; puberty, sexuality, and sexual identity; dealing with alcohol or drug abuse problems; sexual assault; bullying; and so on. If books on these topics leave your classroom without an official record, know that you may have helped someone who had nowhere else to turn. Thus, the library content will change significantly from semester to semester.

- **Rugs:** This is really optional, but old rag rugs can provide a great place for students to sit and read. They also "warm up" a room and, if there is no objection from the administration (some principals freak when they think of kids sitting in or on anything but an official desk), get an inexpensive rug and put it near the bookcase. *Practical tip:* Washable rugs are best.

- **Plants:** Again, this is optional, but plants are great living things to have in a room. There are, thank you, Mother Nature, many varieties that require little care and will flourish under florescent lights and drinking water from the hall fountain. Most everyone responds to the look of plants, and Leila had one or two in every classroom in which she taught. Ken, on the other hand, was always happy enough that his *students* lived through his classes and wouldn't take the additional risk with greenery.

Room Arrangement

For generations students learned in a classroom where the teacher's desk stood centered in front of the board (it used to be black, and now in most schools it is white and can also be electronic). The remainder of the room was filled with students' desks, set in long rows, all facing the front. So what is wrong with this picture? Well, for one thing the teacher's desk impedes the students' view of the board. For another, if the students are all facing front, during discussions they will be unable to see much of anyone else but the teacher. Finally, how do students work in small groups or pairs if they are permanently located in long rows of desks?

Although there is no perfect—nor should there be—room arrangement, you need to consider placing your desk somewhere other than centered in front of the board: the side of the board, either side of the room, and the back of the room are three options, all of which give you a different perspective on the students as they sit at their desks.

Another thing you need to consider is how the students' desks are arranged. There is nothing wrong with students sitting facing the front in long rows when they are taking tests or listening to a short lecture or presentation, but there *is* something wrong with that arrangement at other times. Large-group discussions are not natural when people talk to the back of other people's heads: accordingly, think of putting your students' desks into a horseshoe or in four long rows, two rows facing two rows (Figure 2–1).

If you use the latter, remember to leave space between the left two and the right two of the rows so that you can walk between them comfortably. Walking around the room is a must for teachers, to be able to communicate with students quietly and to ensure students are on task. If you have table-type desks, you can put students in pairs or in a trio or a

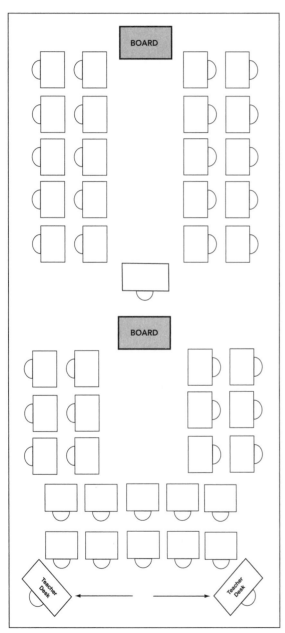

Figure 2–1

quartet; this is, obviously, ideal for small-group work.

And, of course, any desk arrangement can be changed so that three or four students can all work on a project in one general area together (Figure 2–2).

Our feeling is that you should not become attached to a single room arrangement; you should shift the desks in accordance with what the students are doing, not in accordance with some inflexible ideal of order. This may mean, at times, that the desk arrangement changes from class to class; that's OK, too. In fact, it's intriguing to the students. *Practical tip:* If the desks need to be moved at any given time, don't do it by yourself. Ask your students to help: it's far quicker for twenty-five people to do such a task than for a single

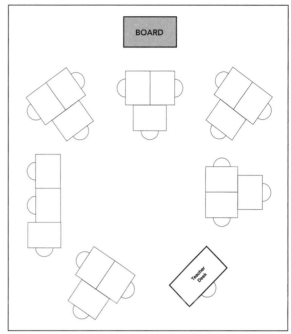

Figure 2–2

individual. But you need to build into your classroom routine that moving desks is to be done quickly and relatively quietly, otherwise your students may think of this as time for a break. Also, if you alter a room arrangement and will not be in that room for the succeeding bell, be considerate and have the students put the desks back as you found them. The teacher who comes in next will appreciate it. Finally, there are some classrooms, such as portables or trailers, where space is very tight, and it is extremely difficult to move desks. If that is your teaching setting, consider moving chairs into circles and letting students hold materials on their laps.

Creature Comforts

Beyond the classroom itself, there is the issue of *you* and what you need to be comfortable as well as productive. Much of this may not be true for the school in which you teach. You can never assume, however, that what you need will automatically be accessible in the building—and in most schools, teachers are expected to stay in the building the entire contract day. In most school districts you can't walk across the street or hop in your car and go buy something for that headache; you can't run home for just a minute to pick something up. Thus try to think of school as a civilized version of camping out: you may be far from home and not able to get what you need at any given moment for your comfort. Depending on your individual needs (use your imagination for all of the varying crises), those items may include any or all of the following:

- some form of aspirin
- some form of antacid tablets or liquid
- eye drops, nose drops, lip balm, breath mints
- Band-Aids and disinfectant, and any allergy or other medication you might need
- bottled water
- if you wear contacts, cleaning solution and, if you wear glasses, an extra pair
- extra sweater or jacket
- tissues and/or paper towels
- hand sanitizers
- emergency sewing kit (needle, black thread, white thread, a few buttons, safety pins)
- extra pants (In a particularly humbling experience, Ken once ripped his pants on a chair while teaching a college course. His wallet got caught on the arm of a chair as he was sitting down, and the pants ripped down the back from belt to thigh, and flapped back and forth like a flag in a windstorm. Ken stayed glued to his chair that whole class. Luckily, his jacket could be tied around his waist, for the walk to the car!)

Keep a permanent supply of these items in your room or desk. You may find, one day, that it makes the difference between comfort and mild misery. *Practical tip:* Teachers are not allowed, in almost any school district in the country, to give students medication, such as aspirin. It may seem really dumb not to share with a student who has an unexpected cramp or headache, but you are placing yourself in some jeopardy by giving out to students, even upon their request, any form of medication. Don't do it. That's what the school nurse is there for.

Food

You will also need to think about eating. For many schools, lunch occurs much earlier than the traditional 12 p.m., and that may affect whether you eat breakfast and what you eat. Be aware early on of your lunch schedule and consider your stomach and your nutritional needs. Further, will you pack your lunch or eat in the cafeteria? Although many people hate making their own lunches, if the cafeteria is really crowded one day, you may find yourself going hungry so you can get to your next class on time. If you have blood sugar issues, you will need to bring your juice or power bar or whatever you require to keep your blood level constant—and, remember, most schools will not allow you to run down the hall during class to do this!

In addition, many people need to drink a significant amount of water during the day. If you are one of those, consider and plan for your trips to the bathroom; and if you cannot get to the bathroom and back to class in time, you'll need to adjust how much water you consume during the teaching day.

Some schools have serious restrictions about eating or drinking in the classroom. If you need, for the health reasons, to do either in class, you will need to notify the administration and, more important, mention to your students why you get to drink or eat, and they can't. It seems like a little thing, but young people are particularly sensitive about fairness, and students can be resentful if they see you eating and drinking, and they can't.

And resentment can engender interesting events, as Leila found:

One day, when I was feeling a cold coming on, I brought a cup of hot coffee into my classroom, never thinking to mention to my students, even informally, why I was sipping away when they were forbidden. About halfway through the period I left the coffee cup, only partially drunk, on my desk, and the class moved into small-group work. At one point while I was circulating around the room, one of my kinder students whispered to me that I should not finish the coffee sitting on my desk as someone—nameless, but someone—had scooped chalk dust into the cup. Although I had few discipline problems with that class, I realized that my coffee had become an instant source of some resentment, and someone wanted to let me know. I quietly thanked the student for her warning, and I never said a thing to the class. As far as I was concerned, lesson learned.

And if you drink a lot of coffee, be prepared to hear your students complain about your coffee breath. Students tend not to suffer in silence.

For Your Journal

This is a list and a chart journal assignment.

Think about your classroom: What would you like to see there? You will have a desk and chair provided, desks for the students, and possibly file cabinets or bookcases. Beyond that, however, most schools leave the furnishings and arrangement up to the individual teacher.

With that in mind, make a list of items you would like in your classroom and then, to the best of your knowledge, attach both a source (yard sale, friends, attic, basement, teacher, or dollar store) and, if you can, a price for each one. How many items are on your list? Where will you get them? How much will they cost? Finally, draw a simple classroom chart: What is located where? How are the student desks, at least initially, arranged? Where is your desk?

A Few Other Things: Getting Started, Openings, Voice, Body, Touch, Dress

Getting Started

It's not just students who have fluttery tummies at the beginning of a school year: teachers do, too. And for you, in your first few years of teaching, getting started can be a bit daunting. Some of the routine and pattern of getting started, even if you have completed a successful student teaching internship, will be new to you, and certainly you are not going to have thought out every eventuality in your classroom. Although you can't decide on the answers for all of the following questions, there are some things you need to consider as you get ready for your first teaching year. We have ideas of our own regarding some of these questions—which are explored later in the book—but here's a list of things you might want to look at and ponder. Where do *you* stand on these topics?

Introductory activities How much time should I spend on introductory (or get-to-know) activities? What activities could I do? What does each accomplish? What do I need to know about these students and about this class?

Rules What class rules do I make? To what extent should students help make the class rules? Should these rules be different for different classes? Can my rules change? What is my policy on students and their materials (books, paper, pencils, notebooks, and so on)? What is my policy on absences? Tardiness? Being excused for the bathroom? What will I do about cell phones? Using earbuds? Where do I go or whom do I call if I need immediate help with a classroom discipline or medical incident? Are my rules consistent with those of the school?

Names and information What do I tell students about me? How do I learn students' names? How do I address my students? How should students address me? What is the school or district policy on friending, following, or connecting with students on social media sites? Do I encourage or allow students to text me or to call my cell?

Starting and running a class Where should I be before the bell rings? What information should be on the board at the beginning of class? How do I begin a class? How will I take up papers and assignments? When and how do I call roll? How do I handle interruptions? How do I handle announcements over the PA? How do I end class and when? How do I assign homework?

Personal How do I dress? How do I speak? To what extent do I use colloquial language in the class or in the hall? How much do I share about myself with other teachers? To what extent do I talk with students about their—or my—individual problems?

If a student tells me something personal that is very serious, what do I do? With whom do I consult in the school building and when? Am I available to students outside class?

Again, you may not have answers for many of these questions and, in point of fact, the answers you have in September may be very different from the ones you might give in March. But thinking about the myriad issues of getting started may help you define what kind of classroom procedures and management you want to establish.

You'll see in many areas in your life and work as a teacher, there are few absolutes. You have a range of options, and it's your responsibility to choose and then reflect on them (now and again in the future) to determine which options are best for your students, for your school, and for you. The consequences of your choices, positive and negative, will be yours to bear.

Openings

Beyond these general questions, the answers to which will often extend throughout the entire teaching year, one of the most important days of teaching is the first day of class. How you set a tone and deal with students that first day can make the rest of the year or the semester a smoother one. Being organized, relatively calm, and prepared your very first day gives students the expectations that this is how you will be the rest of the year. Getting ready, therefore, for the first day may actually take some time: leaving tasks until the last minute—when presemester school meetings and paperwork may interfere—is not a good idea.

But what, besides the handing out of materials and setting up website administrivia, should happen the first day? There are a few things:

1. You need to think of what is important to you and the classroom and **establish and communicate rules or general principles.** If you want students to evince certain behaviors or attitudes, the first day is the day to mention them. Use positive language; giving students a list of don'ts is a surefire route to a negative start.

2. As mentioned earlier in this chapter, you need to **arrange the room** in a way that reinforces what will be going on in your classroom. This includes bulletin boards and artwork, study areas or reading areas, and a quiet corner for a class library. Again, desks should be positioned so students can see each other for large-group activities or, when needed, work individually or in small groups.

3. You need to **provide an introductory activity** that will let students get to know each other as well as you. Here are a few ideas:

   • Interviewing each other and then introducing the other person to the class. As another idea, have members of the class get out of their desks and stand in a large circle. Students place themselves in alphabetical order using the first letter of their middle name. Students go around the circle, taking turns first telling their middle name and then describing how that name was chosen for them.

- Drawing a coat of arms that represents interests and then sharing it. Students draw a symbol or series of symbols that represent the importance they give the following (number five is the most metaphorical):

  1—Outside Interests or Hobbies

  2—Family

  3—School

  4—Reading

  5—My Essence

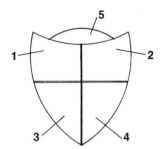

- Giving students a "scavenger hunt" list where they have ten minutes to go around the room and find the names of other students in the class who, for example: live within one mile of school; have traveled in the past year outside the United States; speak a language beside English; have been in a natural disaster such as an earthquake or a tornado; have more than two brothers (or sisters); are a twin; play two musical instruments; have memorized a poem in the last year, and so on.

- Writing a letter of introduction to students and having them do the same to you and their peers.

- Asking students to complete the following statement: I am the only one who _____. As students share, put each phrase on the board so everyone in the class can view the differing comments.

- Filling out a brief interest inventory and then sharing it. Providing fill-in-the-blank statements, such as these, can help:

  When I go online, I like to _____.

  My favorite possession is _____.

  What I like best/hate most about English class is _____.

  My friends value me because _____.

  School would be better if _____.

These activities are ways of letting students establish who they are and who the others are. Certainly every classroom minute counts, but the time spent on these activities will give you useful information about your students and will highlight their crucial importance in the success of the classroom. It will also help you build your class of individual students into a community of learners that will be active the entire school year. Sharing something about yourself will also help students connect with you as a person, not just a teacher. If students do a coat of arms, for instance, you do one, too. If students share the origin of their middle name, you do, too.

4. You need to begin to **learn and use all your students' names,** being very careful to pronounce them correctly or, within reason, to use their preferred names. What is on the roll books may not be what your students want to be called, and your sensitivity to their names will establish a positive and immediate bond. Ken has a trick for learning students' names. In all first-day classes, he gives students a five- to ten-minute in-class writing activity, and, while they are writing, he memorizes their names from a list of names and seats (a photo roster is even better). Throughout the classes, he refers to students by name several times each and then challenges himself to say good-bye to every student by name. When he was a young professional, he could do this pretty well with five classes, though now he finds even his lower-college class load to be a bit challenging. He makes mistakes, but the students appreciate his attempts.

5. You need to **tell students about the class** and how you envision what you will be doing together. Don't forget to use humor and positive terms and enthusiasm. If students think the class will be interesting or fun, they are more likely to work with you and with each other. If you also stress that students will have a say in the class' organization and procedural rules, students will feel that the class is not just yours.

6. Finally, it may seem hard to do both at once, but you need to establish that **you are in charge of the classroom** *and* that **you are a friendly, pleasant person.** Smiling and looking at your students as if you are happy to be with them will, frankly, reassure many of them. On the other hand, being pleasant does not mean that you are a pushover; classrooms need order to proceed, and you are in charge of that order. You have probably heard the old saw about not smiling until Thanksgiving; although some teachers actually take that as serious advice, we think it's silly. You are a human being working with other human beings. Not showing a pleasant demeanor is, to us, self-defeating. Your class is not boot camp, it's school, and you and your students should have a good and productive time together. Students learn the most and the fastest when they are enjoying what and how they are learning. Thus, every class should be fun. But *fun* doesn't mean the opposite of rigorous. We should follow noted educator Tom Romano when he says, "My goal is to present students with a curriculum that will so absorb them that time accelerates" (2009, 31). That's a tough ideal to meet, but the closer we get, the better our students will learn. And that's the point.

Voice

Most of us in this culture associate a commanding presence with a relatively deep voice. Many men have an edge over many women in this department, but its importance seems to us as somewhat of an exaggeration. It helps, however, to use an authoritative or relatively professional tone when trying to get students' attention, particularly, say, at the beginning of a class. Know also that if you speak over students or shout at them—and you'll be tempted—you are establishing an atmosphere that is hard to break or retract. If you use a quiet voice, they will, too. It will help you a great deal if you refuse to continue speaking until all students are completely silent. If you allow a continuous buzz of whispers while you speak, you can expect to hear them always. Instead, take the time to politely but firmly insist that your students listen when you speak. Trust the power of silence; constant talk from you is not helpful; pauses and silence can get students' attention effectively.

Using Your Body

Do not believe people who tell you that to be successful in keeping a class in order, you must be big or tall. The key here is *presence*, and people who are short of stature—both male and female—can have tons of it, and tall folks can have little of it. Remember that your body is a tool and one that you can use effectively. Moving around a class, standing near a student, standing erect, using your eyes to scan a room or to catch a student's attention, using your hands to gesture appropriately can all send messages to students that indicate care, attention, or discipline.

From Leila (5'2" tall) When I taught some years ago in a high school where discipline was an ongoing issue, I made it a practice to stand at my class door and greet or smile at each student as he or she came into the room. It established my presence, it made immediate, individual contact with each person, and, further, students had to pass by me—acknowledge me—to enter the class. Thus the signal of standing at the door was both a personal touch and an order measure.

Similarly, walking around the class can help students—although not to the extent where, in one of my classes, a student told me *just sit down*. My pacing (and in this class, that's just what it was) was making her nervous, and she decided to give me some advice and to attempt to save her relatively shattered nerves. No, I wasn't particularly thrilled to be criticized, but I listened, and I learned from that encounter to be more aware of my own movement and to move a bit less frenetically.

From Ken (6'1" tall) I may be taller, but believe me, I do *not* want to have a classroom presence contest with Leila Christenbury. She's proof that smaller bodies can make a seriously powerful impact in a classroom. I tend to walk around quite a bit in my classes, though not quickly. I move from space to space and stay in each one for a few minutes. It's important that students know I will likely see what they are up to and that I'm listening to them as they are working in groups or having a full-class discussion. Early in my teaching, I learned that teachers can use their physical proximity to, what educator Madeline Hunter once called, raise "students' level of concern" (Hunter 2004, 14). In other words, if students are off task (if they seem not all that concerned about getting their work done), a teacher can change the students' attitude simply by stepping closer to them. Actually, even when I'm standing next to one group, I'm often listening more closely to another group. This takes some getting used to, but it's a good tip. It's also a good idea to stand in a way in which your back is never to any part of the class. Try to stick to outside walls, so you'll be able to see the whole room and notice when a student has a question or wants to give a response. Finally, I suggest that when students contribute to a whole-class discussion, you step away from them (back away, so you're not turning from them). Doing so wordlessly encourages your students to speak loudly enough for the whole class to hear and opens the physical space between you and the student, so your class doesn't become a series of one-on-one discussions with the teacher rather than a true group discussion.

The Personal Touch

Touching is contextually and culturally determined. Much of what we do in class is pretty personal—write about how that makes you feel; discuss in your group if anything like that has ever happened to you. This factor, though, does not give us a license to invade our students' private space, that is, their bodies. Leila's personality lends itself to affection in speech and gesture, but she tries to curb that enthusiasm in school. Ken often holds out his hand as in invitation for a handshake with students as a gesture of welcome, thank you, or congratulations, but he doesn't otherwise touch students. A handshake connotes warmth and professionalism, with little risk of threat. Be aware, however, that some students may not accept a handshake, and that's OK. Some students aren't familiar with the gesture, and for some it may be against their religion to make physical contact of any sort with a person of the opposite gender.

Regardless, it is smart to know students and classes before one ever touches a student. For sure, if you are having a conflict or disagreement with a student, *do not touch them* while you are discussing the issue; it may be seen, rightly or wrongly, as an act of hostility or aggression, and you may get—and deserve—a disproportionate reaction.

In addition, *inappropriate touching* can also be a control issue with students and teachers. As Clary Washington found in one of her classes during her internship teaching, touching signaled a discipline issue:

Yesterday's class made it quite clear to me that I can't be their pal, and that I've inadvertently let them know that I am. One student, Mike, kept grabbing my hands each time I walked past his desk, saying, "I want you Ms. Washington." My reaction (I was totally shocked and forced myself free each time) didn't make it clear enough that this was inappropriate behavior. I could squash this kid like a grape, but that is not even the point. My hesitation to draw boundaries sent him and the rest of the class the wrong message: it's OK to manhandle Ms. Washington. It's not OK.

Male teachers especially need, in this era of heightened sensitivity, to be extremely cautious about touching female *and* male students; culturally the reverse is generally not quite so true for women, but it is still good advice. Although we are human, and some of us have been raised in families where touching is customary, know that our affection and care are not always reciprocated. It is not always understood in the way in which we intend it, and it is an imposition on our part to force a student to accept our gesture, however well meaning. Know before you reach out to touch. If you find yourself talking with a student who is emotionally upset and the correct human response feels to you to be a hug, it's OK to ask, "May I give you a hug?" Those moments should be rare and not often repeated with the same student.

Dress for Context

Dress is another context issue. Certainly two hot topic areas are tattoos and piercings; some schools are tolerant, yet in other school settings administrators do not want to see teachers showing visible tattoos and piercings. So what do you do? Look around you and see what the other teachers come to school wearing and if they show tattoos or piercings. Do not model yourself after the one person on the faculty who everyone thinks is weird or who most assume is repressed or stuck-up and who, others assume, illustrates that by his or her clothing. You can be weird and stuck-up or whatever—later in your career. In the beginning, without wholly sacrificing your own individuality, it is best to take the middle of the road in attire. Frankly, you have enough to concern yourself with without adding your sartorial choices to the mix.

First, with all of this in mind, try to dress in a way that seems comfortable to you. If, as a woman, certain kinds of shoes—such as high heels—make you feel silly, wear flats. If you feel stupid in flats, by all means, wear those heels. For women, the restrictions regarding pants and dresses are often real ones: if no one in your school wears pants (or dresses), understand that you will be noticed if you come to school in such. If, as a man, ties just mean awful stuff, wear a jacket and shirt and no tie. If dress shirts seem stultifying, try more informal ones. If no one on the teaching staff wears jeans or sandals, don't be the first to trot out your pair. Again, if you feel like you can't teach or talk with any authority without a tie, put one on. Real teachers wear clothes that make them feel authoritative, comfortable, and professional. Look at your closet, check out the other teachers, and make your choices. By all means, however, remember that you are a teacher and not one of the students. That may take some wardrobe adjustment for some of you, but you'll get used to it.

Leila I taught in Iowa for a year and came to my first classes dressed as I would to teach in my home state, Virginia. I found my students were truly intimidated by what I assumed to be standard attire; they asked about my clothes before class, and I would often see them checking me out.

Accordingly, I put the suits and skirts and pumps in the back of the closet and came to class in flats, trousers, and sweaters and jackets. My students noticed the change immediately and made approving comments about my "looking nice." They seemed happier; there were fewer comments about my being from "the East"; I felt their ease and was happier in the classroom.

Back in Virginia, when I wore the dashiki friends had brought me from a Caribbean trip, my African American students took time to remark on my appearance. They liked my wearing an interpretation of African fashion, and it made me, to them, seem more personal.

Ken For new teachers especially, it's important that you dress in a way that shows respect for your students and your school, whatever that is. I've noticed in some middle schools, golf shirts and khakis are the general thing for men, where in other schools shirt sleeves and ties are more appropriate. I advise new teachers to dress on the more professional end of the range they see. I generally wear a tie when I teach; it's part of my costume. When I'm in a whimsical mood, I'll wear a tie that has some connection to what I'm teaching (I have ties with dogs, lobsters, lighthouses, smiley faces, rubber duckies, musical instruments, and so on). I have a tie that's covered with big, bright clocks for when I'm giving a timed exam or collecting final projects. (Yes, I have a cruel streak.) As long as you're dressed respectfully and clearly prepared more for a classroom than for a date, you will find you have a range of options for appropriate dress.

Teaching as Failing

This section may be one you'd like to skip; the idea of failing in the classroom may come a bit close to home. As a beginner, you may rightly fear that a great deal of your teaching will be failing. Actually, although that is true, it is also true of veteran teachers, as one of our favorite articles outlines. Richard Hawley (1979) opens his essay with an almost uncomfortably harsh truth:

> Whenever a teacher enters a classroom to engage students in the process of increasing their understanding of some subject, some process, some created thing, some event— that is, whenever a teacher enters a classroom to teach—he or she risks great failure and, regardless of his or her gifts, experiences that failure to a significant extent. (597)

It is daunting and distressing to think that each class will reveal your failure as a teacher, but Hawley is on target. The poet T. S. Eliot wrote in *The Four Quartets* that "The only wisdom we can hope to acquire / Is the wisdom of humility: humility is endless" (1952, 126). Hawley tells us:

> Human beings generally dread the prospect of speaking authoritatively before a group. The dread is greatest when the group being addressed is not particularly receptive or welcoming, when they do not anticipate being pleased. Teachers play to tougher houses than actors do. They also play to them in more intimate settings, and the scheduled run is generally longer, regardless of the reviews. An actor, often with reason, may blame a flat performance on his material. Teachers are less able to do this; it is rarely Euclid's or Melville's fault that a class has fallen flat. Teachers move among their audiences, address them, converse with them. Any inattention, boredom, hostility is clearly visible before them. Because there are normally no co-stars or supporting players, the experience of teaching imperfectly is essentially a private matter. And again, because failure is by nature humiliating, we tend to keep it to ourselves. (1979, 597)

For this reason more than any other, it is necessary that we become reflective teachers and also that we find a teacher friend, a teacher buddy to bounce ideas off. Joining in a professional organization or a listserv or entering an educational chat room can literally be a lifesaver, as with friends it is possible to share what we have done and not done well.

But beyond the concept of failing, there are two other factors intertwined with teaching and failing. Both deal with defenses against classes that "did not go well." The first is blaming the students; the second is blaming the method. The latter is addressed in Chapter 3. And do remember, although the old adage "Of all possible worlds / we only have one" is true of our earth, it is just not true of teaching. Of all possible methods, we may indeed only choose one at one time, but there is a universe of ways to approach a given instructional question. But let's look at the other approach—blaming the students.

Blaming the Students

Blaming the students is counterproductive and probably has a lot to do with teacher frustration. You will have in your career many "difficult" students—which often means they are insufficiently prepared for your class, culturally different from you, learning disabled, emotionally disturbed, somewhere on the autism spectrum, overconfident, or elitist. Yet it is a trap of the first order to blame classes that do not go well on the students. As a beginner, you will, by a grim custom of the schools, often be given the youngest and least tractable students and classes. Tempting though it may be, you cannot afford to blame failure on them. You must be able to move beyond the rather bitter comment of one of Leila's student teachers, who recently remarked after her very first experience teaching a class: "Teaching never follows a perfect plan. The students just seem to get in the way." We can only hope that a student teacher soon changes her mind because as teachers we cannot afford this kind of attitude. We must continue to teach, enthrall, seduce, illumine students *where they are* and *how we find them*. Decrying their lack of attention, preparation, or ability does no good—it is cursing the darkness. Be a lighter of candles, not a curser of the dark; it will save energy, and, further, you and your students just might surmount the problems and learn. And remember, you're paid to help the students learn. The school is there for them, not us.

This is not a perfection business: it is an approximation venture only, and in a rather mystical sense, we teachers are rarely given to know exactly what the outcome of our classes are—what students remember or retain, what comes back to them years later, is really outside our control. It is also really not reflected by the grades they earn, the tests they take, the essays they write, or even our memories of who they were, and what the classes in which they enrolled were like.

Leila's Story: A Few Teacher Moments

Like many teachers, I remember incidents with students that make me squirm: times I misunderstood, mistrusted, did not pay attention to an individual. I lost all patience with Florean Witcher, who, even after being repeatedly advised, just would not look up the term she needed in a book's index. She had the book in hand and knew how to spell the term. I was losing patience. Florean had a legendary temper, and after her third request for help and my third identical reply (*look it up in the index*), she pulled furiously away from me.

I saw the anger—and the frustration—and in a well-meaning but misplaced gesture, I tried to stop Florean from storming to the other side of the class. It was winter, and, as was her custom, she had on her coat even though we were inside. In one of those fateful split-second decisions, I reached for her coat's belt to keep her from moving away. But Florean did not stop, and the belt ripped from its tie. Florean, I, and the class froze; Florean's right hand went into a very convincing fist and, indeed, she was fully capable of flattening me for, in essence, tearing her clothing. She didn't, the moment passed, and I both apologized for damaging her coat and offered to repair it. The apology was accepted, the offer to repair was declined, and the atmosphere cooled.

I then renewed the index discussion and found out that Florean would not look up her term in the index because she had never even heard the word *index*; I was asking her to look something up in an igloo for all she knew. We both became calm and businesslike, Florean learned what an index was, and *I* thought, first, about trying to anticipate students' background and knowledge and, second, about making split-second decisions involving touching and restraining angry students.

And I slowly learned other things. How could I have insisted that Linda Kern's self-confessed nervousness about giving a report in front of the class was overestimated and all that she needed was to just get up and *do it*? She tried, she started, and succeeded, as she had warned me, in becoming so overwhelmed by the experience that there, in front of all of us, she turned and, in her terror, vomited her lunch on the classroom floor. On my knees, as Linda and I cleaned up the remains, I thought about listening to my students.

I could not ever stop the social bullying and name-calling of the physically slight but very smart Tho Dang—the first of the Vietnamese refugees to come to my high school and the first student I had ever taught for whom English was a second language. I also just did not rattle the school's resources sufficiently to get the help he needed to negotiate my remedial English class. Tho struggled on his own—and successfully—without me. He passed all his usage tests with triumph, but it was not due to me, his English teacher, but to his own very hard work and a tutor in the Vietnamese community. When I complimented him on his high scores, he was polite but noncommittal. He knew, I knew, I had not taught him.

In fact, my feeling of failure with Gino Forrest was so strong that, when I saw him in a restaurant years after graduation—he was working as a waiter there—I struck up a conversation with him so that, essentially, I could try to set things right. I told Gino that night how I regretted the day some years past when I upbraided him after class about his consistently comic behavior. The fact was that Gino was a naturally funny guy, had even, after high school, traveled to Los Angeles to try to establish a career as a professional comedian—but I, his English teacher, did not find him at that point very humorous or very helpful with overall class discipline. Looking back on the encounter with Gino after class—I can remember it vividly—I know that I came down on him as hard as I had ever done with a student and was unfair, even harsh. Now I understand my overreaction more clearly: justified or not, I was afraid that Gino was taking away from me the control of that particular class. Regardless, it is still not an incident of which I am proud—surely I could have handled it less forcefully—and I was glad to see Gino so I could tell him so. But this is another interesting aspect of the teaching life—Gino listened to my regretful comments and told me, in all honesty, he didn't remember the event at all.

There is a roll call I have—as all teachers do—of students I have failed in the sense that I did not live up to my obligations as teacher. Like many teachers, I also have had students, years later, tell me brilliant insights or words of advice or encouragement I gave them—good, serendipitous deeds that were wholly individual and that were so context-dependent that I do not often remember, at least not in the same way as the student. But, nevertheless, a number of students have cited crucial incidents in which I, evidently, played an important role.

The failures are dramatic, the good stories are heartening, but some of teaching is a bit more mixed. I also must recount the memorable—and utterly typical—incident when a former high school student of mine, who was then in college and functioning as a summer hostess in a local restaurant, stopped me in the restaurant foyer with exclamations of pleasure and recognition. I was with a group of friends and, actually, rather pleased to have an audience for my student's greeting and such obvious delight. When she wanted to tell me what she remembered most about our class in English those years ago, I glowed with pleasure, somewhat confident that my friends would now hear some stellar incident from the class. I braced myself to accept what she would recount; my friends smiled at each other and at me in pleasant anticipation.

"Oh yes," she recalled, her eyes lighting up with pleasure, "I just never forgot when you told us about your wedding cake and how you decided on it and had it specially ordered."

My dismay, if not my disbelief, was immediate and total; was that, I asked her, what she had remembered?

"Oh yes," she gushed enthusiastically, "it was made entirely of *cream puffs*, and you had ordered it from that new French restaurant."

Well she had me. My wedding cake *had* been made of cream puffs and ordered specially from a new, local French restaurant. But, good grief, had I ever spent class time telling students about my *wedding cake*? About *cream puffs*? What in the world was I thinking to talk about a wedding cake? Even as an aside? Where was my brain that day? Where was my lesson plan?

I squeaked a thank-you and quickly moved with my amused friends through the foyer and out of the door. My wedding cake—on which I had evidently actually spent class time—was what my former student remembered. Humility is endless.

Ken's Story: A Few More Teacher Moments

I have had some "winning" moments as a teacher as well, which I cringe to remember. There was the time I inadvisably moved the bookshelves on my wall and one of them came crashing down on a student during class later that day. The student screamed and yelled, but ultimately, she was fine, thank goodness. Another time, I told an angry student that if she didn't like my class, no one was forcing her to be there. So she left. It was my good fortune that she chose to go to the principal's office. To his credit, the principal never showed a hint of annoyance at me to the student, but he laced into me pretty hard when we were alone. It turns out students *are* forced to be in our classes, and we aren't allowed to invite them to leave—even if we're angry at them. And, as the newspaper advisor, I once decided to let the newspaper staff suffer the consequences of their own actions by allowing the poorly proofread school newspaper to be published as is. The students didn't really notice, but quite a few teachers and parents plus the school superintendent did. Guess who got the heat for that? In a very painful memory from my first few months of teaching, I thought it would be a great idea to put a lot of racist terms on the board so my tenth graders and I could examine the roots of these hateful terms and ensure they wouldn't use them against others. I found out days later that several students in the class began using some of those terms to bully others in the class. My poorly thought-out lesson had failed miserably, and I had to deal with the bullies and apologize to the students whose misery I inadvertently abetted.

We make many, many mistakes as teachers. In a job this challenging, some bad decisions are inevitable. Hawley sums it up well:

> Failure—real failure—is palpable everywhere in the teaching process. We need to name it and to face it, so that we may continue. If we insulate ourselves sufficiently with defenses, we may go unhurt, but we will teach nothing, while providing students models of flight and disengagement. Acknowledging failure and acknowledging defenses, we may come to know as much about our business as the medieval scholastics knew about God: what he is not and that he is necessary. Now off to class. (1979, 600)

And perhaps that is one encouraging aspect of this business of teaching; there is always another class and more students and, thanks to the fates, another chance to teach. As a teaching friend of mine says, "Teaching is the *only* profession where we can clear away all the failures at the end of the school year and start afresh in the fall."

A Final Word from a Poet (and Student and Teacher)

Henry Taylor, a Pulitzer Prize winner, wrote a poem we like to share with our students. It's about failure and domination and a terrible incident in a long-ago but not long-forgotten math class. It presents a bright but not truly confident student and an insecure, overbearing teacher. But the last part of the poem is even more powerful for us, because Taylor, now a teacher himself, writes of what all of us teachers know; we all fail each other and, to a certain extent, we must forgive each other in the classroom:

Shapes, Vanishings

1

Down a street in the town where I went
to high school twenty-odd years ago, by doorways
and shadows that change with the times, I walked
past a woman at whose glance I almost stopped cold,
almost to speak, to remind her of who I had been—
but walked on, not being certain it was she,
not knowing what I might find to say.
It wasn't quite the face I remembered, the years
being what they are, and I could have been wrong.

2

But that feeling of being stopped cold, stopped dead,
will not leave me, and I hark back
to the thing I remember her for, though God knows
how I could remind her of it now.

Well, one afternoon when I was fifteen
I sat in her class. She leaned on her desk,
facing us, the blackboard behind her arrayed
with geometrical figures—triangle, square,
pentagon, hexagon, et cetera. She pointed
and named them. "The five-sided figure," she said,
"is a polygon." So far so good, but then when she said,
"The six-sided one is a hexagon," I wanted things clear.
Three or more sides is poly, I knew, but five only
is penta, and said so; she denied it,
and I pressed the issue, I, with no grades
to speak of, a miserable average to stand on
with an Archimedean pole—no world to move,
either, just a fact to get straight, but she
would have none of it, saying, at last, "Are you
contradicting me?"

    3

A small thing to remember a teacher for. Since then,
I have thought about justice often enough
to have earned my uncertainty about what it is,
but one hard fact from that day has stayed with me:
If you're going to be a smartass, you have to be right,
and not just some of the time. "Are you
contradicting me?" she had said, and I stopped
breathing a moment, the burden of her words
pressing down through me hard and quick, the huge
weight of knowing I was right, and beaten. She
had me. "No, ma'am," I managed to say, wishing
I had the whole thing down on tape to play back
to the principal, wishing I were ten feet tall
and never mistaken, ever, about anything in this world,
wishing I were older, and long gone from there.

    4

Now I am older, and long gone from there.
What sense in a grudge over something so small?

What use to forgive her for something
she wouldn't remember? Now students
face me as I stand at my desk, and the shoe
may yet find its way to the other foot,
if it hasn't already. I couldn't charge
thirty-five cents for all that I know
of geometry; what little I learned is gone now,
like a face looming up for a second out of years
that dissolve in the mind like a single summer.
Therefore,
if ever she almost stops me again,
I will walk on as I have done once already,
remembering how we failed each other,
knowing better than to blame anyone.
                    —Henry Taylor

And so, off to class.

For Your Journal

As you think about your teaching career, what is the one area more than any other in which you would hope you would not fail your students? Is it intellectual? Emotional? Social? Would it have to do with something inside the classroom? Outside? If you could ask your teaching fairy godmother to keep you from one area of failure, what would it be? *Make a wish.*

References

Eliot, T. S. 1952. *The Complete Poems and Plays 1909–1950*. New York: Harcourt Brace & World.

Emmers, Amy Puett. 1981. *After the Lesson Plan: Realities of High School Teaching*. New York: Teachers College Press.

Hawley, Richard A. 1979. "Teaching as Failing." *Phi Delta Kappan* 60 (April): 597–600.

Hunter, Robin. 2004. *Madeline Hunter's Mastery Teaching: Increasing Instructional Effectiveness in Elementary and Secondary Schools*. Updated edition. Thousand Oaks, CA: Corwin.

Lortie, Dan C. 1975. *Schoolteacher: A Sociological Study*. Chicago: University of Chicago Press.

Mack, Nancy, guest editor. 2012. "Preventing Bullying Behaviors." Special issue, *English Journal* 101 (6).

Miller, sj, Leslie David Burns, and Tara Starr Johnson. 2013. *Generation Bullied 2.0: Prevention and Intervention Strategies for Our Most Vulnerable Students*. New York: Peter Lang.

Romano, Tom. 2009. "Defining Fun and Seeking Flow in English Language Arts." *English Journal* 98 (6): 30–37.

Shulman, Lee S. 1987. "Learning to Teach." *AAHE Bulletin* 40 (3): 5–9.

Taylor, Henry. 1985. "Shapes, Vanishings." In *The Flying Change*, 14–15. Baton Rouge: LSU Press.

U.S. Department of Education. 2014. "I Have a Question . . . What Parents and Caregivers Can Ask and Do to Help Children Thrive at School: A Checklist." http://www2.ed.gov/documents /family-community/parent-checklist.pdf.

3 | PLANNING FOR YOUR TEACHING

Order and simplification are the first steps toward the mastery of a subject—the actual enemy is the unknown.

—Thomas Mann, *The Magic Mountain*

Planning for your teaching can seem overwhelming, but it is actually something you will need to learn to do consistently and well. There are so many unpredictable aspects of teaching that can be accommodated when you have a solid teaching plan, and your confidence in your own ability will strengthen as you actually carry out well-conceived plans. Planning is also how you will ensure that what you are asking your students to learn aligns with standards and can be measured in a way that truly evidences your effectiveness as a teacher. Thus planning well is a crucial part of successful teaching. Although most veteran teachers may appear to be sketchy planners, they have developed the ability to plan in great depth without writing it all down. You will also develop these skills, but only if you begin your journey by taking planning very seriously. You will need, in your first few years in the classroom, to map things out fairly explicitly, even if you end up changing those plans as you teach. Further, some school systems like to see teachers' lesson plans on a regular basis and may ask you to submit plans to your department chair or your principal. At any rate, as a beginning teacher there are numerous folks who will take an active interest in the extent—and the presence—of your plans.

In this chapter, we will look at some theoretical aspects of and practical strategies for planning because you will need both on your teaching journey. You'll learn that teachers don't plan in a vacuum. Rather, they think about the models of teaching practices they value and use them as a framework for their planning. So let's start with models of teaching.

Adopting a Teaching Model

Several studies have demonstrated that teachers are most influenced by their own teachers. As you think about teaching, you probably remember back to some of your favorite teachers. But this is a double-edged sword: what we think of as *good teaching* may only have been good for us (not other students), or what we may have thought was good teaching really wasn't. (It's important that you consciously adopt or develop your own model of teaching, based partly on your experience as a student and partly on what you learn from your teacher educators and what research has taught us are the best practices for teaching and learning.)

Each of us has different early experiences that have shaped our models of teaching through the years.

Leila's Story: Creating a Teaching Model

My own teaching model was shaped, first, by what I had experienced as a student and, second, by the experience of my own students as I myself became a teacher. What I remembered—and treasured—from my favorite teachers was their ability to set a stage for discovery and talk. The best of my teachers seemed interested in what we had to say and let us grope through many wrong turns to find out what indeed was not only important to us but what was true. From these teachers I felt I had an opportunity to learn, to find on my own. And I remembered the learning, which was *my* learning, not someone else's.

It was learning to love the questions, for, as seers have often pointed out, we are often not ready for the answers. I still am not ready for some answers—that, by the way, is part of the wonderful discovery of teaching; it is a self-renewing enterprise when it is at its best and, with our students, we explore.

My students helped me develop a model of teaching. Most of them, even the more traditionally polite, had a highly limited patience with listening to *me*. At the extreme, I found students who were not only impatient about listening but who would just not do it. They needed to be involved and active; they needed to find answers and ideas on their own. It was, essentially, an instructional issue for them as much as it was a discipline question.

I found that asking, not telling, was almost always more powerful. Students had to make their own meaning of events or text or writing; it became *our* class, not just mine, and when it was ours, many discipline problems seemed to evaporate. The nonclass-related chatter diminished, and talk revolved around the subject.

Ken's Story: Learning from Experience

I have a vivid memory of the very moment in my first year of teaching that I realized my students did not want me to give them long lectures. I had spent an entire weekend developing a lecture discussing death symbols in Jack Finney's (1956) short story "Contents of the Dead Man's Pockets" for my tenth graders. I was very excited about it because I knew that these adolescents would be fascinated by the clever ways Finney had hidden messages about death in the language of his story. I was about ten minutes in, when Paul—a tall, popular boy in the class sitting on the right side of the classroom toward the back—reached both his arms out in a yawning stretch. His yawn was *so* loud and *so* prolonged, and his mouth was *so* wide open, that you could have driven a small car into it! The whole class turned to him, and we all stared in stunned amazement. I was mad and a little hurt, but deep down I knew poor Paul wasn't trying to be rude. He was just enormously, spectacularly bored. Of course, I was deflated by Paul's yawn, but I made my way through the rest of the lecture and vowed immediately to find a better way. That week I checked out a couple of books on cooperative learning and active learning, and over the next few weeks and months they transformed the way I engaged my students in their own learning.

As I matured as a teacher, I realized Paul did me a tremendous favor. My lesson wasn't really about the students' learning as much as it was about me displaying my knowledge to the students. To this day, decades later, when I talk for too long in one of my classes, I hear the echo of that young man's yawn. (For a longer version of this sordid tale, see Lindblom's "From the Editor: Motivating Students"; 2010, 10–11.)

Moving beyond our individual stories, when teachers are not interested in their students, when their own telling is the most important, we have a classroom as described by student Susanna Field:

> [My English teacher] could have improved her class by coming closer to the students. She could have been more interested in what we had to say. (Because she was not interested, we cared to say nothing.) . . . Also, she could have arranged the desks in a circle, so then we could all discuss with each other, rather than facing the front of the room and merely listening to the teacher.

Thus, we set for you a model of teaching that is almost wholly based on asking and constructing events and opportunities for students to find the meaning. It is a skill that takes some practice; it takes patience, yet it, we think, yields probably the only learning that is worth our energy. If we want students to know facts, they need to consult information sources. If, however, we want students to think and explore and evaluate and understand and weigh and argue, they need an environment in which to come up with their own learning. A popular aphorism states, "Give a person a fish, he eats for a day; teach a person to fish, he eats for a lifetime." We must teach our students to fish, not keep handing them the dead fish *we* have pulled from the stream.

There are several models of teaching—ways of teaching—that are not so much correct or incorrect, right or wrong, but that reflect different *philosophies* or *theories* of instruction and approaches to students and appeal to different personality strengths of teachers. Some of this is individual and essentially neutral in character; some of this is part of good practice. There is, however, an essential approach to teaching that is beyond the kind of individual aspects unique to each of us, *teaching as discovery*, and we present that model here as a goal toward which you should strive. *Teaching as a reflective practitioner* is also an essential model for effective teaching as you will read later in the chapter.

You might find it helpful to explore what these books have to say about various models of teaching:

- Bruce Joyce and Marsha Weil's (2014) *Models of Teaching* presents multiple groups of dozens of separate models of teaching.

- In his study *Twenty Teachers*, Ken Macrorie (1984) sees teachers, regardless of grade level or subject matter, as those doing "good works" in the classroom.

- In the award-winning *The Making of a Teacher*, Pamela Grossman (1990) describes a number of beginning teachers and discusses especially how many of them try to replicate their English major experiences in college with their high school students.

- Robert V. Bullough Jr.'s (1989) *First-Year Teacher* explores the experiences of a beginner and her attempts first to survive the classroom and then to truly become a good teacher.

- *Educating Esmé* (Codell 2009) and *Brief Intervals of Horrible Sanity* (Gold 2003) describe some of the tough times for teachers who are in the classroom for their first years.

- Social studies teacher Stuart B. Palonsky (1986) writes of the strain of teaching in a book appropriately entitled *900 Shows a Year*.

Given the increased national attention on teaching and learning that has come about with wide adoption of the Common Core State Standards (CCSS) and other college- and career-ready standards, there have also been many books written about teachers and teaching that you may find valuable.

- In *Deeper Learning*, Monica Martinez and Dennis McGrath (2014) examine eight schools that have created innovative ways to empower students in areas such as problem solving and, especially, in developing self-direction in their learning (3).

- *Teacherpreneurs* is a book that encourages teachers to be community and national leaders in education (Barnett and Wieder 2013).

- Other books focus on a new reality for teachers of all subjects: all teachers, not just English teachers, are literacy instructors. Patricia Stock, Trace Schillinger, and Andrew Stock's (2014) *Entering the Conversations* is a good one to check out on that topic.

There are dozens of good books about teaching and teachers and, as you get deeper into this business, you may not only want to read them, you may also want to add your voice to the collection. Almost all of these accounts, however, include some of the following models of teaching.

Five Models of Teaching

The following is a stripped-down version of five models you may consider in your own teaching. Please note that some of this is developmental; you will naturally be attracted to certain models early in your career. Some of this is hierarchical; we see the later models as superior to the others. Teaching as telling is the earliest model and the one you should move quickly away from. It is also a very necessary step for a beginner: the other models will come, as they did for us and for many other teachers, with time.

Teaching as Telling

When you first thought of being a teacher, one of the early images in your mind was probably that of you standing in front of a class and telling students about a novel or poem, explaining to them a concept or an idea, and writing on a board while students listened to you or watched what you wrote. The sun is shining through the classroom windows, the room is attractively furnished, the students are quiet, and there you are, at the podium, teaching. Just like in the Hollywood versions of teaching we see in the movies. (See Lindblom [2004] for a humorous take on this.) You are teaching eloquently, and the students are rapt with attention, taking notes and asking, only occasionally, a salient question on the issue. It is an orderly scene, and you are at the head, faced by interested, attentive students.

For many people getting ready to enter the classroom or even for some veteran teachers, teaching is telling, the teacher talking and the students listening. Certainly for most of us early in our career, teaching was a great deal of telling, although as many later found, the longer we taught, the farther we moved from this model of teaching.

If this is your image of what middle school or high school English teaching is, we want you to think about it for a minute. Consider: Who is doing the talking? Who is making the connections? Who is giving the examples? Who is in charge? Who is the active one? Shifting the scene: Who is doing the listening? Who is receiving the connections, the examples? Whose mind may be wandering everywhere? Who is the passive one? An old saying suggests: "School is where children go to watch adults work." Is this what school should be?

How does the teacher know, especially if he or she speaks for a long period—an entire class period—if the students understand, have questions, already know all of the material or part of the material, can extend the material beyond what the teacher is discussing? Is asking "Are there any questions?" or checking to see that students are silent or taking notes sufficient to answer this concern?

Clearly we see severe limitations in the model of teaching as telling; we think it is inefficient, overused, and encourages a great deal of student passivity and intellectual laziness. And, from a teacher's point of view, it is exhausting: the teacher is the center and the one upon whom all are dependent. To take that responsibility, undiluted, five periods a day, five days a week is a recipe for burnout as well as a waste of teacher resource. But it also feels good—especially for a new teacher—and it looks like what many people *think* good teaching is. To be an effective teacher, however, you must realize quickly that teaching as telling is all about the teacher's display of knowledge, not the students' learning.

Better models of teaching put the students' activity at the center. CCSS–related teaching strategies even often suggest that teachers refrain from giving students any background as they approach new texts, instead suggesting that teachers guide students in developing questions about the texts and using their critical analytical skills to find the answers.

Being a talking head is not our idea of teaching, and we have lost faith in the idea of students being a tabula rasa, a blank slate upon which the teacher writes. Similarly, we are concerned about the idea of what Brazilian educator Paulo Freire (1981) criticizes as the "banking concept" of education, where the teacher makes knowledge deposits into students' heads. These ideas of teaching are often attributed to the factory model of the Western Industrial Revolution, in which education was considered analogous to manufacturing; the students were the raw materials, the factory was the school, and the teachers were the workers who shaped the students into some sort of product, or educated person. Nationwide increased emphasis on standardized exams threatens to give this factory model even more influence. All these ideas—teacher as knowledge knower, student as knowledge receiver—sound fairly logical and, indeed, some of them are deeply rooted in our culture. The models, however, are largely based on a few philosophical assumptions that we must analyze explicitly:

✗ It's a teacher's job to funnel specific pieces of knowledge to students.

✗ It's a student's responsibility to absorb those specific pieces of knowledge, much as they would read a book or view a film.

✗ By absorbing those pieces of knowledge, students are being active as critical assessors of the knowledge, and the learning is most efficient.

✗ The specific pieces of knowledge are tailored to students' experience, prior knowledge, and difficulties with the subject.

Many teachers just don't agree with these assumptions. The major problem with teaching as telling is that it is overwhelmingly a one-way street: the person doing the work, including making many of the learning connections, is the teacher, not the student. Listening is rarely an active experience, and listening for long periods of time is downright wasteful, if not impossible to sustain, for most young people. A teacher who talks most of the class cannot tailor the knowledge or the insight to all of his or her students; students, moreover, do not have the experience of questioning, arguing, and putting into context what they are hearing if the overwhelming activity is simply receiving a teacher's talk.

This is not to say that there aren't times when a teacher does need to give students instructions, history, or major points. There is a place for minilectures on the use of imagery in modern poetry, for the uses of the semicolon, for the difference between alliteration and assonance. But rarely should these extend beyond ten minutes or so, and very soon after a minilecture, it is time for students to take the information and use it, question it, incorporate it, illustrate it, do *something* with it so that the knowledge does not remain solely the giver's point but their own. Bloom's famous taxonomy of levels of critical engagement is not just a list of options for assignments but a guide for teachers to help their students take ownership of new knowledge. As one young man in student teaching, using his first student groups as an effort to help him break the teaching-as-telling mode, wrote:

> Tuesday, April 3
>
> English Literature Class: 3rd Period was motivatingly scary. The students worked in groups (another way for me to cut down on talking). I feel I am actually getting the message of why it's ineffective to talk too much to students. They received their instructions, played some, and talked some, and laughed, and joked, and worked some. And when the groups were presenting their answers, they did it as if they had actually learned what I had intended.
>
> —Ronnie Fleming

If you find yourself doing more talking than your students, you're probably operating in a teaching-as-telling model. Work on changing that. Remember: your students' learning, not your telling, is the goal.

Teaching as Inspiration

We have taught a number of students who were rather successful in their own school careers and, understandably, took that skill with them into their new lives as teachers. For many of these students, however, they also took their ability to "wing it" and used that ability in the classroom. We know that there is surely a place for inspiration—changing the direction or focus of an activity in response to what happened in a previous class, or, indeed, what is happening in that very class at that very moment—but we urge you to reconsider the model of teaching as inspiration. Teaching as inspiration works effectively only when it grows from the in-depth planning that has already been done. Planning is really the foundation to good teaching, and although no one can realistically map out everything that will happen in every class—nor should they—relying on inspiration and waiting until the last minute to pull a class together won't do you or your students much good.

Teaching as inspiration is based on the following assumptions:

✘ Getting students excited is more important than leading them to some sort of intellectual conclusion.

✘ Things always have a tendency to "work out" in a classroom setting.

✘ The freshness of inspiration is always superior to the certainty (read: *dullness*) of planning.

Certainly, there are times when it will strike you that an activity could change or be added to right here and right now, and that will help you with your classes, but relying *solely* on teaching as inspiration will not substitute for mapping out instructional activities before class, making sure the activities align to required standards, and ensuring that you'll assess the students' learning in some meaningful way. You may observe excellent teachers who seem to view teaching as inspiration as an appropriate model, but you aren't seeing the careful planning they have done first, which makes the lesson seem so effortless and spontaneous.

There is also the simple matter of professionalism. Teaching a short story you have not read, asking students to do exercises you have not reviewed, showing a film you have never seen, or having to make up a classroom activity on the spot is proof of poor planning and can result in some tense classroom moments and some potentially embarrassing instructional gaffes. Further, it is likely that some smart student will know just how unprepared you are.

Part of your job as a professional is to come to class prepared; relying on inspiration is a sloppy way to run your teaching life, and—most important—it will shortchange your students.

Teaching as Maintaining a Creation

In the opening of her groundbreaking book *In the Middle*, 2015 Global Teacher Prize–winner Nancie Atwell (1998) describes herself early in her career as an organizer and planner who carefully, minutely created a class and its organization and then, essentially, maintained that creation throughout the year. With the best of intentions, she set a complicated system "in motion" and simply made it endure throughout the school year. Atwell writes:

> I confess. I started out as a creationist. The first days of every school year I created; for the next thirty-six weeks I maintained my creation: my curriculum. From behind my big desk I set it in motion; then I managed and maintained it until June. I wanted to be a great teacher—systematic, purposeful, in control. . . . I didn't learn in my classroom. I tended my creation. (1998, 3)

A teacher, such as Atwell describes herself, is indeed in control and manages a classroom much as one would manage any system. As she writes in another article, "Sitting there at my big desk, developing new assignments and evaluating the results, I remained oblivious to . . . my students' ideas, experiences, and expertise. I remained in charge" (1985, 35).

Teaching as maintaining a creation is based on the following assumptions:

✗ Teaching has more to do with well-regulated, consistent systems and patterns and rules than with the shifting demands of students' learning.

✗ Once a classroom organizational pattern is established, it can successfully guide an entire semester or year of the class.

✗ A teacher can successfully anticipate student needs to the point that any organizational pattern that he or she establishes will be durable for a fixed period of time.

The problem is, of course, what Atwell describes: *I didn't learn in my classroom*. It is not just spineless sentimentality or softheartedness that leads us to believe that, yes, our students can teach us. Indeed they do—different ways of approaching and different aspects of knowledge. As Atwell describes, we can, and should, shift away from teaching as maintaining a creation:

> Today I learn in my classroom. What happens there has changed, and it continues to change. I've become an evolutionist. The curriculum unfolds as my kids and I learn together and as I teach them what I see they need to learn next . . . my practice evolves as my students and I go deeper . . . Learning with students . . . has made me a better teacher to them than I dreamed possible. (1998, 3)

Although setting a class' agenda is part of teaching, we have to strike a balance between being the organizer and being the dictator. The latter is not only inefficient—all responsibility falls on the teacher—but it also often means that the students' interest is not captured and capitalized upon. Being in charge, absolutely, always, can stifle our students and box us into an unshakable role as sole authority. In a way, this model is the opposite of teaching as inspiration. For the teacher bent on maintaining a creation, planning and organizing too rigidly can become a trap: we fall so in love with our own system for our classes that we neglect to revise, adjust, or change to accommodate our students.

Teaching as Discovery

We now come to the model we believe will be the most enduring for you as a teacher. A teacher who uses discovery

- doesn't necessarily avoid questions to which there is no answer or mind saying, "I don't know"
- lets students talk, and creates an atmosphere and assignments that encourage student talk

- allows pauses in the talk—just like in a real conversation, which means there are periods of thoughtful silence in the classroom

- asks, asks, asks and falls out of love with telling

- starts teaching with where the students are, not where the book is or where the teacher is.

It is not as efficient, as many suppose, to be told the point and then find the examples to support it. It's like being told the punch line and then trying to re-create the joke to fit the end. Using the discovery method, we learn and we internalize that learning by finding the point ourselves, by making it our own, by saying it, by stumbling toward it, and by making some use of or value from it. We avoid overt didacticism, as our knowledge is not our students' knowledge, our revelation about a poem or play or language principle is not our students'.

If we adopt this teaching model, we must stop asking our students to admire the fine conclusions we have reached or to be in awe at our knowledge of any given subject. Instead, we allow them to lurch through to their own, as we act as guides and assistants in their journeys. This is one of the most powerful aspects of the act of teaching. We often wonder if, actually, it is the only one.

Teaching as a Reflective Practitioner

All good teachers must also be mindful of the results of their teaching. It is important that you add into your teaching life the concept of reflecting on what you do in your classes and what your students do and what seem to be the outcomes. The aphorism "Those who do not know history are doomed to repeat it" may have some bearing on this discussion: if you are unaware or do not consider not only why a class was unsuccessful but why it was *successful*, it would seem virtually impossible for you to progress in your teaching life. In fact, the whole idea of a teacher being a researcher within the context of his or her own classes is a large part of being a reflective practitioner.

The field of reflection can be summarized, perhaps, by four very salient questions. Researcher Bud Wellington cites them:

1. What do I do? ("observational description of practice")

2. What does this mean? ("principles of theories-in-use . . . which underlie and drive the described practice")

3. How did I come to be this way? ("forces our awareness beyond the classroom . . . correctly reveals educational practice as essentially political")

4. How might I do things differently? ("gives us the call to action") (Wellington 1991, 5)

Wellington notes that these questions "are not intended as rhetorical . . . for casual consideration over tea. Rather, they are intended to raise consciousness, to challenge complacency, and to engender a higher order of professional practice" (Wellington

1991, 5). Teacher educator Julie Gorlewski suggests that teachers should gather data in their classrooms to critically reflect upon the success of their teaching and to avoid what researchers call "confirmation bias" (the act of only acknowledging data that support one's desired outcome, such as when a teacher asks if students understand something and the teacher is satisfied that most students nod yes). Data can be a simple exit slip on which students write a sentence that demonstrates they have learned how to, for example, use iambic pentameter. In her aptly named "Seize the Data," Gorlewski asserts that "Classroom data—collected, analyzed, reported, and acted upon by teachers—offer the possibility to enhance instructional effectiveness" (2011, 102).

When we ask these questions and gather data about our classes and our teaching—before we embark on a class or after it, as evaluation and follow-up—we are being reflective about our models of teaching. When we alter our teaching in response to the answers to the questions, we are being responsible and responsive.

At this point we have offered five models of teaching, but we have clear preference for a model that incorporates the final two. As you make your teaching journey, we hope you'll find your stops in the discovery and reflection models will leave lasting impact for you and your students.

Teaching *Their Eyes Were Watching God* and the Five Models

So, let's take a piece of literature and look at it from the point of view of each of the five models.

Writer and anthropologist Zora Neale Hurston's ([1937] 1990) *Their Eyes Were Watching God* has become popular in many high school English classes. Although its use of dialect, mature themes, and frank language makes it unacceptable in most middle school settings (and, indeed, those factors can also prevent it from being used in secondary schools), it is nevertheless on a number of reading lists across the country and is listed as an exemplar text for the CCSS. The novel, set in Florida and originally published in 1937, is a strong one that deals with important questions; it has feminist underpinnings, uses beautiful imagery, and carries a clear message regarding love and endurance. *Their Eyes Were Watching God* is also characterized by a powerful and gripping plot, and its protagonist, Janie, is memorable. Further, important issues of race, class, and poverty are all part of the novel.

If the teaching model were *teaching as telling*, a teacher using *Their Eyes Were Watching God* would more than likely engage in the following activities:

- Give students a brief lecture on the definition and characteristics of the regional novel and ask them to find examples in *Their Eyes Were Watching God* to illustrate those characteristics.
- Cite the major themes of the novel and ask students to find illustrative incidents.

- List the major characters of the novel and ask students to define their roles.

- Give students worksheets with important quotations and have students explain why those quotations are significant.

- Review the parts of a plot for students and have them identify the rising action, the falling action, and one climax.

If a teacher were relying upon *inspiration*, he or she might make a few notes on the novel and start the class hoping that someone would bring up important issues. The teacher would follow the students' lead and pursue whatever came up. The length of the "study" might be one day, might be a week; it might lead to other literature or not. The assessment for the novel probably wouldn't be written until it became clear to the teacher what the main thrust of the class discussion was.

A *maintaining-a-creation* model would likely involve *Their Eyes Were Watching God* as part of a thematic unit or genre study, orchestrated and integrated with other pieces and following the same pattern of discussion and investigation as pieces of literature in the previous part of the unit. The topics to be discussed would be strictly established as would the time spent on each topic or activity. It would not be unusual for the test on the novel to be written before the actual teaching of the novel, and it would also follow that nothing that happens in the class would change that assessment. That is clearly a misguided practice as it means that classroom discussion and emphasis have no effect on how the learning is assessed. We believe that we can't be so tied to our creations that we forget that classes are dynamic, living entities that will shift and grow as time moves forward; the lesson should serve the students, not the other way around.

A *discovery* model would look very different. Instead of the teaching-as-telling assignments listed above, instead of assuming some form of inspiration will strike, and instead of meticulous mapping out of the topics and time, the teacher would change the focus and emphasis to guided exploration and critical discussion. The topics to be lingered on and for how long and the specifics of the final evaluation would not be immediately established; they would rely on the students. With discovery as a conceptual frame, the teacher might go in any of these directions:

- Ask students about the dialect in the novel: Was it difficult? Was it essential? What would happen if the novel did not use any dialect at all? Can you rewrite one section of dialogue using standard English and then compare and contrast the dramatic effect? What is gained? What is lost?

- Ask students about the theme(s) of this novel: What evidence in the text leads you to know what the themes or theme are? Which seem the most or least important? Why?

- Ask students about the characters: Is this novel about more than one character? (Janie? Tea Cake? Jody?) How do you know? How can you tell? To what extent is it important to decide? Why?

- Ask students to select three quotations that seem important: Why are these quotations important?

- Have students read some of the criticism that suggests *Their Eyes Watching God*, written decades ago and brought back into print and popularity in contemporary times, just doesn't deserve the attention and praise that it is given. What do you think of that argument? To what extent do you think this novel deserves/does not deserve the attention it is currently receiving? If you were giving a literary prize, what would you select as criteria?

- Ask students about the feminist, race, and class issues and other political aspects of the novel: What appears to be the message regarding love between men and women? Marriage? Commitment? How does the novel speak to contemporary struggles and debates about social justice?

- Ask students to determine if there is a climax to this novel: Is there more than one climax? What in the text makes you think that? What, by the way, is a *climax*?

A *reflective practitioner* would also consider what to do and why in teaching *Their Eyes Were Watching God* and would be sensitive to options (how might I do things differently from last time?). If a reflective practitioner used the discovery activities listed above, he or she would be attentive and make adjustments; the literary merit question, for instance, which assumes that students have an interest in literary prizes, might be tedious to answer and puzzling for real students. It also raises issues of racial discrimination and might be complicated, especially if the teacher is of a racial majority making the inquiry of a class largely of minority students. Adjustments, research, and refinements would need to be made. These changes, for a reflective teacher, would be reflected in the class immediately and again in future plans to teach the novel. This teacher would also collect data (through an exam or some informal response writing) during the lessons, and then use that data to understand and improve the effectiveness of future lessons for helping the students learn. Reflective teachers are always learning and evolving. It's one of the greatest joys of the profession.

For Your Journal

Pick a piece of literature or a language arts skill and consider it from the point of view of the teaching models. If you were to teach it by *telling*, what would you do? If you were to rely on *inspiration*, what might be the shape of the lesson? If you taught the concept in the frame of *maintaining a creation*, what might you ask students to do? Finally, if you had students *discover* the concept, how would you structure the class? Then, as a *reflective practitioner*, what questions would you ask yourself about any or all of the above teaching models and their effectiveness?

It Didn't Work

Teaching as Considering Instructional Options

Another aspect of teaching, especially beginning teaching, is the seductive—but false—idea of teaching as correct or incorrect. Beginning teachers, like beginning anything, tend to think in terms of *right* and *wrong* when it comes to classroom practice. Having sat in on the classes of dozens of student teachers for some twenty years, we have yet to find a novice who is not concerned about what he or she did that was in terms of *correct* and *incorrect*. It's maddening news for the beginner, but it's true: there is very little right and wrong in this business. It is, actually, almost wholly a matter of options, the choice of any one of which yields different outcomes. And the best option always depends on the individual students in the particular classroom at a particular time. Good teachers learn to use their knowledge and expertise to size up a classroom situation and plan the best practices for their students. In this era of increasing standardization of assessments and curricula, it is particularly important for developing teachers to understand this.

Teaching is not right or wrong; things don't just "work" or "not work." It is, both happily and unnervingly, much more complicated than that, as Stanford University professor David F. Labaree notes:

> [T]eaching remains an uncertain enterprise [because of its] irreducible complexity. What we know about teaching is always contingent on a vast array of intervening variables that mediate between a teacher's action and a student's response. As a result, there is always a ceteris paribus clause hovering over any instructional prescription: This works better than that, if everything else is equal. In other words, it all depends. (2005, 53)

What in the world does Labaree mean? Let us explain: If we could hypothetically assume a lesson plan that would be identically presented to two different classes of students in the same grade in the same school, the outcomes and student learning of those classes would be, despite all efforts of the teacher, very different. The variables are crucial: not only are the students different but their "mix" is different; the sheer number of students is different; the time of day of the class period is different; different things happened the day before in class (and in each student's home); and so on. Some of those factors are choices made by the teacher about subject matter and methodology, but some are simply indigenous to school, the varying classes a teacher deals with every day, and the fact that we teach real people, not robots.

As experienced teachers know—sometimes intuitively, sometimes through bitter trial and error—the same lesson plan, technique, or instructional approach cannot be used successfully with all students semester after semester or even from period to period. This may come as an unhappy surprise if you were hoping that after the first year or two your lesson or unit plans would become sort of unchangeable blueprints on which you could rely for many years. Certainly experience will be helpful to you as a teacher, but you will not be able to replicate from year to year or semester to semester entire class plans. Change and adjustment to the many factors that make up a class and a group of students is part of successful teaching, and there are many factors to consider. But cheer up: you'll rarely be bored.

The Variables Involved

What can make a successful class? What can contribute to a less than successful one? There are a variety of components, all of which you should know and recognize. As a beginner, however, it is useful to know that there is rarely a single reason for a successful or unsuccessful class. Although you may be tempted to point to one thing, it's not just you, the teacher; it's not just your students. It's not only what anyone is studying or how they are studying it or even how long they have spent on it. It's rarely just the school or even the weather. It is a little bit of all of these; every one of these factors can and does interact with and affect learning outcomes and learning environment. Let's look at the variables one at a time.

One variable that can affect a classroom is *subject matter*, its *nature*, *amount*, and *purpose*. The nature of subject matter is a factor because that which is familiar and that which is not can affect not only learning but student attitude and classroom environment. For example, sometimes literature that is difficult can be more intriguing to students than that which is readily accessible; on the other hand, starting with familiar material and then moving to the more difficult can give students a sense of security that they might not have if they immediately started with the difficult material.

The amount of subject matter is also a crucial variable in classroom success. How much is enough, and how much is too much? A day of poetry can be wonderful; five straight days of poem after poem might be tedious and boring, taking all of the surprise and newness out of the genre. On the other hand, two days writing an essay may leave students puzzled and confused; three days might give them more time to revise and rework. We don't intend any of these examples as general rules for instructing particular concepts. The point is, there *are* no such general rules.

The purpose, *why* someone is learning something, can affect attitude, actual learning, and student engagement and thus the smoothness and effectiveness of any lesson. Required material that students must learn for a standardized test may be viewed very differently from material they have chosen. The International Reading Association (IRA) (now known as the International Literacy Association, or ILA) and National Council of Teachers of English (NCTE) Standards for the English Language Arts include a standard specifically on this point: "Students use spoken, written, and visual language to accomplish their own purposes" (1996, 32); and the November 2011 *English Journal* is devoted to this standard.

Methodology, another variable, is just not successfully interchangeable with all classes. For example, students who are used to working in small groups will, with direction, continue to function efficiently and productively in those groups. On the other hand, abruptly putting students who have been fed an exclusive diet of worksheets into small groups can be a disaster. In another area, verbal and assured students will often respond well to a large-group discussion; for some students, however, large groups are intimidating or alienating, and the opportunity to talk as a whole class may not be successful. It's important to incorporate many methodologies into a class, but knowing when to apply them and how much time the students will need to function effectively in that method is a crucial part of planning. The EngageNY.org website includes a useful list of classroom activities (they call them *Protocols*) that might invigorate your thinking about available teaching methods (Expeditionary Learning 2013).

Setting or school context can also affect classes. As outlined in other chapters, knowing who your students are and what their lives are like outside school can give you crucial clues about what links to establish in making material relevant and what material to select or emphasize. To give a fairly low-level example, students in rural midwestern settings may need background information if they read a short story set in New York City; western urban students may need background information regarding poetry about southern fields and farms.

Veteran teachers also know that at a certain time of the day (a split period broken by lunch, for example) or at a certain time of the year (late spring, for instance) certain activities will be more successful than others. To illustrate, creative dramatics, which requires movement and noise and expressiveness, might best be avoided when students are already really excited or keyed up. The first school day after a holiday and the last period of a Friday are times when creative dramatics might not be such a good choice. Then again, students can be sleepy in morning classes or during their post-lunch crash; these classes often go better with more physically active lessons. Even what time of year to introduce particular content matters. Scheduling the completion of the senior research paper in late spring is not very smart. Most seniors by that time of year and at that late date of their high school life really don't have their minds set on research or the format of a bibliography. It is better to schedule the completion of such a long, meticulous project in the late fall or winter.

Time is another variable, especially as it relates to the amount spent on a single topic. Although many teachers love certain topics or pieces of literature and want students to know every aspect and understand almost everything before they consider the text "covered," numerous days or class periods spent on a single topic can engender boredom and restlessness. Less in this case is more—it is usually advisable not to spend huge chunks of instructional time on single topics. Despite its great appeal to you, a month of study on *Romeo and Juliet* will make most students crazy; two weeks on the persuasive essay may be overkill. CCSS strategies encourage teachers to use sections of texts, rather than exhaustively covering every work from cover to cover. Effective teachers understand the importance of time as a variable in their classrooms.

Another variable is you, the *teacher*. Your degree of experience, your enthusiasm for and knowledge of any given subject, even your mood on a particular day can truly affect your classes. Imagine that you are, for example, still unsure of the difference between restrictive and nonrestrictive clauses and yet you are going to give fifth bell a ten-minute minilesson on the subject. All other things being equal, just how relaxed do you anticipate that ten minutes will be? How receptive do you think you might be to a possible barrage of questions from puzzled students? Chances are, with the best of intentions, what you present will be tight, to the point, and not very expansive. And, as you can imagine, that type of presentation might have an effect on your students and the class atmosphere. Contrast this in your mind with a class period talking about one of your favorite plays. Can you imagine how your attitude might affect the class itself? Finally, you may have had personal issues or problems that are worrying you; leaving your own problems, however legitimate they may be, at the classroom door is a habit you may just be learning.

Of course, the *students*—their experience, background, and maturity—are a powerful variable in the success of any classroom. Knowing and adjusting to your students is vital in making instruction "work."

The teaching act, as experienced teachers know and beginning ones quickly learn, is a complex event and is influenced by a myriad of variables: when novice teachers report that "it didn't work," they are actually talking about numerous factors.

To recap, the problem begins with the nebulous *it*. Is *it* the interest or appropriateness of the subject matter? The success of the students' activities? The teacher's instructional methodology? The students' learning outcomes? The students' responses and general satisfaction?

We also need to look at the even more vague *work*. What didn't *work*? Did the majority of students fail a test? Did the students seem confused about a concept? Did class discipline disintegrate? Was the teacher simply dissatisfied with the lesson or unit?

There are a number of variables involved, and although "it didn't work" is not an unimportant or easily resolved worry, understanding what works or doesn't work in a lesson can be more readily handled with a conceptual framework that breaks teaching and learning into component parts.

A Paradigm for Analyzing the Teaching Act

Let us imagine a paradigm for learning that is, essentially, A producing B or B resulting from A:

A Paradigm for Analyzing the Teaching Act

> *Subject matter* of this nature
> in this amount
> for this purpose
> with *methodology* of this type,
> in this *situation* or *setting*,
> and for this *time* of instruction,
> with a *teacher* of this disposition
> this background
> and these qualities,
>
> } A

PRODUCES

these *patterns of affective and cognitive learning,*
in *students* at this level of development and maturity
with this level of experience and
with this kind of background.
(Christenbury 1980, 233–39)

⎫
⎬ B
⎭

Without belaboring what may appear as a perfectly self-explanatory model, let's look at some obvious (if not simpleminded) questions to highlight the components.

Subject matter of this nature To what extent is the complexity of British seventeenth-century metaphysical poetry accessible to all students? What kind of ethnic studies can be/should be taught in a community? What kind of student response will there be to an intensive consideration of spelling rules? How useful will students find the formal argumentative essay?

Subject matter in this amount Should a teacher present multiple punctuation rules in an intensive unit or intersperse them with other material? Should novels be read and taught extensively or intensively? Do students learn more producing a final draft of a piece every week or every other week?

Subject matter for this purpose Is there a difference between teaching something as a review or because students requested it? How do students respond if a teacher spontaneously adds material to a class? If a subject is taught as part of a curricular requirement, to what degree can student interest be affected?

Methodology Do some classes enjoy large group discussion? Do some classes respond well to small-group work? Do some students seem to engage well in silent reading and working alone? Is work at a computer successful with the majority of students? How can pair work be used? How can we tailor the various methods we use so the students are learning most effectively?

Situation or setting Is the last period or bell of the day appropriate for certain types of instructional activities? In what ways are the bells that are usually usurped for assemblies and pep rallies affected by the disruption? Should the approach for a class right before lunch be different from that for first period?

Time Considering the students in a particular class, are two days enough to review imagery? Is one month too long for the reading of a novel? Are three weeks sufficient for the reading of a play? How many days do students need to work on a rough draft?

Teacher Do a teacher's experience, academic qualifications, and personality characteristics affect a class? To what extent can his or her level of confidence and ease with students be a factor in teaching success? Can all teachers readily adapt to all teaching methods?

Patterns of affective and cognitive learning Are all groups of students equally able to understand texts of all levels of complexity? Do some students understand material but remain disengaged? Can some students thoroughly enjoy some material but not completely comprehend it? Should a teacher demand emotional (or affective) responses of any kind? A mix of cognitive and affective? Cognitive only? When? Why? What kinds of scaffolds or support must a teacher use to enable student learning of particular material?

Students Do some students, regardless of chronological age, seem more mature than others? What forms does this maturity take in the classroom? Do high-achieving students react differently and learn differently than less-capable students? Are urban and suburban students alike in their instructional needs? What about students for whom English is a second language?

Now that you are completely depressed and overwhelmed by these questions, know that they are the issues that veteran teachers perhaps never fully answer but do learn to consider, especially when we wonder why something didn't "work" in the classroom. Knowing the questions in this case may be more important than knowing the answers, and it may help you when you know that a class didn't go well or, yes, just didn't work. It will also help you develop as a reflective practitioner. When your lessons feel like they went well and you have results (and data) to support that feeling, you will know why your lessons are effective and you can apply that success in your future lesson plans.

For Your Journal

There are a great many factors that go into a successful lesson, a lesson that students find worthwhile and develop lasting knowledge from. What factors do you feel most prepared to deal with? What factors are you most concerned about, and what can you do to learn more about ways of addressing them?

Creating Activities

There are excellent books available on planning, writing objectives, and addressing CCSS and other state standards. There are also, especially from NCTE, hundreds of journals, books, and newsletters full of teaching activities. The Read/Write/Think website includes hundreds of peer-reviewed lesson plan ideas (with free downloadable materials), and The Teacher Channel site offers videos of real classes, so you can see lessons in action, while the teachers reflect on them. These resources and the good ideas of your fellow and sister teachers will often help you with your planning (note that your school and school district may ask you to follow a certain outline for all your plans). You also need to know how to do it yourself. In general, then, you need to plan a class with the following components in mind:

- Objectives: What do you want students to learn or be able to do as a result of this class? What seems important to highlight about this strategy or skill or piece of literature? What relevant standards are you addressing?

- Method: How are you going to get your students to achieve these objectives? What activities will they engage in? Will the students write? Discuss? Work in small groups? Read and then respond? Act something out?

- Scaffolds/Student Supports: What directions, graphic organizers, model texts, examples, or other materials will you offer students to help them achieve the objectives? Will you give all students the same supports, or will you create a variety of supports for different students in your class, differentiating your instruction? As teachers are asked to raise the level of rigor in all classes, we must give all students help in achieving at those high levels. What will you do to support English language learners or students with special needs?

- Materials: What will you need? Cards? Books? Films? Interactive whiteboard? Tablets or smartphones? Art materials? Props?

- Outline of Tasks and Times: What will be the general procedure for the class? How will you introduce the objectives and activities in a way likely to engage students and ensure they understand the value of today's learning? What comes first? Second? How much time will you need for each activity? How will you end the lesson in a way that gives students a chance to reflect on their learning?

- Evaluation/Assessment: How will you judge how well your students have achieved the objectives? Understood new concepts? Appreciated new genres to which you have exposed them? If you give a test, what will be on it? If students write, what will be the content and focus? How long will it be? What kind of rubric will you use to grade it? If students discuss or work in small groups, how can their contributions be evaluated? By frequency? Importance? Originality? Will this be a formative assessment (which students will use to improve their work) or a summative assessment (which gives final feedback to students)?

Additionally, it helps to remember three principles of creating activities: simplicity, relevance, and specificity.

Simplicity A simple teaching idea is not a simpleminded one, but one that has a major thrust and focus. Teaching ideas that rely upon multiple, complex components—most of which, necessarily, would be interconnected—can fall apart due to their own elaborate nature. Both teachers and students can get hopelessly confused if a teaching activity has too many parts, too many concepts, too many grading rubrics, too many components. Keeping an idea and its attendant activities simple—and thus central—will make the idea more successful in almost any setting. Using *Their Eyes Were Watching God* as an example, you would want your students to do something that is fairly small scale. Bringing in a local social worker to discuss spousal abuse is probably more complicated than necessary and, further, deflects attention away from the novel. When designing activities you need to keep the focus direct and simple.

Relevance Relevance is a highly complex topic and, in this context, does not relate to the contemporary or applicable nature of an activity. Relevance is a characteristic that means that the *activity itself is directly tied to the text or the concept*. Although this caution may seem self-evident, it is often lost when we try to make an otherwise interesting activity fit a piece of literature or when we fixate on a subordinate aspect of the literature and use it as a major springboard for discussion or research. For example, it may seem outrageous, but some beginning teachers might think that any assignment would be adaptable to *Their Eyes Were Watching God*. Having students research the economy or geography or even weather patterns and prevalence of hurricanes in Florida in the early twentieth century versus today would not, for instance, be that significant to the study of the novel. Nor, in addition, would an exploration of how this remarkable book was "rediscovered" and brought back into print. Activities need to be directly related to the novel and its study. Ensuring that your objectives, activities, and assessments are closely aligned to specific standards can help your teaching be appropriately focused and relevant.

Specificity If you want students to write, tell them the general direction and the length. Similarly, if they are to do an art project based on the novel, list the components needed. Too many specific directions can be stultifying, but giving students no directions ("Write about what the novel meant to you"; "Draw a picture based on *Their Eyes Were Watching God*") is unfair. Such vagueness will also, as you can imagine, lead you into difficulty when you have to evaluate and grade such assignments. Further, specificity in assignments will help you clarify what you want from students and also make you consider how long students need to successfully complete the activities. Remember that when we ask students to attempt new or unfamiliar activities, they can often appear reluctant, possibly even uncooperative. What many of us fail to remember is the fear that almost all students have of trying something new—and failing. Accordingly, part of our job as teachers is to extend student skill, to nudge them into new territory, so we must be willing to give students clear explanations and, when appropriate, specific models of what we want. Interpreting Russian psychologist Lev Vygotsky's zone of proximal development, many educational theorists have called such help *scaffolding*. Just as someone changing a lightbulb in a ceiling lamp needs a stool (or scaffold) to stand on to reach it, our students need something to help them reach new heights in their learning. Of course, students are eventually able to reach these new heights on their own, so the tasks must be made more rigorous, and students will need new scaffolds. This is unlike someone trying to change a lightbulb, who'll probably always need that same old stool.

The House on Mango Street: From Chapter to Plan to Class

Leila's Lesson

Sandra Cisneros' (1984) *The House on Mango Street* is an accessible novel that is widely used in many schools across the country. It is a first-person memoir of a young girl, Esperanza Cordero, who tells of her neighborhood, parents, friends, school, and, most importantly, her wishes and dreams. The format of *Mango Street* lends itself to classroom use as most of the almost three dozen chapters—which could also be accurately termed *vignettes*—are exceptionally short and also feature helpful and, at times, evocative titles. Written in a deceptively simple style, *Mango Street* combines prose craft and emotion. Here, in its entirety, is the three-paragraph chapter entitled "Those Who Don't":

Those Who Don't

Those who don't know any better come into our neighborhood scared. They think we're dangerous. They think we will attack them with shiny knives. They are stupid people who are lost and got here by mistake.

But we aren't afraid. We know the guy with the crooked eye is Davey the Baby's brother, and the tall one next to him in the straw brim, that's Ross's Eddie V., and the big one that looks like a dumb grown man, he's Fat Boy, though he's not fat anymore nor a boy.

All brown all around, we are safe. But watch us drive into a neighborhood of another color and our knees go shakity-shake and our car windows get rolled up tight and our eyes look straight. Yeah. This is how it goes and goes.

There are many useful things that we could do with our students using the above chapter. Certainly its subject matter, prejudice and the disparity between appearance and reality, is immediately obvious. Consideration of this topic could spark a number of discussions and responses where students not only look at what Cisneros has written (and her character, Esperanza, has articulated) but also make links to their own perceptions and experiences with such prejudice and assumptions. Students may also be able to share other pieces of literature they have read that address similar concerns. And, you could use the occasion to share with them a piece of a more complex text (literary or informational) that is relevant to these concerns, encouraging the students to approach difficult texts with confidence and intellectual curiosity.

Additionally, there is also the craft of the prose in "Those Who Don't." Having students look at the language that, even in this very short piece, is both simple and highly effective could be interesting. Students could note the memorable rhyme ("all brown all round"), the distinctive adverb *shakity-shake*, the two sentences that start with the conjunction *but*, and the one-word sentence *Yeah* and how it functions.

But I would also make a case that "Those Who Don't" could be used effectively to teach logic and organizational structure. What I would like students to do is consider how the speaker sets out her thesis, gives relevant examples, and then switches the concentration from the others, "those who don't," to herself and what she and her neighbors and friends do. This kind of structural analysis, though it is taking place in the context of a fiction piece, is also relevant to nonfiction and informational texts, in particular persuasive essays. And, I might find a nonfiction piece or two to demonstrate how the strategy works in a nonliterary genre. I would want to spend about thirty to forty minutes of a class doing all this, thirty minutes which include reading, discussion, filling in a template, and beginning a similar persuasive essay. This essay could easily be used with younger students, but let's assume we concentrate on students in grades 9 and 10. How would I try to achieve this? Here's what I would plan.

Objectives
- The students will appreciate "Those Who Don't" by discussing and understanding its theme, attending to unfamiliar terms and complex language in the text.
- The students will consider the relation of what the chapter describes to their own lives and to other pieces of literature they have read.
- The students will explore the prose craft in the chapter, deepening their understanding of the organizational and argumentative structure of "Those Who Don't" by first sketching the sequence of the major points and using that sketch to write a similar piece, a short persuasive essay.

Standards
In my state, Virginia, the pertinent Standards of Learning would be

- 9.4 (for grade 9), The student will read, comprehend, and analyze a variety of literary texts including narratives, narrative nonfiction, poetry, and drama
- 10.4 (for grade 10), The student will read, comprehend, and analyze literary texts of different cultures and eras.

Both of these standards have about a dozen subset activities, and almost all of them would be applicable to the consideration of "Those Who Don't."

Methods

- large-group discussion
- pair work
- individual writing
- large-group sharing

Scaffolds/Student Supports

- I have prepared discussion questions that will assist the students in understanding the theme of the text.
- I have created a template sheet, "Looking at the Logic and Organization of 'Those Who Don't,'" that will assist the students with their analysis of the logic of Cisneros' argument.
- The students will work in pairs on the template sheet, allowing them to use each other for support. This will provide extra support for all students, including those with special needs or who are English language learners.

Materials

- whiteboard and pens (or interactive whiteboard)
- copies of *The House on Mango Street*
- copies of template sheet, "Looking at the Logic and Organization of 'Those Who Don't,'" for students

Outline First, I would tell students that we're going to read a chapter from *Mango Street*, and I would write the chapter title, "Those Who Don't," on the board. I would ask students what they predict this chapter might be about and why, and I would record three or four answers on the board. We would then take out our copies of *Mango Street*, turn to "Those Who Don't," and I would ask for a student volunteer to read the chapter aloud.

Time: 5 minutes

After hearing the chapter read aloud and following it in our books, I would ask the students what they now thought this chapter was about, what its themes were. I seriously doubt many students would miss the point of "Those Who Don't," and as we discuss the fears of those who are in an unfamiliar neighborhood and of what they might be afraid, we would move to one of the speaker's major points, that there is little indeed to fear. How do we know this? For textual evidence, students would likely point to the second paragraph of "Those Who Don't" and cite the human beings the speaker describes behind the possibly scary exteriors.

Time: 5–7 minutes

At this point, many students would be through with "Those Who Don't" (*been there, done that, got it*). It is important, though, to continue on. Cisneros, in fact, complicates the entire issue in her third paragraph, when Esperanza turns the tables. What does Esperanza tell us in paragraph three? How is this important? How does it relate to her previous contention that although "stupid people" who wander into *her* neighborhood have unreasonable fears, when she and her friends go into *other* neighborhoods, their fears are real? So who is right and who is wrong? Are Esperanza and her friends also "stupid"? (It's very important that I have these specific questions prepared in advance, so I'm not just telling the students what to think.)

Time: 5 minutes

At this juncture, students may not have any real answer to the questions posed about whose perceptions are correct, and for this lesson such is not essentially important. What is important is to move students into an analysis of how Cisneros makes her persuasive argument, an argument that is three points in three linked paragraphs, using the signal word *but* to indicate shifts in concept.

To make this clear, I would hand out this template and ask students, in pairs, to fill in the blanks. In all cases, they are to use the language of "Those Who Don't," not a paraphrase of what Cisneros writes. This template is a scaffold to help the students *analyze* the argument Cisneros is making; that is, break the argument down into its parts to understand how it works. I could just tell them all this, but I want them to do it for themselves, and this template is my way of helping them with that complex intellectual work.

Looking at the Logic and Organization of "Those Who Don't"

Paragraph #1

Point #1 _____

Examples illustrating Point #1   _____

_____

_____

Paragraph #2

Point #2 _____

Examples illustrating Point #2   _____

_____

_____

What word is used to signal new point? _____

Paragraph #3

Point #3 _____

Examples illustrating Point #3   _____

_____

_____

What word is used to signal new point? _____

Conclusion _____

Time: 10 minutes

I would now ask students to write their own "Those Who Don't" using this structure, a short persuasive essay of three paragraphs with three different points, examples illustrating each of the three points, and some sort of signal word between paragraphs two and three and to indicate a shift (or extension) in logic. Students would write alone, and can start using Cisneros' words: "Those who don't know any better _____."

After working alone, students can then share their drafts in the large group.

Time: 10–15 minutes

Evaluation/Assessment Students would receive credit for turning in their completed template (with both names on the sheet) and for their final three-paragraph "Those Who Don't." Using a 100-point scale for this activity, students could receive 40 points for the completed template and 60 points (20 points a paragraph, modeled after the template) for the short persuasive essay. If this were a longer writing assignment, I would create a rubric for the evaluation, and I might give out that rubric as an additional scaffold if any students needed it.

"I'm Nobody! Who are you?" From Poem to Plan to Class

Ken's Lesson

Emily Dickinson (1830–1886), a mostly solitary woman who lived her entire life in the same house in which she grew up in a conservative, Christian town in Massachusetts, wrote hundreds of seemingly simple poems. Dickinson stored her writings in carefully wrapped packages of poems that she put in her attic. Though she published only ten poems during her lifetime, her great productivity as a writer was discovered soon after her death, and she has since become one of the most important figures in American literature. It may be hard for students to believe that Emily Dickinson, whose poems are often about personal relationships and nature, is actually a biting social critic, who writes about religion, death, natural splendor (or ferocity), and human failings. Her creative gifts for finding or inventing the perfect word or phrase and for using the sound of language (especially the "feel" of words in the mouth) to connote a particular mood or shift in meaning are enduringly fascinating. Even in the twenty-first century, she reads freshly.

An especially good poem for students to work with is "I'm Nobody! Who are you?" (2005). Its themes of comfort with an ordinary identity and its sharp criticism of those who seek celebrity tap well into the insecurities and questions many young people have as they are developing their own adult identities. Although Dickinson could not have imagined a world of Instagram, text messages, Twitter, and Facebook, the poem also dovetails well with ongoing discussions of social media. Just how much should people share with the world regarding their tastes, habits, and friends?

I'm Nobody! Who are you? (260)

—Emily Dickinson

I'm Nobody! Who are you?
Are you — Nobody — too?
Then there's a pair of us!
Don't tell! they'd advertise — you know!

How dreary — to be — Somebody!
How public — like a Frog —
To tell one's name — the livelong June —
To an admiring Bog!

For this lesson, I would focus on the ways in which Dickinson uses metaphor to underscore an unexpected claim: that fame is undesirable and that an ordinary life is far preferable to celebrity. I would also ask students to examine the ways in which Dickinson's use of figurative language (including metaphor and rhyme, particularly "off rhyme," or "slant rhyme") creates a conspiratorial mood and a close relationship with the reader. In future lessons or, if it comes up organically in the class discussion I arranged for today's lesson, I would ask students to consider how Dickinson might feel about how Facebook, Twitter, and Instagram—and other social media platforms—have encouraged public "croaking" and what new consequences (and benefits) arise in our very open Internet era.

Objectives

- Students will work together to discuss the ways in which Dickinson uses words and images in her poem to convey a theme about the value of an ordinary/private versus a public identity.
- Students will be able to explain how Dickinson uses figurative language to connote specific meaning and tone and to develop a personal relationship with readers.

Standards

- CCSS RL.2: Determine central ideas or themes of a text and analyze their development; summarize the key supporting details and ideas.
- CCSS RL.4: Interpret words and phrases as they are used in a text, including determining technical, connotative, and figurative meanings, and analyze how specific word choices shape meaning or tone.
- CCSS L.5: Demonstrate understanding of figurative language, word relationships, and nuances in word meanings.

Methods

- large-group reading
- individual writing
- fishbowl discussion
- pair work

Scaffolds/Student Supports

- I will provide time for students to write about their own thoughts regarding an ordinary versus a celebrity identity.
- I have prepared discussion questions to facilitate a fishbowl discussion; during the fishbowl discussion, students will be able to make use of each other's ideas and insights to fuel their own.
- I have created a graphic organizer that will help students work in pairs to identify and explain Dickinson's figurative language. I have filled out the first row of the graphic organizer to show students what I am looking for in their answers.

Materials

- interactive whiteboard (or whiteboard and pens)
- copies of "I'm Nobody! Who are you?"
- copies of graphic organizer "Analysis of Figurative Language in Emily Dickinson's 'I'm Nobody! Who are you?'"

Outline First, as students walk into the room, I would have the words *I'm Nobody* on the board, and I would ask students to write for a few minutes about what those words mean to them. I would ask for a few volunteers to talk about what they wrote, and I predict most students would discuss negative aspects of people feeling like "a nobody"; that is, most students would see being "a nobody" as a negative.

Time: 5–7 minutes

After this brief discussion, I would hand out copies of the poem and show one on the board. I would ask two student volunteers to read the poem out loud, so we would all have a chance to read and hear the poem together twice.

Time: 3 minutes

Students might expect that following a reading of a poem, the teacher would tell them what the poem means. Instead, I will arrange a fishbowl discussion and focus the students on questions that will allow them to explicate the meaning of Dickinson's poem.

Questions for Fishbowl Discussions (written on the board, revealed as students complete one question and are ready for the next)

1. To what extent does Emily Dickinson think being a "nobody" is a good thing or a bad thing? Similarly, to what extent does she think being a "somebody" is a good thing or a bad thing? What words in the poem make you believe that?

2. What does Dickinson mean when she says, "They'd advertise"? Who is "they"? What would they "advertise"?

3. How is a "somebody" like a frog? What does Dickinson mean when she says a frog "tells its name"? Do frogs actually talk?

4. What is a *bog*? (Students might need access to a dictionary for this answer, especially if they don't live near watery areas where frogs congregate.) How is it that a frog might tell its name to an "admiring bog," and how is this like a public person, what Dickinson calls a "somebody"?

5. How does the poem shift in tone between stanza one and stanza two? What words connote tone in each of the stanzas? (Following the fishbowl discussion, I would briefly inform the students that the phrase *you know* at the end of the first stanza is an example of "off rhyme," or "slant rhyme," and that it marks a change in tone; sure enough, the poem's tone, which begins with a conspiratorial friendliness between the poet and the reader, shifts to one of biting social critique in the second stanza. Imagine calling famous people "frogs" who are croaking all the time to a bog full of sycophants!)

Fishbowl Discussion Directions

- To arrange my class for a fishbowl discussion, I would position six chairs in a circle in the middle of the room, and I would arrange the other desks to form a larger, multilayered circle around the smaller circle. I would ask six students to volunteer to be in the small circle at the beginning. Only the students sitting in the circle of chairs in the middle (the fishbowl) may speak; everyone else (including the teacher) may only listen. Students in the outside chairs may "tag out" one of the students in the middle and switch places with them. Students should be encouraged to self-monitor their discussion to allow everyone a turn in the fishbowl, while also allowing a truly in-depth discussion. Students who are tagged out are welcome to tag back in, if they feel they have something to contribute.

- Once the students are arranged in their seats and prepared to begin the discussion, I would reveal on the board the first discussion question (see previous list), and I would not move to the next question until the students have fully analyzed the aspect of the poem raised in the question. I would inform the students that they should all take notes on their answers to the questions, as those notes will help them in the next part of the class.

Time: 20 minutes

Following the fishbowl, I would ask students to work in pairs and refer to their notes to fill out the following graphic organizer. As you will see, I have the first row filled out to give the students an example of what I am looking for in terms of their answers. You will also notice that the graphic organizer asks the students to go into more specific depth about the figurative language in Dickinson's poem.

Analysis of Figurative Language in Emily Dickinson's "I'm Nobody! Who are you?"

Word(s) from poem	What do people generally think of when they hear this term or phrase?	What does Dickinson mean by this term or phrase?	What is the figurative significance of this term or phrase?
Nobody	Someone unimportant Someone who has never done anything worthwhile	Someone who is not a celebrity, isn't well known Someone who does not talk about themselves all day	Dickinson turns what one expects to be a negative (being a nobody) into something positive (being someone who doesn't care about being a celebrity or bragging about themselves all the time)
Somebody			
Advertise			
Public			
Frog			
Tell one's name			
Bog			

Time: 10 minutes

Once time is up, I would call the students' attention, and ask them to put their names on their graphic organizers and turn them in for a grade. If some students aren't done, I would let them to take the organizer home to finish and turn in the next day.

Evaluation/Assessment Students would receive credit for turning in their completed graphic organizer. Students could earn up to 100 points based on the quality and depth of their answers. I might also keep a count of student participation in the fishbowl discussion, making sure each student spoke at least once, and I would give each student a fishbowl participation grade (1–5, with 5 being the highest).

A Brief Word on Creating Tests and Test Items

Although in your first few years of teaching you may rely heavily upon tests and test items that are provided in the teacher's edition, on a CCSS module, suggested by the textbook publishing company, found on a website, or even given to you by other teachers, you will, as you become more sure of yourself, start to alter those tests and test items and, eventually, make up tests on your own. Creating your own tests can be very positive because when you craft your own tests, the items will more accurately reflect what you actually taught or discussed in a given class. Whether, however, you are revising tests and test items or creating your own from scratch, you want to remember a few points, some of which may seem so obvious but are often overlooked by beginning teachers. If you follow these points, you will find that grading your tests will be simplified and that student concerns—or even objections—will be minimized.

When you are creating a test or test items, remember to:

- test what you have actually taught
- test more than recall and memorization (use Bloom's Taxonomy to create questions that require higher levels of critical thinking)
- make sure all test items total your target figure (100 is standard but not mandatory, but don't get caught up in complicated, time-consuming scoring schemes)
- indicate for each test section the number of points the question or questions are worth
- consider providing extra credit items (but ensure that your students' scores are still accurate reflections of their learning, and be sure not to let extra credit become a large percentage of the final test grade)
- write clear, unambiguous directions for all test questions and test sections

- leave sufficient space on the test for essay and short-answer items if the students are to write on the test itself
- put a blank line on the first page of the test for the student's name
- if you are hand scoring your test, make sure the blanks for multiple choice, matching, and so on are lined up so that you can easily grade multiple tests at one time
- proofread your test carefully.

Before the test:

- review with students for the test
- give students fair warning about when the test will be given.

During the test itself:

- allot sufficient class time for the test to be completed
- make sure students know your procedures regarding taking tests (including talking to other students, asking you questions during the test, having materials on the desk, turning the test in, what to do if they finish the test early, and so on)
- warn students during the test as to when time will be up
- make sure you are aware of school policies for students who may be entitled to additional time; a separate, quiet space for test taking; or another accommodation as a result of an Individualized Education Program.

When you grade the test:

- discount test items if a significant number of students fail to answer correctly (This is a good sign that the question isn't clear or you didn't teach that concept well.)
- check your arithmetic so that the final grade is accurate.

When you return the test to your class:

- take class time to go over the test with your students so that they understand what items they missed as well as what they did correctly
- be willing to meet with and talk to students one-on-one if they have questions regarding your grading.

Finally, if most of your students do not do well on your test:

- retest if necessary
- learn from your own tests and continue to refine them, as reflective practitioners do.

And, if you are creating your own test items, remember that

- *true-or-false* items are not truly discriminatory unless students are asked to explain their choices
- *multiple choice* and *matching items* need to have sufficient options to be challenging (multiple choice needs to have more than three options; matching should not feature equal numbers of concepts)
- *fill-in-the-blank* items must be phrased very carefully *or* you must be prepared to accept multiple answers *or* the fill-in-the-blank must mimic a matching item format
- *short answer* items need to be specifically phrased so that students know what you are asking
- *essay questions* must be precisely phrased, and, as noted above, sufficient time must be allotted to answer them.

The purpose of testing is to determine how well your students have achieved objectives that you have set. Don't get so tied to the rules and regulations of your tests that you lose sight of the purpose. When your tests are unclear or if they reveal that your students did not learn what you wanted them to, be flexible about eliminating questions and reteaching and retesting as necessary.

The Place of Standards in Your Planning

In the past few years, there has been a revolution in K–12 education involving standards. States that did not adopt or have dropped the CCSS (National Governors Association Center for Best Practices, Council of Chief State School Officers 2010a) have developed their own standards, which are more specific than they've been in the past and, like the CCSS, focus on making students "college- and career-ready." As of this writing, the CCSS are very controversial nationally, so what should someone just starting out as a teacher think about all the political fervor surrounding them? The answer is probably not much, at least when it comes to what goes on in your classroom, although teachers should understand such standards and be prepared to explain how their teaching speaks to the standards.

Ultimately, any set of standards can be a valuable resource for a teacher. The CCSS for English teachers may be found in a document titled "CCSS State Standards for English Language Arts & Literacy in History/Social Studies, Science, and Technical Subjects." Treated as a resource, standards can help teachers design lessons, assignments, and assessments that will educate students at an appropriate level and for specific, appropriate purposes. If you align your lessons carefully to standards, you can have confidence that your lessons are professional and responsible and that your ideas and methods for teaching could withstand scrutiny. If a parent, a student, an administrator, or even another teacher challenges your lesson, you'll be glad to have a set of respected standards on your side.

One of the reasons why the CCSS are controversial is because they were not instituted by educators but rather by the National Governors Association (made up of the nation's state governors). How involved educators were in the development of the standards is a point of controversy. There are other standards, however, that can also help teachers ensure they are serving their students well. For example, you should consult the IRA/NCTE Standards, which were developed by members of those organizations, all of whom are educators. And, though it is primarily intended as a resource for postsecondary education, the "Framework for Success in Postsecondary Writing," a collaboration of the Council of Writing Program Administrators, NCTE, and the National Writing Project, is another valuable resource.

Whether or not your state has adopted the Common Core, it has probably adopted some form of college- and career-ready standards. For that reason, looking closely at CCSS is worthwhile for all early career teachers. Let's look closely at one CCSS Anchor Standard.

This is number 2 in the "College- and Career-Readiness Anchor Standards for Reading":

> Determine central ideas or themes of a text and analyze their development; summarize the key supporting details and ideas.

CCSS are often written in shorthand. The standard above would be notated as "CCSS R.2." This anchor standard is one of ten standards for reading. This anchor standard alone makes sense and probably needs little explanation. But to be crystal clear, let's say this standard requires that students can read a text of any kind (a poem, an essay, a chart) and understand how it uses language to create an argument (or some assertion), and the student can list and describe the ways in which the text uses language and evidence to carry forth that assertion to readers. Any English teacher would agree that this is an important skill for literate people.

The CCSS helpfully give us more direction in the grade-specific breakdown of the anchor standards. And, in addition, because CCSS require students to read literary and informational texts, there are separate standards for each. So here are the grade-specific standards for RL.2 (Reading Literature) for grade 6 and for grades 11 and 12 (there are also standards for RI [Reading Informational Text], but we'll deal with them in the chapter on nonfiction and informational texts):

> RL2.6: Determine a theme or central idea of a text and how it is conveyed through particular details; provide a summary of the text distinct from personal opinions or judgments.

> RL2.11–12: Determine two or more themes or central ideas of a text and analyze their development over the course of the text, including how they interact and build on one another to produce a complex account; provide an objective summary of the text.

You can see how students' ability to determine a central theme from a text should include increasingly greater depth, complexity, and objectivity, as they move from sixth grade to senior high school. If we were to use Leila's lesson on Cisneros' *The House on Mango Street* as an example, her lesson addresses this standard well for sixth grade by asking students to closely examine the words and phrases (including unknown terms) and to restate the meaning of the text, taking care to focus on the actual language of the text (textual evidence). As Leila moves on in her lesson, asking the students to examine how the meaning of the chapter changes (shifts in point of view from paragraphs 1 and 2 to paragraph 3) and encouraging them to see the power of the chapter's speaker's position in the narrative, the lesson begins to address the higher-order critical reading skills described in the standard for grades 11 and 12.

The CCSS provide grade-specific standards for every anchor standard in Reading, Writing, Speaking & Listening, and Language. They can be very useful guides for understanding what your students should know and be able to do. Your state and school will in all likelihood have additional information available that will help you fill out your curriculum for the year.

At some point very early in your career, you should make yourself familiar with your state and or/school district standards for English language arts, regardless of whether they follow the CCSS State Standards. In your school, you will be asked to indicate specifically which standards you are addressing in your lesson plans and, as across the nation, your state's standards will also surface eventually on the state test. This kind of linked consistency may well help you and your students, because for most of us, regardless of locality, English language arts standards are generally reasonable.

But where to start? You might think of taking some time to assess your state or local standards from the perspective of a single grade level. If so, think about the following:

I. Choose *one grade level* in secondary English Language Arts (grades 6 through 12) and download or photocopy your state or school district standards for that *one grade level*. These standards are, essentially, your instructional map for the year.

II. Consider each of the standards and answer, *for each, four questions*:

1. To the best of your understanding, to what extent is this skill *appropriate or inappropriate* for this grade level?

2. To the best of your understanding, to what extent is this skill *important or unimportant* in the broad context of mastery of English language arts?

3. If you had to *teach* this standard to your students, *what activity and/or content* would be appropriate to help students master this standard?

4. If you had to *test* mastery of this standard with your students, what kind of *test item or mastery demonstration* would you use with your students?

Although two of the questions are theoretical (numbers 1 and 2), two are very practical.

How to teach a specific skill using an activity or reading and how to test that skill is the heart of the matter. Taking a bit of time to review your district and/or state standards and to assess them may save you some panic as you enter the whirlwind of the school year and plan your teaching.

For Your Journal

Select a grade level and look at the English language arts standards for your state. Consider the four questions in the shaded box on page 120, especially the one on activity/content and test items or mastery demonstration. How difficult was it to come up with ideas? To what extent were you able to imagine multiple activities and mastery assessments for a single standard? Share your ideas with a friend. What is similar? Different?

Preparing Students for College and Career Readiness and an Uncertain Future

In a factory model of education, it's important that educators know exactly what their students must know and be able to do to create products (students) that are fully functional for the adult life they will lead. However, in the twenty-first century, the pace of change is so fast and so revolutionary (particularly in areas of communication and global interchange), that it's becoming more difficult to predict exactly what students need to know and be able to do to be successful. To be honest, we have no idea what's to come in the next five years of technology and global politics, never mind what today's twelve-year-olds may face twenty years from now. So, it's useful to consider *enduring* skills and attitudes that adults should have if they are to be successful in such an uncertain, and frankly exciting, time.

The CCSS and some other standards focus on preparing students to be successful in college and/or on a career track of their choosing. So, what do college- and career-ready students look like? According to CCSS, they have the following seven attributes:

- They demonstrate independence.
- They build strong content knowledge.
- They respond to the varying demands of audience, task, purpose, and discipline.
- They comprehend as well as critique.
- They value evidence.
- They use technology and digital media strategically and capably.
- They come to understand other perspectives and cultures. (National Governors Association Center for Best Practices, Council of Chief State School Officers 2010a, 7)

Few would disagree that these are admirable goals for any English teacher to have for students. And they correlate well with the eight "habits of mind" crucial for college success spelled out in the "Framework for Success in Postsecondary Writing":

- *curiosity*—the desire to know more about the world
- *openness*—the willingness to consider new ways of being and thinking in the world
- *engagement*—a sense of investment and involvement in learning
- *creativity*—the ability to use novel approaches for generating, investigating, and representing ideas
- *persistence*—the ability to sustain interest in and attention to short- and long-term projects
- *responsibility*—the ability to take ownership of one's actions and understand the consequences of those actions for oneself and others
- *flexibility*—the ability to adapt to situations, expectations, or demands
- *metacognition*—the ability to reflect on one's own thinking as well as on the individual and cultural processes used to structure knowledge. (Council of Writing Program Administrators National Council of Teachers of English National Writing Project 2011; http://www.ncte.org/positions/statements/collwritingframework)

Educational theorist Howard Gardner, famous for his theory of multiple intelligences, has more recently identified five "minds" that convey the kinds of thinking skills that are important for the future:

- *The disciplinary mind*: the mastery of major schools of thought, including science, mathematics, and history, and of at least one professional craft
- *The synthesizing mind*: the ability to integrate ideas from different disciplines or spheres into a coherent whole and to communicate that integration to others
- *The creating mind*: the capacity to uncover and clarify new problems, questions, and phenomena
- *The respectful mind*: awareness of and appreciation for differences among human beings and human groups
- *The ethical mind*: fulfillment of one's responsibilities as a worker and as a citizen. (2009)

We share these lists of attributes, habits, and minds, not to overwhelm you with information—though, it's perfectly understandable if you feel that way right now—but rather to help you understand how complex the task of teaching English really is. These lists can remind you why we teach what we teach and how we teach it. There's a reason why English teachers must be so smart, so focused, and yet so imaginative in their work. We are helping students develop extremely complex sets of skills, knowledge, and attitudes. Don't let this task overwhelm you; let it energize you.

Finally, the CCSS also require English teachers to make several so-called "shifts" in their thinking about English content. Unless you've been taught within a CCSS school yourself, you might find you need to think about these shifts as you imagine what your teaching will look like.

1. *Regular practice with* complex texts *and their academic language:* Students are being asked to read more difficult texts at earlier ages, and the CCSS requires that they develop knowledge of the specialized terms and linguistic constructs found in more sophisticated texts.

2. *Reading, writing, and speaking* grounded in evidence from texts, *both literary and informational:* The Common Core focuses very heavily on textual evidence. Students will move from developing opinions in younger grades to developing skills of critical analysis and argument in later grades, but all grades will highlight using specific evidence from texts.

3. Building knowledge *through content-rich nonfiction:* English teachers will still be expected to teach literature, but they will be incorporating an increasing amount of nonfiction, particularly informational nonfiction, in their courses. By the time a student reaches twelfth grade, seventy percent of his or her school reading and writing should be in nonfiction. (National 2010a, 5, emphasis in the original)

Standards Are Guides, Not Restrictions

Some educators are concerned that lists of standards tell teachers *how* to teach. This is not true. In fact, the CCSS state explicitly, "The Standards define what all students are expected to know and be able to do, not how teachers should teach" (6). Another CCSS document takes the issue further, stating it is a myth that the CCSS tell teachers how to teach: "Teachers know best about what works in the classroom. That is why these standards establish what students need to learn but do not dictate how teachers should teach. Instead, schools and teachers will decide how best to help students reach the standards" (National Governors Association Center for Best Practices, Council of Chief State School Officers 2010b). However, not all is roses and rainbows. The standardized exams that will be used to measure what students have learned have the potential to drive and even to narrow the curriculum, and they may encourage some teachers to engage in rigid test prep rather than rich, authentic teaching and learning. In states like New York, where students' test scores are used directly in teacher evaluations, the pressure will be even stronger. If you're interested in learning more about the more controversial aspects of CCSS and the planned assessments, a good place to start is the November 2014 *English Journal* (NCTE) themed "The Standards Movement: A Recent History."

We discuss the CCSS and other standards important for English language arts throughout this book. Chapters on teaching literature, writing, language, and oral communication will deal explicitly with appropriate standards. And, there are vast numbers of other useful resources available, including these:

- Smith, Appleman, and Wilhelm's (2014) *Uncommon Core* gives excellent advice about of the value of prereading strategies, which are discouraged by some CCSS proponents.

- Sassi, Gere, and Christenbury's (2014) *Writing on Demand for the Common Core State Standards Assessments* helps teachers address the challenges of test writing.

- *Common Core CPR* by Lent and Gilmore (2013) offers in-depth discussion of strategies for approaching CCSS teaching.

- Stuart's (2014) *A Non-Freaked Out Guide to Teaching the Common Core* is a quick, fun read that highlights the CCSS Anchor Standards.

- A particular favorite is *Supporting Students in a Time of Core Standards*, by Sarah Brown Wessling, Crystal VanKotten, and Danielle Lilge (2011), which includes a helpful Q & A about the standards and offers excellent, classroom-tested strategies for approaching them.

Points to Keep in Mind About Standards

- You should know and value professional standards as resources and guides, but don't let them keep you from treating your teaching as a creative enterprise in which you engage students' minds and imaginations.

- Aligning your lessons clearly to professional standards can help ensure that your teaching is appropriately rigorous and will help you prepare students for their future and for standardized exams.

- All the political drama about the standards—even though you should be aware of it and perhaps even be engaged in it—need not distract you from your important work as an English teacher with your students.

Using standards and professional statements, such as the "Framework for Success in Postsecondary Writing," can help teachers ensure that their lessons are philosophically sound and intellectually rigorous. Don't think of standards as handcuffs that restrict your teaching; think of them as guidebooks that you have in your back pocket throughout your teaching journey.

A Final Caution About Planning

Despite all the exhortations about the importance of planning and how it will help you in your teaching, remember that plans can—and should—be changed depending on context. Loving the plan, following it as a script, regardless of what is actually happening in your classroom, will not ensure learning. Make your plans, but remember that you may need to be flexible, as Brian Durrett realized at the end of a week of student teaching:

It hit me like a ton of bricks while I was driving home Friday afternoon. My cooperating teacher had been telling me over and over that I should try straying from my lesson plan or improvising a little when I felt that things were not going well. I listened to what she said but I was not hearing her. It finally sunk in when I was reflecting on what had happened that day. When things began falling part in my classes, I would tend to barge on and get through what I had planned. I did this even though I had become completely frustrated with the students for not paying attention and following my instructions. I never really asked myself how I could make this any better. I would keep driving my point home because I had the plan written down; people told me that my plans were well thought out so I assumed that they would work. For some reason, I never considered all of the elements that could thwart a lesson plan. I just knew what I had planned and that was what I was going to do in the classroom . . . [but] the best laid plans will not always work. The students are dynamic. Some days they are very receptive and are eager to tackle what I throw out to them. Other days, even the coolest lesson goes over like a lead balloon because it is warm and sunny outside or there is a tension that causes the students with the shorter fuses to explode at the smallest thing. Being able to read the students and doing what they can handle makes me happier because I am not doing battle throughout the class. It makes the students happy because I'm not trying their patience and pushing them beyond their limit.

Planning for your teaching may at first seem hard to do, and knowing when to deviate from the plan may, at first, be even harder. Certainly your early life in the classroom may have a different rhythm and a different reality than what you may remember experiencing as a student. The classroom will, though, also reveal itself to you as a very intense and wonderful place where plans are made but also unpredictable and exciting things occur, new insights, significant conversations, real learning, real connections. It may be a little moment, but it happens to all teachers. Beginning teacher Beverly Garner describes it well:

There have been days when I've had second thoughts, and days when I've felt exhilarated. Right now, I'm feeling horrible with a virus and an accompanying secondary infection, so I'm a bit down. What bolsters me, though, are those FACES, when they're LISTENING, and something is CLICKING between them and me—those times when they're laughing, or arguing even, let me know there's something going on, and it's a great feeling.

Some afternoon soon you too will find yourself standing at the end of a full and good teaching day—although you may be doubtful at this point, you will indeed have a number of these. You will look around your room and think of what you planned and what you and your students then said and did in class. You will not think of the difficult times when you felt you were facing the unknown. Some afternoon it will strike you, at least on that day, that teaching is actually a rather wonderful way to spend your life.

References

Atwell, Nancie. 1985. "Everyone Sits at a Big Desk: Discovering Topics for Writing." *English Journal* 74 (5): 35–39.

———. 1998. *In the Middle: A Lifetime of Learning About Writing, Reading, and Adolescents.* 2nd ed. Portsmouth, NH: Heinemann.

Barnett, Ann Byrd, and Alan Wieder. 2013. *Teacherpreneurs: Innovative Teachers Who Lead but Don't Leave.* San Francisco: Jossey-Bass.

Bullough, Robert V. Jr. 1989. *First-Year Teacher: A Case Study.* New York: Teachers College Press.

Christenbury, Leila. 1980. "A Paradigm for Analyzing Components of the Teaching Act." *English Education* 11 (4): 233–39.

Cisneros, Sandra. 1984. *The House on Mango Street.* New York: Vintage.

Codell, Esmé Raji. 2009. *Educating Esmé: Diary of a Teacher's First Year.* Expanded edition. Chapel Hill, NC: Algonquin Books.

Council of Writing Program Administrators National Council of Teachers of English National Writing Project. 2011. "Framework for Success in Postsecondary Writing." www.nwp.org/img /resources/framework_for_success.pdf.

Dickinson, Emily. 2005. "I'm Nobody! Who are you?" In *The Poems of Emily Dickinson*, edited by Ralph W. Franklin. Cambridge, MA: Harvard University Press.

Expeditionary Learning. 2013. "Appendix: Protocols and Resources." EngageNY.org. https://www .engageny.org/sites/default/files/resource/attachments/appendix_protocols_and_resources.pdf.

Finney, Jack. 1956. "Contents of the Dead Man's Pockets." *Good Housekeeping* (June). www.is .wayne.edu/MNISSANI/20302005/Deadman.htm.

Freire, Paulo. 1981. *Pedagogy of the Oppressed.* New York: Continuum.

Gardner, Howard. 2009. *Five Minds for the Future.* Cambridge, MA: Harvard Business Review Press.

Gold, Elizabeth. 2003. *Brief Intervals of Horrible Sanity: One Season in a Progressive School.* New York: Penguin.

Gorlewski, Julie. 2011. "Seize the Data: Embracing Information." *English Journal* 100 (6): 99–102.

Grossman, Pamela L. 1990. *The Making of a Teacher: Teacher Knowledge and Teacher Education.* New York: Teachers College Press.

Hurston, Zora Neale. (1937) 1990. *Their Eyes Were Watching God.* New York: Harper & Row.

International Reading Association and National Council of Teachers of English. 1996. *Standards for the English Language Arts.* www.ncte.org/standards/ncte-ira.

Jackson, Shirley. (1948) 1982. *The Lottery: And Other Stories.* New York: Farrar, Straus & Giroux.

Joyce, Bruce, and Marsha Weil. 2014. *Models of Teaching.* 9th ed. New York: Pearson.

Labaree, David F. 2005. *The Trouble with Ed Schools.* New Haven: Yale University Press.

Lent, ReLeah Cossett, and Barry Gilmore. 2013. *Common Core CPR: What About the Adolescents Who Struggle . . . or Just Don't Care?* Thousand Oaks, CA: Corwin.

Lindblom, Kenneth. 2004. "Everything I Really Need to Know About Teaching I Learned from Television and Movies." *English Journal* 93 (3): 84–87.

———. 2010. "From the Editor: Motivating Students." *English Journal* 100 (1): 10–11.

Macrorie, Ken. 1984. *Twenty Teachers.* New York: Oxford University Press.

Mann, Thomas. 1927. *The Magic Mountain.* New York: Knopf.

Martinez, Monica R., and Dennis McGrath. 2014. *Deeper Learning: How Eight Innovative Public Schools Are Transforming Education in the Twenty-First Century*. New York: New Press.

National Governors Association Center for Best Practices, Council of Chief State School Officers. 2010a. *Common Core State Standards for English Language Arts & Literacy in History/Social Studies, Science, and Technical Subjects*. Washington, DC: National Governors Association Center for Best Practices, Council of Chief State School.

————. 2010b. *Myths vs. Facts*. Washington, DC: National Governors Association Center for Best Practices, Council of Chief State School Officers.

NCTE. 2014. "The Standards Movement: A Recent History." *English Journal* 104 (2).

Palonsky, Stuart B. 1986. *900 Shows a Year*. New York: Random House.

Sassi, Kelly, Anne Ruggles Gere, and Leila Christenbury. 2014. *Writing on Demand for the Common Core State Standards Assessments*. Portsmouth, NH: Heinemann.

Smith, Michael W., Deborah Appleman, and Jeffrey D. Wilhelm. 2014. *Uncommon Core: Where the Authors of the Standards Go Wrong About Instruction—and How You Can Get It Right*. Thousand Oaks, CA: Corwin.

Stock, Patricia Lambert, Trace Schillinger, and Andrew Stock. 2014. *Entering the Conversations: Practicing Literacy in the Disciplines*. Urbana, IL: NCTE.

Stuart, Dave Jr. 2014. *A Non-Freaked Out Guide to Teaching the Common Core: Using the 32 Literacy Anchor Standards to Develop College- and Career-Ready Students*. San Francisco: Jossey-Bass.

Wellington, Bud. 1991. "The Promise of Reflective Practice." *Educational Leadership* 48 (March): 4–5.

Wessling, Sarah Brown, Crystal VanKotten, and Danielle Lilge. 2011. *Supporting Students in a Time of Core Standards: English Language Arts, Grades 9–12*. Urbana, IL: NCTE.

4 | THOSE WHOM WE TEACH

We need to hear adolescents, and not when we are shouting at them or when they are shouting at us. They need to be heard when sitting face to face with someone who is interested in them as individuals . . . The point is not simply that good kids can be bad, or that the school system needs fixing, but rather that labels so easily planted on teens obscure their more interesting reality. In fact, one of the most powerful themes exposed through the simple act of taking the time really to know . . . kids that they have enormous potential.

—Patricia Hersch, *A Tribe Apart: A Journey into the Heart of American Adolescence*

In the end, teachers will only learn about their students by listening to them and hearing about their strengths and struggles, about their perceptions of the work they are expected to do. Too often we wonder about what is going on with our students, why they are acting a certain way or not doing something we want them to do. Rather than speculate, we can get the answer directly from the source. We can ask students what they need and want from us as teachers.

—Sophia Sobko, "Academic Self-Sabotage: Understanding Motives and Behaviors of Underperforming Students"

Sophia Sobko is a first-year teacher who writes eloquently of how her students underperform and what we can do about it. Patricia Hersch is not a teacher. Although Sobko details her teaching in a high school in California, Hersch is a journalist who spent three years observing eight young people in school and out and talking with them about their lives, their beliefs, and their dreams. One of Hersch's (1999) major conclusions in *A Tribe Apart: A Journey into the Heart of American Adolescence* is that young people need more—not fewer—adults in their lives and that, as you might have suspected, for us to have any effect on them, young people need to have a positive relationship with adults, both teachers and nonteachers:

> It is a popular notion that adolescents career out of control, are hypnotized by peer pressure or manipulated by demons for six years or so, and then if they don't get messed up or hurt or killed, they become sensible adults. That's ridiculous. The youngsters I have spoken to are trying the best they can in the present world to do what is right for them. . . . An eighth grader explains: "We're kind of like adults. We've learned how to run our own lives, think for ourselves, make decisions for ourselves." . . . The turbulence of adolescence today comes not so much from rebellion as from the loss of communication between adults and kids, and from the lack of realistic, honest understanding of what the kids' world really looks like. The bottom line: we can lecture kids to our heart's content but if they don't care what we think, or there is no relationship between us that matters to them, or they think we are ignorant of the reality of their lives, they will not listen. (1999, 365)

Sobko (2014) would agree. And if students will not listen, they also will not learn. For sure, students are our profound partners in the classroom, and our willingness to understand them and our sense of connection with them constitutes a large part of teaching success. We knew this early in our teaching, but Leila got a chance to relearn it.

When she returned to teach high school after many years at a university teaching other people how to teach, she found, not surprisingly, that her students in English 11 were very different from those students she taught years ago. Leila knew that an ability to adjust and change is important: getting into an instructional rhythm with these students, trying to take their perspective about assignments and grades, understanding their motivations to work—or not to work—were crucial to her teaching success. And when she had difficulty connecting with some of those students in the high school class, she understood clearly how serious that problem might be. Ignoring or minimizing students, teaching around them or in spite of them, are just not options. If we are to be conscientious and successful teachers, engaged students are at the heart of our work.

What Is Adolescence?

So who are these young people you will teach and with whom you need to connect? Generalities are misleading—and young people as a group despise being labeled and classified—but some observations are in order. And do remember that even though you may right now be close in age to those you teach, their experience at this moment in school is not yours, and your past experience will soon not be up-to-date. Like most adults, you will rapidly—inescapably—have to be reeducated by your students regarding the here and now, what is going on in their lives, and what is important to them.

Some factual information may help capture a snapshot of students today. A large-scale survey of young people in the Washington, DC, area—a very urban/suburban and multicultural, multiracial, and multilingual area—describes teenagers this way:

> They're a generation in a hurry, hurling headlong to adulthood but not yet shed of youthful innocence or naïveté. They're mixed up—and the girls in particular are stressed out. They view the future through cracked rose-colored glasses, anxious about the direction of the country and the world. Most predict another terrorist attack as big or bigger than September 11 sometime in their lives. One in four expects a nuclear war . . . at the same time [they] are brimming with youthful optimism and self-confidence about the world they will inherit. . . . Sometimes their confidence borders on delusional: The vast majority say it's likely they will be rich. Sometimes it is poignant: Most are convinced they will be married to the same person till death do them part. But more often their expectations are sensibly realistic: Most expect that just about everything, from a new house to a college education, will cost more when they are their parents' age. (Morin et al. 2005, 14)

What do teenagers in this survey cite as fears? The survey lists pollution, AIDS, drug abuse, immorality, divorce, war, the economy. What do teenagers in this survey value? By percentage and topic, the researchers found the following:

75 percent value being successful in a career.

65 percent value having a family of your own.

65 percent value having lots of close friends.

64 percent value making a difference in the world.

62 percent value having enough free time to do things you want.

And there are, understandably, gaps by race and gender. In general, African American teens feel "the country's best years are in the past" although only a fraction of white teens agree. Boys view the future positively; a majority of girls are not as optimistic and also think about a recurring terrorist attack. Girls in this survey feel far more stress than boys, especially regarding school issues; a majority of black teens believe they will be famous someday, but whites are not as confident. Most of the teens surveyed would consider interracial marriage, and a significant number had dated or were dating someone of another race. Finally, the importance of religion in everyday life was a positive factor for over one-third of all teens surveyed.

How exposed are these teens to the harsh realities of life? It may be indicative of the metropolitan nature of Washington, DC, and not all teens across the country may respond in the same manner, but almost half the teens surveyed know someone who is in a gang, and a fifth have had a friend who was killed or injured by gun violence and personally have been a victim of crime or violence. Interestingly, the results of a separate national survey were not very different: "one of the biggest surprises of the [two] surveys was how closely the attitudes of [Washington, DC] area teens mirror the view of high school-age teenagers across the country" (Morin et al. 2005, 17).

Similarly, in a federal study reported in 2009 (Federal Interagency Forum), although 67 percent of students surveyed lived in two-parent households, most single-parent homes were more likely to live in poverty (Planty et al. 2008). In addition, the composition of students we teach continues to shift from the old paradigm of majority white and Anglo culture. Culturally and linguistically diverse students are the fastest-rising group of K–12 public school students, rising 43 percent since the late 1990s, with white students declining in percentage of the whole and students of color increasing (Valdez and Callahan 2011, 4).

Perhaps none of this is a surprise to you, but these shifts affect our schools and any preconceived notions regarding whom we teach.

Again, we consider what adolescence is. We have all been adolescents and we all probably think we know a lot about adolescents. But it's possible that what we know about adolescents is based more on myth and assumption than on fact. In an *English Journal* article, Sophia Tatiana Sarigianides, Mark A. Lewis, and Robert Petrone (2015) describe how a book they read jolted them into rethinking adolescence and developing what they call a "youth lens" for examining literature and culture. For them, Nancy Lesko's (2012) *Act Your Age! A Cultural Construction of Adolescence*, was a wake-up call, as they "found [their] previous beliefs about adolescence reflected in everything Lesko critiqued. . . . Her book exposed these dominant ideas as stereotypes tied to a racist, sexist, class-based history, and discussed the varied ways these ideas bound, or constrained, youth, especially minority youth" (Sarigianides, Lewis, and Petrone 2015, 15). To combat these issues, Sarigianides, Lewis, and Petrone suggest bringing a "youth lens" (their own construct) to bear on discussions, particularly of young adult literature. They ask questions such as these:

- What determines "adult" versus "adolescent" behavior in a text?

- Are inner-city minority youth portrayed differently than suburban majority youth?

- How are religious teens who observe celibacy until marriage depicted with regard to "raging hormones"? (17)

For us, the lesson from this is that we should treat our students as individuals. Yes, they are all adolescents. But adolescence is no more a monolith than adulthood is. Our students are different people, they have different experiences, and they are susceptible to prejudice, misrepresentation, and injustice, just as we all are.

No One Ever Said It Was Going to Be Easy

Interacting with students is the heart of the teaching process: when that interaction is lively and relatively smooth, the joys of teaching come easily to mind. When, however, the interaction is strained, awkward, or even unpleasant, teachers often wonder why they got into this in the first place. Teaching is, as you suspect, a terribly *intimate* business, and when we and our students are not in sync, the level of discomfort can be frighteningly high. Yes, the days and weeks of teaching can go by in a very routine manner, but there will be days when things go wrong between teachers and students and when the entire enterprise becomes remarkably difficult. It is, first, that students are in groups and identify in ways different from adults; it is also that some students don't identify very much at all.

If you have been a visitor in a teachers' lounge recently and no one particularly worried about your presence there, the remarks you overheard might have surprised you. In many teachers' lounges across this country, in countless school workrooms and offices, relatively sharp and unflattering remarks are made about students by teachers. Much of that talk is the release of tension by people who interact intensely and over sustained periods of time with large groups of young people. Thus, much of that talk means little. Some of it, though, can be cynical and cruel. The latter is not worth your sustained consideration and often comes from adults who are overwhelmed and very tired and disappointed by the entire enterprise of teaching. But where in the world does the former come from?

The cynical comments come from the difficulty of teaching as we define it in this country in the public school system: teaching people in same-age groups, teaching people in groups, and the political act itself of teaching people. The fact that these patterns can make teaching difficult is probably not very surprising to you, especially when you recall your own life as a student. It is naïve to expect that your teaching career will not have some hard moments. Teaching students can be a tough business; it can have ugly times. This does not involve just you and your classroom. Over the past few decades, we have seen regular instances of school shootings in almost every state in this country and in schools at almost all levels, elementary through high school. Although some of the shooters are adults from outside the school community, many are students who return to settle old scores or to make a grisly impression through media coverage. You will teach students who could be in that category. Some of our former students—males and females—are in jail, some are dead, and each of us has had at least one student who committed murder. Some are hard to remember fondly.

The Tough Times of Teaching

Leila's Story: Apathy and Violence

For all of the wonderful experiences I have had in the classroom and the countless satisfying and even exhilarating encounters with students, like many teachers, I have also had my share of rough moments.

Fighting student apathy is part of my history as a teacher: I have been unable to motivate every student in my classroom. Some, for a variety of reasons, have refused to engage, be involved, or attempt to do assignments. They were what some term "risk averse" and could not be enticed into more active learning. Some slipped in and out of my classroom more like ghosts than real people, only temporarily there, perched, just waiting to move on. Some were so quiet, so removed, I almost forgot they were on my roll and, after some months of trying to get them involved, I turned my energies and efforts elsewhere.

Despite my attempts, my energy, and my enthusiasm, I have seen students turn away from an activity, a learning contract, a book. I have had students who have, without exaggeration, done virtually nothing in class for days at a stretch. I have asked students to sit up in class and not sleep, to open books that have remained resolutely shut, to bring a pen or pencil or paper to class, to get up and actually *sit* with their group. I have had students who made themselves so unobtrusive in class that very soon after our time together I could not begin to recall their names. This happened in my early teaching career and then again when I returned to teach high school.

I, like many teachers who have taught for some time, have also had more dramatic difficulties with students. I have been threatened physically and cursed, and I had my car damaged. I have had my locked classroom broken into and test materials stolen. I have had bulletin boards I assembled and for which I bought or made the artwork defaced or vandalized. Some of this was directed at me personally; some of this was directed more generally.

I was hit "accidentally" in the act of shielding a slightly built student from the class bully; sadly for me, the larger student's fist went into my stomach but, thankfully, not into the other kid's face. While standing in the hall during a class change, I was slammed into a door by a student I did not recognize and who was trying to get away from a pursuing assistant principal. On hall duty, I was knocked out of the way while walking a confused and drug-dazed student to the school infirmary; his friends, observing the scene, feared any intervention and did not want a teacher involved. The student was taken away from me forcibly and spirited somewhere across the school campus.

When I was taking over a hospitalized colleague's study hall, I was warned that the group had been a problem in the past. Sure enough, the second day of my assignment I was backed up against the classroom door by a student who wanted to leave the room before the bell rang. Cheerfully, I stood at the door, but the encounter changed character quickly; the game became one of seeing whether the student could frighten me by producing a lighter and threatening to set my long hair on fire. With his face inches from mine and his arm blocking my movement, the student, with a fascinated and repelled audience behind him, watched to see whether I would back down. I did not, would not; there seemed to be too much at stake. But I was scared. In this case, the fates were merciful: the lighter stubbornly refused to operate (Did the student know this? Was this part of the game?), the bell finally rang, and study hall ended.

Ken's Story: Interesting Times

Adolescence is a difficult and confusing time for people because they are just learning how to think about themselves as adults. Their bodies may be more mature than their minds or vice versa, and they may be experiencing emotions, thoughts, and responses from their peers and adults that they are simply not prepared for. At the same time, there are students who are quite mature (physically and emotionally), and there are other students in the school who are far less mature. Putting so many people experiencing all this confusion and uncertainty in as rigid and crowded an environment as school is a recipe for some very, let's say, *interesting* times.

Like Leila, I have experienced some extremely unpleasant moments in class. I've had students throw things at me when I've turned my back and written demeaning things about me (and my mother) on their desks. I've been cursed out by students almost as many times as I have been by my family (just kidding). I have been called a "mother" so many times that I still expect to get cards on Mother's Day. More seriously, I've been physically threatened by students and even had to secure a legal order of protection from a particularly angry student. In the most frightening situation of my professional career, I was teaching in front of the class when a student stood in the middle of the room, pulled out a (what turned out to be a fake) gun, took a stance, and in a two-hand hold pointed it directly at me. More on that complicated student later.

I've also worked with students who have had psychotic breaks and both serious and minor mental illnesses. All of these situations contribute chaos to a classroom and can stir up or push aside the attitudes, needs, and responses of other students. And you never know what will happen that will be out of your control. I once had a student who hated working with me no matter what I did, and I did everything possible to appease, cajole, or deal this student into working. Finally he confessed to his counselor that I reminded him of his uncle (who had abused him); he was quickly moved into another teacher's section and he did fine.

Then there are the many students who simply see their teachers as the embodiment of the education–industrial complex, just cogs in a huge machine designed to crush their dreams and deaden their lives with boredom and irrelevance. I've certainly worked with my share of these students, and although I've come up with strategies for dealing with them, they haven't always worked. We do our best. And when things spin out of control, we make our best judgments, call for the help we need, deal with the fallout. And then we prepare for our next class.

The reasons for these events vary: some involve individual students and their responses not only to teachers but to situations; some reasons involve reactions to school as an institution and teachers as representatives of that institution. Many arise from students' response to situations not related to schools or teaching; students can "act out" against family or community problems and can do that acting out in school. And today it is not just students who can bring this anger to school: often parents, when dealing with administrators and teachers, are similarly hostile. Certainly you may have many serene years in the classroom without anything such as the experiences we have recounted, student apathy, and physical and verbal assaults on teachers. On the other hand, the occasional flare-up of anger or hostility is actually fairly commonplace in schools across the country. We have mentioned school shootings. On a lower scale, vandalism is also an issue for school systems, as is maintaining an atmosphere not only of relative civility but of some form of mutual intellectual engagement. But why does this occur? Why in the world would such an atmosphere exist in school?

We need to look at how school is a frightening and even hostile place for some of our students and why the we/them dyad can be one of the most damaging of relationships. You, the beginning teacher, are *them*. Many students see themselves absolutely as *us*. For some students that will mean withdrawal, apathy; for others it will involve a more active and combative role. For both types of students, school is foreign territory and they come with their defenses up, committed to getting over, getting by, and ultimately, mercifully, getting out.

Two Researchers on Students: William Glasser and Linda M. McNeil

There are two classic books you might want to know about: Linda M. McNeil's (1986) *Contradictions of Control* and William Glasser's (1985) *Control Theory in the Classroom*. Both researchers have studied schools and students and conclude that, in

Glasser's words, the whole game needs to change. Glasser, a psychiatrist, sees school as a place where students do not feel part of the process:

> The problem is that at least half of all students are making little or no effort to learn, because they don't believe that school satisfies their needs. To make school harder—to increase the length of the school year or the school day, to assign more homework, to require more courses . . . is not going to reach those students. . . . We can't do anything to people, or really even for people, to get them to produce more. We have to change the school itself, so that students look at it and say, "In this school and with these teachers I can satisfy my needs, if I work hard." (Gough 1987, 656)

The Common Core State Standards (CCSS) and the standardized assessments and teacher evaluations connected to them do not acknowledge these very real pedagogical challenges. For better or for worse, teachers and schools are left to address them on their own.

For McNeil, the enterprise has become seriously poisoned at the source—at what teachers actually present to students in the form of content. McNeil writes that teachers, in an effort to maintain a semblance of power or control in school, actually diminish what they teach—their content—and create "brief, 'right' answers, easily transmitted, easily answered, easily graded [in order to conform] . . . to a school where their only power came from the classroom" (1986, 157). Glasser advises cooperative learning to counter this lack of control. For McNeil, however, Glasser's control theory has some insidious implications, which she outlines below in *Contradictions of Control* (and reiterates in a later book, *Contradictions of School Reform* [2000, 11–17]):

> Adults who visit high-school classrooms are often struck by the dullness of the lessons. Those who visit systematically note the overwhelming prevalence of boring content, dull presentations and bored but patient students. . . . The dull presentations are not caused merely by poor teacher preparation or teacher burnout, but by deliberate, often articulated, decisions teachers have made to control the students by controlling the content. . . . Defensive, controlling teaching does more than make content boring; it transforms the subject content from "real world" knowledge into "school knowledge," an artificial set of facts and generalizations whose credibility lies no longer in its authenticity as a cultural selection but in its instrumental value in meeting the obligations teachers and students have within the institution of schooling. . . .
>
> As the course content is transformed into "school knowledge," there is little incentive for the student to become involved in that content. It is there to be mastered, traded for a grade and, as some students have said, deliberately forgotten afterward. (1986, 191)

At times we wonder if there aren't ways in school that we can literally set up situations where kids become—or are encouraged to become—stupid. When we insist that all students know—and repeat back to us—minute details, when we place emphasis on senseless tasks or minor aspects of assignments, when we ask questions that are not worth answering, we set students up for compliant passivity. When the whole point of a school year is to pass multiple high-stakes tests, we narrow the curriculum and the student's sense of intellectual engagement. When we demand strict obedience to all behavioral regulations, when we, in essence, try to micromanage all student interaction, we can create classrooms where students become cowed and passive, where even the "good students" are at best compliant and others are profoundly resistant. In his aptly named *Beyond Discipline: From Compliance to Community*, well-known education critic Alfie Kohn points out that such a "teacher-directed model [is] one in which expectations, rules, and consequences are imposed on students. And it is typically driven by a remarkably negative set of beliefs about the nature of children" (2006, introduction). Once we make it clear that students are to fit themselves into narrow boxes, we can rarely expect that they will exercise much of an intellectual life: questioning, challenging, exploring. If, on the other hand, we decide and convey to our students that they do have minds and lives (desires, ideals) of their own, that in a way they are not so different from us, their teachers, then we can create vibrant classroom situations. How will you ensure you become and remain one of these encouraging teachers?

For McNeil, "the very relations within classroom[s] and within schools will have to be transformed" (1986, 215) for real knowledge and school knowledge to become one. And this leads us to one of our great concerns, the alienated student.

For Your Journal

At this point in your career, you have observed some high school or middle school English classes. Reread McNeil's comments about visiting high school classrooms and consider them in light of what you have recently seen. Do you agree with McNeil's characterization of many classes as models of "defensive, controlling teaching"? If so, what, in specific, did you see? If, on the other hand, this is not your experience and observation, what kind of positive, intellectually challenging teaching did you observe? What did the teacher do? How did the students respond? How will you emulate or change what you've observed when you're teaching?

The Alienated Student: Not Always Who You Think

Susan Beth Pfeffer, a writer of adolescent novels, has lightheartedly defined what she calls the "basic rules of teenage life." Some of them include *My Family Is Awful, Anyplace Would Be Better Than Here,* and *It Is Inconceivable That I'm Going to Survive This Awful Moment.* Her most important rule, however, is *I Am the One True Outsider.* Pfeffer notes that "no matter how popular teenagers might be, they always know that they and they alone are the one true outsider" (1990, 6).

Even though Pfeffer is being humorous, the issue is a serious one. Certainly it is a hallmark of many young people to feel like the outsider, the only one, the stranger. Adults have a tendency to smile at this feeling, knowing that, in some measure, it is rarely a perennial condition that persists into mature years. On the other hand, the power of feelings of alienation cannot be minimized by us as teachers in the classroom. Sam M. Intrator and Robert Kunzman, looking at what students say about school, make this observation:

> [O]ur schools struggle to engage adolescents in the formal curriculum. Although learning and succeeding in school require *active engagement,* a term used to describe the degree to which students are psychologically and emotionally connected to what is transpiring in their classrooms, data from a wide range of studies focused on reporting youth perspective suggest that students are generally bored and disengaged in school. (2009, 31)

Intrator and Kunzman go on to note that "when adolescents critique their academic experiences as boring and disconnected from their lives, their feelings can be understood as a catch basin for other, more nuanced critiques" (2009, 31) of school itself. This is certainly borne out by a series of issues of *English Journal,* in which a number of teachers wrote about their experience in the classroom with what they termed "alienated" students. Daniel A. Lindley Jr. wrote, "We know who they are, and we know what they do to us, the alienated ones, those students so far removed from our values, our beliefs, our whole way of life" (1990, 26). Lindley asked teachers to distinguish between the "possible" and the "impossible" because we know that a teacher can control or influence only certain aspects of school and life that might contribute to a student feeling alienated. Certainly we cannot bring students home with us, give them money, trade places with their parents, get them off drugs, make them motivated, or even learn for them. But we can, within our classrooms, make contact with them as human beings and provide opportunities for them to succeed and participate.

What are the factors that make it likely students will not do well in school, and as a last resort, drop out? Most studies cite a familiar list of markers as indicators. These are taken from a 2004 National Center for Educational Statistics study and, in particular, point to possible reading and achievement difficulty:

- a household income below the poverty level
- a language other than English as the primary home language
- a mother with less than a high school diploma or with a GED degree
- a single-parent household. (United States Department of Education 2004)

How are these findings important to us? Notice that family income is only one of the risk factors; notice also that most of the factors are not under the control of the school. This latter issue is of great concern to educators who, when held singularly responsible for student achievement, cite other complicating factors in addition to instruction within a classroom—in other words, is the playing field always level for all students who are judged on achievement? On the other hand, students whose families exhibit these characteristics may well be in our classes in great number, and it is our responsibility to teach them and teach them well—even though we must acknowledge that some students will have far more barriers to overcome than others.

Characteristics of the Alienated Student

What kind of students will you be teaching who might have reason to feel alienated in school? Although teen pregnancy appears to be declining or leveling off, you may be teaching people who are parents, who have a baby at home. You will be teaching people who have parents who are in the midst of divorce or bankruptcy or emotional breakdown. You will be teaching people who feel they live, despite material comfort, in emotional poverty. You will be teaching people who are finding identity in gangs, who are trying to see if sexual intimacy can lead to psychological intimacy, who are escaping with drugs or alcohol or even compulsive shopping. You will be teaching people who are repeatedly told that they have everything—and who feel that they have nothing. You will be teaching people who, at their age, profoundly suspect that life doesn't hold a whole lot for them—and, for sure, that school is not going to help them make it any better. You will be teaching people who wonder if they will be the next generation to see another set of twin towers fall in the smoke and fire of yet another terrorist attack, who wonder if the world will even exist when they become adults. You will be teaching people who are told that getting into college is the most important goal of their lives and who know they will not be admitted—and people who are sure they will get into college and question whether that will mean very much at all. You will be teaching people who are told that this is the best time of their lives—and who wonder, if that is true, what in the world do the succeeding years hold?

You will be teaching people in the great and dramatic process of growing up, a growing up that often is marked as much by fear and danger and unhappiness as by joy and discovery. For some of our students the latter feelings are intermittent and transitory, lasting a few days or weeks; yet for others, the feelings are relatively permanent.

For many students, school and our classes are arenas where they do not feel safe or a part; they do not want to be there. Surely there are always exceptions to the following generalizations, but these are the students who only put in their time in school, who want to get out as soon as possible, and who will occasionally "act out" if pushed or challenged. Alienated students, both the truly apathetic and the more combative, do not talk a lot in large-group discussions, do not do much homework, do not see themselves as any part of the life of the school—either during the day or after the last bell. Consider this description Johnathan gives of himself in high school:

> I was what I think one would call a "problem child." . . . In my junior English class . . . I sat in that back corner of the room as always. I could never stand the feeling of people looking at the back of my head. This class was a little strange for me because there was not one person in the room that I was friends with. And, of course, I never participated in class discussions. This meant that I never spoke in class, I never said a word.
>
> This has been, over the years, a very typical situation for me. And once the silence starts it becomes increasingly difficult to say anything. The silence builds such a momentum that in order to utter one word I would be facing a mountain of shame, and at once losing my anonymity, drawing attention to my paralysis.

One day in this English class we had a test. I had forgotten to bring a pencil. Class had already started, the door was closed, I was trapped. I thought about asking the people near me for something to write with; I thought about asking the teacher. Instead, I just made writing motions with my finger the entire period and turned in a blank test, face down, quickly as I left the room.

The next year English class was better. One of my best friends was in the class, and he sat next to me in the back corner of the room. I still never said anything in class. The other students were just faceless heads, masters of all social situations. The teacher was someone whose gaze I averted for fear he might think I was interested and call on me. I didn't have to worry.

—Johnathan Morris

Preservice teacher Jack Conte could also have been described as an alienated student in middle school. But a lot was going on the mind and life of this young man who appeared sullen and apathetic:

I was a cognitively bored, socially terrified, and academically alienated child. After years of elementary school teachers who found my dyslexia too challenging to deal with, and bullying by bigger, more popular students, I had developed serious trust issues in school. I wouldn't say I didn't have any friends—I just had dull sepia toned friends to match everything else in my dull sepia filtered life. I was so bored and jaded I would fight just to see some color, just to give me some form of challenge. And as I began to come around, trouble at home drew me back into my shell. Over those three years I couldn't hear a single word a teacher said. I did less than half of my homework, what I did do was on the bus that morning, IF I was on the bus that morning. I wasn't someone who skipped school or anything, I wasn't cool enough for that—just someone who was constantly late because I refused to leave my bed. Not for lack of trying, my then undiagnosed autoimmune disease did most of its legwork in those years, and chronic pain isn't a great tool for academic concentration. Yet someone decided, instead of challenging me or giving me engaging work, to track me into a special advanced class—and tell me they made the class just for me. And little me of course thought this meant I was mentally handicapped, because I didn't know the existence of, or even imagine I would be in, an advanced class. So clearly, I did even less work, and yet through a devious nature and natural tendency to test my luck just for the thrill, continued to "get away with it." A phrase that would become my motto for years to come.

—Jack Conte

Alienated students are often like Johnathan and Jack, the ones who, at least in class, are likely sitting by themselves, who are apt to try to sleep or otherwise withdraw from the life of the class, who are absent from school more than the average, who consistently forget or lose their instructional materials. With some exceptions, these are the students who just don't turn in major assignments and who don't complete even minimal parts of tests. These alienated students are those who are termed "at risk" and who are often extreme underachievers.

Jeffrey Landon describes a young woman he encountered in his student teaching who fits the at-risk description and whose behaviors outside school as well as in it are cause for concern:

Jewel is a sophomore, six feet tall, and she walks hunched over to disguise both her height and her chest. Her skin is the color of an acorn, and her cheeks are acne-scarred. I have never seen her talk either in class or out; in class, she is almost invisible.

I have read two short essays by Jewel. In the first she talked about Christmas, and how it depressed her. Her parents live in another city, but she hasn't seen them in two years. She writes, "they are too busy." She thought she would see them on Christmas, but it didn't work out. Instead they sent her a yellow dress two sizes too small for her body.

On New Year's Eve, Jewel injured herself, falling down some stairs while holding onto a butcher knife. It was called an accident by her grandmother (who she lives with). Jewel required many stitches. Apparently, she had accidentally (and repeatedly) punctured her stomach and sliced open at least two veins in her arms. . . . In another essay comparing herself to a figure in literature, Jewel wrote, "I always wanted to have a happier life, but that won't happen I guess. I don't want to hurt myself, because I care about myself. But sometimes I can't stop what they do."

During his student teaching, Brett Groneman learned that voicing frustration about an apathetic student can make a bad situation worse:

I had a student who was difficult to work with, and was often hostile toward me. After many days of constantly warning this student about his behavior and work ethic, I made a comment to the rest of the class that the student I was having a hard time with was "a lost cause." While this comment was intended in jest, the student immediately began to spew expletives at me, unleashing a lot of obvious pent-up frustration. In that moment I realized what I had done, I had let him think, if for just a moment, that he was worthless. I under-stood too late the damage I had done with that comment and the next day, went to the student with an earnest apology and some articles to help him with an essay he was writ-ing. Luckily for me, he accepted my apology and our working relationship became quite positive after that. We had few issues after that point, and I owe that mostly to the fact that we were both able to understand the importance of that moment. I had lost my patience with him, and he wasn't able to accurately communicate to me his needs in the class. After viewing each other as human beings, the walls came down and the learning could begin.

For Clary Washington, a student teacher in a suburban high school, Derek put a human face on the alienated student. Upper middle class, ostensibly bright and prom-ising, surrounded, in fact, by concerned adults, Derek was nonetheless on his way to trouble. After numerous discipline incidents in Clary's class, Derek failed a research paper. Outraged by his grade, he threatened to write a complaint letter about his "hor-rible," "awful" student teacher, Ms. Washington. Clary writes in her journal:

While he put absolutely no effort in [his] paper, last week Derek asked me how he did, apparently believing that I was not bright enough to figure out that he didn't write what he took credit for. What was really sad was that what [he] essentially copied was full of misspelled words and punctuation errors due to sloppy transcription. . . . What is almost amusing (if it weren't so sad) is that [Derek] could write a letter complaining about me as a teacher, and few would take it seriously because he cannot write. . . . His mother wants him to be considered learning disabled, and there has been discussion of possible brain damage due to Derek's car accident late last year. (After the accident Derek tested positive for alcohol and cocaine.) . . . I'm obviously not a medical expert, but Derek's attitude is what I see standing in his way—not an impaired brain. If he's given special treatment, he'll just assume that he'll be taken care of for the rest of his life, something that was confirmed when I asked him what he planned to do after high school, and he said work for his father. He's got everything figured out at 17. Almost 18 he keeps reminding me. Old enough to go to jail, I think . . . [Later] Derek told me in class, "You're going down, Ms. Washington, you're going down. You'll never work in [this county]. I'll see to that. I can." . . . When Derek first came in the class, I didn't want to stereotype him as the "bad boy," but he really fulfilled his reputation. I don't like him, and it has perhaps taken me a while to really become comfortable with this notion. He really made part of my [student teaching] experience miserable. His problems are really too numerous for me to tackle alone.

You may, in your teaching, have students such as Derek.

Alienation, Gender, Race, and Class

There is also research evidence that gender, race, and class can be alienating factors. Researchers Carol Gilligan, Nona Lyons, and Trudy Hanmer (1989), as well as psychologist Mary Pipher (1994), have found that female students seem to lose a sense of confidence and assurance as they move through the middle school years. Many girls become silent in our classes and doubtful of their intellectual strength as they become high school students. Female students begin to perceive and become troubled by the contradictory roles they will face and are currently facing as women. Many are puzzled by these changes and, as the book title *"We Want to Be Known": Learning from Adolescent Girls* notes, girls often feel relatively invisible and that they and their needs are not necessarily "known" (Hubbard, Barbieri, and Power 1998, 198). Often girls will not participate vigorously in class and will not challenge either male students or the teacher. In fact, one survey of 2,400 girls and 600 boys in fourth through tenth grades showed that "adolescent girls experience genuine, substantial drops in self-esteem that far outpace those reported by boys [and have] less confidence in their academic abilities and fewer aspirations to professional careers" (Bower 1991, 184).

Some of this may be what child psychologist Mary Pipher sees as the issue of girls and adolescence: "With puberty girls crash into junk culture . . . [a culture that] is just too hard for most girls to understand and master at this point in their development. They become overwhelmed and symptomatic" (1994, 13). And often we see this in our classes.

For boys, there is similar pressure, and a spate of books (Smith and Wilhelm's [2002] *"Reading Don't Fix No Chevys"*; Tatum's [2005] *Teaching Reading to Black Adolescent Males*; Brozo's [2002] *To Be a Boy, to Be a Reader*; Maynard's [2002] *Boys and Literacy*; Newkirk's [2002] *Misreading Masculinity*) explores how school—and the English classroom—mirrors more perfectly female values and interests than those of males. For former eighth-grade teacher Alfred Tatum, writing in *Teaching Reading to Black Adolescent Males*, "schools are hostile and unpredictable environments for many black males, who come to view themselves as nonachievers and nonparticipants in society because of what happens to them there" (2005, 33). Tatum outlines how young men adopt a "cool pose," which is "a ritualized form of masculinity, uses certain behavior, scripts, physical posturing, and carefully crafted performance to convey a strong impression of pride, strength, and control" (29). Tatum observes, though, that the ritualized forms of masculinity, the "cool pose as a coping mechanism," can carry negative aspects as they encourage a refusal to get involved in experiences; a disinclination against self-disclosure that makes it difficult for teachers to know how to help; an avoidance of institutions and activities—such as school, museums, and churches—which, though they could help with personal turmoil, are seen as terminally uncool (29). In addition, those who feel they are the representatives of their race can also feel tremendous pressure. In *A Tribe Apart*, Patricia Hersch describes Charles, whose parents are black professionals and whose high expectations have inculcated in Charles a special burden: "He never feels at ease in his classes because he is never free of the burden of proving he is Mr. Perfect Black" (1999, 87), the flawless representative of his race. For Charles, and for many other racial minorities who choose to embrace school and all it represents, who wish to achieve on the terms of the mainstream, there can be real alienation:

> Charles' dilemma represents the word of the striving black middle-class adolescents. It is a life lived on the defensive, a constant tightrope to be navigated between two cultures: a white culture that never fully embraces them, and a black peer group that disdains black achievers. If hip-hop extols the black underclass, then where does a kid like Charles belong? (88)

In a 2015 article, a group of English education professors discuss how adolescents of color aren't necessarily thought of in the same ways that white adolescents are:

> [W]hen youth of color "resist" or "rebel against" the status quo in or outside of school, they become criminals—"public enemies," "menaces to society." Similarly, youth of color don't have "normal" curiosities about sex or natural sex drives; instead they are "hyper-sexual," oversexed, their desires base and carnal. And youth of color don't have peer groups or caring adults in their lives: they have gangs. (Groenke et al. 2015, 36)

We must be mindful of how dominant cultural assumptions can insidiously influence our views of students. Becoming and remaining aware of stereotypes and how they perpetuate mischaracterizations of youth of color should be an important and constant effort of all teachers.

Economics and assumptions about class can also wreak havoc on a student's feeling of school as a welcoming place. In two separate appearances at Leila's university, a recent state teacher of the year cautioned her audience that what a teacher says can have wholly unintended consequences, often with devastating results. An ambitious and good student for all of her high school years, this now award-winning teacher recalls an offhanded comment from one of her favorite teachers about not acting like someone from the local, and relatively notorious, trailer park. At the time, other students in the class laughed and understood the reference; those who lived in the trailer park had long been caricatured as impoverished, violent, and unemployed. The future state teacher of the year, however, was shocked and never trusted her high school instructor again. She lived in that trailer park and now understood that even a favorite teacher would, if she had known, most likely have held it against her and made false assumptions about her and her family. A decade later, with that one incident far behind her and many academic and professional achievements to boast of, this was a central story she wanted all of us to hear.

Other Sources of Alienation: Teachers/Administration/School Size

Other, perhaps hidden, sources of alienation are not only the shapes of our students' personal lives and the composition of the student body itself but you, the teacher, and your school's administration.

It is likely that you, the reader of this book and the beginning teacher, are Caucasian and middle class. It is also likely that you are a female. Further, it is also probable that most of your colleagues in your school will share these characteristics. In other words, you the teacher and your school administration are largely homogeneous in class and race. This is not to imply that Anglo teachers cannot deal effectively with students of color or that female heterosexual teachers are limited in their connection or that middle-class values are always at odds with those of other classes. The issue is, however, that the power structure of schools—of which you are or will soon be a part—is usually overwhelmingly represented by the white, middle class, heterosexual, and female. When your students are different, there can be conflict and misunderstanding, issues that although not your sole responsibility are nevertheless your predominant responsibility to attempt to bridge. Carol Smith Catron remembers the magic of a teacher who seemed to bridge that gap:

> Junior year I had [a teacher] who I loved. My favorite thing about her class was that there were no favorites. We had everyone in that class from a guy named Wendy with a pierced nose and chains on his boots to a girl named Julie who was head of the cheerleaders and won every beauty contest to come her way. And then there were all the people in between, like me. I felt like I was this teacher's favorite person in the world. So did my friend Vanessa, and my fiancé, John. And, no doubt, Wendy and Julie felt the same way. There were no "shadow" people, or people who dominated every discussion. Everyone was called upon in class and everyone's answers were given respect and consideration.

Within her class, the teacher Carol Smith Catron recalls made all of her students individuals. On the other hand, you must remember that because of the way middle and secondary schools are organized, you will be seeing upwards of 100 students a day in a school of anywhere from 1,200 to 2,000 students. Many schools attempt to ameliorate the drawbacks of such "largeness," but students can, as a well-respected National Council of Teachers of English (1990) statement notes, feel "lost in the crowd." It is quite possible to hide in such large configurations and, quite possibly, to feel even more apart and disengaged.

Another Possible Source of Alienation: Student Identity

Not all of the factors discussed here mean that a student will feel alienated, but it is helpful to remember, once again, the great range of pressures that confront young people. Being a minority racially—Caucasian students in predominately African American student bodies, Latino students surrounded by Anglos, Asian Americans in a sea of Caucasians—and the reverse of each—can engender a certain sense of aloneness. Students for whom English is a second language can also feel much apart from school culture. Muslim and Jewish students are often the exception in a student body of Christians; Roman Catholic students can be a small proportion of a largely Protestant group. Gay, lesbian, and transgender students can also feel alienated, and those for whom sexual identity is an evolving issue can feel isolated. It is too easy for us to look at those youthful, clear faces, those expressive clothes and hairdos, those tattoos and piercings, and assume that what is in our students' lives is equally cheerful and well balanced. The appearance can often belie the reality.

Finally, there are occasionally mental health issues. As Jeffrey Benson articulates, "Students with emotional and mental health problems aren't bad people, and they aren't beyond redemption. In too many cases, their anxiety around powerful adults is a well-earned outcome of their life experiences. By committing ourselves to being predictable, organized, reasonable, and able to listen, teachers may represent these students' best hope to grow into their better selves" (2015, 45).

Alienated Students: Stories from Our Classrooms

The following stories are based on real people and, in one case, on a composite of two people; Ken and Leila taught them, and they were all, in their own ways, alienated students who were attempting to grow into better selves.

Ken's Story

Like many teachers, I have had to handle mental health crises with students: I once walked into a classroom in which a student cowered in the corner because he saw a pool of blood in the middle of the room; as I moved toward him, to his eyes I walked through this invisible puddle of blood, getting it all over myself, and he screamed violently for me to stay back. I've worked with two young men who had psychotic breaks related to undiagnosed bipolar disorder, both of whom suffered delusions of grandeur: one was convinced he could see people's souls through auras and that he could learn any language he wanted simply by thinking about it. One time a student came to my office complaining about chest pain and then started speaking rapidly and in a rambling fashion about teachers out to get him and his parents who secretly wanted him to fail; he got progressively more and more anxious until I had to call for an ambulance for his own safety. And a number of female and male students have confided in me—through writing or in conversation—that they had severe suicidal thoughts. An especially painful memory for me is the student who seemed happy and on top of the world—a good-looking, very smart, popular young man—who for reasons still unknown to me one weekend fastened a hose from his exhaust pipe into his car window and asphyxiated himself; I learned this from the Sunday morning newspaper. All these situations were frightening and upsetting at the time, and they are even now as I look back on them. Through those experiences, I've learned to ask for help when I need it and I've learned more than I thought I'd ever need to know about mental illness. I've also learned to look at every student as precious and to do my best to ensure that even the difficult, hard-to-like students feel respected and cared for.

Leila's Story: Marianna, Antoine, and Marc

Once I had a student who had very pale skin and pale, wispy blonde hair. She had a pretty, sweet face with watchful eyes that would widen enormously. She was shy, had no friends I could discern, ate alone in the cafeteria, and walked alone between classes. She was, at sixteen, undergoing a difficult period in her own life and with her alcoholic mother. When she took an overdose of pills between classes, the rescue squad came and carried her from the girls' bathroom floor to the hospital. A month later, she returned to school and was placed in one of my classes. I knew her recent history but was cautious about treating her differently from the others. But equal treatment was hard for two reasons: Marianna was virtually incapable of speaking above a soft whisper. Almost no one in the class, even those sitting right around her, could hear her comments, and no one, including me, her teacher, could induce her to raise her voice. But it got even more complicated because when she turned in her first writing assignment, I realized I was in the presence of one of the brightest students I had ever seen in my teaching career. Whispering and writing, the troubled and brilliant Marianna was in my class.

Once I had another student whose almost angelic features, mocha skin, and dark eyes belied a volatile temper. It was never clear to most of his teachers and even many of his friends what would "set off" Antoine, or why he would decide at a given juncture in class to raise his voice in question, protest, or complaint—or stalk out of the classroom, slamming the door behind him. (Teacher Rafael Velazquez Cardenas

[2014] calls these outbursts "yell-outs," and, if you are interested, his classroom research done during his first year of teaching is fascinating.) When he did his work, Antoine was a wonderful student, and he could be a strong addition to any class discussion. He was aware, smart, and explosively under pressure.

One day he came into class ten minutes late, a fairly usual behavior. But in the missed ten minutes, Antoine had not heard the class introduction of why the day's reading, the South American short story, was paired with the Biblical story of the Good Samaritan. Standing up to announce, "This is no religion class," Antoine once again stalked out and slammed the door behind him. Not very much later, no one was happy—or even terribly surprised—when, one Saturday night, Antoine returned to an after-hours club to retaliate for a perceived slight. Antoine's father, who had taken him to the club, had been insulted, the story went, and Antoine went back to the club ostensibly to retrieve his coat—but actually to shoot the owner dead. On bond and awaiting trial for murder, and later after he was convicted, awaiting the beginning of his jail sentence, the volatile and very bright Antoine was, like Marianna, in my class.

And once I also had a student who didn't exactly look like James Dean—he was too stocky and his cheekbones weren't as prominent—but wanted to act like him. When he bothered to come to school (he attended only about two-thirds of any given week), Marc either would not bring his books to class or, when he did bring them, would not open them. He would not answer questions, turn in homework, take tests, or do much of anything but slouch in his desk and watch the class. Whenever he decided he had "had enough," he would get up and walk out. He was moody, abrupt, and in the middle of his fifth year of a well-known and tempestuous love relationship with a classmate. His sole interests were Angie and motorcycles; the rest was irrelevant. When Angie, pregnant, withdrew from school, Marc stayed to get more Ds and Fs. Putting his face down on his desk with his jacket pulled over his head, bereft of his girlfriend, Marc was also in my class.

Ken's Story: David

Earlier in this chapter, I referred to a student who aimed a gun at me in class. It turned out to be fake, but I didn't know it at the time. In these post-Columbine days when school shootings are not as unheard of as we'd wish, one can imagine a swift, decisive response to a student with even a fake gun. At that time, however, it was not something anyone had thought much about, especially in the upstate New York suburban district in which I taught.

This student, I'll call him David, was very smart—very, very smart—and yet he was completely unmotivated by school, and as a result of his frequent misbehavior he had spent most of his years in classes intended for students who struggle academically. (It's not uncommon that students are misplaced in academically inappropriate classes due to behavior problems.) When I met David in my eleventh-grade English class, he was used to being the most capable student, and he could complete the assignments quickly and well (when he chose to), or he could blow them off entirely and still keep up with the class. He cared nothing at all about his grades and had no interest in being moved to a more academically challenging level. His single parent, for whatever reasons, challenged any move the school or a teacher tried to make to inspire David, and meetings with counselors, administrators, David, his parent, and (always) their lawyer were common. No one at the school could figure out what motivated David, but the school was obviously not addressing his needs, could not address his needs, and yet he and his parent wanted nothing done about it. It was a sad, frustrating, and deeply disappointing situation, especially to an enthusiastic, early career teacher like me.

David's grades got to the point where there was a possibility that he might be left back at the end of the year. Repeating a grade was not in his plans, and he began arguing with me for any point on any assignment he did not receive a perfect score on. After a heated discussion about yet another grade, David sat in class while I stood at the front, speaking to the class about whatever it was. (I can see the moment with crystal clarity, but I have no idea what I was talking about.) Out of the corner of my eye, I saw David stand, take what seemed to me a professional stance, and aim a handgun directly at my head. Utterly exposed, there was absolutely nothing I could do. My pulse rate rose, my stomach fell, and I'm still surprised I didn't lose my faculties. But I remember thinking the best thing to do was ignore it and keep teaching. I knew if he pulled the trigger, I'd be gone before I heard the shot. So I just kept talking. I'm sure there was a change in my tone, but no students reacted at all. After what felt like a very long time, but was probably about ten seconds, David shrugged and sat down. I was very shaken up, but as any teacher will tell you, something else takes over in such moments, and your concern about your students becomes paramount. I got the students working on some writing, and I went to David and asked him, in my best version of friendly curiosity, "Wow! You really scared me. Is that a real gun?" He showed me that it wasn't, and I was relieved. Immediately after class, I told the vice principal about it, and the gun was taken from him shortly thereafter. He was written up and given yet another detention.

Believe it or not, that was not the final straw in David's unfortunate journey. After yet another heated discussion about a grade, in front of an entire class, David threatened to punch me. I braced for the blow as he cocked his arm. I was so fed up with him at this point that I decided the blow would be worth taking, because he'd be immediately expelled. He seemed to read my thoughts—remember, he was very, very smart—and he just smiled and walked out of the room. Threatening me and leaving class without permission was the act that finally ended our relationship. Later in this chapter, I will tell more of David's story.

Teacher Reaction to the Alienated Student

In a newspaper years ago, we read a study of nurses and how they treated their critically ill patients that we think has some bearing on teacher reaction to alienated students. Researchers found that registered nurses would spend a considerably shorter period of time interacting with and caring for patients who were critically, often terminally, ill. The researchers concluded that because such patients were less rewarding to deal with, the nurses, more than likely unconsciously, spent less time with them. So it is, too, with us as teachers. In fact, the subtitle of the Lindley (1990) article on alienated students, "For Teachers of the Alienated," is "Three Defenses Against Despair," which, although a rather melodramatic phrase, captures the intensity of the issue. Most of us will tend to avoid the truly alienated student because he or she is often not rewarding to be with. We can make a number of efforts, but it is not axiomatic that they will be successful. And, in fact, some teachers, fearful of burnout, make it a point to be less than fully engaged with such students. Others have experiences that confirm that the school, as it is currently organized, cannot be effective with such students.

For example, it is with no little shame that Leila recounts her encounter with the alternately vacant-eyed and occasionally giggling student whose behavior was a complete puzzle. Her hair was unkempt, her skin blotched, and her inexpensive and somewhat tattered clothes were held together by a dozen or so safety pins. Even in Leila's less-than-affluent school, this student stood out as poorly and inappropriately dressed. She insisted, though, that she had big plans for the immediate future: she would be on a plane to Hollywood the next week. The movies were her goal, she asserted, and she was only in Leila's class as something to pass the time before she set out for California. And her instructions were equally direct: she told Leila to leave her alone, put her desk away from the others, and not speak to her. She would not cause any problems, she assured Leila, if Leila would just cease and desist.

As Leila recalls, that's just what she did. The student dropped out of school in a month or so, for the system's resources and Leila's energy were no match for her problems.

For a colleague facing a different situation, there was also little recourse, but, in this case, she made a better effort than Leila feels she managed with the student just described:

> Nothing prepared me for the day two of my students, who had killed a cat, wore the bones to school around their necks. One gleefully described how he had killed the animal while his classmates alternated between disgust and laughter. I asked him why he had killed the cat. He told me that his god was calling out for a sacrifice. A week later he wore the cat's skull to school on a string, complete with a red cross painted on top.
>
> I exhausted all of the channels possible—guidance counselors, department chairman, administration. The facts seemed to be that unless the two had killed the animal on school property, there wasn't anything that could be done.

Tell that to the cat.

Tell that to the parents in the school district.

Tell that to the next teacher who hasn't a notion how to handle this. . . . If we can't deal with students in crisis we are potentially turning them away from possibly the only place where they may be influenced positively. If we sit in class and fervently hope that [such students] will drop out, we are being woefully shortsighted.

On the other hand, caring is just not enough; these students need different sorts of strategies to bring them into the life of the classroom. And, as in the case of Leila's Hollywood-bound student, we are not doing our job if we just, as Leila did some years ago, give up and turn away.

Guidelines for Dealing with the Alienated Student

Perhaps it is more a sense of degree than kind when we think of guidelines for dealing with alienated students and an effort to individualize our approach with them. Certainly there is no magic set of activities that will turn apathetic students into involved ones or calm the disaffected student. Certainly many of those students do succeed with minimal—even no—intervention. For many of them, however, extra help is necessary, and we need to do more than just leave students alone. Here are a few guiding principles:

- **Refuse to ignore your alienated students**: Let them know that you know they are there in the class and that you are aware of them and their performance and want to see it improved. *Things to do*: Speak to these students every day, make eye contact with them, begin with a friendly smile, ask them how they are doing. Do not avoid them; it only reinforces their behavior.

- **Maintain expectations for the alienated student's academic performance**: Regardless of the origin of the "problem," the student must be held accountable for his or her own achievement. *Things to do*: Remind these students where they are in terms of assignments and deadlines; look for opportunities to tell them when you genuinely expect they will do well or be interested; praise them when they have earned it, without letting them know you really feel "it's about time." If your school has a tracking model, make sure your students are at the appropriate level for their abilities. A class that's too challenging or too easy encourages students to "check out."

  Remember that a student's outward appearance may be little more than a shield against an unfair, punishing outside world. Outrageous clothes, hairstyles, makeup, piercings, tattoos, facial expressions, and attitudes may be aesthetic choices, or—as they were for the fictional Lisbeth Salander in Stieg Larsson's (2008) *The Girl with the Dragon Tattoo* trilogy—they may really be a form of battle armor for an essentially shy, awkward, or even fearful adolescent.

- **Use performance contracts to shape behavior**: Written contracts can define behavior and goals for students. Yes, this is an old idea under the heading of behavioral modification; it may seem prescriptive, but sometimes short-term, highly specific goals can help students get on track. Contracts work well, in part, because they are very clear—so there's no room for ongoing and futile debate— and they are infused with a realism that those disenchanted with schooling seem to appreciate and respect. *Things to do*: You and the student agree that answering so many times in class will equal such and such a reward, that so many assignments completed with such and such requirements will equal such and such a grade; you establish a written contract or form, and both you and the student sign and date it.

- **Make deals**: On large (such as the performance contracts) and small issues, give students a sense that they can exert some control over their in-school lives. *Things to do*: Tell students that if they turn in homework two days in a row they can wear their earbuds during independent reading or writing time or choose an alternate assignment in the future; if they answer questions on Monday you will not call on them on Tuesday; and so on.

- **Remember that variety in curriculum and flexibility in instructional style is probably more important to your alienated students than to others**: The lack of choice can be numbing to alienated students. *Things to do*: Tell students they can read either this or that; they can do one of these four projects. As much research has shown, building choice into your lessons is very likely to increase engagement among all students.

- Finally, without creating a wholly artificial situation, **try to structure activities with which students can be engaged and can legitimately succeed**.

These principles can be helpful as they play out in students' school lives. A 2004 research study looking at students who believed they had a voice in their classroom decisions showed the benefit of this kind of student engagement. When queried, the students felt that they were "supported and respected by teachers"; that what they learned in school was "useful"; that they felt "safe at school"; that they worked "harder than they expected to work in school"; that they took "pride in their schoolwork" and that they placed "a high value on learning" (Intrator and Kunzman 2009, 33). We could ask for no more.

Leila's Story: What Happened to Marianna, Antoine, and Marc?

With Marianna, whose whispered, virtually inaudible speech was a problem in class, the first step seemed to lie in her great strength in writing. I encouraged her to write out her comments rather than speak, and after some discussion, on an occasional basis I asked her to read her writing aloud. I also put Marianna in group and pair work where speaking in front of many others would not be such an issue. When these two strategies seemed to be consistently successful, I initiated a step-by-step attempt to get Marianna to speak audibly in large-group discussions. Along the way I realized that I had, inadvertently, reinforced Marianna's behavior pattern not only by physically moving closer to her to hear what she had said but by asking her to reiterate her comments and then praising her rather effusively when she did repeat them. I stopped those behaviors and started calling on Marianna as I would any other student. If her speech was only partially audible, I accepted it as she presented it, although other students would occasionally insist that she speak up. The combination of techniques seemed to work, and Marianna became more a part of the class, not the whispering student she had been before. This procedure took about two semesters; it was my impression Marianna gathered some confidence and seemed to shed her "speaking aloud" block. By the time of graduation she was headed to college some states away and seemed more confident.

I was not able to do anything about Antoine's outbursts of temper. Convicted and sentenced as an adult to a prison term, Antoine was allowed to stay in school until the end of the marking period. While he was awaiting jail, however, his behavior became understandably subdued. We worked out a reading list/project contract that directly addressed the years he would be spending in prison, and Antoine made excursions into sociological studies on crime in America and the penal system. Antoine did the best work he had ever done in class, and his written reports were careful and detailed. As tragic and sad as his situation was, his work allowed him to pass his English class. If nothing else, he went to prison with very recent academic success, not to mention some factual knowledge of what awaited him.

Marc and I consistently struck deals. Although it was against departmental policy for juniors in British Literature to write a research paper on anything but British literature, I threw out the rules. Marc's research paper, a major part of his year's grade, detailed the history and production schedules of the Harley Davidson Company, complete with specifications and descriptions of all the current models. I used the successful research project to build on other behavior; Marc now had a chance to pass my class despite his previous academic deficiencies, and we worked out an arrangement for minimal participation. Marc agreed to answer at least twice a week in class if left alone otherwise; he was not allowed to put his head down in class, but he did not have to bring his book and could share with someone else. He was absent a great deal and would not take unit tests. He also initially refused to take the final exam, but I got Angie to intervene, and Marc did, just barely, pass for the year.

Ken's Story: What Happened to David?

David's and my unhappy adventure together did eventually end. After dealing with several significant outbursts in my class, I worked with an assistant principal (AP) to set clear behavioral guidelines for David, which he flouted again and again, including when be brought his fake pistol to school. What David didn't know was that I had also been carefully documenting his classroom behavior and submitting reports to the AP. After David threatened to punch me in front of our class, the AP decided it was time to call another meeting with David's parent, and as always, their lawyer joined us.

During the meeting, the AP asked me to begin reading the careful log I had kept of our classroom interactions. I read something along the lines of "September 15, Period 3, 11th Grade English: David came to class ten minutes late and announced, 'I don't want any bullshit today.' The other students laughed and began jeering each other and high-fiving David. After five minutes, I was able to return the class to the lesson. The bell rang fifteen minutes before my planned lesson was concluded. September 17, Period 3, 11th Grade English: David refused to join the group I assigned him to for a lesson on *Of Mice and Men*, chapter 5. Rather than disrupt class, I allowed David to work independently. During the time for group work, he shouted to several students from a distance, disrupting the groups' discussions on the assignment." I read my notes for about five minutes, when the lawyer called me to a halt and asked all but the parent, the AP, and himself to leave the room. After about twenty minutes, they came out and said the matter had been resolved. I never saw David again.

David was withdrawn from our public school, and I heard he was moved to a private school that specialized in students with behavioral difficulties. Neither I, nor to my knowledge anyone else at the school, ever learned what became of David. I hope he found something that allowed him to embrace learning, develop his considerable intellect, and build a future he could be proud of. But at the time, I was relieved that the documentation I had created, with the assistance of that AP, allowed me to remove a significant obstruction from my other students' learning. And, I was also very relieved I wouldn't have to deal with David again. This is not a happy or fulfilling ending for a teacher, but it is what it is.

The Place of the School Counselor, the Parents, the Administration

It is likely that when a student shows up in your class and appears to be apathetic or disaffected—or alienated—someone else in the school is aware of that student and his or her difficulties. It is not a given, however, and when you perceive, as a teacher, that the student is displaying signs of relatively desperate behavior, you must inform your counseling staff, make an effort to call the student's parents, or otherwise alert your administration. To this day, Leila still worries about her Hollywood starlet; she feels she let her slip away. Leila decided not to expend the energy, and it's hard to know if the intervention of a counselor would have helped the student cope more successfully with reality.

In the case of Marianna, other students were well aware that she was teetering on an emotional edge and were the ones to get a teacher involved as soon as she overdosed and slumped onto the girls' bathroom floor. In her case, her parents, who had problems with their marriage and their drinking, had not been heretofore helpful, and because Marianna was a student who had never been any "trouble," she had escaped the notice of most of us. When she returned to school, however, it was under a certain amount of supervision and care. She was also placed in a foster home through the efforts of the counseling staff.

For Antoine, the school was not directly responsible: he got a gun and shot the nightclub owner on the weekend and off school property. There had previously, however, been little organized effort to intervene in what escalated into a major problem and left one person dead and one life shattered. Antoine's outbursts were not recognized for what they eventually became; instead, his behavior in school and difficulty with teachers were perceived, possibly cynically, as fairly typical for a teenage African American male.

With Marc, parents, school counselors, and administration were aware of his difficulties in school, and, as a strategy, all three had resorted to reward structures, threats, and a variety of punishments. All three seemed ineffective: it was only when the rules were bent, deals struck, and his girlfriend Angie enlisted into the struggle that Marc showed improvement.

And just recently, it was teamwork with a parent that seemed to make the difference for Leila's student Susan.

Leila's Story: Parent–Teacher Intervention with Susan

When I returned to teach high school, Susan was one of the students in my class I worried about the most. She was a pleasant young woman but extremely quiet and self-effacing, one who would not share anything in large-group discussion and who, in small-group work, always paired with folks who seemed to be more energetic than she and could accomplish the work. At one point she appeared to give up in class, put her head on her desk, and just refused to be engaged.

She completely stopped writing in her journal, even though all of us, myself and the students, wrote for ten minutes at the opening of every class. What was the problem? Previously Susan had written a strong journal entry on her father, a man who had ceased to be in her life some time ago and who, even on holidays and her birthday, failed to acknowledge her presence. His new family and younger children seemed to be his focus, and it hurt Susan immensely. I talked with her during and after class—I too had had a difficult time with my own father—but got almost nothing from her but averted eyes and mumbles. Her behavior was beginning to alarm me; I checked with other teachers, and there were rumors about her health and her love life, both of which could have explained her lack of affect in school. There was an older boyfriend for whom Susan had, alarmingly, made two court appearances because she appeared to be involved in some of his difficulties, but, despite all that and her indifference to work, she believed firmly that in a year or so she would escape high school and be a student at a university (her heart was set on Louisiana State University [LSU]). Using any "in" I had, I talked to Susan about LSU and asked her about the connection she might see between her grades in school and her admission to college-level work. But Susan was not buying my teacher version of reality: she was going to LSU, and somehow whatever she did or did not do in our class was beside the point.

As the semester continued, Susan's work was so marginal and skimpy that when the second midterm grades were given, I called her mother yet another time. Susan's mother was one of the parents with whom I connected positively and strongly, and she appreciated my efforts to keep in touch. This crisis, however, was getting serious, and over the phone we discussed what we could do. All other approaches had failed—and at home Susan went into her bedroom, closed the door, and would not talk to her mom. So Susan's mother and I plotted and planned and arranged for what we both hoped would be a small but effective shock. Without warning Susan, her mother arranged to come early to school so that we could call Susan out of class and sit down jointly with her. Perhaps the surprise of the two of us—making an impromptu, tag-team intervention—would cause some change.

Certainly Susan registered surprise when she was called to the office during first period, only to see both myself and her mother waiting for her, but the effect was not as I had hoped. We three sat in the empty cafeteria, and it was cold in all senses of the word. The earnest (and rehearsed) presentation made by the two of us to Susan was greeted with silence. Susan listened but would not respond, had no answers, offered no reasons, and made no promises to do anything different in class. I was saddened; the whole effort seemed a waste of time. So on we went, and I concluded I had done what I could do for Susan.

Life, however, can be surprising. Just a few weeks later as part of a class project, Susan chose a young adult novel, and a breakthrough appeared to come. She actually read the novel she selected and, for the first time in the entire semester, elected to work alone. She chose one of the creative projects I had offered and made an ABC book based on the novel. Using different markers and type styles, she put her phrases on carefully trimmed construction paper, tying the pages together with yarn. Susan had raided her mother's sewing kit to put on each page pearls, sequins, sparkles, beads, and all sorts of glitter. The content was not remarkable, the presentation was messy in places, but the entire effect was wonderful, full and consistent with the spirit of the book itself. It was, in many ways, a triumph. More to the point, it was the first completed work Susan had done in months, she had done it on her own, and it was pretty good. I couldn't praise her enough.

To what extent the intervention/discussion with myself and Susan's mother had been the catalyst or not, after that there seemed some shift in Susan, and, thanks in part to her good grade on the ABC book project, she did just barely pass the semester. I can't prove it, but I do believe that somehow the mother–teacher teamwork and our dogged refusal to ignore her finally made an impression on Susan and helped her to succeed on one small project. She never did go to LSU—I followed up on her a year or so after I left the high school—but, for me, getting Susan's attention and getting her to engage at least once was a small victory.

One Teacher's Strategy for Dealing with Alienated Students: "Big Bucks"

The students described and the strategies devised to help them represent attempts to deal with alienation in school. In the following account, however, an individual teacher had an entire class that was relatively unmotivated and certainly apathetic. What can a teacher do about a *group* that might be termed *alienated*? This teacher decided to use a behaviorally oriented plan that depended on extrinsic reward; for her, the solution was successful, and although it may not represent any sort of plan you would like to implement in your classroom, it is worth detailing. "Big Bucks" offers a tangible, real-life reward for school activities, and in this school context, it worked.

One of the saving graces of the second half of Leila's teaching career in high school was the friendship and guidance of a buddy down the hall. Nancy Rosenbaum, more than most anybody she knew, could come up with systems that worked and that were directly related to a student or instructional problem. Leila always admired Nancy for the crafty way she could adapt a principle or a concept to her students.

They have stayed friends through the years and share personal and school-related news. At one point in her teaching, Nancy had a crisis of sorts. She had moved to a new school and just did not like what was going on in one of her classes. Here was her situation: she was teaching Project College, an intensive reading course to prepare athletes and others who were not particularly motivated or geared to go on with their education. Built within the class were a number of field trips and guest speakers to give students an idea of what was "out there" in the world. It seemed a relatively ideal structure.

But the students in Nancy's Project College class turned out to be a highly unmotivated group of juniors and seniors. As a group, they consistently came to class late and without materials. A disproportionate number wanted to go to the bathroom immediately when class began; some of them insisted on using class time to study for what they perceived were more important tests in other subjects. They were not convinced about going to college or getting jobs; for a few, an athletic scholarship might be an entry ticket, but even that was a bit remote. They were not angry or hostile: they were just indifferent, disaffected, and tuned out. They did not want to do a whole lot of work; for many, even participation in field trips was declined because it would mean makeup work in other, missed classes. For a number of students in this group, very little that was going on in school related to what they perceived as the reality of the world. And, as Nancy knew, they might just have been right.

What to do?

It was during a routine weekend trip to the local office supplies store that Nancy had a vision. Browsing in the aisles, she spied oversized note pads with a reproduction of a $500 bill on one side and space to write a grocery list or a memo or whatever on the other. It was a gimmick to jazz up ordinary note pads, but to Nancy it seemed to open a door. Big bucks, she thought. Hmm, big bucks. She bought a lot of them. She made some notes, did some planning, and was ready to institute a barter-and-reward system in her class, a strategy she called "Big Bucks."

The next week in class she put the stack of $500 memo pads on her desk. Gesturing toward them, she began. What, she asked her students, do you have to do to earn Big Bucks? What, after these final years in school, can you do to get those greatly desired Big Bucks?

The class perked up; here was a subject they were interested in. Students brainstormed, they brought up illegal activities, they snickered, they got serious.

OK, the students concluded, to earn Big Bucks you have to do something fairly extraordinary—or maybe something pretty well for a sustained period of time. The students knew from their class that college graduates make hundreds of thousands of dollars more over a lifetime than high school graduates do. They even cited some of the guest speakers they had had in their class who could command higher fees in IT, engineering, and medical fields for just those types of achievement. And, of course, with those Big Bucks you can have at least some of what most people call "the good life"—the conversation moved a bit to cars, houses, jewelry, vacations, and the like.

Nancy then gestured toward the note pads and outlined how students could earn the $500 "bills," one at a time, for certain behaviors or achievements:

- being on time to class four times in a row: $500
- showing a 10 percent improvement in score from pretest to posttest on certain subjects: $500
- sharing great ideas with the class, including study techniques that really worked or memory tricks for any subject: $500
- quizzes with scores of over 98 percent: $500 each
- being exceptionally polite and pleasant: $500
- keeping a semester calendar for assignments and deadlines: $1,000, payable the last day of class
- going on field trips that required makeup work in other classes: $500
- meeting deadlines, getting money and/or permission slips in before the due date: $500.

Nancy then outlined what her students could do with the Big Bucks they earned, a list that was directly related to the issues of this particular class:

- Going to the bathroom during class cost $500.
- A trip to the media center to study for something else was $3,000 for half the class period, $5,000, for the whole period ("not cheap," Nancy noted, "but a bargain if you need it").

- School rules dictated that four tardies to class equaled one after-school detention; a student could be tardy to class, without further penalty, for $500.

- The big-ticket item: buy all or parts of the final exam. For Big Bucks, students could purchase their year-end Project College English exam ahead of time and study accordingly. The entire exam sold for $9,500; individual sections cost varying amounts.

As Nancy set up "Big Bucks," students could lend money to others or give their money away. They could not, however, borrow from the teacher, forge the Big Bucks (Nancy initialed and dated each bill), or get their money replaced if they lost it. And a student who had purchased all or part of the final exam could show it to others who hadn't been able to. That decision was left entirely up to the individual.

The point of this one teacher's strategy for dealing with the alienated is that it was based on an established order all of us, students and teachers, intimately understand—money. It may have been symbolic—note pads with enlarged $500 bills—and it may have relied a great deal on extrinsic reward, but it took on a power and a reality of its own. And in this one class, Big Bucks reinforced good behavior, study habits, esprit de corps, and a very good final exam. Nancy also observed, "Most of these students had jobs, and occasionally I'd hear one remark that this was just like life; as soon as they had a payday, they'd have a bunch of bills that used it all."

In hindsight, what would Nancy change? She wrote:

> The use of Big Bucks cut the tardies and bathroom trips even more effectively than I first thought it could. It gave me a chance to reinforce behaviors I think will help students—sharing study ideas, practicing on quizzes with each other to get the 98 percent, keeping a calendar so that deadlines do not totally sneak up on them, consciously thinking of the extra politeness or helpfulness that may help them in their relationships with others. It also did not make every reward a grade.
>
> Students suggested things to earn and spend Big Bucks on that I could never have thought of, and some of them were great ideas. . . . Students also can save!! During second semester, everyone's priority was accumulating the $9,500 first—everything else could wait. When they had their nest eggs, spending could begin.
>
> At the end of the semester (and sometimes before), students could be incredibly generous with each other. One girl was the surprised recipient of $l,000 from a student who gave or "loaned" Aimee the money because Aimee needed it right then.
>
> I never had any big quarrels or fights about money. Students did like to keep up with how much they had and how much other people had—a couple of people counted their "cash" at the end of the period every day. But the emphasis was never all money—money was a bonus. (Rosenbaum, personal communication, 2005)

Although the administration had to be notified, Nancy wrote that members of "the administration, including the department chair, came to observe when I was first beginning with Big Bucks and were very interested and supportive" and the program then went along on its own. It is one teacher's solution to a problem in one disaffected class, a solution that relates to the class—and also uses what we so frequently refer to as the outside and "real" world.

Instead of Money, What About Games in the Classroom?

Right now, some teachers are experimenting with "gamification" of instruction—transforming assignments into "quests" and giving "badges" or "resources" as rewards for success—to encourage their students to engage more actively in their own learning. In his *The Multiplayer Classroom: Designing Coursework as a Game,* Lee Sheldon (2012) describes how he modeled a college course on the popular online game *World of Warcraft,* and a related blog gives more information (https://gamingtheclassroom .wordpress.com/). Students begin the course with an F, but they can work to "level up" all semester, up to an A.

There are also classroom management strategies that follow game rules. One of Ken's former students, William, who now teaches in New York City, uses the website Classcraft to gamify his classroom. He's done it to help students learn to be mindful, rather than just to follow rules:

Students are able to "level up" and earn stars for being mindful, recognizing mindfulness in others, supporting each other, being focused and on task, self-managing behavior, and making academic progress. They are then able to redeem these stars for different things, such as a "replay" on homework or points on a test. In addition, they receive a "quarterly adventure" to monitor the assignments they complete and have the opportunity to earn more stars at the end of each quarter if all assignments are complete. In addition, there is an online program called Classcraft that is a true video game for the classroom, which has also proven to be truly motivational.

> In the beginning of the year, I am in charge of leveling students up, but as the year goes on and they become more independent and mindful, a student who is facilitating a Socratic Seminar, for example, can "level-up" their peers. As a result, the foundations of mindfulness and the use of videogame theory are a way of motivating and engaging the most reluctant learners because the classroom itself becomes a positive place they want to be in.
>
> —WILLIAM MEEHAN

Using gamification strategies to encourage engagement and positive behaviors may be effective in controlling a classroom, but Alfie Kohn cautions us that such strategies are based in behaviorism. Think chickens pecking for pellets in a Skinner box. They don't encourage intrinsic motivation, and they don't help to develop independent, critical thinkers who are prepared to participate fully in an activist democracy. (See Kohn's *Beyond Discipline* [2006] and *Punished by Rewards* [1999] for more.) Bottom line: Use these methods mindfully.

The Average Student: Lost in the Middle

At one point in American history, a large group of citizens was characterized as the "silent majority." That phrase still has some power and can be applied to what are often termed *average* students: the ones in the middle who are neither characterized as gifted nor alienated and who do not otherwise call attention to themselves. These students are the majority of those we teach in middle school and high school and are tracked and labeled as average. When they are flanked either in a single class or in our teaching day by others at the extremes, it is easy to gloss over them and to forget that they, too, are a vital part of our teaching life. Although most of the activities in this book are directed at average students, it is helpful to consider them as a group with as much definition as our alienated students. Kids who don't cause any trouble, who largely do their assignments and cooperate, can be given short shrift by us as teachers. We need to remember that these students also require attention, praise, reinforcement, and, indeed, an acknowledgment that what the system may call an average student can be highly misleading. Within your average group can be startlingly original thinkers and, conversely, kids who are in over their heads academically. Being seen as average is not necessarily a pleasant experience, and for some students it can also be a conscious strategy to keep notice from being called to oneself, a way to hide. We as teachers need, as best we can, to remember to examine the labels we so often glibly place on or readily accept for our students and not lose our responsibility to our average students.

An eloquent comment on this subject came to Leila in a letter. A young woman preparing to be a teacher had read *Making the Journey* and wanted to talk further about average students. Ashley Ruff (personal communication, 1998) observed:

> I have often been lumped into that category [of being average] myself, and it tends to be glossed over more frequently than any other category. I have found that within my own high school "the average student" is often treated very different in relation to the other preexisting tracks. We already knew that we would have to read a lot more literature than the basic track. We also knew that we wouldn't be going on as many field trips as

the gifted class. I remember feeling in high school that I simply didn't fit into a category anywhere. I felt as if I wasn't smart enough to be gifted, and I wasn't slow enough to be basic. I simply was just another "average student."

Being a face in a large crowd or being considered unremarkable is not always an enviable position. Teachers need to consistently challenge students who are tracked as average in academic ability and to provide them with the same kinds of stimulation they provide so-called gifted students. Getting by, unremarked and unnoticed, is the goal of a number of average students, and it is not something with which we as teachers should glibly cooperate.

The Gifted Student: Burdens and Responsibilities

The pinnacle of success for many teachers is to be given a class of "gifted" students, those who have risen, at least at a given point in their school lives, to the top academically. Some enjoy this teaching immensely and find it very satisfying to deal with motivated, competitive, college-bound students, either in classes or in programs such as Advanced Placement (AP) or International Baccalaureate (IB). Such students, however, have their own special challenges, and not all of them are academic.

There is for these students often an incredible pressure to produce, succeed, and, in some cases, to be relatively "perfect" in a variety of other areas, notably social and athletic. Some of this pressure comes from parents and teachers, but a great deal of it also comes from the students themselves.

It was during Leila's teaching of AP English that she had her most extensive contact with students who could be termed "gifted." Although not every one of those was truly gifted, the majority was academically talented. These students needed intellectual stimulation but also an atmosphere of mutuality and cooperation, rather than one of competition and aggression.

In almost all cases, the students needed to consider their own paths to success and, in the case of the AP class, the limitations—perceived or not—of their segregation from the rest of the student body.

Accordingly, Leila tried to use more cooperative learning with these students and, to an extent, to deemphasize what was for many of them the major motivating force of their lives, the grade. It was possible with these students to make a convincing case for postponing a tangible reward or to use participation and completion as benchmarks.

Keeping in touch with the gifted students' parents was as important as keeping in touch with the parents of less successful students and helped, in some cases, to soften the pressure from home.

And we need to remember that gifted students are as varied as all our other students. Jill Williamson recalls her AP English class and paints a portrait of the varied gifted students:

Shawna and Amy were best friends, but their personalities were entirely different. Amy spent most of her time popping gum and cracking silly jokes and took her poetry quite seriously. Shawna worshipped her GPA yet did the very least amount of work she could to get by. And Shawna had the most beautiful head of long, wavy, red hair. I was so jealous. Jason, Jim, and Jeff always became the teachers' pets. Jason was my modern-day Adonis. Jim slept most of the time but was quite charming nonetheless. And Jeff missed class frequently to celebrate Jewish holidays, and he always seasoned his speech with multisyllabic words. T. J. was sensitive and had a quiet laugh. York had the quickest wit of all of us and had seven brothers and sisters. Greg was our token burly, slow-witted jock, and Sean was our token surfer dude. Jennifer came from a broken home and her expression was blank most of the time, yet she wrote the most eloquent and creative short stories. John was my favorite classmate. On the outside he was a Virginia gentlemen, but secretly he spent quite a bit of time drawing phallic symbols and telling dirty jokes. He was also a terrible speller. Nikki was my manic-depressive friend who spent way too much time reading Ayn Rand and stopped coming to school about halfway through our senior year. I was the class spelling champion.

Students as varied as Jill's friends in her AP class will be in your class, too.

The Delicate Contract with Students

Dealing with and getting along with your students is a central priority of teaching; depending on your personality, you may not enter into any sort of love fest with your students. Regardless, there needs to be a sense of mutual respect and care and feeling on both sides that this endeavor is worth embarking on. Although indeed school is compulsory and your language arts class is required, there is also a necessary mutuality to this business. School requires student assent, or it's just a facade.

Despite the "level" of the class, the degree of alienation, giftedness, or averageness, students can decline to cooperate. What if, we might wonder, we held class and nobody came? What if the teacher asked a question and nobody, but nobody—ever so sullenly or ever so politely—answered? What if a test was distributed and nobody picked up a pencil and took it? It is a delicate contract because, indeed, there is little we can do if students, at the extreme, absolutely refuse to cooperate or, at the not as extreme, change the class expectations until they are virtually meaningless. This lack of faith can occur with any level of students, and in some ways it is a teacher's worst nightmare. So how do we make sure that the students in our classes do not say no, do not decide not to participate? It is, indeed, a delicate social contract. We need to remember four things:

1. We need to be reasonable, to offer students activities that are meaningful, doable, and have real connection to skills and knowledge.
2. We need to articulate why what we are studying or writing or reading or discussing is important.
3. We need to listen to students and to accord them the same courtesy we would accord our own peers.
4. We need, finally, to remember that school, enduring as a concept, is perennial largely because the majority of students have come to our classes over the decades with a certain hopeful belief that they will learn from us and that the learning will make their lives better.

For Your Journal

One of the ways we can work more successfully with students is to think not of rules and regulations, but of options for that delicate contract. Look at the following classroom situations. How many options can you suggest to deal with such typical classroom/student events? What do you predict would be the result of each of the options?

1. A student repeatedly comes in late and disturbs the class in progress.
2. A student consistently uses materials from your desk without asking but, when confronted, always apologizes and promises to replace the materials.
3. Two students, best friends, consistently whisper loudly whenever you are giving directions. When you confront them, they begin to text each other instead.
4. A student gets into an argument with another student and, when you intervene, calls you an obscene name.
5. As you are explaining the details of a new project, a student complains that you are giving the class too much work and that the project is "stupid" anyway. Other students nod and appear to agree.
6. At least half a dozen students constantly interrupt others in the course of large-group discussions, disrupting the flow of conversation and also dominating the discussion.
7. When you teach a one-to-one class (in which each student works on his or her own laptop), several students check and respond to email instead of working on their assignments.
8. A student refuses to cooperate in group work and wants to work alone.
9. A student consistently comes to class without materials or books or with the wrong materials and books.
10. A student has a habit of not turning in homework assignments, citing a lack of clarity from you regarding directions and/or deadlines.
11. Almost once a week this student comes to class, puts his head on the desk, and resists participation in class.
12. Often, right before the bell rings and class starts, a student needs to talk to you about why she does not have her assignments or about difficulty she had completing the assignment. You try to give her attention, but the bell rings, and the class waits for both of you to finish your conversation.

Leila's Final Story: Tanya and Barry

Despite Ken's and my stories of difficult students and failed expectations, I end this chapter on a positive note.

An exceptional benefit to teaching—a benefit that perhaps I have not emphasized enough—is that working with students is often close to magical. Not every month, not every semester, not even every year, but often, often enough to keep you going, you will meet and work with students who shape and positively influence your life. You will remember these students and even keep in touch with some of them—as I still do with two I have written about in this chapter, Marianna and Angie. You will receive from these students kindness, consideration, and often genuine affection. They may make you laugh, and they will make you feel, perhaps as only those who work with the young can regularly feel, that the world is indeed a big and exciting and glorious place.

And beyond the parting hugs and handshakes and occasional tears, beyond the letters of appreciation and the little gifts from classes and groups—the necklace from the literary magazine staff, the locket from Advanced Placement, the coffee mugs and blank journals and books and glass apples and pens from the homeroom, the junior class, individual students—beyond all the little tokens and tributes that I, like most teachers, have received over the years, beyond the tangible gifts are those moments when your students often reveal to you their trust and friendship. I have chosen, of those students, two who affected me in memorable ways.

Tanya and I kept a running argument going for three years: first in sophomore homeroom, then in a junior English class, and finally in her senior year in my AP class, where she was one of a handful of African American students in the pilot course. She was terribly bright and very sarcastic, and although I knew she was both vulnerable and talented, she could occasionally bring out the worst in me, her teacher. I loved Tanya's spirit, but she also had a way of asking the wrong question at just the wrong time, of challenging at precisely the vulnerable moment when the class was ready to have one bright member take on the teacher. Sometimes I could appreciate Tanya's wit and verve and really admire it: with the roll of an eye or a quip or just a well-timed question, Tanya could turn a class around. Sometimes, however, she tried my patience.

A good student for her sophomore year despite some run-ins with other teachers, Tanya became a *very* good student her junior year and learned to play the politeness game. In Advanced Placement during her senior year, she was aggressive in discussion and bright, and I especially enjoyed her writing. She and I tried to rise above our differences.

And it was Tanya who called me at home late one night with a very adult and truly serious personal crisis. She called, she said, to ask my advice. I would not betray her, she said, and she wanted to know what I would do in her situation. She was brisk and almost businesslike. I was mildly stunned—Tanya and I were more worthy adversaries than friends—but I gave her what insights I had, and we talked frankly on the phone for a half hour or so. Back in school, Tanya waited some weeks before she told me that the crisis had been resolved. I was relieved for her and, operating in a rather new sense of relationship, under a truce of sorts, Tanya and I went on to finish the semester together. She graduated with honors, and as I shook her hand in congratulation, I felt a renewed sense of affection and concern for this complicated and smart young woman who had, surprisingly, possibly all along, trusted me. Her graduation was bittersweet: I was happy to see Tanya leave high school for a very prestigious university, but, honestly, I seriously doubted her chances for success. And I knew, of course, as with many students, that I would never know the outcome.

It was fully four years later when a graduation invitation from that prestigious university arrived in the mail. I could scarcely believe the name on the return address: it was from Tanya. After four years of silence, she had sent me the news. Of course, it was typical Tanya; written on the back of her calling card was her one-line comment, teasing, jaunty, and proud: *Ha! Ha! Bet you're surprised!* Indeed I was and touched that, years later, Tanya knew that I would want to know the news.

Tanya taught me something about students and teachers, about influence that is not always obvious, and about relationships that are forged over the years. Maybe I had failed to see it all along, but my sparring partner, the bright and aggressive Tanya, had turned out to be a student with whom I shared a bond and who seemed to know that I cared. And Tanya continued her triumphs; she is now a physician.

Barry was a new student to my high school who did not get along very well with school rules or policies. Very early in the semester he had been in a difficult situation with a number of his teachers. Typically, he and I had had a series of confrontations in my third-period class, which escalated so quickly that I really wondered if we could stand to work together for the rest of the semester. I tried to talk to Barry, but he blew me off pretty convincingly, and I decided to exercise a rare option in our school. I asked, on the basis of personality conflict, that Barry be transferred to another teacher and another class. It was probably a cowardly move on my part, but there was something about the challenge of Barry I did not feel equal to that semester; I felt I had enough to handle with five classes and 140 students. Regardless of my motives, Barry saw the request as an insult, and, possibly on general principles, was enraged. In a subsequent conference about his schedule—and his behavior in my class and others—he assaulted an assistant principal and was immediately suspended from school.

When I saw him in the halls after he returned to his classes—and his new English class—I stayed clear; Barry was one student whom I had crossed and, inadvertently or not, my transfer request was the precipitating event that resulted in his suspension. Barry, I suspected, would be more than willing to retaliate. But the year went on quietly, and I saw little of him.

It was, then, with some serious trepidation that I found myself, with other teachers and students, on a bus with Barry. My high school had arranged a modified Outward Bound experience, and I was one of a dozen teacher volunteers to go into the mountains with students who had been, for varying reasons, identified as at risk. The

Outward Bound day was an exercise in communication and trust building, centered around physical tests of strength and endurance that were performed in teacher–student teams. Barry, of course, was a prime and logical candidate and was, with some of his friends, on the trip.

I had no control over the activities or grouping. There was some risk in some of the "events," and participants were warned about the danger of falling or slipping—teamwork was essential to preventing injuries. At any rate, teachers and students were randomly placed in teams for varying tests of strength, agility, and trust building. My team's turn came to scale a horizontal crossbar held twelve feet above the ground by two vertical uprights. The whole structure, crossbar and uprights, had no ropes, no handholds, no ladders, and certainly no safety features, such as a net. As luck would have it, I was selected to be the first to be launched over the top and handed down to an opposing team working on the other side. I hated the look of this activity, the height and the possible danger, but I just couldn't be the teacher/coward of the team.

Fearfully but doggedly, trusting my team members as I was encouraged to do, I climbed up the back and on to the shoulders of a volunteer. Standing on his shoulders and balancing the best I could, I stood up and reached for the crossbar, twelve feet above the ground and some two feet above my head. I jumped, grabbed for dear life, threw a leg over, hugged the crossbar, and desperately looked to the volunteer on the other side to help me get down.

I must have been more concerned about breaking my neck than I had realized, because I hadn't noticed the members of the other team. I literally couldn't trust my eyes—on the other side of the crossbar and the only thing between me and the void was my former student Barry.

He reached for me. I had a real sense of fatalism, twelve feet above the hard-packed earth, and possibly for that reason I felt I had to say something. Who knows, it might have been my last words before I went to the hospital with my broken leg or arm or both, and anyway, Barry and I had not talked since he had been removed from my class and suspended.

I looked at him. Barry was expressionless. *It's a long way down* was all I could think. And then I just blurted out what was really on my mind, "If you want to get even, here's your chance." Certainly here was his chance: this was one of the most dangerous of the day's activities, and the accidental slip and fall of a volunteer, though regrettable, would not necessarily be that suspicious. Some of these facts had been outlined before this trip; I knew it, and I supposed Barry did, too.

For an eerie moment Barry remained expressionless and silent but then, twelve feet in the air, he smiled, shook his head, and grabbed my arms. Not gently—but not roughly—he delivered me safely to the members of his team—and the ground. I did not look back as I walked away and went on to the next activity, but I remember my legs were shaking.

Later that day during a break I went looking for Barry. I found him, sat down with him, and we talked. I thanked him for not dropping me, and that opened a very intense twenty-minute conversation. Barry was, as I guess I should have known, about as decent a person as I had ever met. He hated school, he didn't get along with his parents, he worried about his life and his girlfriend. I told him I was sorry about what had happened in my class; he told me he was sorry, too. We shook hands, went our separate ways to finish the day, and, later, when we saw each other in the halls during the remainder of the semester, we waved and smiled. We were, in a way, friends who had done something together, shared something important. I almost hoped I would have Barry in class the next year, but his parents moved out of the area, and I never saw him again.

I never forgot Barry or that day, though, and I think about how frustrated and angry he probably was, how tempted he could have been to have an "accident" with a hated teacher, and how he, with every temptation to get even and every possibility he could get away with it, refused to. To this day I wonder, if given a similar situation, I would have resisted as he did. I learned something from Barry, something about doing the right thing regardless, and his example stays with me after all these years. In fact, most of our students, like Tanya and Barry and many others, believe that we, their teachers, not only know something but are people of good will and will treat them fairly.

And, in a way, the belief of the young in us, their teachers, and their belief in what we represent, the power of education, is both heartening and heartbreaking. It is the essence of optimism and faith, and, unfortunately, it is often not confirmed by experience. If we take this business seriously, however, we are bound, to the best of our abilities, to never disillusion our students or dishonor what is nothing less than a sacred trust. This can be a hard assignment, this stuff of teaching, but the people before us in our classrooms and the lives they represent are briefly, yet profoundly, entrusted to us. As daunting—terrifying even—as that may be, it is also our little piece of immortality.

For Your Journal

Think of your middle and high school friends or of some students you may have recently observed. Can you find ones who possibly could be characterized as "alienated"? "Average"? "Gifted"? What behaviors do or did those students exhibit? What kinds of assignments or teachers appealed to them? Did not appeal to them? What variations or refinements would you make on the three categories of students presented in this chapter? If you care to, how would you describe yourself, in middle school or in high school, in relation to those categories?

References

Benson, Jeffrey. 2015. "How Not to Be a Mountain Troll." *Educational Leadership* 73 (2): 42–25.

Bower, Bruce. 1991. "Teenage Turning Point: Does Adolescence Herald the Twilight of Girls' Self-Esteem?" *Science News* 139 (March 23): 184–86.

Brozo, William G. 2002. *To Be a Boy, to Be a Reader: Engaging Teen and Preteen Boys in Active Literacy*. Newark, DE: International Reading Association.

Cardenas, Rafael Velazquez. 2014. "'Why You Gotta Keep Muggin' Me?' Understanding Students' Disruptive 'Yell-Outs' in Class." In *The First Year of Teaching: Classroom Research to Increase Student Learning*, edited by Jabari Mahiri and Sarah Warshauer Freedman, 166–77. New York: Teachers College Press.

Federal Interagency Forum on Child and Family Statistics. 2009. *America's Children: Key National Indicators of Well-Being*. Washington, DC: U.S. Government Printing Office.

Gilligan, Carol, Nona P. Lyons, and Trudy J. Hanmer, eds. 1989. *Making Connections: The Relational Worlds of Adolescent Girls at Emma Willard School*. Troy, NY: Emma Willard School.

Glasser, William. 1985. *Control Theory in the Classroom*. New York: Harper & Row.

Gough, Pauline B. 1987. "The Key to Improving Schools: An Interview with William Glasser." *Phi Delta Kappan* 68 (May): 656–62.

Groenke, Susan L., Marcelle Haddix, Wendy J. Glenn, David E. Kirkland, Detra Price-Dennis, and Chonika Coleman-King. 2015. "Disrupting and Dismantling the Dominant Vision of Youth of Color." *English Journal* 104 (3): 35–40.

Hersch, Patricia. 1999. *A Tribe Apart: A Journey into the Heart of American Adolescence*. New York: Random House.

Hubbard, Ruth Shagoury, Maureen Barbieri, and Brenda Miller Power. 1998. *"We Want to Be Known": Learning from Adolescent Girls*. York, ME: Stenhouse.

Intrator, Sam M., and Robert Kunzman. 2009. "Who Are Adolescents Today? Youth Voices and What They Tell Us." In *Handbook of Adolescent Literacy Research*, edited by Leila Christenbury, Randy Bomer, Peter Smagorinsky, 29–45. New York: Guilford.

Kohn, Alfie. 1999. *Punished by Rewards: The Trouble with Gold Stars, Incentive Plans, A's, Praise, and Other Bribes*. New York: Houghton Mifflin.

———. 2006. *Beyond Discipline: From Compliance to Community*. Alexandria, VA: Association for Supervision and Curriculum Development (ASCD).

Larsson, Stieg. 2008. *The Girl with the Dragon Tattoo*. New York: Random House.

Lesko, Nancy. 2012. *Act Your Age! A Cultural Construction of Adolescence*. New York: Routledge.

Lindley, Daniel A., Jr. 1990. "For Teachers of the Alienated: Three Defenses Against Despair." *English Journal* 79 (6): 26–31.

Maynard, Trisha. 2002. *Boys and Literacy: Exploring the Issues*. New York: Routledge.

McNeil, Linda M. 1986. *Contradictions of Control: School Structure and School Knowledge*. New York: Routledge and Kegan Paul.

———. 2000. *Contradictions of School Reform: Educational Costs of Standardized Testing*. New York: Routledge.

Morin, Richard, Liz Mundy, Kevin Merida, Claudia Deane, Lisa Frazier Page, and Jose Antonio Vargas. 2005. "What Teens Really Think: A Poll of Washington Area Kids Gives Us a Piece of Their Minds." *Washington Post Magazine* (October 23): 14–29, 32–50.

NCTE. 1990. *Lost in the Crowd: A Statement on Class Size and Teacher Workload*. Urbana, IL: NCTE.

Newkirk, Tom. 2002. *Misreading Masculinity: Boys, Literacy, and Popular Culture*. Portsmouth, NH: Heinemann.

Pfeffer, Susan Beth. 1990. "Basic Rules of Teenage Life." *The ALAN Review* 17 (Spring): 5–7.

Pipher, Mary. 1994. *Reviving Ophelia: Saving the Selves of Adolescent Girls*. New York: Putnam.

Planty, M., W. Hussar, T. Snyder, S. Provasnik, G. Kena, R. Dinkes, et al. 2008. *The Condition of Education 2008* (NCES 2008-031). Washington, DC: National Center for Education Statistics, Institute of Education Sciences, U.S. Department of Education.

Sarigianides, Sophia Tatiana, Mark A. Lewis, and Robert Petrone. 2015. "How Re-thinking Adolescence Helps Re-imagine the Teaching of English." *English Journal* 104 (3): 13–18.

Sheldon, Lee. 2012. *The Multiplayer Classroom: Designing Coursework as a Game*. Boston: Cengage.

Smith, Michael, and Jeffrey Wilhelm. 2002. *"Reading Don't Fix No Chevys": Literacy in the Lives of Young Men*. Portsmouth, NH: Heinemann.

Sobko, Sophia. 2014. "Academic Self-Sabotage: Understanding Motives and Behaviors of Underperforming Students." In *The First Year of Teaching: Classroom Research to Increase Student Learning,* edited by Jabari Mahiri and Sarah Warshauer Freedman, 73–89. New York: Teachers College Press.

Tatum, Alfred. 2005. *Teaching Reading to Black Adolescent Males: Closing the Achievement Gap*. Portland, ME: Stenhouse.

United States Department of Education. 2004. *National Center for Educational Statistics: The Condition of Education 2004*. Washington, DC: U.S. Department of Education (NCES 2004-077).

Valdez, Veronica E., and Rebecca M. Callahan. 2011. "Who Is Learning Language(s) in Today's Schools?" In *Handbook of Research on Teaching the English Language Arts*, 3rd ed., edited by Diane Lapp and Douglas Fisher, 3–9. New York: Routledge.

5 | THE WORLD OF LITERATURE
Teaching and Selecting

And gladly wolde he lerne and gladly teche.

—Geoffrey Chaucer, Prologue to *Canterbury Tales*

The Fear of Not Knowing Enough

Leila's Story

I am back in my high school, standing in a wide and empty corridor. It is time to go to class; in fact, I am late, and behind the closed doors are other students already seated and working. I need to go to class; I have a test today. Funny thing, though, I have not been to class in months, have done no homework and no studying. I know I am going to fail the test, fail the course, and not graduate from high school. I just hate that class; I don't understand the subject and have avoided it until now. Right this moment, however, I would give anything to have been working all along; the feeling of fear and impending doom is overwhelming.

This, of course, is my dream, my special, recurring anxiety nightmare. Like many people, this dream comes periodically to visit me, and I think it stands for fear of failure or worry about achievement and preparation. Although you may not have such recurring dreams, you are probably a bit apprehensive about how much you know as you prepare to enter the classroom.

There is hardly a one of us on the eve of teaching or in the first few years in the class-room who felt that she or he knew *enough*. All of us are haunted by the worry that we are ill prepared, underread, insufficiently educated, ignorant about a number of crucial areas. And the fact is, we probably are. Bluntly put, the amount and depth and breadth of knowledge that we need to be fully conversant with all aspects of language arts is just not possible for most of us to achieve in the preparation years before teaching. It is also not reasonable to expect that level of expertise in the first few years.

However, the fallacy of the fear of being ill-educated is the unspoken assumption that our reading and study should really be completed by the time we become teach-ers. Most teachers know that the first year in the classroom simply marks the start of a new phase of education and, indeed, that we will never "own" pieces of literature or facts about language or grasp writing principles so firmly as when, year after year, we handle and manipulate and use and create activities based on those elements of language arts. We have to, it is true, be a teacher from the very first day; but as veteran teachers know, we do not have control over all of our subject matter for some years to come. As the title of this book insists, we also continue to *become* teachers, and that includes expanding our knowledge and our skill in the classroom.

We do, as Chaucer reminds us, not only "gladly teche" but also "gladly lerne" (1. 308). And for those who see Chaucer's oft-quoted phrase as more of a definition of a political stance regarding teaching, it is, interestingly enough, also a pure practi-cality: teachers, to teach, really must continue to learn. Unless one makes a conscious effort to resist, teaching and learning are symbiotically related.

The idea that you don't know enough, that your learning is continuing—possibly, in one sense of the word, just starting—may be a depressing thought for you. If you look at it another way, it also might be relatively heartening. It would be, in the long run, horrifically boring if you could really know everything, master everything almost immediately. There might be more surety than you are feeling now, but how emptily the teaching years would stretch before you! There is also the undeniable benefit (es-pecially in literature) of discovering with your students and thus seeing somewhat with fresh eyes, which may be what sustains you during the first few years in the classroom when, with mounting panic, you realize that you will occasionally be teaching some-thing over which you yourself have only marginal control.

Take heart, new teacher, and forge ahead: the excitement of learning will probably outweigh the sheer fear. You will also have the pleasure of watching your own tastes change and expand as you add to your storehouse of learning authors and ideas and techniques. Unless you are very different from almost all teachers, you will, as the years go on, become far more accomplished—and educated—than you can really imagine right now.

And, of course, it almost goes without saying: if your own education has left you deficient in some area, it is your responsibility as a teacher, as a professional, to make up that deficiency. And, at this stage in the game, it really doesn't matter whose "fault" the deficiency may be; you didn't take the course or the teachers were not effective or you just didn't think the information was that important. It is, however, up to you to get yourself up to speed.

If you are confused about assonance and alliteration, look them up and learn them; if you've never gotten point of view straight, start studying now; if the rhetorical triangle isn't a concept you're comfortable with, improve the situation on your own; if you don't know the difference between the Middle Ages and the Enlightenment, you can read about them; if somehow you've missed the major American twentieth-century novels, select a reasonable number and set aside some weekend time to enjoy them. If the distinction between phrase and clause eludes you, if you are not certain what a parallel construction looks like, you can learn it. You will now gladly learn as well as gladly teach. It comes, happily, with the territory.

Literature: The Heart of Language Arts

The days of literature, fiction, poetry, and drama occupying the lion's share of the curriculum may be on the wane. But literature, the reason most of us are English teachers—and the area with which we are usually the most familiar—remains the backbone of English language arts.

Although not all our students will appear to react with the same enthusiasm regarding all the literature we read and respond to in the classroom, literature is, for most of our students, the most enjoyable part of language arts, for at least these four reasons:

- It is an opportunity for them to escape, to literally lose themselves in reading. It is an old-fashioned phrase, antiquely put, but Emily Dickinson's belief that "there is no frigate like a book" (poem #1263) is indeed apt; a book, like no other vehicle, is stunningly equipped to carry us somewhere else.

- Students find themselves in other characters and learn about their own beliefs and about who they are.

- Through literature, students can experience other lives and other eras. As Umberto Eco has said, "The person who doesn't read lives only one life. The reader lives 5,000. Reading is immortality backwards" (quoted in Romano [2016]).

- Reading literature can be an opportunity to experience the sheer art of a well-crafted plot, the delineation of a character, the unfolding of an important theme. This aesthetic appreciation is often considered the most important reason for reading literature, but by placing our entire emphasis on aesthetics—how a piece of literature achieves what it is—we can destroy the reading and the pleasure of literature.

It goes back to a cynical statement cited in Chapter 1, "English class ruined every good book I ever read." We do our students a great disservice if we confine all of our discussion and attention—and testing—to aesthetic appreciation. Which leads us to literary criticism, reading through different lenses, and another reason you need to spend time with your students and their response to all aspects of literature, not only the pure aesthetics.

For Your Journal

Considering the four reasons for reading literature, think about when and how you can relate to each reason. Perhaps a specific novel or short story or poem might stand out as being the major example. What do you remember about yourself as a reader and each of the four reasons for reading? Can you link any pieces of literature to specific reasons? Are there books you read that, for you at least, fulfill all four of the reasons for reading?

Reading with Different Lenses

What do students want from their reading of literature? When Leila returned to teaching high school, she asked her twenty-two junior-level students what they expected from the class. The responses, conveyed anonymously, specifically requested exciting, interesting, and in-depth discussions in class. A few students also wrote suggestions about literary analysis; one wanted to learn to "analyze/interpret literature properly." Another asked that the class "discuss hidden meanings and things like that." A third cited, "All I really expect is that you give us direction, but don't limit us creatively or in our interpretation" of literature. These students understood that various literary theories raise different questions about literature, and they were interested in exploring them. And you can encourage your students to pursue numerous avenues of interpretation—to use a variety of lenses—as they read. To read more about using literary lenses, you might look at these books:

- Lisa Eckert's (2006) *How Does It Mean?* explores five approaches (archetypal, objective, reader-response, biographical, and thematic).

- *Doing Literary Criticism* by Tim Gillespie (2010) details no fewer than eleven such lenses (reader response, biographical, historical, psychological, archetypal, genre, moral, philosophical, feminist, political, and formalist).

- English teachers find Deborah Appleman's (2009) *Critical Encounters in High School English* valuable for exploring literary lenses.

As you become more comfortable with a text and your own teaching, as your students raise questions in your classroom, you may want to explore and experiment. In the meantime, however, let's look at just a few of these literary lenses.

If your teachers spent a great deal of time giving you information regarding the era the literature was written, the context in which it occurred, and who else was writing then, those teachers were concentrating on *historical* or *literary background*. For some teachers, that background is of less interest than the life of the author; if you remember being asked to pay attention to a writer's birth and death dates and other such information, your teachers were probably emphasizing *author biography*.

A third approach has been called the New Criticism, in which the centrality of literature's pedigree—where and when and even by whom a piece of literature is written—is ultimately irrelevant. When viewed using a *New Critical* lens, literature is considered a piece of art; very little other information is important or even of interest. For decades this was a highly influential way to approach literature and was used almost exclusively across all levels of literature down to the high schools. It also featured intense examination 4 lenses erns, known generally as *close reading*. New Critical theory is experiencing a resurgence through the close reading advocated by proponents of the Common Core and similar college- and career-ready standards, as teacher Ellen C. Carillo observes:

> In the last several years, a sentiment long associated with the New Critics reemerged as the Common Core State Standards were developed and implemented across the country. . . . [Common Core] insists that the center of literacy instruction must be the "text itself" and "surrounding materials should be included only when necessary so as not to distract from the text itself" . . . [The focus is] on objectivity rather than the role of the reader in the composition of meaning. (2016, 29)

You may find that you're encouraged not to assign students prereading activities or to tap into students' prior knowledge before assigning them a text to read. If so, you're experiencing the very sentiments to which Carillo speaks. We'll have more to say about this later in the chapter.

Yet another way to approach literature—another lens through which to view—is to ask students to relate literature to themselves, their lives, and what else they have read. This lens is a *reader response* approach, and the emphasis here is on what the reader brings to the piece. The lenses of historical context, author biography, and New Critical/close reading are seen as less relevant. When using the lens of reader response, teachers ask students how the literature intertwines with what they know, who they are, and what they believe. Clearly, a reader response approach is less concerned with the factual information of a literary or historical emphasis; it does not address the author's biography, and the New Critical considerations are relevant only as they influence a reader's understanding of the text. The central focus in this lens is that of the reader and his or her experience. Reader response contends that most readers approach pieces differently, and responses can shift not only from reader to reader but through a person's reading of the same text at different times in his or her life.

The Four Lenses: What to Do?

There are valid reasons for multiple approaches and, given a perfect world and more than enough time (to paraphrase Andrew Marvell's "To His Coy Mistress"), we as teachers would skillfully combine all four (and add other lenses, such as feminist, archetypical, genre, philosophical), shifting our emphasis in response to the demands of the literature and the interests of our students. After all, each of the four lenses offers positive directions and possibilities for creative, critical thinking. Such comprehensive blending and adjusting, however, are not possible in most classrooms. Thus, to make informed choices about what to spend class time on, we need to ask ourselves as teachers: What is served by each of these approaches?

New Critical approaches to literature came about because of serious dissatisfaction with extensive concentration on historical context and author biography. Whether the poem was the first or the last of a writer's career or was written after the artist's midlife nervous breakdown seemed not only irrelevant but also to deflect from the consideration of the work itself. Whether the literature occurred in response to some historical or topical event seemed equally unimportant. Certainly there are clear exceptions to this: students probably need to know, for example, why Jonathan Swift was so outraged by events in Ireland that he would write the scathing "A Modest Proposal." Students might also need to understand that Nathaniel Hawthorne's *The Scarlet Letter* is not a historically accurate account of the Puritans but is a highly selected, highly filtered, nineteenth-century interpretation of a period of history. Do they need, however, to know Swift's or Hawthorne's biography? On the other hand, the colorful and tragic life of Edgar Allan Poe often seems to inspire students to wade through his dense prose and to attempt to understand it; the incidents surrounding Samuel Taylor Coleridge's "Kubla Khan," whether reported truthfully by Coleridge or not, are intriguing to most readers and lend some further depth to the magical, mysterious poem. The problem comes when such information usurps—and it can, very quickly—the point of the reading. If students spend the bulk of class time learning about history and biography, where is the time to actually engage with the literature? As an alternative, many English teachers learned in their literature study to love the close reading of poetry and prose. Using this lens, literature is seen as a relatively isolated object to be discussed and analyzed, almost as one would turn a multifaceted object, such as a cut diamond, and consider it from all points of view. The diamond itself would not be altered by the turning and handling; it would retain its entire integrity as an object. Thus the New Criticism, as defined in John Crowe Ransom's (1979) book of the same name (originally published in 1941), was literature without the influence of the reader, the historical context, or the personal history of the author.

Yet teachers find that, despite obvious advantages over other lenses, New Criticism (close reading) does not translate well into the middle school and high school English classroom. Purely analytical reading, a celebration of the intricate art of literature, can become for students a bloodless dissection of an already difficult text, robbing it of joy, making it a task rather than a connection to life. Reader response is an alternative to this approach, and Louise Rosenblatt is the major voice of transactional, or reader response, theory. Her *Literature as Exploration* (1976), first published in 1938, offers a very different view from that of Ransom.

Transactional Theory and Reader Response

Rosenblatt reminds teachers of their "responsibility to the students as well as to the discipline" (1976, ix) and cautions us:

> We go through empty motions if our primary concern is to enable the student to recognize various literary forms, to identify various verse patterns, to note the earmarks of the style of a particular author, to detect recurrent symbols, or to discriminate the kinds of irony or satire. Acquaintance with the formal aspects of literature will not in itself insure esthetic sensitivity. . . . Knowledge of literary forms is empty without an accompanying humanity. (52)

connect to everyday life

Rosenblatt maintains three points:

1. The literature itself must have some connection to the students' lives.

2. The approach must, to capitalize upon the students' lives, be inductive.

3. Students must be involved, must be engaged to the point where the discussion leads them, as Rosenblatt writes, "to raise personally meaningful questions . . . [and] to seek in the text the basis for valid answers." (1976, ix–x)

What does it mean for a teacher and students to use the lens of reader response? It means a radical transformation, that "analysis of the work, . . . acquisition of new insights and information, will have value only as it is linked up with the student's own primary response to the work" (120). What Rosenblatt means—what a reader response lens demands—is that we and our students do far more with what is read in a classroom than look for patterns and devices and even comprehension or answers to multiple-choice test items on the state exam.

Rosenblatt insists that ⌈literature is engagement, response, and search for insight.⌉ Ultimately, the study of literature can be both individual and idiosyncratic as it is heavily, necessarily dependent upon what every reader brings to the text. And that profound faith in what the reader brings—what the reader has a right to bring—is continuingly radical, startling, and disruptive of the hierarchy of the traditional classroom. Rosenblatt gives us the very definition of a democratic classroom. Such a classroom can be destabilizing, as Rosenblatt well knows: When "teachers and pupils . . . [are] relaxed enough to face what indeed happened as they interpreted the printed page," the dominance of the teacher is ceded. Rosenblatt tells us:

> Frank expression of boredom or even vigorous rejections is a more valid starting point for learning than are docile attempts to feel "what the teacher wants." When the young reader considers why he has responded in a certain way, he is learning both to read more adequately and to seek personal meaning in literature. (1976, 70)

What a conjunction Rosenblatt offers us—not only to read but to seek meaning. Is she telling us that the two are complementary, even inseparable? Indeed she is.

Leila's Classroom Study: Characteristics of a Reader Response Classroom

You may hear that reader response methods are eschewed in new college- and career-ready standards for the teaching of reading and literature. Ken and I believe these attitudes are based on a misunderstanding of the power and rigor of well-designed reader response approaches. In fact, we encourage reader response as an important, even essential, approach for literary study.

In a study completed some years ago, I taped and analyzed classes of two teachers who use a reader response philosophy in teaching literature. The teachers, in two different schools in different sections of the same urban area, had their students discuss a trio of contemporary poems. A detailed look at what was said within the classes revealed five characteristics of a classroom that uses a reader response orientation:

1. Teachers encourage students to talk extensively.
2. Teachers help students make a community of meaning.
3. Teachers ask, they don't tell.
4. Teachers ask students to make links to personal experience.
5. Teachers affirm student responses, and encourage them to link their responses back to evidence in the text.

I also found that the discussions refute two common objections to the implementation of a reader response methodology in the classroom: first, that attention to student response to literature will deflect seriously from any literary analysis of the work itself; and second, that a reader response approach, in and of itself, takes too much instructional time to be efficient—it is quicker to tell students than to ask them to explore their own interpretations or reactions to a text. Let's take a brief look at the following three poems on young people and their fathers and how two classes discussed them:

Breakings

Long before I first left home, my father
tried to teach me horses, land, and sky,
to show me how this kind of work was done.
I studied how to be my father's son,
but all I learned was, when the wicked die,
they ride combines through barley forever.

Every summer I hated my father
as I drove hot horses through dusty grass;
and so I broke with him, and left the farm
for other work, where unfamiliar weather
broke on my head an unexpected storm
and things I had not studied came to pass.

So nothing changes, nothing stays the same,
and I have returned from a broken home
alone, to ask for a job breaking horses.
I watch a colt on a long line making
tracks in dust, and think of the kinds of breakings
there are, and the kinds of restraining forces.

> —Henry Taylor, *An Afternoon of Pocket Billiards*

Those Winter Sundays

Sundays too my father got up early
and put his clothes on in the blueblack cold
then with cracked hands that ached
from labor in the weekday weather made
banked fires blaze. No one ever thanked him.

I'd wake and hear the cold splintering, breaking.
When the rooms were warm, he'd call,
and slowly I would rise and dress,
fearing the chronic angers of that house,

Speaking indifferently to him,
who had driven out the cold
and polished my good shoes as well.
What did I know, what did I know
of love's austere and lonely offices?

> —Robert Hayden, *Angle of Ascent*

Black Walnuts

The year my father used the car for hulling
was the best. We cobbled the drive
with walnuts gathered in baskets
and cardboard boxes, then rode with him
down that rough lane, forward and backward,
time and again, until the air was bitter to breathe
and the tires spun in the juice.
For years after, every piece of gravel
was dyed brown, and the old Ford
out on the open road would warm up
to a nutty smell, especially in winter
with the windows closed and the heater blowing.

Crouched over hulls mangled green and yellow,
we picked out corrugated shells
even the car's weight couldn't crack
and spread them on the grass to dry.
My father, on his hands and knees, happy
over windfall, talked of how good
the tender meats would taste; and in that moment
I wished with all my heart that he might live forever,
as leaves ticked down around us
and the fresh stain darkened on our hands.

—Neal Bowers, *North American Review*

Teachers encourage students to talk extensively If engaging in a transaction with literature (having students make the literature their own) is an instructional goal, then students must be able to join in a conversation. This is to be distinguished from a series of responses to a teacher's question, responses that are ultimately regulated, guided, and abbreviated within the class context. Students must, if they are to thrive in a reader response classroom, really talk, converse, speak at length, pause, argue, question. They should not be confined to one-word, one-phrase answers in response to a teacher's question and in a pattern determined by the teacher. In a reader response classroom, teachers encourage students to talk extensively.

In the two classes studied, the discussion is lively. Students remain on task with the three poems during the entire class period, and the teachers do not have to guide students "back to the subject." In fact, student responses in both classes are not always one-word or one-phrase answers but extended sentences (largely in clusters of five to seven seconds with a dozen or so twenty-second responses). When students do make brief-phrase answers, they are in the context of a rapid-fire argument/discussion with other students that seem to come in response to the drama and tension of the discussion.

Teachers help students make a community of meaning Because each student's response will draw on individual, even idiosyncratic, personal background and experience, and because exchange and exploration are the goals, reader response teachers must be patient with factual misunderstanding. Eventually, individual misconceptions are corrected in a community of meaning. In a reader response classroom, nevertheless, paramount attention is not focused on right answers.

Accordingly, both classes studied are characterized by open discussion and exploration of multiple interpretations. For example, about five minutes into the discussion of the first poem, "Breakings," Teacher A initiates a discussion on a passage that refers to the breaking of a colt. The colt's experience is metaphorically linked to the poem's speaker's own "breaking" by life/reality, but the teacher waits as the students struggle with the meaning. Although they (as a whole class) later understand the poem's major point, it is a journey of interpretation. As in discussions outside of school, meaning is found and lost and found again:

TEACHER A: What does it ["Breakings"] mean, James?

JAMES: He learned how to be a farmer on his dad's farm and then he left first to find a new job, and he got—he couldn't find nothing better—he couldn't find nothing good—so he had to go back to working on the farm and hopefully . . . (*Garbled*).

KAY: He left his dad and the dad wanted the son to be just like him—so he got tired of it.

TEACHER A: What do you think he's learned at the end [of the poem]?

BILL: I thought he was at a racetrack.

TEACHER A: What made you think that?

JAMAL: Because it said—the colt—he's kicking up dirt. I thought he was at a racetrack.

TEACHER A: What's he doing with the colt on a long line?

JAMES: He's plowing.

KAY: He's breaking.

JAMES: He's plowing . . . he's training.

KAY: He's training.

ANN: He's trying to get it so that he can break the—

TEACHER A: He's trying to break the colt? . . . Ann, you work with horses, don't you? Have you ever seen them when they put them on a long line—what are they trying to do?

ANN: It's a *lunge* line. They're trying to get them to—have them get used to . . .

TEACHER A: Get used to the thing around their head—what do they call that, a *halter*?

ANN: Yeah. They call it a halter.

TEACHER A: So what else could they be breaking here?

BILL: Breaking him into a plow . . . getting him used to a plow.

TEACHER A: Breaking on the plow. What does a plow do?

BILL: It plows the field.

JAMES: It breaks up the ground.

TEACHER A: Does it break up anything?

BILL: It breaks up the dirt.

TEACHER A: OK. What does this guy say about his feelings about his father?

As the discussion goes on, much is said about what the speaker feels about his father. It may first appear that the students do not immediately understand the metaphorical significance of *breaking*, but they eventually come to the following conclusion:

TEACHER A: What do you think this title, "Breakings," means?

MARY: Breaking of him.

ANN: Breaking the horses.

CURT: Breaking both [of them].

A community of meaning is made.

Teachers ask; they don't tell Teachers who tell students, who talk most of the class time, do not have reader response classrooms. It must be the students who struggle with the literature, who give the answers, and who make the meaning—their own meaning—of the text.

The major tool in these discussions is the question. Although one teacher in this study does give vocabulary synonyms and the other speaks extensively on a related aspect of one of the poems, the teachers resist almost all direct instruction. When confronted with a student question, both teachers turn to other students rather than become the answer giver. Teacher A does not provide students with a list of prese-lected terms but asks twice for words the students do not understand ("Find another word that you don't know the meaning of"), asks for confirmation regarding terms ("Ann, what do they call that, a *halter*?"), and, when she actually looks up one word for a definition, asks students to give her the spelling of the word. She encourages students to struggle to find meaning themselves and, in a typical exchange, tells a student: "Look at *corrugated* in context. . . . Have you ever seen corrugated card-board?" When the student responds, "That word doesn't make sense," the teacher does not correct her or argue but acknowledges the fact and tells the student, "We're going to find out why it doesn't make sense." When confronted with a twenty-second silence regarding the meaning of "Breakings," Teacher A gives two prompts but waits for student answers—which do come, from three students. Even when asked for clarification, the teacher turns to her students.

TEACHER A: What do you think changes in the roles that the dad and the son play?

Anything?

ANDRE: What do you mean by the *roles*?

TEACHER A: Does anyone know here what I mean by the *roles*?

She receives responses to this question, as she does when she asks for an interpretation of a line in "Those Winter Sundays."

TEACHER A: He says in here, let's look down at this bottom line, "speaking *indifferently* to him." What do you think that means?

MIKE: Not any differently than . . .

BOB: Not in a different language.

CURT: Same as everyone, everyone else.

TEACHER A: Why would that be that significant if he's talking to his father the same as everyone else?

ALAN: All fathers are like . . .

CURT: It's probably that same weekend routine.

BILL: Does that mean like *indifferently* to, like than what he usually does—or just to everybody?

TEACHER A: I don't know . . . what do you think?

BILL: It's everybody—he should be talking to his father differently because his father.

Similarly, Teacher B, when asking, "Which of these three [poems] seems to be a *father poem*?" receives two student questions: "What do you mean by that?" and "Which one do you like?" She does not answer, however, letting students argue as to the definition. And the students do subsequently argue in what is the most heated discussion of their particular class.

Teachers ask students to make links to personal experience Requesting that students make links to personal experience is the paramount activity in reader response classrooms. In capable hands, however, it becomes more than students simply venting their opinions. Two events are simultaneous: personal experience is shared and cited, but the students in both teachers' classrooms also pay close attention to the text of the three poems, using it to buttress their points.

One teacher asks students in two separate instances to relate to the anger of the speaker against his father in "Breakings" and receives multiple answers—some students link their assigned household tasks (such as mowing the lawn) to the speaker;

some discuss their general anger toward their parents. During the latter, three students share responses, one for twenty-two seconds.

Certainly the fact that the three poems are central to students' lives—they all have parents, if not on-site fathers—makes such an insistence on linkage of personal experience possible. All of the students have stories and opinions and a history in this area; the discussions, as cited here, might not be as rich if the topic were about building highways or going to war. Yet, as the discussions reveal, the students do more than simply link the poetry to their own lives and experiences. Most of the students return to lines, concepts, and ideas in the literature and—with the teacher's encouragement—they relate to the text as well as doing a capable job examining and even analyzing it.

Teachers affirm students' responses Another characteristic of the methodology of a reader response classroom discussion is that teachers affirm student response to the literature. They can affirm response by overt praise or agreement, but these two classes show that the teachers reinforce their students' responses through three major instructional methods: by referring to student comments in discussion, by asking other students to respond specifically to those comments, and by helping all the students tie their responses back to evidence in the texts. Such actions give powerful confirmation to students that their ideas, their responses, their understandings are legitimate.

In one section of the discussion, approximately seven students respond for a total of three relatively teacher-uninterrupted minutes, taking turns looking at the phrase in question. Another student then moves the discussion to the "speaking indifferently" section and talks, without interruption, for almost one and one-half minutes.

Teacher B repeatedly moves students to respond to other student observations—at least a half-dozen times during the class period. In "Breakings," for instance, she notes: "Jim said you break the spirit of the colt. If we make an analogy here between the father and son, does that make the son bitter—as Rick said?"

The technique has the effect of inspiring students to continue to respond to each other. From this very heated, wide-ranging argument there emerges a question of whose poem is it anyway, a discussion that is about reader response. Theresa starts the discussion, and her comment is almost lost in the uproar. The teacher does not repeat it for the class, but signals the other students to listen.

> **TEACHER B:** Check out Theresa's remark, and let's hear if you agree.
>
> **THERESA:** I think it [the interpretation of the poem as about fathers and sons or fathers and daughters] is determined by the reader and not the poet.
>
> **JOHN:** Yeah, it's neutered. (*Garbled voices; Teacher B calls the class to order.*)
>
> **TEACHER B:** Do you agree that there's a different meaning for the reader, that that's possible?
>
> **THERESA:** Yeah.

RICK: Yeah. Sometimes the poem—you put these allegorical meanings [in it], then it can. But if you just write a straightforward poem, it can't be disputed then. There's, like, no second meaning.

TEACHER B: What kind of poem is a "straightforward" poem?

RICK: What the poet wants to write.

ROB: Like a descriptive poem.

KAREN: Like when he says *he*.

ROB: Like a haiku.

KAREN: Yeah.

JOHN: I think you can interpret it however you want—but you may well be *wrong* in your interpretation. Because I think the poet had a set audience in mind and what he was remembering and what he was trying to get out. So if you want to think of it as a father–daughter thing, you may be wrong, but you're welcome to your own opinion.

JIM: The poet's a man.

KAREN: But you don't know the poet.

RICK: But if the author like released what this . . . pamphlet, this book, . . . is about, is meant to mean, that would take all the fun out of discussing it.

ROB: Well, you see the poet is writing for the poet himself, and that's how he is interpreting it. But other people can read it, and that's how they interpret it.

And how they interpret it, and the very excitement, the very pleasure of discussing it, is at the heart of this reader response classroom. Certainly there is a place for the literary lecture and for an author's biography. Certainly the close reading and New Critical examination of that well-wrought urn can also be an illuminating and rewarding activity. But as Rosenblatt reminds us, when we consider our middle school and high school students and their engagement with literature and the formation of their joy of literature, we must allow them not only the discussion floor itself but also the authority of their own thoughts and instincts. We must also, lest this description be too unduly sunny, be prepared for a classroom where discussions can "pull on differences" and "make trouble":

> One of the killers of good classroom dialogue is students' reticence about noticing the differences in their positions . . . going for consensus in dialogue can often just repress minority views and diverse perspectives. The norm of everyone agreeing just makes the people who think differently shut up. . . . [As teachers we should] help students accustom themselves to participating in civil discussion where differences are visible instead of hidden. (Bomer 2011, 139–140)

The teachers in this study know and convey that different readers can have different interpretations. What they do is not mysterious or arcane or overwhelmingly difficult. What they do, however, is mandatory if we care about literature and about developing our students into lifelong readers. It is an "emotional work for many students, part of learning to be in quality conversations . . . becoming comfortable with disagreement" (Bomer 2011, 149).

TECH TALK: Goodreads Reviews

Goodreads.com is a website dedicated to book lovers of all kinds. Along with many lists of titles and recommendations of books for different ages on different topics, Goodreads also allows participants to track their own reading, follow the reading of their friends, and—best of all—read and write short reviews of any book. On Gooodreads, students can write authentic book reviews for a real audience and receive feedback in the form of comments on their reviews from anywhere in the world. Reviewers can give a book 0–5 stars and can attract their own fans if they write useful and engaging reviews. In the hands of a creative teacher, Goodreads.com can become an occasion for students to generate enthusiasm about reading, writing, and communicating about books.

Reader Response: Uses and Abuses

Especially after reading these exciting give-and-take conversations of the students, it may be hard to think of reader response being abused in a classroom, but a few cautions are in order.

Many well-meaning teachers cite Louise Rosenblatt and reader response theory but are not sure what Rosenblatt has written and what reader response activities mean in a classroom. Certainly reader response does not imply that any student response under any circumstances carries complete authority. Reader response asks the student to bring his or her experience to the literature, and it honors that *connection*. It does not simply use the text as a springboard into irrelevant anecdotes or fanciful thinking, but rather it brings the individual's life experience into dialogue with what the texts says. Reader response maintains that an individual reader can shape a piece of literature through his or her own interpretation, although the limits of that shaping are crucial to delineate. Using a reader response approach in a classroom is *not* an invitation to students or teachers to do any of the following:

✗ Ignore completely what is in the text.

✗ Read into the text facts or inferences that are clearly not present or not defensible.

✘ Insist that "well, that's my opinion" constitutes the last—and unassailable—word on the discussion.

✘ Reveal sensitive aspects of their personal lives as a necessary justification to discuss the literature or defend their points.

A reader's response must be intelligent and thoughtful and have some legitimate tie to the text, however tenuous that might first appear. To consider a discussion in which students do not have to pay any attention to what they have read is not reader response—it's irresponsible.

On the other hand, we cannot insist that students reveal responses to literature that may violate their sense of privacy. Much literature that is worth reading and discussing deals with mature issues. Students can have legitimate responses to that literature—and experience with those issues—but prefer to keep the specifics to themselves. Asking students to make general connections or to discuss if they know of anyone else who has been in a similar situation or felt a similar way can relieve the pressure to reveal. Teacher as *voyeur* is an ugly sight; we do not want to extract from our students, in the name of reader response or any other approach to literature, personal revelations that they would prefer to keep outside the classroom. On the other hand, you may find some students are eager to use your classroom as a way to reveal (to you or to the entire class) very personal details about their own lives. As a teacher you must encourage students to develop an appropriate sense of decorum. You must also be alert for signals that one of your students is experiencing trouble and may need help; in those cases, a consultation with a guidance counselor, a school psychologist, or a trusted administrator or senior colleague is in order.

We must attempt to create a classroom climate where students can bring their own lives and beliefs to the text. Balancing and adjusting that climate is part of the craft of the teacher.

For Your Journal

Pick a short story or poem or play or novel you have read and might like to teach. Think about it from the perspectives of the four lenses: historical or literary background, author biography, New Critical, and reader response. Make a list of questions you might want to ask students that reflect each of the four. Now, look at the questions you developed and write a brief entry on which of the four interests you the most as a teacher/learner. Why? How do you think your students will respond?

Organizing Literature

You may find, especially in the beginning of your teaching, that you follow a textbook's organization of literature and go from Chapter 1 to June 1. You may, practically speaking, be a bit too overwhelmed to do much more creative shaping. As you become more self-assured, however, as you continue not just to be but to *become* a teacher, you will want to experiment and play with how you organize literature for your classes. Such experimentation will help you respond to what your students may be interested in pursuing. After all, ninth-grade or seventh-grade or any-grade English, even when you and your students have a curriculum guide and some form of literature anthology/textbook, can include many different—and wonderful—things not only to read but to discuss and write about.

Let's consider. Most textbooks are arranged in standard patterns. Textbooks—and teachers—typically organize the study of literature in one or more of these ways:

- chronology (such as the Romantic Period, the Harlem Renaissance, and so on)
- author (James Baldwin, F. Scott Fitzgerald)
- theme ("Discovering Oneself," "What Is True Friendship?")
- genre (the short story, poetry).

There are, as you can imagine, benefits to all four patterns. Certainly in survey courses of American and British literature the chronological pattern is the most frequently used; in more general literature courses, theme and genre are popular. Some classes focus on individual writers for brief periods of study. By dipping in and out of chapters, though, by taking some pieces from one section and some from another, the organizational pattern can be adapted. Some textbooks even list in the (often unread) introduction or teacher's manual suggestions on how to use the literature in different configurations. Obviously, you can also mix up the categories and study, for instance, a more complicated version of one pattern by adding to it.

Let us consider poetry (genre) by adding to it:

- modern (late-twentieth and early-twenty-first century) poetry (chronology and genre)
- modern poetry by American writers (chronology, genre, and authors)
- modern poetry by American writers who focused on the loss of the American Dream (chronology, genre, authors, and theme).

What such a series of combinations may do is enrich the consideration and discussion of the literature. Making connections intellectually is what much of our reading is all about; when students are confronted with one of these combinations, they make connections they would not otherwise see.

Theme and Genre: Pleasures and Pitfalls

Asking students to consider literature under the umbrella of a *theme* can be very helpful as students try to make sense of a poem or a novel or a play. It can connect what could otherwise seem so disparate it is impossible to grasp. Linking, for example, pieces of literature that come from different countries and different eras—but that all have a similar theme—may also help students see connections and stimulate questions that might not otherwise be so obvious. Thematic approaches to literature are very popular, and you may find many lists of "text sets" in articles or on websites about teaching literature.

Certainly the three poems discussed in the section on reader response ("Breakings," "Those Winter Sundays," and "Black Walnuts") all share, loosely, the same theme of fathers and children. On the other hand, we need to be very aware that by asking students to see or find a predetermined theme, we can be circumventing their discovery of the literature. And this caution regarding theme does not necessarily mean students should seek some terribly far-out interpretation in the name of rampant individuality. Literature is essentially made new by new readers, and we need to create a classroom atmosphere where, although there is guidance, there is not a preset determination of what a work or poem just might be about. The point is to use a framework such as theme in a rather loose manner. Your students may see themes you have not anticipated and may possibly reject the thematic relation of two pieces of literature—and for good reason. Announcing or insisting that a certain piece or pieces of literature have a set theme is intellectual hostage taking.

In a similar way, the very act of looking at literature only as representative of a specific genre can be as limiting as it can be helpful. Literature is traditionally categorized into *genres*, a term that attempts to capture the marvelous and myriad universe of writing. You recognize the three major terms: *prose*, *poetry*, and *drama*. Prose is further defined/refined into fiction (novels, short stories) and nonfiction (literary nonfiction, such as essays and longer pieces; informational nonfiction, such as contracts, reports, research studies; more on this in Chapter 6).

All of this is helpful in a way but also misleading. You will find, as will your students, that genre—particularly literary genre—is tricky at best. One of Leila's favorite activities is to make three columns on the whiteboard, each headed by the names of the three genres: prose, poetry, and drama. She then asks students to brainstorm characteristics that they think are appropriate for each genre. Students rarely hesitate as most can recall with little difficulty a few characteristics of a play they have seen or a poem or a novel they have read.

After about twenty minutes of coming up with terms and descriptors and moving from genre category to category, she stops and asks students to look, without comment or elimination, at the lists they have made on the board. Students generally find that each genre shares almost identical characteristics, and they realize that when you think about it, it is truly difficult to *define* a genre or type of literature. In fact, each genre often has the characteristics of the others, and sometimes we may feel as if we are, in this game of definition and codification, reduced to saying, "I can't define it, but I know it when I see it."

This argument may seem negative to you, but think about how the questions of the genres can be manipulated into wonderful discussion departures. Consider these intriguing contradictions:

- Fiction vs. Nonfiction: How true is fact? How false is fiction? Where can you draw the line between story and account? What makes fiction fiction? Nonfiction nonfiction? What is the place of creative nonfiction? Given controversies surrounding the "facts" in some nonfiction memoirs (*A Million Little Pieces*, *Three Cups of Tea*), what are the ethics of presenting imagined information as nonfiction?

- Prose vs. Poetry: How much poetry uses flat, proselike statement? Which prose uses figurative language? How compressed is language in poetry? In prose? What makes prose prose? Poetry poetry? What are prose poems?

- Short Story vs. Novel: What makes a short story a short story? A novel a novel? Is a short novel (a novella or a novelette) really a long short story? Why or why not?

- Drama vs. Fiction: What is the drama of a play? Why isn't the dialogue in a short story or novel—or a piece of nonfiction, for that matter—playlike? What makes drama not fiction? Fiction not drama?

Talking about genre in these ways can be interesting to students and can, further, get them to look more critically at what they are reading. And now let's turn to the major genres and how you can select and teach each of them.

Teaching and Selecting Novels and Short Stories

Both contemporary and classic fiction are staples of the English language arts curriculum. Many classic novels used in secondary English classrooms are Western European, specifically, British (such as George Orwell's *1984* or Mary Shelley's *Frankenstein*) and American (such as William Faulkner's *As I Lay Dying* and John Steinbeck's *Of Mice and Men*). There are a number of other recent novels written outside the Western European tradition and used in secondary English classrooms—one such widely read African novel is Chinua Achebe's *Things Fall Apart*—but British and American still tend to dominate in secondary curriculum.

Short stories also have their classics, and although some famous ones are in translation—such as those by Guy De Maupassant—British and American short stories are widely anthologized in many textbooks across the grade levels: Kate Chopin's "The Story of an Hour," Edgar Allan Poe's "Cask of Amontillado," Shirley Jackson's "The Lottery," and that old chestnut, Richard Connell's "The Most Dangerous Game." In addition, there are numerous contemporary short story collections that you can use with your students. (Teacher Don Gallo has compiled a number of wonderful young adult short story collections, and the titles are cited in the Literature Cited section at the end of this chapter.) Regardless of the piece of fiction, however, there are three major issues teachers must consider before approaching a novel or a short story: background, length, and focus. (For further discussions of approaches to novels, see Chapter 3 for *Their Eyes Were Watching God* and *The House on Mango Street*).

Literary Background

What will students need to know to appreciate the novel or short story? When Leila returned to teach high school, the classic she and her students read and studied was F. Scott Fitzgerald's *The Great Gatsby*. As she realized (and recounted partially in *Retracing the Journey* [2007]), all was not well.

Leila recalls: Although I thought I had prepared my students for the 1920s setting and characters—not to mention telling them that the book was an American classic and filled with shimmering language—it was clear that I had not done so sufficiently. My students had little problem with the vocabulary, but they needed more background than I anticipated. About a third of the way through the novel, in class discussion the students showed that they were clearly flummoxed by characters who spent all day entertaining themselves and were so wealthy that they never needed to work or clean the house or do the usual mundane chores that most of us perform. How had I missed stressing this essential point about economics? We went back to talk about it, but I feel that my misjudgment regarding the need for extensive background preparation made the reading of this novel not as powerful I had hoped. Many of the students genuinely disliked the movie we saw after our reading, but it did give them a visual on which to focus and made the setting of the novel far more explicit. In hindsight, I should have used the movie earlier to capture for students the wealth and opulence of Gatsby's life and the setting of the novel. Sadly, my misperception about the background my students needed made the reading of *The Great Gatsby* tedious and puzzling.

As with Leila's experience teaching *The Great Gatsby*, other novels also cannot be taught effectively without giving students careful background understanding. Teaching Twain's *The Adventures of Huckleberry Finn* without a clear understanding of the culture of the time of the novel, for example, risks reinscribing racism in readers instead of enlightening audiences to injustice, as it did when Twain first wrote it. And asking students to simply dive into a Shakespeare play without some understanding of the language and the setting of the play is bound to result in confusion, frustration, and probably boredom.

It's a bit different with short stories that often give readers everything they need regarding background in the first few paragraphs and are rarely as tricky as novels. Some short stories can, though, require prereading and contextual information. Regardless, try to look at the piece as if you were reading it for the first time—what will your students need to know before reading or very quickly into the reading so that they do not become frustrated? To understand the setting of a short story such as "Cask of Amontillado" (written some 150 years ago), students will need to know about wine and wine cellars as well as what Poe calls "the supreme madness of the carnival season" (not all of your students will be familiar with Carnival and Mardi Gras). Chopin's "The Story of an Hour" may need some vocabulary glossing for, despite its very short and straightforward tale, words such as *aquiver, bespoke, elixir, importunities,* and *grip-sack* may interfere with student understanding. Before reading a story like Charlotte Perkins Gilman's "The Yellow Wallpaper," today's students may need more information about the marriage conventions of the time as well as legal rights regarding husbands and wives.

Length

Short stories are rarely longer than a dozen pages, and this brevity is part of their great utility and interest. You and your students can read a short story in one class and respond and discuss it fairly efficiently. Novels, however, are often a different matter, and keeping students motivated and reading can be tough. If the novel is a long one, such as *Frankenstein* or *Beloved,* you need to think of pacing for your students. Having some students responsible for some chapters—using a jigsaw arrangement where students in groups read selected chapters and then become experts who teach other students about the chapters—and limiting your time is important. If the novel is short, it may well be possible to read much of it aloud or in class. Study guides for chapters—those that ask questions that highlight complicated, interesting themes and plot points—can also be helpful, especially if students create them themselves. In the high school class Leila taught, student groups crafted guides and picked out, on their own, important vocabulary, interesting quotations, striking poetic passages, the latter of which was especially appropriate for *The Great Gatsby.* And from these study guides, shared in class, students as a group were able to select items for the final novel test, making the test far more student-centered than a teacher could have created alone. As noted before, the class as a whole did not like *Gatsby,* but the study guides were helpful, and the test grades were high.

In his tenth-grade classes, Ken taught a lesson centered on feminism that included three dramas: Ibsen's *A Doll's House,* Glaspell's "Trifles," and Douglas Johnson's "Plumes." Ken arranged six groups, each of which read only one of the three plays, and then they answered questions about feminism. The groups then jigsawed to teach each other about the plays they read (each group had members who read each of the plays), and they worked together on presentations on different aspects of feminism. Breaking up and sharing the reading of long or difficult texts and incorporating relevant projects can enliven literary study and embed the development of important skills.

Focus

If you worry about being a conscientious English teacher, you think that you need to cover all of the major "parts" of a novel or short story, that is, plot, character, theme, setting. Don't forget, though, that all fiction is not alike; some writers are great on plotting and moving characters through intricate settings; some use a bare plot and concentrate on character. Setting is important in some fiction and purely backdrop in others. So what do you do? Pay attention to the literature you choose, adapt your plans appropriately, and try to resist trotting your students through every literary element.

Use state and NCTE learning standards to help plan where to use what literature to achieve which objectives. And remember, too, that for some students new to the literature, there will be insights and emphases that you had not anticipated. It is powerful when you can follow students' interests, because they may choose to focus on an aspect of the fiction that you had not anticipated. These are some of the very best moments for English teachers!

One final caution about reading classic novels and short stories: with the wide availability of summaries on myriad websites—SparkNotes, Cliffs Notes, GradeSaver, and other such "study aids"—many of your students will surely read commercial summaries rather than the literature itself. If nothing else, this is a real reason to look beyond canonical, classic literature and choose something recently written for which there are no prepackaged materials. In addition, keep this very much in mind if you ask your students to write formal essays or responses on works such as Richard Wright's *Native Son* or Jane Austen's *Pride and Prejudice*; there are countless standard research papers for sale on the Internet, and some students will not be able to resist the temptation. You might even consider ways to include commercial summaries into your teaching, so students learn to think of these as enhancements rather than as replacements for reading the texts. And, by all means, talk with your students about the importance of academic honesty and how purchasing prewritten papers ultimately hurts them. New emphasis on standardized exams has unfortunately given rise to many cheating scandals, and it's a good idea to address these matters with your students at several points throughout the year.

Teaching and Selecting Poetry

Let's tell the truth: many teachers are scared of poetry. Some feel that every poem has a set meaning and that if they do not teach and convey that meaning in their teaching, any work with the poem is incomplete. In addition, because many teachers are fearful of the "meaning" of poems, they often deflect the issue entirely by spending most of their time teaching literary terms and making sure that every student knows the two metaphors, the one instance of assonance, and the rhyme scheme of the poem. Obviously, we don't agree: poems don't need owner's manuals before they can be read and appreciated. In fact, you can teach poems that are puzzles (think of Emily Dickinson's poems, many examples of which are deliberately ambiguous and tantalizing) and not necessarily explain to students—or even know yourself—every aspect of every line. Further, we think that to enforce the knowledge and identification of all literary terms in a poem seems to us artificial and counterproductive. Reading poetry and talking about it can enrich your class—and if every student and even you are not sure exactly what every line means or cannot pinpoint every image in the piece, you can still fill your classroom with the music and magic of poetry. Poems can touch students in ways that fiction and nonfiction and even drama do not, and when you add poetry to your literature teaching, everyone is enriched.

Textbook anthologies, either hardbound or electronic, routinely contain poetry classics, and although your favorite piece may be something by Gwendolyn Brooks or Walt Whitman or John Keats, remember that contemporary poetry is a treasure trove and you should think of bringing in poems from other sources. Billy Collins, Mary Oliver, Rita Dove, Nikki Giovanni, Robert Pinsky, Naomi Shihab Nye, and others have numerous, accessible fine poems that students can readily read and understand. Regardless, as with any literature, you need to be sure that students have sufficient background if the poem makes important (and obscure) allusions. W. B. Yeats' "The Second Coming" cannot be read without some sort of introduction to the poet's world view as well as Christian theology (think of "slouches toward Bethlehem," for instance), whereas Robert Frost's central image of "two roads diverged in a yellow wood" requires little prior discussion. At any rate, if you tackle something as complex as John Donne's "A Valediction Forbidding Mourning," know that you cannot just hope students will get the poem on their own. For truly mature and older poems, your expertise will be needed or students will be frustrated and turned off. And, frankly, that is one good reason to use poetry that is more accessible than the canonical poems of the greats. Yes, we want to get our students to know and appreciate canonical literature, but doing so requires using more accessible literature as stepping stones, scaffolds, to these more challenging texts.

How can we use poetry in our classes? Teaching extensive poetry units is not a good idea because reading and studying numerous poems over an extended period of days can exhaust even the most enthusiastic of students (see Limit Your Time in the teaching tips section later in this chapter). But poetry can be used in many different ways and dropped into classes or studied and read for a day or two. For example, Chapter 6, on nonfiction and informational texts, shows how a single poem can be used as a "texture" or "context" text while students read a longer work on a similar theme. In addition, poetry can be its own object of study, a companion to or extension of other literature, a vehicle for literary appreciation, and, happily, an inspiration for creative writing. Let's look briefly at each one in turn.

Poetry as an Object of Study

Some poems are true classics, such as many of the sonnets of Shakespeare, the nature poetry of Williams Wordsworth, and the poetry that emerged from the Harlem Renaissance. If you are teaching one or more of these poems, poetry can indeed then be an object of study. Its historical placement may be of real interest, and the background of the author may also be important to include. Poetry as an object of study can also include genre consideration—yes, how in the world do we define a poem? What kinds of features do we most often find in poems? And, in this case, consideration of the huge range of poetic devices and their effect is appropriate. Poetry can also, however, be beautifully paired with other literature.

Poetry as a Companion to Other Literature

Poems can also be used as parallel pieces to prose and drama, and some poems can be linked to characters or themes. The range of this possibility is huge; your students can search out poems that they think represent themes in something they have read; they can select a poem that they feel the main characters would appreciate and tell why. One obvious pairing is Langston Hughes' "Dream Deferred" and Lorraine Hansberry's play *Raisin in the Sun*. But also think, for instance, of Emily Dickinson's poem that begins, "Hope is the thing with feathers": Which of the Loman family in Arthur Miller's *Death of a Salesman* might like that poem especially and think it represents his or her life? Which characters might find it irrelevant?

Poetry as a Vehicle for Literary Appreciation

It may seem a bit odd to suggest that you could read a poem aloud at the beginning or end of a class and just let it be heard, not discussed or tested or written about, but poetry can serve just that kind of function in the English classroom—as it also can do outside the classroom in any kind of organized poetry slams. Nonsense poems and poems with strong rhyme work well for this activity, as do poems that capture current happenings or conditions. For instance, Leila shared Mary Oliver's "First Snow" one fall when an unexpected two inches of the white stuff fell in Virginia; Ken's students in New York don't think of fall snow as unusual (or, for that matter, particularly inspiring). In addition, performance of poetry can help students appreciate the sound of poems; acting out in pairs or larger groups, students can experience the drama and music of large numbers of poetry. Poetry slams and performances in settings outside school, such as local bookstores, show students that poetry is not just restricted to a rarified atmosphere. Even national poetry recitation contests, such as Poetry Out Loud, can inspire your students to make poetry something powerful and meaningful for them.

Poetry as an Inspiration for Creative Writing

They may not win any prizes, but most students enjoy attempting a variety of poetic forms: haiku, acrostics or name poems, sonnets, poems that are in shapes (think of George Herbert's "Easter-Wings"). Found poetry, the making of poems by breaking prose into lines (news articles are good sources as are some sections of novels), can also intrigue students and show them the close relation of prose and poetry. We also occasionally like to make a game with poetry writing. We prepare four grab bags, and students must choose slips of paper from each and then write a poem. One recent selection by students yielded an animal, elephant; a color, scarlet; a sound, boom; and a taste, salty. Writing in response to poems and using a genre other than the essay or journal entry—such as a letter, a diary entry, a series of questions—can be similarly intriguing. Poetry is meant to uplift and inspire; using it in this manner can open writing and creative expression in your students.

TECH TALK: *Composing Haikus and Acrostic Poems*

NCTE's Read/Write/Think website, described in a previous Tech Talk, also includes interactives that help students and teachers write poetry. Try the haiku poem interactive—http://bit.ly/1m9x5I0—which gives students a space to list brainstorming words and the number of syllables in them, and then provides a chart in which to write the lines of haiku. Finally, the program allows students to select a text style and background so they can print out an artistic version of their haiku.

The acrostic poem generator—http://bit.ly/1cTPeA4—helps students write poems that begin with a topic word and list a word or phrase that begins with each letter in the topic word and that relates to the topic word. The generator guides students through a brainstorming phase and then allows them to print out their results.

When you begin to work with poems, remember that even though students have a copy of the poem in front of them or projected on a screen, all poems need to be read aloud. The sound and the music of the words is essential to their understanding and appreciation of the poem, and if all your students do is read the poem silently, many of them may not hear the emphasis and may struggle unnecessarily with the craft of the lines and the meaning. A quick Internet search will help you find many ideas for choral readings and other creative ways to have students read poems aloud together in ways that also facilitate critical reading. And if the poem is not a complex classic that requires preparation and background and you still are puzzled about approaching it, after it is read aloud ask your students to follow these quick and sensible suggestions from *Do I Really Have to Teach Reading?* by Cris Tovani:

- Circle passages you like.
- Write three questions about the poem.
- Make a connection from this poem to a personal experience.
- Look at the title of the poem; how does it seem to relate to the poem itself? (2004, 119)

Teaching and Selecting Plays

Leila's Story

Drama is one of the most positive factors in a school curriculum, and many students find that experience with acting changes their attitude toward school life and toward themselves. Certainly that was true of me: working with all sorts of drama was an activity I treasured, and my junior and senior English teachers encouraged our participation in musicals and plays and even, as a project, had us write and stage an original play. I started acting and singing in junior high school, continued it in high school and college, and also did some directing. In my very first teaching situation, I was named the drama coach—and although the rehearsals and performances added many hours to my already full schedule, and I'm not sure I knew as much as I needed to do the job, I found that working with kids and plays was almost exhilarating. Students who were not responsive in class came alive on stage, and those who would not turn in homework really did learn their lines. Shy students seemed to become bolder when they interacted with characters on stage, and I experienced a level of trust with students that at times was hard to achieve in my own English classroom. (For more information on drama in the classroom and its effect on student learning, see Betty Jane Wagner's [1998] *Educational Drama and Language Arts: What Research Shows*; Paula Ressler's [2002] *Dramatic Changes* outlines how gender identity issues can be approached thorough drama.)

Ken's Story

I took two theatre courses in college, and I acted in one play, but I'm a pretty bad actor, and I was much better the semester I was the stage manager. (Turns out I'm a real ham only when I play myself.) But I absolutely loved teaching drama in high school. I enjoyed that students could read parts out loud, that we would all experience turns in plots and sudden reveals together, and I delighted in teaching Shakespeare. My favorite play to teach was *Julius Caesar*, a staple in our tenth-grade curriculum. The other teachers spent a few weeks on the play at most, but I was infamous in the school for spending more. I was fascinated by the intrigue of Cassius' plotting, Brutus' naïveté and constant dithering, Caesar's blinding ambition, Calpurnia's and Portia's strength and wise (and also completely ignored) advice, Marc Antony's fiery eloquence, and Cicero's aloof wisdom. I incorporated texts about rhetoric and public speaking and about ancient Rome and that era's forms of government and warfare. I confess it was probably all too much for the students, some of whom were antsy that we weren't getting through the play fast enough. I also tried to time it so we would act out the assassination of Caesar on March 15th, the Ides of March. We'd have an Ides of March party, complete with Roman food (bread, cheese, grapes, and olives—with red grape juice "wine") and toga costumes. In hindsight I know that party was fun, but it didn't actually promote much student learning. Doing it again, I'd try to tie my teaching of the play—and the Ides of March party—closer to objectives to embed more learning into the fun.

Drama does indeed have power, and you do not have to launch a full play or know about blocking and lighting to use it effectively in your teaching. When you select or use a play, though, know that it is not just a short novel with dialogue and those pesky interruptions of stage directions. Drama comes alive only in its natural element, performance. So whether you have students take parts and read lines as they are seated or standing in front of the class or if you have small groups act out selected scenes in your room or even on a stage with props and lighting, plays must be *heard and seen* to be understood. Certainly student reading is important, but this is one reason that many teachers also use filmed versions of plays so that students can see how those stage directions actually work and how emphases on lines can be varied. Although the language and plot and character of drama are all worthy of examination, the *play* is the thing indeed, and you are not honoring the power of drama unless you actually use it as it was intended—performance. Lawrence Olivier's 1944 film adaption of Shakespeare's *Henry V* is especially interesting because it begins as a staged performance in the Globe Theatre and then transforms into a more stylized, modern film production. The first part gives students a real sense of what a play staged in Shakespeare's time was like.

But what plays can you use? There will be some in your textbook anthology and probably some play sets in your English department office. Here are some other ideas:

- Classic plays include *Twelve Angry Men* by Reginald Rose, *The Crucible* and *Death of a Salesman* by Arthur Miller, *Raisin in the Sun* by Lorraine Hansberry, *Our Town* by Thornton Wilder, and *A Doll's House* by Henrik Ibsen.

- Somewhat more contemporary plays include *Lost in Yonkers* by Neil Simon, *Driving Miss Daisy* by Alfred Uhry, and August Wilson's *Fences*.

- If you are looking for a variety of short dramas, try Don Gallo's *Center Stage* or Judith Barlow's *Plays by American Women*.

- *Beyond the Bard: Fifty Plays for Use in the English Classroom* by Joshua Rutsky is focused and gives solid teaching suggestions for half a hundred plays.

Regardless of what play or plays you choose, remember that drama is not just another text to be read and discussed. Short or long, classic or contemporary, let the lines and the characters live in your classroom. And don't feel that students need to read all of a play aloud; having them prepare small portions to present is as powerful. Especially with complex plays, asking the class to attempt an entire work can be overwhelming. For suggestions about warm-ups before reading and performance, see Let Them Act It Out in the teaching tips section later in this chapter.

And now to the most widely read playwright in the secondary English curriculum, Mr. William Shakespeare.

Teaching and Selecting the Plays of Shakespeare

Shakespeare's work is challenging, iconic, difficult, rewarding, and magic. Despite the centuries between the inception and contemporary readers, his plays and poetry are eminently worth your time and that of your students. Teachers in almost all schools in this country teach a Shakespearian play or two almost every year; it's a staple of most

English language arts curricula, and there are many ways, as you will see, to use—and learn to love—the Bard.

Giving Your Students Background

Let us caution you briefly about background when reading and discussing the plays. Although your students may benefit from knowing something about the Elizabethan Age—the language, the culture, the politics—we have always felt it misguided that many teachers spend too much time on that subject, taking time away from the literature. Further, what English class has not been subjected to countless lectures on *where* Shakespeare's plays were physically performed—the Globe Theatre, its construction and layout—if not asked to construct detailed models of that theatre? Nothing is wrong with some attention to historical context, but, again, it can usurp the major point of studying Shakespeare at all—and the point is the text. So give that background briefly: if it takes over a quarter of the time you have allotted for Shakespeare, you need to reconsider the proportion of classroom time spent on background. Some great references for brushing up your Shakespeare include the following:

- E. M. W. Tillyard's (1943) *The Elizabethan World Picture* is a classic, packed with information, and brief.

- Stephen Greenblatt's (2004) *Will in the World* is similarly illuminating and also speculates on the personal life of Shakespeare.

- The Folger Shakespeare Library's website is a veritable candy store of excellent lesson ideas, video clips, and more.

- A 2009 *English Journal*, guest edited by Michael LoMonico, celebrates the Folger's Teaching Shakespeare Institute's twenty-fifth anniversary with an issue full of great ideas for focusing students actively on Shakespeare's language.

Shakespeare's Language

One of the major reasons many teachers love teaching Shakespeare is the language. Across the centuries, it stands and endures and calls. Shakespeare has crept into our conversation, our phrases, quips, and titles—from "all the world's a stage" (*As You Like It*) to "green-ey'd jealousy" (*Merchant of Venice*) to "hark, hark, the lark" (*Cymbeline*) to "double, double, toil and trouble" (*Macbeth*) to "how sharper than a serpent's tooth it is / To have a thankless child" (*King Lear*). Our students know to "beware the ides of March" (*Julius Caesar*); they can complete the line "Romeo, Romeo, wherefore art thou Romeo" (*Romeo and Juliet*); and "the winter of our discontent" (*Richard the Third* and as borrowed by John Steinbeck) may strike a vague chord of recognition. Most of our students, consciously or unconsciously, know some Shakespeare. On a more elevated level, the words of Shakespeare have a freshness and sharpness that is worth our students' attention and study.

Using Quotations to Teach Shakespeare

Along with strong imagery, gripping plots, and believable characters, Shakespeare gives us, as teachers and students, an utterly ringing collection of phrases, aphorisms, and quips. There are thousands of memorable quotations from Shakespeare's plays, and they illumine not only the plays but life itself. As Pope (1961) writes in "An Essay on Criticism," "True Wit is Nature to advantage dress'd, / What oft was thought, but ne'er so well expressed" (l. 297). Shakespeare is the essence of true wit to advantage dressed. Studying quotations can be a helpful tool to organize discussion of his plays in the English classroom.

Using quotations to teach Shakespeare

- makes students focus on the specifics of the language

- helps students deal with the complexity of the plays by using smaller units to discuss and focus

- provides a structuring device of part for the whole, and

- encourages students to memorize—or own—the language.

The broad range of the plays can be highly intimidating to our students. Reducing a scene to the consideration of a single quotation can help students "manage" the play and, further, consideration of the smaller idea within the quotation can help them get a handle on the larger theme. Although it is, of course, a fallacy to blithely assume that the part can stand always and conveniently for the whole, a more limited observation or a more circumscribed comment can illumine a wider field. Finally, close work with a small number of quotations can encourage students to familiarize themselves with if not actually memorize the language—students can thus "own" the words of Shakespeare, and the effect can be long range and electrifying.

Quotations and scene summaries A common and pragmatic technique to help students understand the bare bones of the action is having students, after reading a number of scenes, summarize the events/facts by writing a one-sentence précis for each scene. Students have three choices of how they could write their scene summaries: standard English, Elizabethan English, or a home dialect of English (African American English, working-class vernacular English, or a regional dialect of English). Each choice can yield somewhat different results and adds a bit of creativity to the assignment.

From our experience, summaries in standard English are more geared to student understanding or attempted understanding of the facts of the scene. Summaries in Elizabethan English offer this same advantage, but the students' approximations are not only often hilarious, they can be wildly inventive and occasionally almost astoundingly close to the original. Summaries in the latest versions of fast-paced hip-hop, tough-talking working-class vernacular, or upper-class East Coast gentility often offer witty revelations of the students' factual appreciation of the action; in addition, this unusual language occasionally comments subtly on the play. Obviously, however, such an emphasis on scene summaries—on what happened—tends to make students concentrate on plot, requiring them to digest and understand more of the action than the subtlety of subtext.

Teaching of Shakespeare changes accordingly. A teacher can move away from summary to quotations. Students pick from each scene the single line or lines they feel are the most significant. Students then write a brief paragraph of justification, including who said what to whom, in what context, and why this quotation has been chosen over others.

The instructional advantage of using quotations, as opposed to the summaries, is that students can then discuss what they picked and why. Displaying two or three most frequent choices and opening the floor for large-group discussion or having students who chose the same—or very different—quotations work in groups yields lively discussion and talk. Let's see how this works specifically with a quotation from *Othello*.

A quotation from Act V, Scene ii of Othello After students have read or acted out scenes in class, it is also possible to have the class as a whole agree on a central quotation and discuss why it merits being the majority choice. Why, for example, in Leila's class, did students argue that, in Act V, Scene ii of *Othello*, "I that am cruel am yet merciful; / I would not have thee linger in thy pain" (ll. 86–87) was a more significant line than the famous "Put out the light, and then put out the light" (l. 7) and the even more well-known "one that lov'd not wisely but too well" (l. 344)? Just what was cruel, what was merciful, and what Othello perceived as lingering in pain were part of the discussion. The light imagery and all its resonance of putting it out was not, for this class at least, of interest; perhaps the very famous loving wisely but too well comment seemed hackneyed and, furthermore, so patently false it was not worth consideration: How could this murderer be accused of loving, at least on a surface interpretation, "too well"?

In addition, Leila's students also passed up from that scene Emilia's poetic and powerful incremental repetition of "My husband!" as she listens incredulously to Othello's accounting of just how he knows of Desdemona's betrayal; students similarly gave barely a glance to the "as ignorant as dirt" (l. 164) quotation (an insult still used widely in many regions); they did not select the powerful justification Iago makes for his own perfidy ("I told [Othello] what I thought, and told no more / Than what he found himself was apt and true" [ll. 176–77]). For these students, the "cruel yet merciful" quotation was of central importance: it relates to Othello's assessment of his own character and actions and his stubborn refusal, at this point in the scene at least, to see the truth of Desdemona's fidelity. The discussion of the quotation also leads to the kind of close reading we can do in class, examination that is essential to this kind of selection.

TECH TALK: *Composing Illuminated Texts*

To engage students in close reading of poetic or other literary texts, have them create what former Stony Brook University methods instructor Mike LoMonico calls "illuminated text." Traditionally, an illuminated text (often from the medieval era) has brightly colored initials and letters, gilded edges, or even illustrations of scenes that mark particularly important sections of the book. LoMonico's version asks students to create hyperlinks within a short text that make interesting and illuminating insights about the text. Links might be made to photographs of animals or people mentioned, to maps or photos of places, informational sites, or anything else a reader finds will lend analysis or interpretation to a text. Any simple blog program, such as Wordpress.com, works. Here is an example from one of Mike's former students, Sasha Guirindongo, who is now a reading coach in New York City: http://bit.ly/1USCmEd.

Acting out quotations The use of dramatics, performance-based teaching of Shakespeare, is an indispensable part of considering the plays. As discussed previously in this chapter, drama is not meant just to be read but to be heard, seen, and performed: the words should be felt in the body and in the mouth. Using quotations, students can experiment with inflection and intonation as they perform the quotations they choose, performances that necessarily reflect alternative interpretations. Miriam Gilbert, in her "Teaching Shakespeare Through Performance," recommends "deprivation" exercises: not only miming the lines rather than speaking them but also "telegramming" them or "reducing [the lines] to the smallest number of words that will convey the message" and then performing them. She reminds us that "performance-based teaching needs to work toward discussion" (1984, 605) that will reveal the number of interpretations any group of students will find in Shakespeare's lines.

Quotations and tests As quotations can be used to discuss the plays and their implications, so also can they be used with essay tests. It is possible to present a number of quotations to students, have them pick out a requisite number (for example, five out of ten or seven out of fifteen), and ask them to write on each one. In their essays, students should include who said the lines to whom at approximately what juncture in the play. Students should then discuss the significance of the speech and its wider meaning. Context—who is speaking to whom when—can be most interesting, and even if students are mistaken in their memory or judgment, it can invite them to consider just what that line or lines might mean and why they were spoken. The wider significance is helpful in that it asks students to consider the ramifications of the lines both before and after the actual incident.

In selecting such a list of quotations, it would seem that students should have some familiarity with the range of lines before the test; to present students a list of relatively unknown quotations—regardless of the possibility of choice—is self-defeating and anxiety producing. The point is to look at the line or lines and see context and wider dimension. Similarly, students can choose a limited set of quotations—one for each act is a possibility, a central single line is another—and write on why that quotation or quotations is/are important.

For Your Journal

Pick a Shakespearean play you like or have enjoyed before. Pick an act and reread it: what quotations seem important to you? Why? What discussion questions could come from those quotations? Which quotations could be used to act out parts of the play or from which to create an illuminated (see Tech Talk) text? Is there any quotation students could write about? What should students focus on as they write?

Teaching and Selecting Young Adult Literature

There has been, even before the advent of the "dime" novel in the nineteenth century in this country, literature that has been specifically written for and marketed to the younger reader, the young adult. Known first by the term *juvenile* (which has unfortunate contemporary connotations and has slipped out of usage as a term simply synonymous with *young*) and then alternately by the terms *young adult*, *YA*, or *adolescent*, this literature started in modern form in 1967 with the publication of sixteen-year-old S. E. (Susie) Hinton's novel *The Outsiders*, the gripping story of two embattled groups of teenagers, the Greasers and the Socs. Realistic dialogue, a strong plot, and compelling characters are all part of *The Outsiders*, and the novel, somewhat akin to J. D. Salinger's *Catcher in the Rye*, struck a chord with young readers. Susie Hinton's first effort signaled an avalanche of writing that continues, unabated, to this day and goes by the term *young adult* (YA) literature.

For many teachers, especially those unfamiliar with quality YA literature, the whole field seems unnecessary or, possibly, necessary only for students who are unable to handle the intricacies of "real" adult literature. That argument ignores the fact that many of our students just stop reading around the middle school years and never take the habit back up. It also dismisses the fact that excellent, sophisticated literature has been written by YA novelists, including Laurie Halse Anderson, Christopher Crutcher, Sharon G. Flake, A.S. King, and many others. Developing lifelong readers is tricky, and for some young people, the shift from elementary school to middle school and above leaves their reading far behind. YA literature can provide an important and crucial bridge.

To keep our students reading, YA literature provides a useful and quality transition. Certainly there is formula fiction. R. L. Stine's Goosebumps and Fear Street series are still popular as are Ann M. Martin's Babysitters Club series and Francine Pascal's 152-book series Sweet Valley High, but they form only part of the YA genre. More challenging YA work is reviewed in national journals and newspapers, critiqued by professors and librarians and professional writers, and awarded honors and medals, such as the Newbery, the Coretta Scott King, the Michael L. Prinz Book Award, the Orbis Pictus, and others. The Harry Potter series stands as the biggest of them all with tens of millions of readers worldwide, but other series books are strong: Hunger Games, Divergent, Uglies, Twilight, Vampire Academy, and Mortal Instruments also count millions of readers and, in some cases, a similar number of viewers of the successful movies based on the books. YA author John Green is a current very hot ticket, and *Looking for Alaska* and *The Fault in Our Stars* are at the top of many young people's reading lists. Veteran YA author Jacqueline Woodson has scored both a Newbery award and a National Book award for *Brown Girl Dreaming*. In addition to the blockbuster series books, there is a startling variety in the field: poetry, short stories, plays, nonfiction, and, of course, novels of adventure, romance, horror, science fiction, historical fiction, fantasy—all in almost any conceivable area of interest.

Definition of YA Literature

What makes a YA novel YA? Until the publication of J. K. Rowling's Harry Potter series, there were reliable and consistent characteristics, which included a stripped-down plot with very few, if any, subplots; a limited number of characters; a compressed time span and a restricted setting; and an approximate length of 125 to 200 pages. Although there are still many YA books that fit this definition, it is no longer the standard. Rowling changed the game of the YA genre, and other writers followed suit. Individual books in her Harry Potter series are as long as 900 pages and feature numerous subplots, multiple characters, and, for the series as a whole, a time span of over seven years with wide-ranging settings and flashbacks. So, again, what makes a YA novel YA? Now, the most consistent and important indicator is a single factor: the protagonist is a teenager or young adult.

This can make selecting YA literature somewhat tricky, but it may help to consider what YA is *not*. For sure, young adults, your students, will read "classics" with teen protagonists—such as Mark Twain's *Huckleberry Finn* or William Golding's *Lord of the Flies*; such novels are, however, not considered YA literature. Similarly, contemporary novels popular with adults and young people, such as those written by Danielle Steel, John Grisham, David Baldacci, Nicholas Sparks, and much of the work of Stephen King, are also not in the category of YA literature. Commencing with the publication of *The Outsiders* and written for and marketed to young people, the YA genre is somewhat apart. It is also a unique genre that can lead students (many of whom are not ready to make the shift from children's literature to adult literature, from *Charlotte's Web* to *Jane Eyre* and *Great Expectations*) into reading and the enjoyment of literature.

Concerns About YA Literature

There is no fudging the fact of the matter, though: YA literature, at least in the schools, has still not entered the curriculum in any widespread way. Four issues are the more than likely culprits:

- the question of quality
- the concern for the classics
- the subject matter and language in YA novels
- text complexity and YA literature in the era of new college- and career-ready standards.

The question of quality As mentioned before, many people, especially those who have not read YA literature, worry that the novels are just not well written. Certainly those novels that earn the Newbery Medal are not in this category, nor are those that make the best lists of the numerous journals that review YA literature, among them the *ALAN Review, School Library Journal, Booklist, VOYA, English Journal, Horn Book Magazine*, and *Journal of Reading*. The fear persists, however, especially for those who are unfamiliar with YA literature, that these "junior" novels are nothing other than monuments to mediocrity and not worth students' time. According to these critics, students will stay mired in the worst of this literature and never develop a taste for more mature works.

Our experience both as readers and teachers does not confirm this belief. Our students need to read a whole lot, and not all of what they read should necessarily be immortal prose or poetry. G. Robert Carlsen, a strong voice for YA literature, wrote years ago in *Books and the Teenage Reader* regarding what he called *subliterature* and suggested that students need to read such material and would move beyond it. Very little YA literature could be termed *subliterature*, but the point is a valid one. Our reading has to go through stages, and when we tell our students that one year it is quality children's books, such as *The Phantom Tollbooth*, and the next it is a classic, such as Nathaniel Hawthorne's *The House of Seven Gables*, we may lose a number of readers and never regain them.

The concern for the classics Another fear is that if students read YA literature, they will not read the classics. This implies an either/or situation in which students have a highly limited time to read and does not seem to be borne out by the experience of real readers. In fact, it would appear that many readers read both genres simultaneously, just as adults often relax with light (some term it "mindless") reading and keep at their bedside more serious works. Pairing young adult novels with classic novels, as bridges to each other, is also an effective way to use both kinds of literature, and there are numerous resources that offer suggestions and lesson plans for taking more traditional books and putting them with quality YA novels.

At any rate, insisting that students read classics or nothing often results in the latter: students, confronted with literature with which they can make little personal connection, choose, often quietly but often permanently, to stop reading altogether—or to confine reading to only that which is required by English class.

The subject matter and language in YA novels Along with other issues such as the place of the classics and young adult literature, the question of censorship is a very real one when teachers consider using YA literature in class. All of the hot topics—sex, drugs, suicide, parental tensions, race, poverty—are touched on in much YA literature, and often the characters speak in realistic dialogue incorporating slang and an occasional obscenity. In fact, the realism of much of YA literature may be part of its popularity with young people. Again, the issue is polarized: all good literature addresses the hot topics, but for many people, unfortunately some teachers and librarians included, hot topics are acceptable in antique dress but not in today's clothing. There is nothing Sherman Alexie's frequently censored *The Absolutely True Diary of a Part-Time Indian* discusses that William Shakespeare or Nathaniel Hawthorne or Herman Melville avoids. Put the same themes in modern times, however, and discuss them in contemporary language, and many people become wary and worry that young people will be exposed to something they might otherwise never learn—or will learn sometime in that distant future when they can "handle" it. Truth be told, life is not that way, and young people need truth in today's language as much as in the language of yesteryear.

Keeping students reading is one of the gifts of YA literature; it is a powerful tool we can use both in and outside the classroom and can provide a bridge to more sophisticated, lengthy and complicated reading.

Text complexity and YA literature in the era of college- and career-ready standards One of the most controversial aspects of the Common Core State Standards implementation is the rather simplistic way it encourages raising the average text complexity of works recommended for each grade level. Many classic texts have simply been dropped two to three years from where they have been traditionally taught, so that, for example, *The Odyssey,* which has been traditionally taught at eleventh or twelfth grade, is now recommended for ninth or tenth grade. As a result, teachers are being encouraged to teach complex masterpieces to the exclusion of more engaging, accessible texts. In truth, students will never read works they dislike or don't understand with as much effort as texts they find engaging and that make them feel successful. That doesn't mean pandering to students or falling victim to low expectations, but it does mean we should provide students with a wide range of texts to read. By all means, include difficult, challenging texts—and scaffold them properly. But using YA literature as bridges to these texts and as worthy on its own is an important ingredient in getting students to develop the mature, sophisticated skills that reading, understanding, and appreciating complex texts require.

New Kid on the Block: The Graphic Novel

Although YA literature occupies a corner in some English classrooms, graphic novels have not been widely accepted into many school district curricula. The genre is rapidly developing, however, and it is expanding into wider spheres. For instance, Scholastic, a well-respected and long-established publisher of young adult and other fiction, launched Graphix, a division devoted solely to graphic novels (such as Jeff Smith's classic, funny, and appealing Bone series) and to student creation of and interest in comics. The American Library Association (ALA) features a "Great Graphic Novels for Teens" list among its more traditional book lists and book awards and regularly updates nominations to the list. Scholarly and historical books, such as Scott McCloud's (1994) *Understanding Comics* and Stephen Weiner's (2003) *Faster Than a Speeding Bullet: The Rise of the Graphic Novel*, provide background and frame for this unusual genre.

Some of this may be a surprise to you, and some of it may not. Certainly you may know graphic novels from two examples that have been more widely read in schools, Art Spiegelman's Pulitzer Prize–winning *Maus* (followed by *Maus II*) and Marjane Satrapi's *Persepolis*. Despite the comic book format of frames and dialogue and animal characters (the latter in *Maus* in particular), the subjects are deadly serious, one a fable of Nazi Germany where the Jews are portrayed as mice and the Nazi as cats, and the other a story of oppression in 1970s Iran. There is, however, more range to the field than the examples cited here might suggest, including the huge influence of Manga, Japanese graphic novels that feature superheroes. Many also know the field of graphic novels largely through American-based super heroes (such as Spider Man, X-Men, Batman, Wonder Woman, and the Hulk), and graphic novels also include horror, realistic fiction, science fiction, fantasy, nonfiction, and literary adaptations and interpretations. It is a rich field.

From a teacher's perspective, graphic novels provide an innovative combination of art and prose, and the many unusual topics of graphic novels make them interesting choices for supplementary reading in the classroom and as lures for students who would otherwise be reluctant to pick up and finish a traditional book. In addition, graphic novels' extensive use of dialogue and unusual narrative form can be studied and replicated in the classroom. Good graphic novels are master works of minimalist text coupled with intensely meaningful visuals with a complex code that might surprise you. Interested students can both transform parts of traditional prose works into short graphic novels and can also assess the art and its effect in graphic novels.

What else can a teacher do with a graphic novel? Depending on the novel's subject matter, there are actually a number of things.

Compare protagonists to classic heroes Many graphic novels feature very strong main characters who can be women, men, teens, children, or some otherworldly creature. They often follow classic character arcs inspired by some of the heroes of ancient literature, such as Ulysses, Beowulf, and King Arthur. Graphic novel characters are rich personalities that can be compared and contrasted productively with protagonists from any classic work already in your curriculum. Consider using this method to help your students engage more deeply in both forms of literary work.

Use graphic novels that are based on classics Reading a graphic novel version along with the classic it is based on has dramatic possibilities for interesting assignments. Ask students to read a graphic novel adaptation in comparison to some of the original work. What is changed? Preserved? How does the graphic presentation enhance or alter the original prose? This is also a great way to differentiate instruction for a class with a wide range of reading abilities. And, for students eager to go to SparkNotes rather than read the original, your class will provide an entrée into the wonderful experience of reading classic masterpieces.

Contrast the graphic novel to the film Hollywood has discovered the graphic novel, and there are recent (and future) films available based on Hellboy, Batman, X-Men, *The 300*, and *Road to Perdition*, just to mention a few. Ask students to view both and compare and contrast in particular the visuals. To what extent does the film mimic or alter the graphic novel? Which is more effective and why?

Approach difficult subjects Like *Maus* and *Persepolis*, some graphic novels are very serious, and Gene Luen Yang's *American Born Chinese* is hard to beat for a consideration of friendship, racism, and ethics. Told in parallel and ultimately interwoven tales, one featuring a Chinese myth and the other taking place today, this is a finely plotted and executed piece of literature that scores a powerful point. Another strong book you might want to look at is Shaun Tan's *The Arrival*, a compelling and highly artistic wordless graphic novel that tackles immigration and all its rewards and stresses. Adrienne Tomine, whose stylized drawings have graced several *New Yorker* covers, has written graphic novels that deal with adolescent and adult relationships. *Summer Blonde* is an interesting read, but it does contain mature subject matter.

For Your Journal

YA and many (but not all) graphic novels are not lengthy, and you will probably be able to read one in a brief period of time. Read a YA work or graphic novel and write about it briefly: How did you react to it? Who do you think would like to read such a book? How do you assess it in terms of tightness of plot, believability of characters, realism in dialogue, appropriateness of setting, importance of theme, accuracy of information? Regarding the graphic novel, what do you notice in terms of art, color, and placement? To what extent does the presentation enhance the subject matter? Can you think of any adult or "classic" work you could pair this book with? What similarities/differences do you see?

The Specter of Censorship

Whenever a teacher uses a poem, a novel, or a play in a classroom, he or she is open to the question of censorship. There is—the evidence is virtually irrefutable—no piece of literature "safe" from challenge and censorship. From all kinds of popular magazines to the most revered of the classics, reading material is regularly questioned and occasionally removed from library and classroom shelves. Sometimes the courts, as high as the Supreme Court, are involved in censorship cases. Most times the challenges are handled at the individual classroom, school, or school board level.

Although few of us would relish such a battle or the attack on our professionalism, we as teachers need to be prepared to give a rational defense of why we are asking—or, as some people might think, allowing—our students to read certain materials in our classes. ALA and NCTE have many resources available to teachers and schools regarding challenged books. NCTE's Intellectual Freedom Center (www.ncte.org/action /anti-censorship) has much of what you may need, including full text of the important publications *Students' Right to Read, Guidelines for Selection of Materials in English Language Arts Programs,* and *Rationales for Teaching Challenged Books.* Additionally, the following five suggestions may help you.

1. **Find your school's materials selection policy and procedure for dealing with books that are challenged.** Get a copy. If none is available, raise the issue: through these documents, schools are prepared to deal quickly and effectively with a parental or public complaint.

2. **Find out if your department has a file of rationales for books that are taught in classes.** Making up rationales and keeping them on file are powerful pieces of ammunition when parents and members of the public question books. Printed rationales or techniques for writing your own are available from ALA and available on the NCTE Intellectual Freedom Center website.

3. **Get a copy of NCTE's publication "Citizen's Request for the Reconsideration of a Work of Literature" (from the NCTE publication cited, *Students' Right to Read*).** It is a workable and usable form to give parents and others who question a work you might be teaching.

4. **As you teach and select, do keep in mind what merit you feel the material has for your students.** If you really don't know why you are using something, even if it is in mandated curricular guides and/or materials, maybe you don't need to teach it. Conviction is important in this business, and there are so many great things from which to choose that are highly defensible.

5. **Finally, if a work you have selected or allowed is questioned, it is in your best interest to always assume that the challenger is a person of good will.** Civility, respect, and helpfulness are characteristics you should strive for, even in

such an emotionally charged situation. Remember, parents and members of the public do have the right to ask questions and receive answers. Sometimes the underlying reason for their inquiry is simply that they are uninformed or unsure about the merit of literature with which they are unfamiliar.

If your school has a materials selection policy and a procedure for dealing with complaints, and you have a rationale on hand, the issue can usually be resolved amicably. On the other hand, if you find yourself without those resources, there are others who can help you—your local education association, your local language arts association, or, as mentioned, ALA and NCTE. The attempt to censor and restrict is almost as old as writing itself; you may have never thought of it in this way, but for both librarians and teachers it is an ongoing effort to keep library shelves freely stocked and students reading widely. In no case, however, should you stand alone. Censorship challenges can be emotional and scary (the Nat Hentoff YA novel *The Day They Came to Arrest the Book* tells one such story), and teachers need to avail themselves of outside resources.

Nicole Galante tells the story of a serious, unexpected challenge she faced as a high school teacher in New York several years ago when she applied to teach Mark Haddon's *The Curious Incident of the Dog in the Night-Time*:

> We acquired the signatures of teachers and parents, which would usually all but guarantee approval, but the proposal ran into resistance when we took it to the school board. The board rejected the book, citing reasons that ranged from "I wouldn't let my 14-year-old daughter read this trash" to "What do students get out of this book? That if you're a little 'off' you split your parents' marriage up?" to "Can't you just teach another book?" I couldn't believe it. This was a fight against the kind of seemingly well intentioned ignorance that prevents English teachers from doing their most important job: teaching the people who are our students; teaching them empathy and character through analysis and giving them ways to express a shared understanding through writing about their interactions with literature. (2013, 102)

Galante's essay describes how she effectively dealt with this situation, including getting help from English faculty at a local university and making a strong, professional case with the school superintendent, who ultimately made the right decision. Galante took considerable risk facing down this book challenge, and she was a seasoned teacher when she made it. The point here is she didn't try to do it alone.

When we discuss this issue, it is almost impossible not to cite John Milton's stirring and still very apt *Areopagitica*, his defense of writing against the censor. Milton wrote this pamphlet in 1644 in response to the censorship prevalent in seventeenth-century England. Addressed to the British Parliament for the "liberty of unlicensed printing," Milton thundered about protecting the reading public through "a fugitive and cloister'd vertue, unexercis'd and unbreath'd" (691). He argued that even in a restrictive, theocratic society, reading would not sully anyone; he concluded it was better to kill a person than a book—because a book was so akin to a likeness of the divine:

> as good almost kill a Man as kill a good Booke; who kills a Man kills a reasonable creature, God's Image: but hee who destroyes a good Booke, kills reason it selfe, kills the Image of God, as it were in the eye. (681)

On a less elevated—but no less compelling—plane is E. B. White, who wrote in 1949 in the *New Yorker* regarding the New York Board of Education's criteria for selecting books. The criteria are strongly reminiscent of today's concerns:

> The Board of Education has twenty-three criteria for selecting textbooks, library books, and magazines for use in the public schools. We learned this by reading a fourteen-page pamphlet published by the Board explaining how it makes its choice. One criterion is: "Is it [the book or magazine] free from subject matter that tends to irreverence for things held sacred?" Another criterion is: "Are both sides of controversial issues presented with fairness?" Another: "Is it free from objectionable slang expressions which will interfere with the building of good language habits?" (1990, 140)

White worries in his essay that "these three criteria by themselves are enough to keep a lot of good books from the schools." He goes on:

> Irreverence for things held sacred has started many a writer on his way, and will again. An author so little moved by a controversy that he can present both sides fairly is not likely to burn any holes in the paper. We think the way for school children to get both sides of a controversy is to read several books on the subject, not one. In other words we think the Board should strive for a well-balanced library, not a well-balanced book. The greatest books are heavily slanted, by the nature of greatness. (1990, 140)

We wish we had written that.

Using Literature: Some Teaching Tips

There are a number of principles to keep in mind when you think of using literature.

Limit Your Time

Covering every aspect of any piece of literature is deadening, and furthermore, real readers don't approach literature that way. Why is it in the classroom we beat poems and short stories and novels to death, exhausting every avenue of discussion and, in the process, our students, too?

Think about limiting the time you spend on what your students are reading and try to fall in love with the concept that it is better to leave them wanting to discuss more, do more, than to end a unit of study with everyone cranky and worn out and just sick of the piece. It's the extensive versus intensive debate, and we always opt for the former. We would rather range over a wide variety of works than spend significant portions of time exhausting a single text. From our experience, extensive, not intensive, reading seems to give students a wider range of ideas and facility.

Practically, what does this mean? As mentioned in the poetry section in this chapter, it means that with the Godiva chocolate of literature, poetry, less is definitely more. Five straight days of poetry could drive you and your students crazy; think of a maximum of two or three, and never, never do a complete "unit" of poetry, as it makes poetry too solitary, too distant from all other ways to communicate. The literature is too condensed for most younger readers—middle schoolers and high schoolers—and should be interspersed with other forms of literature. It may seem like heresy, but, as we have noted in this chapter, it is helpful to "drop in" a poem every week or so: duplicate one, read it aloud, briefly discuss it, and move on. Sometimes, of course, even brief discussion is unnecessary; poetry, like those delicious Godiva chocolates, needs to be sampled and savored.

With longer works, such as multiact plays and novels, a few weeks—three to five block days of instruction—is a reasonable limit. And, yes, this means Shakespeare, too: most students' enthusiasm will flag, as will yours, if you spend class period after class period on the same, single work of literature. Even the most dedicated of classes will wilt if, day after day, you and they mine the piece for every bit of gold it holds. There's nothing wrong with having students read only excerpts of certain works, skipping some sections (reading summaries instead), or dividing sections up between students and having them share the work with each other. Remember that it's our job to help develop capable, thoughtful, critical lifelong readers, not to make students specialized experts on just a few long books.

Short stories, particularly when they relate thematically or chronologically to other pieces of literature, are highly useful for "breaking up" poetry and longer pieces of study. Short stories, like poems, can also provide vehicles for "self-contained" classes in which in one period, one day, students can read and respond to a piece of literature. This not only avoids homework—which in some school settings or at some junctures is difficult, if not impossible, to have all students complete—but it also provides an impact that is hard to replicate when the literature is read outside class.

Prereading: Give Them a Context and Lead Them In

Many beginning teachers forget how puzzling a piece of literature can be, how it can seem, especially on first reading, to come from absolutely nowhere. They often assume that students will "get it" more quickly than is realistic; accordingly, in their classroom discussions or activities involving literature these teachers just start—often seemingly out of thin air—as if the mere act of having heard a poem read aloud or having read a short story as homework was a sufficient introduction.

Always think about how to lead your students into a piece: call it a *hook*, a *warm-up*, an *anticipatory set*, call it what you will, but do it. Give students some sort of context for what they will be dealing with, and try at the onset to help them puzzle out a connection.

For example, in Samuel G. Freedman's (1990) *Small Victories*, the story of students in New York City's Seward Park High School, English teacher Jessica Siegel talks about how she uses a number of techniques. To introduce "Walden," the Henry David Thoreau essay on leaving the complications of civilization to live simply in the country, she opens the class discussion by asking "What's a luxury?" and uses student answers to set the stage for what Thoreau would describe as going into the woods to "live deliberately" and, necessarily, without luxury. To open a unit on early American literature that encompasses writing about what the early settlers hoped for in the New World, Siegel asks her students, predominantly the children of relatively recent immigrants, why their parents came to the United States. She then uses their answers to link today with the seventeenth-century first settlers of America. For "Upon the Burning of Our House, July 10th, 1666," which is about the destruction of seventeenth-century American poet Anne Bradstreet's house by fire, students write in their journals a brief description of their favorite possession. Following this, Siegel asks students to imagine their feelings about the destruction of that favorite possession. In all three cases, students are encouraged to think of a concept or an idea that ultimately relates to the literature.

In her first few months student teaching, Debbie Martin did a similar activity:

Today I probably had my best day of teaching yet. I mean real teaching. . . . I wrote on the board: Defining death is a very difficult task. If a six-year-old asked you, "What is death?" what would you say to him/her? Students had ten minutes to respond. They were told that we would share answers.

Which we did. I had no trouble getting students to share. They wanted me to read their writing first, but once I did they eagerly volunteered. I let those who wanted to read, read and those who just wanted to tell me their ideas, tell me.

When they did so I made very little comment. I didn't need to. The remainder of the class jumped in. We even had quite a disagreement between two students in one class. As long as it was rational and kind, I let it go on for a few moments. I ended it by saying that a definition of death was often tied to religious beliefs and that in any case [it] was tied to beliefs that were very personal. Further, that if we had the time to really get into it, more than likely not one of us would agree.

We then read John Donne's "Sonnet X" or "Death, Be Not Proud." The relationship between the writing and the sonnet were crystal clear. One of my students who does nothing said later, when I mentioned a review, "We don't need to review this one; we've practically memorized it now."

Although there is a danger, as with the pitfalls of theme, that such openers, warm-ups, or anticipatory sets will steer students only too precisely into what *we* want them to see in and believe about a piece of literature, the opposite is probably more dangerous, especially for younger and unsure readers. Leaving students to flounder, repeatedly confronting them class after class with literature that seems relatively contextless, is to invite disaffection and unease. The luxury of no context and discovery may be more appropriately left for college and graduate school, where more adept readers are not so confounded by what they are discussing. By and large, our middle school and high school students, many of whom are pretty new to this game of looking at unfamiliar literature, may need to be pointed in a general direction. What Jessica Siegel and Debbie Martin do in their classrooms seems to have far more benefits than disadvantages.

If your school or school district is heavily influenced by the Common Core or similar standards, you may find you are actually discouraged from offering students any context at all for the literature they read. Like us, Michael W. Smith, Deborah Appleman, and Jeffrey D. Wilhelm (2014) believe this is a serious mistake. In their *Uncommon Core: Where the Authors of the Standards Go Wrong About Instruction—and How You Can Get It Right*, they suggest prereading activities are essential and that focusing too heavily on leading students through an analysis of literature without a context to work from encourages teacher- rather than student-centered classes (2014, 79). They suggest prereading strategies such as giving students prior context, "opinionnaires" (in which students are asked their opinion on issues related to a theme forthcoming in a book), "essential questions," "jigsaw groups," and something called "floorstorming," in which students work on the floor to group and categorize photos and images related to the text (47–49). Babirad (2015) wrote a useful, free-access review of this book that is valuable if you don't have time to read the original right away.

If these ideas seem too focused or complicated, consider doing one or more of the following:

- Ask your students to speculate on the title: What does it mean? How do they know? Can they provide synonyms? Can they create a parallel title?

- Read them the first line of the poem or the first paragraph of the prose, and ask them to write about what they expect will happen next. Ask them to share their answers and discuss.

- Excerpt a slice of dialogue from the play; have a number of students read the parts, and ask students what is going on. Have another duo or trio read the same lines and ask the question again. Do the readings differ in tone and interpretation? How?

Let Them Create It—Within Reason

A way into poetry is encouraging students to write their own; similarly, short skits can also help students appreciate drama and feel its power. Be very wary, however, of asking students to write epic poems or multiple-act plays; although there are some classes and some students who may be able to do it, insisting that an entire class embark upon a complete work of literature may not invite creativity so much as despair. In the same way, asking students to write an entire short story is an assignment many teachers rather routinely give, and the results are very rarely satisfactory. Unless you are committed to helping students work through the process of creating a long work, stick to more attainable goals. It is one thing to do a very short, self-contained piece; it is another to piece together prose that features, in the case of the short story, setting, characters, and dialogue, not to mention theme and coherent plot with conflict and climax.

As an alternative, consider having your students create short pieces of text that are related to the original. For instance, shifting genre, you can ask students after reading a novel to respond by writing two original twenty-line poems, rhyming or unrhyming (your choice), stanzas or no stanzas (your choice), which reflect the spirit and intent of the novel. The first student-written poem should relate to the first half of the novel, and the second poem should relate to the second half of the novel. The poems should show knowledge of the novel, appreciation of it, and some creativity. You can also think of this as a form of "fan fiction," a form of creative writing that has taken on a world of its own on the Internet. Have students write stories, poems, and essays using the characters, themes, and settings from whatever literary works you've recently read in class.

With a chapter from a novel or with a short story, students can look at plot, setting, and character. For example:

- Have students *pick a favorite or pivotal scene*. Then let them add a character, delete a character, or alter a piece of dialogue by changing a crucial word or key phrase. Ask your students to rewrite that one scene and share it by reading it aloud and discussing how it changes the plot.

- Have students *write a new ending or a sequel* by extending the ending by one hour, one day, one week, one month, one year. For some pieces of literature, what happens immediately after the final period is of great interest; for other pieces, what the characters are doing after a year is more realistic. Have students share their new endings and discuss how they arrived at them. As an alternative, have students write a letter as the main character, five years after the end of the novel, to someone significant who may or may not know what happened in the novel. The letter should show understanding not only of the novel itself but of the implications of the events of the novel five years later.

- Have students *do a new beginning to the literature*—in media speak, a *prequel*—that begins an hour, a day, a week, a month, a year before the literature actually starts. Again, have students share.

- Let students *change the title* and *rewrite the opening paragraph* and/or the closing paragraph to reflect that new title. How did they come up with the new title?

- Have students *rewrite the setting* of a section. Setting can be a snooze to students, but what if a section of the literature is set in a different era? In the country rather than on the street corner? In spring instead of winter? Have students discuss the changes they make.

- Let students *rename characters, change the gender of characters, change a major personality trait or physical characteristic* of a character, and then have them rewrite a section. Character is pivotal in most literature. What happens when one of these characteristics is changed? Why?

- Ask students to *write up scenes from a work that are referenced* but that do not take place on the pages. Or, have students imagine new scenes, subplots, or alternative scenes.

Use Literature Circles

Literature circles allow students to work together in small groups and to talk about a single book, often a book that the students themselves have selected. Although you can give your students real guidance as they work in their circles (you can offer lists of books from which to choose and procedures for discussion), literature circles allow students to be more autonomous than they might be in a whole-class configuration. Think of literature circles as a sort of small-group book club where students, not the teacher, run the show. Guidelines, journal checks, and teacher visits to the group can help students stay organized.

Do remember that literature circles need preparation. Sometimes students are not ready to talk among each other day after day—or even a few times a week—without some specific direction. Assigning students small-group roles (facilitator, recorder, timekeeper), giving them possible lists of things to talk about (yesterday we considered the main character; today let's list possible themes), giving students incremental deadlines (by the end of the week each group member will need to have completed two journal entries) are all part of your job structuring literature circles. Harvey Daniels' (2002) book *Literature Circles* is devoted entirely to the subject and offers many more ideas for small-group roles; you might want to check it out (see also the Bonnie Hill, Nancy J. Johnson, and Katherine Noe [1995] text) if literature circles seem appealing to you in your classroom.

Let Them Act It Out—After They Have Warmed Up First

Creative dramatics can make magic in a classroom, and certainly students can base short skits not only on full-length plays but also on poems, short stories, and pieces of nonfiction. Regardless of what you base your creative dramatics on, do not forget the human being in all of this; just because your students are young does not mean they have no inhibitions. Just telling students to "get in front of the class and act it out" is a recipe for disaster. Students need some help; like most people, they need to get ready. First, students need to be warmed up. This can involve breathing exercises, movement exercises, and games. Students can then, in groups or pairs, work on brief skits or do impromptus and present them with much less inhibition and fear.

To expect students just to *do it*, to perform on *your* moment's notice, is unfair and something, frankly, you most likely would not want to do either.

Add Art and Music

As response through creative dramatics can inspire students, so also can the use of art and music. Letting students who like to draw or paint or put together collages interpret or respond to literature through that medium can unlock a world of connection that might otherwise not exist. One project students enjoy is making an ABC book based on a novel. Using the letters of the alphabet, students make an ABC book/list using each letter of the alphabet and citing appropriate events/ideas/concepts. Here's an example for *The Great Gatsby*:

> *D* is for **DAISY**, who was Gatsby's love and inspiration.
>
> *E* is for **ENIGMA**, the mystery that was Gatsby.

Like Leila's student Susan, described in Chapter 4, students can illustrate the alphabet book or use different typefaces to make it visually appealing.

Likewise, our students are often fiercely loyal to certain groups or styles of music, and using the lyrics of their favorite songs or raps and asking them to connect reading with what they listen to can also make literature real or illuminating in a way that would not be otherwise possible. A book on this topic is *Hip-Hop Poetry and the Classics for the Classroom* in which poems are paired to hip-hop songs for analysis and comparison. Teacher-authors Alan Sitomer and Michael Cirelli (2004) link, for instance, Dylan Thomas' "Do Not Go Gentle into That Good Night" with Tupac Shakur's "Me Against the World"; "Harlem" by Langston Hughes with "Juicy" by Notorious B.I.G. The lesson plans are specific, and poem texts and excerpted song lyrics are provided. If your students love hip-hop, check it out. A 2016 issue of *English Journal,* themed "Imagination, Creativity, and Innovation: Showcasing the 'A' in English Language Arts," was produced with the help of members of the Conference on English Education's Commission on Arts and Literacy. If you're looking for innovative ways to bring the arts into your ELA classroom, consult this issue.

A key to success in using art and music with literature is allowing students some freedom and yet being specific with expectations. Asking students to respond to literature with art or using music and not giving them any other boundaries can result in poorly focused projects. Instead, ask students to select a certain number of songs and discuss how the lyrics relate to the literature; give students dimensions or a number of elements to be incorporated into art projects.

Give Them a Choice Whenever Possible

Even the most well-thought-out activity, one that has worked for other teachers and in other classes, can fall flat with a specific group of students. Giving students choice regarding what they will do with literature is often essential to student motivation and success, and there are many sources of ideas that can help you provide your students a menu of activities they will find appealing. Diana Mitchell, who is one of the most creative teachers Leila knows, offers a number of inventive suggestions in their book *Both Art and Craft*:

- *Yearbook entries* where students imagine what characters in the literature were like in high school and create, for each, a yearbook entry that includes a picture, a nickname, school activities, clubs, sports they might have participated in, a quotation that the character might have selected, favorite colors or foods, plans after high school.

- *Creation of a web page* (or Facebook profile) where students create an appropriate electronic site that a character might have. Students must use appropriate background, pictures, information, and at least five links to sites that the character would be interested in. Students need to justify all choices.

- *Creation of a group chat* (or Twitter chat) in which a character has found other people to talk with. Students should describe the chat the character is in and why the character would be drawn to the kind of group that operates the chat room. Students can also construct a conversation the character has with others while in the chat.

- *Creation of a childhood* for a character where students include the character's earliest memory; the character's memory of being scared, embarrassed, happy; the character's biggest worry; the one thing the character really dislikes; the one thing the character wishes his or her parents had realized about them. (Mitchell and Christenbury 2000, 53–58)

If They Can't—or Won't—Read It

Who says that reading aloud to students is just for elementary school? The pleasures of *hearing* literature are manifold and, indeed, can help students who are struggling with material too difficult for them to comprehend easily. Hearing a piece read and seeing it simultaneously on the page can double comprehension; it can also give you the opportunity to gloss, or define, words that you are relatively sure your students would not readily understand. In her teaching, Leila read aloud most of the Edgar Allan Poe short stories her students studied; her cadence and vocabulary synonyms helped them get through a lot of the difficult, vocabulary-rich nineteenth-century prose. Reading aloud any text, even less challenging pieces, offers support to classes that feature reluctant readers or virtual nonreaders.

Many English teachers love to read aloud. We can also occasionally, though, ask students to take turns reading literature whose syntax and vocabulary would not be a torture for a volunteer. Reading aloud adds to the drama of the literature and provides, especially with short works, an impact and power that only a single, sustained reading can provide. If your students can't read or if they really struggle over certain kinds of literature, read it to them or have relatively confident volunteers read all or part of it.

Reading aloud is also very important in drama and poetry. Reading a poem a number of times is part and parcel of the experience of the genre, and even if students have looked at a piece in preparation for a discussion or for homework, they should hear it again—aloud—before discussing or writing or anything.

Reading aloud can also help address another issue: that of students not doing homework or reading outside of class. Certainly for schools that feature high absentee rates, the expectation that students will prepare their reading before class can lead to serious teacher frustration when a small percentage of students—if any—come to class actually having read what was assigned. Although this accommodation may strike you as caving in to a bad situation—weak student reading skills and excessive student absences—we would defend it as at least part of a realistic compromise. Faced with failing absentee students who could never catch up or working with the reality of these students and the school, we choose the latter. Further, we believe many of the students learned something along the way as they listened.

Students not completing assigned reading is a frequent problem for teachers, and there's no one-size-fits-all approach to this challenge. Engaging students through motivating prereading activities, using reading journals throughout the reading of a text, incorporating group discussion and collaborative projects, and designing enjoyable in-class assignments that require students to have read the work (or otherwise must participate in a less interesting, solitary assignment) are methods that can encourage students to read. If you feel you must use reading quizzes, please make them *educative* by asking complex, truly useful questions, rather than simple recall questions. It's also important that you get to know your students well enough so that if there's a problem actually preventing the student from doing the reading—for instance, the student can't read at the level of the assigned text, the student doesn't have a quiet, safe place to read outside school, the student works too many hours after school to have the stamina to stay awake while reading—you, the teacher, can identify and help address it.

If You Don't Like It Either

Both of us have read the sentiment before and happen to agree with it: if you really don't like a piece of literature—and this is particularly true of poetry—you probably shouldn't teach it. As self-indulgent as that may seem, it is good advice and, within some limits, we follow it ourselves. We're lucky in English that if one text doesn't tickle us, we can always find another that will meet the same learning objectives. The point is that enthusiasm is catching. The reverse is also true. To give one example, if "To the Virgins to Make Much of Time" seems impossibly silly to you, skip it and maybe even Robert Herrick altogether. There is surely some other seventeenth-century British poet whom you can present to your students in an effective and enthusiastic manner. On the other hand, don't assume that what one year you absolutely could not bring yourself to teach will remain on your "yuck list" forever: your tastes will change as you teach, and you need to give literature a second look every year or so. You might surprise yourself.

Remember Why You're Doing This

When you're faced with objectives and those very official-looking textbooks, curriculum and pacing guides, and multiple classes of thirty students or so each, it is hard to remember just why you are reading literature. Don't forget the sheer *joy* of it, the possibility that at least some of your students will become lifelong readers due in part to what happens in *your* class. Don't forget the laughter and the excitement; it's why you are doing this.

For many beginning teachers the curriculum requirements and what it seems the school or the school system expects can become an overwhelming weight; there is the fear, reasonable or not, that you will be judged by how much material you cover or how efficiently you cover it. For some teachers, the scores their students make on large-scale exams are also a concern.

But at some point, although you cannot wave away or minimize these very real issues, you also have to make some choices about what the school expects versus your responsibility to your students. To some people, even some teachers in the classroom, a "free" reading day once a week would seem a waste, even frivolous. But what you are about is more than pages in the textbook and passing scores on literature tests. As highbrow as it may seem when you contemplate the down and dirty realities of third period, you are in that class to invite reading and thinking, to give students with minds and hearts and psyches windows onto the world we know is in books. You are a guide to something bigger than the state competency test, the unit exam, the departmental requirements, or even admission to college. It is not always true that there will be conflict between reading and talking and thinking and what the school "expects," but at times there may be. And when that occurs, remember why you are a teacher, why you got into this business in the first place.

Long after the multiple-choice test on *Beowulf* has faded, long after the students can no longer identify who wrote about a raisin in the sun or tell with certainty what happened to Willy Loman or Heathcliff, this connection to literature will endure. Thus your guiding North Star is not the curriculum guide; you need, while trying to be responsible to the demands of your job and the expectations of the system, also to hold true to your vision for yourself and your students. It's a lot to ask; it's also very important. Without holding true to that vision, you may find yourself relatively lost and feeling, as some do, that you are in the classroom "delivering" a package of instruction at someone else's behest. That's not what you want to spend any part of your life doing; although balancing the expectations may be the tightrope act of your life, the stakes are huge, and the effort is worth it.

Keeping your focus on your own purposes for teaching literature is also an excellent way to ride the waves of curricular reform as they come and go. The enduring task of helping students build a relationship with reading and texts is always the center, no matter the pedagogical flavor of the month or the standardized test du jour. When you keep your principles at the center of your teaching, you will make the best of all the opportunities that come from educational reform without allowing yourself to compromise what you know is best for your students' learning.

For Your Journal

Pick a favorite piece of literature—a play, a poem, a short story, a novel—that you think you could teach in middle school or high school. How would you prepare students for this piece of literature? Think about three or four activities you could do during or after the reading; write about them. Can you imagine this piece of literature being challenged or censored? For the sake of argument, imagine it is. What reasons would you advance for using it in the classroom?

A Final Note on Choosing Literature

If we want our students to respond to literature, then it is crucial that we choose literature—or let them participate in choosing literature—to which they can have a response. Much of the literature you use in your classroom will be dictated by the texts provided, the curriculum, and pacing guides, yet there are ways you can expand beyond what text has been selected for your students. There is just not time for you to duplicate or scout out a parallel text for everything, but on the other hand, in addition to young adult literature and graphic novels, don't forget these rich and often overlooked sources of reading:

- magazines of all types
- paperback books (from the school bookroom, students' attics or basements, second hand bookstores, yard sales)
- newspapers and tabloids
- catalogs of all sorts
- pamphlets, booklets, informational brochures.

Although we have a contractual obligation to adhere to what the school system and our English language arts department encourage or mandate that we "cover," we also need to remember that we have a similar obligation to our students to give them reading to which they can truly respond. It is not revolutionary to have a classroom library of materials such as those listed and to let students read and browse through them at specified times. Devoting an entire class period to free reading can encourage students who would not otherwise spend—or find—the time. The reading can be supervised, academic credit can be given, but it can come from the *Guinness World Records*, *Road*

& *Track*, *Sports Illustrated*, *People*, *Seventeen*; a maintenance manual; horror, sports, and romance novels; and technical brochures and catalogs. Real readers are omnivorous; if we insist that reading means only one thing—that is, "good" literature of which we specifically approve and the "best" literature, which appears on sanctioned lists—we are not only lying to our students, we are in our own way discouraging the young reader.

To open the world of the printed page to our students, we must open the covers of all kinds of reading matter, *Hamlet* to *Hemmings Motor News*. Making a reader is a broad and messy business, and we need to become inclusive, not exclusive, in our own tastes and in what we offer to our students and encourage them to read.

Leila's Story: Thurman and *Architectural Digest*

Thurman was tall, had long, blond hair that fell below his shoulders, wore sunglasses most of the year (in class as well as out), and sported the chains, boots, and studded jacket that in my school signaled his membership in a group of rather tough white males who endured school rather than enjoyed it. Thurman lived in a public housing project and hung out with a group who had a reputation for drugs and trouble. With most of his teachers he was silent, almost mild-mannered, but he actually had a strong temper and a violent streak; he had been suspended a number of times from school and, out of school, he was prone to explosions. Too many fights and a final assault conviction led him to a thirty-day jail sentence. But the judge wanted Thurman to stay in school, so the sentence was served on weekends. He checked into the city jail on Friday afternoon and checked out to return to school on Monday morning.

Thurman was in my English class and was struggling with his reading, if not his behavior. He usually wanted to be let out of our afternoon class early; between jail, his job, and his personal life he didn't feel he had much time to waste. It was a request I almost always refused, regardless of the urgency or sensibility of reasons, and Thurman would eventually settle into work. For some reason—one of the mysteries of teacher–student chemistry—we got along very well, and he became one of my absolute, all-time favorite students. After a semester or so of contact, I thought he was wonderful, and he, in his own often elusive way, seemed to like me, too.

Maybe that was why he would be one of the first to wander to the back of the room during our regular Friday free reading times and leaf through the collection of magazines that I provided for students who forgot something to read or who had little access to a wide variety of reading material. He seemed to have a sense of loyalty to me as his teacher and could, most times, be enticed to try something because I recommended it. After all, I had listened to his favorite rock group of the time and even, on his recommendation, bought one of their albums. We had, of a sort, a deal.

Loyalty aside, Thurman was not a strong reader. He stumbled over words; he refused to complete outside reading. His writing was careful but jerky and unsure. It was, however, on one of the Friday afternoon reads that Thurman intersected with *Architectural Digest*, the pricey journal of multimillion-dollar homes and furnishings I had scrounged from relatives who could not only afford the hefty subscription price but who could occasionally purchase some of the cheaper items featured in it. Although I had been really reluctant to add the journal to my class library—its relation to almost anyone's real life was pretty tangential—there were issues and issues of *Architectural Digest*, they were free, and I needed variety.

What possible connection could *Architectural Digest*, this monument to gold-plated faucets of the stars, sunken living rooms of the mega wealthy, marble and terrazzo floors of the famous, have with a hot-tempered white kid from the projects? Photographs and text, it was a bombshell to Thurman; he read intently, steadily; he borrowed copies between Fridays. He didn't want to talk about it at first; he just, ravenously, miraculously, wanted—to read. He looked at the pictures, read the captions, and graduated into the text. When he did talk, and it wasn't for some time, he wanted to know about such homes, such designs, such lives. He had, he admitted, no idea that the world in *Architectural Digest* had ever existed. And I could tell, thankfully, that that fact did not depress him a bit; he was filled with understandable wonder, but with a young person's optimism, he was also filled with exhilaration. This was a world of excess, to be sure, but also of beauty and grace where the aesthetic was discussed seriously.

When Thurman wandered out of my life—he did pass my class, graduate from high school, get a job, stay out of jail, and eventually marry—I felt the loss of a favorite student. But also I felt pretty good. Thurman had looked, he had read. I never would have guessed that magazine and that young man would intersect. But they did. And I felt overwhelmingly happy and convinced, once again, that hooking kids into reading is a wide-ranging, broad-moving experience. If *I* had selected reading material for Thurman, it never, in my wildest dreams, would have been *Architectural Digest*. He made the selection himself; all I did was give him a little freedom and some time to read, and then get out of the way. I wonder if that isn't quite enough.

When I was president of the NCTE, part of my work was traveling around the country to give talks and workshops. One early fall I was the keynote speaker for a two-day session involving all the middle and senior high school–level English teachers in a large school district in Maryland. The teachers were a committed and interested group of professionals, and I outlined my deep belief that we must widen the definition of reading and give students more than classics, that we must try to entice them into the world of literature by offering other choices. I talked about the variety of magazines, the range of nonfiction, and urged those present to encourage those works in their classroom curriculum and, more to the point, to give students credit for work done with this kind of literature. The members of the large audience listened avidly, and at the end there were numbers of questions. One teacher asked about my allowing students to read magazines—I had specifically mentioned car magazines—in English class. I answered his question from the podium but, after the talk, he came up to see me one-on-one. He was incredulous and told me he thought that I was surely not doing my job as a teacher to allow such material in an English classroom and to give students credit for it. I made my point again, but I know I did not convince him that morning, either answering his question from the audience or talking to him individually. Invited to speak to a large professional group, having prepared carefully, I want to be well received, and at times for me resulting conflicts and criticisms can be unsettling. But I left that conference and that one teacher with hardly a backward glance. I kept thinking of Thurman, and I knew, deep and sure, that I was right.

References

Appleman, Deborah. 2009. *Critical Encounters in High School English*. 2nd ed. New York: Teachers College Press.

Babirad, Robert. 2015. Review of *Uncommon Core: Where the Authors of the Standards Go Wrong About Instruction—and How You Can Get It Right* by Michael W. Smith, Deborah Appleman, and Jeffrey D. Wilhelm. *English Journal* 105 (2): 117–18.

Bomer, Randy. 2011. *Building Adolescent Literacy in Today's English Classrooms*. Portsmouth, NH: Heinemann.

Carillo, Ellen C. 2016. "Reimagining the Role of the Reader in the Common Core State Standards." *English Journal* 105 (3): 29–35.

Carlsen, G. Robert. 1980. *Books and the Teenage Reader*. 2nd ed. New York: Harper & Row.

Christenbury, Leila. 1990. "Creating Text: Students Connecting with Literature." In *Literature and Life: Making Connections in the Classroom: Classroom Practices in Teaching English,* edited by Patricia Phelan. Vol. 25. Urbana, IL: NCTE.

———. 1993. "What Oft Was Thought But Ne'er So Well Expressed: The Use of Quotations in Teaching Shakespeare." In *Teaching Shakespeare Today: Practical Approaches and Productive Strategies*, edited by James E. Davis and Ronald E. Salome. Urbana, IL: NCTE.

———. 1997. "Problems with *Othello* in the High School Classroom." In *Teaching Shakespeare into the Twenty-first Century*, edited by Ronald E. Salomone and James E. Davis. Athens: Ohio University Press.

———. 2000. " 'The Guy Who Wrote This Poem Seems to Have the Same Feelings as You Have': Reader-Response Methodology." In *Reader Response in Secondary and College Classrooms*, 2nd ed., edited by Nicholas J. Karolides. Mahwah, NJ: Lawrence Erlbaum.

———. 2005. "Rosenblatt the Radical." *Voices from the Middle* 12 (March): 22–24.

———. 2007. *Retracing the Journey: Teaching and Learning in an American High School*. New York: Teachers College Press.

Daniels, Harvey. 2002. *Literature Circles: Voice and Choice in the Student-Centered Classroom*. 2nd ed. York, ME: Stenhouse.

Eckert, Lisa Schade. 2006. *How Does It Mean? Engaging Reluctant Readers Through Literary Theory*. Portsmouth, NH: Heinemann.

Folger Shakespeare Library. "Teach & Learn." www.folger.edu/teach-learn.

Freedman, Samuel G. 1990. *Small Victories*. New York: HarperCollins.

Galante, Nicole. 2013. "The Audacity of Empathy: It's *Still* the Students, Stupid!" *English Journal* 102 (6): 102–103.

Gilbert, Miriam. 1984. "Teaching Shakespeare Through Performance." *Shakespeare Quarterly* 35 (5): 601–608.

Gillespie, Tim. 2010. *Doing Literary Criticism: Helping Students Engage with Challenging Texts.* York, ME: Stenhouse.

Gorlewski, Julie, and David Gorlewski, eds. 2016. "Imagination, Creativity, and Innovation: Showcasing the 'A' in English Language Arts." *English Journal* 105 (5).

Greenblatt, Stephen. 2004. *Will in the World: How Shakespeare Became Shakespeare.* New York: W. W. Norton.

Hill, Bonnie, Nancy J. Johnson, and Katherine Noe, eds. 1995. *Literature Circles and Response.* Norwood, MA: Christopher-Gordon.

LoMonico, Michael, guest editor. 2009. "Teachers Set Free: Folger Education and Other Revolutionary Approaches to Teaching Shakespeare." *English Journal* 99 (1).

McCloud, Scott. 1994. *Understanding Comics.* New York: Harper.

Mitchell, Diana, and Leila Christenbury. 2000. *Both Art and Craft: Teaching Ideas That Spark Learning.* Urbana, IL: NCTE.

National Council of Teachers of English. Intellectual Freedom Center. 2014. *Guidelines for Selection of Materials in English Language Arts Programs.* www.ncte.org/action/anti-censorship.

———. *Rationales for Teaching Challenged Books.* www.ncte.org/action/anti-censorship.

———. 2012. *Students' Right to Read.* www.ncte.org/action/anti-censorship.

Ransom, John Crowe. 1979. *The New Criticism.* Westport, CT: Greenwood Press.

Ressler, Paula. 2002. *Dramatic Changes: Talking About Sexual Orientation and Gender Identity with High School Students.* Portsmouth, NH: Heinemann.

Romano, Carlin. 2016. "The Irrepressible Lightness of Umberto Eco." *The Chronicle Review,* B5 (March 11).

Rosenblatt, Louise. 1976. *Literature as Exploration.* 3rd ed. New York: Noble & Noble.

Sitomer, Alan, and Michael Cirelli. 2004. *Hip-Hop Poetry and the Classics for the Classroom: Connecting Our Classic Curriculum to Hip-Hop Poetry Through Standards-Based Language Arts Instruction.* Beverly Hills, CA: Milk Mug Publishing.

Smith, Michael W., Deborah Appleman, and Jeffrey D. Wilhelm. 2014. *Uncommon Core: Where the Authors of the Standards Go Wrong About Instruction—and How You Can Get It Right.* Thousand Oaks, CA: Corwin.

Tillyard, E. M. W. 1943. *The Elizabethan World Picture.* London: Chatto & Windus.

Tovani, Cris. 2004. *Do I Really Have to Teach Reading? Content, Comprehension, Grades 6–12.* York, ME: Stenhouse.

Wagner, Betty Jane. 1998. *Educational Drama and Language Arts: What Research Shows.* Portsmouth, NH: Heinemann.

Weiner, Stephen. 2003. *Faster Than a Speeding Bullet: The Rise of the Graphic Novel.* New York: Nantier Beall Minoustchine.

Literature Cited

Achebe, Chinua. (1959) 1994. *Things Fall Apart.* New York: Anchor Books.

Alexie, Sherman. 2007. *The Absolutely True Diary of a Part-Time Indian.* New York: Little, Brown.

Austen, Jane. (1813) 1996. *Pride and Prejudice.* New York: Penguin.

Barlow, Judith, ed. 1981. *Plays by American Women: The Early Years.* New York: Avon.

Beowulf. 2001. A New Verse translation by Seamus Heaney. New York: W. W. Norton.

Bowers, Neal. 1988. "Black Walnuts." In *North American Review* 273 (June): 19.

Bradstreet, Anne. 1972. "Upon the Burning of Our House, July 10th, 1666." In *The Women Poets in English*, edited by Ann Stanford, 52–53. New York: McGraw-Hill.

Brontë, Charlotte. 1971. *Jane Eyre*, edited by Richard J. Dunn. New York: Norton.

Chaucer, Geoffrey. 1961. *Canterbury Tales.* In *The Works of Geoffrey Chaucer*, 2nd ed., edited by F. N. Robinson. Boston: Houghton Mifflin.

Chopin, Kate. 1990. "The Story of an Hour." In *Introduction to Literature*, 2nd ed., edited by Dorothy U. Seyler and Richard A. Wilan. Upper Saddle River, NJ: Prentice-Hall.

Cisneros, Sandra. 1984. *The House on Mango Street.* New York: Vintage.

Clare, Cassandra. Mortal Instruments series. New York: Margaret K. McElderry.

Coleridge, Samuel Taylor. 1951. "Kubla Khan." In *Selected Poetry and Prose.* New York: Holt, Rinehart & Winston.

Collins, Suzanne. Hunger Games series. New York: Scholastic.

Connell, Richard. 1970. "The Most Dangerous Game." In *The Most Dangerous Game and Other Stories of Adventure.* New York: Berkley Highland Books.

Dickens, Charles. 1969. *Great Expectations.* New York: Collier.

Dickinson, Emily. 1960. *The Complete Poems of Emily Dickinson*, edited by Thomas H. Johnson. Boston: Little, Brown.

Donne, John. 1962. "A Valediction Forbidding Mourning." In *Donne*, edited by Richard Wilbur. New York: Dell.

Faulkner, William. (1930) 1964. *As I Lay Dying.* New York: Random House.

Fitzgerald, F. Scott. (1925) 1995. *The Great Gatsby.* New York: Scribner.

Frey, James. 2003. *A Million Little Pieces.* New York: Random House.

Frost, Robert. 1961. "The Road Not Taken." In *Modern Poetry*, 2nd ed., edited by Maynard Mack, Leonard Dean, William Frost. Englewood Cliffs, NJ: Prentice-Hall.

Gallo, Donald R., ed. 1990. *Center Stage.* New York: HarperCollins.

Gilman Perkins, Charlotte. 2007. "The Yellow Wallpaper." In *Literature for Composition: Reading and Writing Arguments About Essays, Fiction, Poetry, and Drama*, 8th ed., edited by Sylvan Barnet, William Burto, and William E. Cain, 765–75. New York: Pearson Longman.

Glaspell, Susan. 1985. "Trifles." In *Plays by American Women: 1900–1930*, edited by Judith E. Barlow, 70–86. New York: Applause.

Golding, William. 1962. *Lord of the Flies.* New York: Coward-McCann.

Green, John. 2002. *The Fault in Our Stars.* New York: Dutton Penguin.

———. 2005. *Looking for Alaska.* New York: Dutton Children's.

Haddon, Mark. 2003. *The Curious Incident of the Dog in the Night-Time.* New York: Vintage, Random House.

Hansberry, Lorraine. (1959) 1994. *A Raisin in the Sun.* New York: Random House.

Hawthorne, Nathaniel. 1983. *The House of Seven Gables.* New York: Viking.

———. 1990. *The Scarlet Letter*, edited by Brian Harding. New York: Oxford University Press.

Hayden, Robert. 1975. "Those Winter Sundays." In *Angle of Ascent*, 113. New York: Liveright.

Henry V. 1944. Directed by Laurence Olivier. London: Two Cities Films.

Hentoff, Nat. 1982. *The Day They Came to Arrest the Book*. New York: Dell Laurel-Leaf.

Herbert, George. 1962. "Easter-Wings." In *Herbert*, edited by Richard Wilbur. New York: Dell.

Herrick, Robert. 1964. "To the Virgins to Make Much of Time." In *Seventeenth Century Poetry: The Schools of Donne and Jonson*, edited by Hugh Kenner. New York: Holt, Rinehart & Winston.

Hinton, S. E. 1967. *The Outsiders*. New York: Viking.

Hughes, Langston. 1994. "Dream Deferred." In *The Collected Poems of Langston Hughes*, edited by Arnold Ampersad and David Roessel. New York: Knopf.

Hurston, Zora Neale. (1937) 1990. *Their Eyes Were Watching God*. New York: Harper and Row.

Ibsen, Henrik. (1879) 1992. *A Doll's House*. New York: Dover.

Jackson, Shirley. (1948) 1982. "The Lottery." In *The Lottery: And Other Stories*. New York: Farrar, Straus & Giroux.

Johnson, Georgia Douglas. 1985. "Plumes." In *Plays by American Women: 1900–1930*, edited by Judith E. Barlow, 162–70. New York: Applause.

Juster, Norton. 1961. *The Phantom Tollbooth*. New York: Alfred A. Knopf.

Martin, Ann M. Babysitters' Club series. New York: Scholastic.

Marvell, Andrew. 1990. "To His Coy Mistress." In *Selections*, edited by Frank Kermode and Keith Walker. New York: Oxford University Press.

Mead, Richelle. Vampire Academy series. New York: Penguin.

Meyer, Stephenie. Twilight series. New York: Little, Brown.

Miller, Arthur. (1953) 2003. *The Crucible: A Play in Four Acts*. New York: Penguin Classics.

———. 1977. *Death of a Salesman*. New York: Penguin.

Milton, John. 1950. *Areopagitica*. In *Complete Poetry and Selected Prose of John Milton*. New York: Modern Library.

Morrison, Toni. (1988) 2004. *Beloved*. New York: Vintage.

Mortenson, Greg, and David Oliver Relin. 2006. *Three Cups of Tea: One Man's Mission to Fight Terrorism and Build Nations . . . One School at a Time*. New York: Penguin.

Oliver, Mary. 2004. "First Snow." In *New and Selected Poems*. Vol. 1. Boston: Beacon Press.

Orwell, George. 1949. *1984*. New York: Harcourt Brace Jovanovich.

Pascal, Francine. Sweet Valley High series. New York: Penguin Random House.

Poe, Edgar Allan. 1964. "Cask of Amontillado." In *Great Tales of Horror*. New York: Bantam.

Pope, Alexander. 1961. "An Essay on Criticism." In *Alexander Pope: Selected Poetry & Prose*, edited by William K. Wimsatt Jr. New York: Holt, Rinehart & Winston.

Rose, Reginald. 1983. *Twelve Angry Men: A Play in Three Acts*. Renewed version. Woodstock, IL: Dramatic Publishing Company.

Roth, Veronica. Divergent series. New York: Katherine Tegan Books.

Rowling, J. K. Harry Potter series. New York: Scholastic.

Rutsky, Joshua. 2001. *Beyond the Bard: Fifty Plays for Use in the English Classroom*. Boston: Allyn & Bacon.

Salinger, J. D. 1951. *The Catcher in the Rye*. Boston: Little, Brown.

Satrapi, Marjane. 2004. *Persepolis: The Story of a Childhood*. New York: Pantheon.

Shakespeare, William. 1942. *The Complete Plays and Poems of William Shakespeare*, edited by William Allan Neilson and Charles Jarvin Hill. Boston: Riverside Press.

Shelley, Mary. (1916) 1984. *Frankenstein*. New York: Bantam.

———. 2005. *Frankenstein: The Graphic Novel*, adapted by Gary Reed. New York: Puffin Graphics.

Simon, Neil. 1993. *Lost in Yonkers*. New York: Samuel French.

Smith, Jeff. 2005. *Out from Boneville*. New York: Scholastic.

Spiegelman, Art. 1986. *Maus: A Survivor's Tale. Vol. 1: My Father Bleeds History*. New York: Pantheon Books.

Steinbeck, John. (1937) 1993. *Of Mice and Men*. New York: Penguin Great Books.

Stine, R. L. Fear Street series. New York: Scholastic.

———. Goosebumps series. New York: Scholastic.

Swift, Jonathan. 1984. "A Modest Proposal." In *Jonathan Swift*, edited by Angus Ross and David Woolley. New York: Oxford University Press.

Tan, Shaun. 2007. *The Arrival*. New York: Arthur A. Levine.

Taylor, Henry. 1975. "Breakings." In *An Afternoon of Pocket Billiards*, 3. Salt Lake City: University of Utah Press.

Thoreau, Henry David. 1971. "Walden." In *The Writings of Henry David Thoreau: Walden*, edited by J. Lyndon Shanley. Princeton, NJ: Princeton University Press.

Tomine, Adrienne. 2003. *Summer Blonde*. Montreal: Drawn & Quarterly Publications.

Twain, Mark. 1985. *Adventures of Huckleberry Finn*. Berkeley: University of California Press.

Uhry, Alfred. 1987. *Driving Miss Daisy*. New York: Dramatists Play Service.

Westerfield, Scott. Uglies series. New York: Simon Pulse.

White, E. B. 1952. *Charlotte's Web*. New York: Harper.

———. 1990. *E. B. White: Writings from* The New Yorker, *1925–1976*, edited by Rebecca M. Dale. New York: HarperCollins.

Wilder, Thornton. (1938) 2003. *Our Town: A Play in Three Acts*. New York: Harper Perennial.

Wilson, August. (1983) 2010. *Fences*. New York: Samuel French.

Woodson, Jacqueline. 2014. *Brown Girl Dreaming*. New York: Nancy Paulsen Books.

Wright, Richard. 1940. *Native Son*. New York: Harper & Row.

Yang, Gene Luen. 2008. *American Born Chinese*. New York: Square Fish.

Yeats, W. B. 1961. "The Second Coming." In *Modern Poetry*, 2nd ed., edited by Maynard Mack, Leonard Dean, William Frost. Englewood Cliffs, NJ: Prentice-Hall.

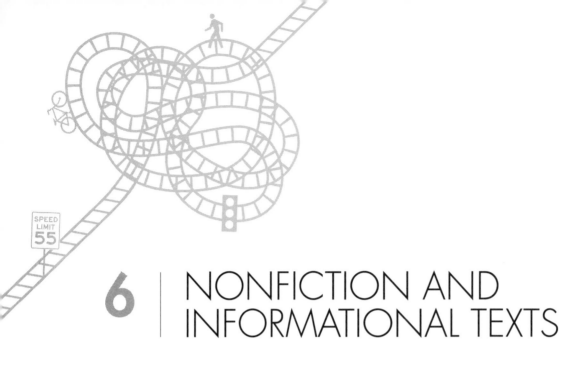

6 | NONFICTION AND INFORMATIONAL TEXTS

Knowledge is power. Information is liberating. Education is the premise of progress, in every society, in every family.

—Kofi Annan, Secretary General of the United Nations (1997–2006)

It may seem really strange, but not so long ago the reading of fiction, plays, novels, and poetry was seen as damaging. Only "true" literature, literature based on fact or advocating religious belief and practice, was considered worthy of reading. Plato worried that those who did not write about facts were liars and, in *The Republic*, he advocated banishing the poets and dramatists so that, in his ideal society, young people could be suitably protected. The issue resurfaced in the 1730s, when public libraries were established in the United States. In fact, in an 1876 Philadelphia conference, members of the newly formed American Library Association discussed whether novels should even be allowed on public library shelves. As a control measure, numerous libraries in the country strictly limited the number of books young adults could check out, thus restricting the reading of "damaging" fiction.

We are now a long way from this fear of fiction. Fiction has become not only acceptable in the typical English language arts (ELA) classroom but required. In fact, reading lists for many classrooms include *only* fiction. But for many, truly worthwhile reading is reading for fact and information. Today, the focus of new college- and career-ready standards have emphasized the importance of nonfiction, especially informational texts, and this renewed attention to nonfiction, although welcome to some readers, has worried some English teachers, who believe it will cause a deterioration of attention

228

to fiction, poetry, and drama. This is just not the case. Fiction and nonfiction can indeed coexist, and in this chapter we will show you effective ways of incorporating nonfiction, including informational texts, in your English classes. We don't want to restrict the more imaginative genres—we certainly don't want to banish the poets and dramatists—but we do want to open literature and reading to more than fiction, poetry, and drama.

Harnessing the Power of Information

Nonfiction is powerful, and informational texts are texts that make things happen. Written well, these texts can, as Kofi Annan implies in the speech quoted at the start of this chapter, "liberate" us from injustice, from tyranny, from fear, from ignorance. They are blueprints for better ideas, goals, and outcomes for the future. They are stories of real people facing obstacles in their societies and contending with social, economic, political, and racial forces. They are accounts of historical movements and the implications of policy decisions. Nonfiction and informational texts marshal facts and data to make claims, push agendas, suggest new directions, and outline actions. As readers and teachers, it is we who must unveil the action of these texts to reveal the understated power they contain and help students fully understand and even harness the power of information.

For many of our students, nonfiction is the only real deal, transcending their interest in any form of fiction, poetry, or drama. We believe nonfiction—both literary nonfiction and informational texts—needs more attention in our classes and needs more acceptance by us as teachers. Further, the very nature of nonfiction means that much of it is contemporary, and that can be a real boon to balance or explain classic fiction that is set decades or even centuries in the past.

On the other hand, you may have heard some grumbling from English teachers about giving more time in ELA to informational texts. This is understandable. We live in a period in which the humanities are taking a backseat to what are considered by some to be the more immediately practical and necessary disciplines of science, technology, engineering, and math—what you may also know as the STEM disciplines. Not since the launch of Russia's *Sputnik* in 1957 has the American public (and government) been so narrowly focused on these areas. However, we are very happy that there are those who are interested in physics, mathematics, and similar fields. Every time we drive over a bridge, take a train through a tunnel, turn up the heat, or discover an exciting new classroom app, we are grateful for the minds that create and maintain these wonders.

But it's also important to remember that humanities teachers have a great deal to contribute to, about, and by teaching informational texts. According to a recent study conducted by researchers at Northeastern University, "despite the recent focus on STEM degrees, most Americans and particularly business leaders say it is more important for graduates to be well-rounded and possess broader capabilities such as problem solving and communication skills" (2013, 3). Even STEM professionals need the ability to understand, analyze, and explain the technical details of their specialized knowledge. Those skills are the basics of English ELA. Recently Ken, who teaches at a research university known worldwide for STEM education, asked his colleagues about their opinions of humanities education. To a person, those engineering, math, and science educators said they valued a humanities perspective even in their STEM students.

Thinking Creatively About Information

One of the most common words in current professional discourse is *innovation*. We read stories of companies that didn't innovate and died (Blockbuster Video, Borders Books), and we hear about companies that continuously innovate, changing with the times and new technologies to not only survive but thrive (Netflix, Amazon, Starbucks). Innovation in STEM leads to discoveries that save lives, create new technologies, decrease pollution, and more. But how do people develop the ability to innovate? According to educator George Couros, "innovation is *a way of thinking*. It is a way of considering concepts, processes, and potential outcomes; it is not a thing, a task or even technology" (2015, 19–20, emphasis in the original). Critical, imaginative thinking is what English teachers do best. And, if we can help students develop the capacity to apply their imaginations even to technical texts and tasks, we can help create smarter, better STEM workers. Even as unexpected a source as *The 9/11 Commission Report*, in which a group of U.S. congressional representatives explain their finding after an exhaustive study of the tragic 9/11 attacks, focuses on the importance of imagination. The report blames a failure of imagination for U.S. intelligence agencies' lack of foresight. Though in hindsight all the information was there for the United States to imagine the plans and proportion of the 9/11 attacks, no one foresaw it (2004, 339–47). The report's authors call emphatically for the importance of imagination in future intelligence operations. This is something English teachers do quite naturally. We create multitudes of exercises to increase students' capacities for flights of fancy, and we help students harness those flights for their own practical ends, be those ends analyses of stories, creative correspondence, or drawing new, original inferences about the world around them—setting themselves apart from groupthink. Applying these forms of thinking to informational texts will expand our students' reach and further develop their critical capacities to innovate in whatever field they pursue. (For more on English teachers' responsibilities in the wake of 9/11, see Lindblom [2005].)

Developing a Preference for Good Information

Finally, and possibly the most important thing English teachers can teach their students is to encourage a *disposition for using good information*. Since the ancient Greeks and possibly long before, educators have known how important it is to instill in students not only the skills of effective argument but also the desire to use those skills effectively and ethically. We should develop students who *want to* populate their arguments, reports, and all their writing with only the best, most useful, and most rigorously ethical information they can find. Perhaps we cannot teach students to be ethical people, but we can certainly help them understand the importance of academic honesty and fair dealing, and the strength of rigorous information and evidence. Some people fall victim to faulty logic (as producers and as consumers) not because they are evil, but because they don't know any differently. As professional educators we are duty-bound to ensure students know how to recognize and use good information in responsible ways, and we should do everything practical to encourage them to prefer ethical approaches to informational texts.

Nonfiction Text Types

Nonfiction is not a single genre. It's far more complicated than that. In fact, if you think about it, the term *nonfiction* only tells us what it is not, not what it is. In the following sections, we discuss many forms of text that are properly considered nonfiction, and you'll see that they fit loosely into two broad categories: literary nonfiction and informational texts. *Literary nonfiction* includes biographies, autobiographies, and memoirs—texts that are intended to be aesthetically appreciable narratives based on factual evidence. *Informational texts*, on the other hand, are primarily intended to communicate specific, often technical, information as clearly and engagingly as possible. Literary nonfiction has long been part of the ELA curriculum. Informational texts, however, have taken on a far more prominent role in ELA, especially given new focus on college- and career-ready standards.

Literary Nonfiction

For teachers, nonfiction—whether it be a full book or an article or an essay, whether it be letters, diaries, memoirs, speeches—can also be a vehicle to give students practice with important skills. Although many ELA teachers are first and foremost lovers of fiction, literary nonfiction is powerful and highly useful in the classroom. English teachers are generally comfortable teaching literary nonfiction, which includes work in the following genres:

- exposition
- argument
- personal essays
- speeches
- autobiographies

- opinion pieces
- biographies
- memoirs
- news and feature stories (journalism)

To find work in these genres, book lists, such as those compiled by the American Library Association and by the National Council of Teachers of English, as well as sources such as Joyce Carol Oates and Robert Atwan's *The Best Essays of the Century* and articles such as Larry R. Johannessen's "When History Talks Back: Teaching Nonfiction Literature of the Vietnam War" are helpful. Other regular essay collections are useful to consult, such as Ariel Levy's *Best American Essays 2015* and *The Best American Science and Nature Writing 2015*, edited by Rebecca Skloot and Tim Folger (2015).

Many well-written nonfiction books on a wide variety of topics are available. Students may be interested in reading some of these examples:

- Truman Capote's account of murder and motivation in *In Cold Blood* was one of the first nonfiction books written in a style closer to a novel than an informational text.

- A nonfiction classic, Jacob A. Riis' *How the Other Half Lives*, is a portrait of tenement poverty in 1900 New York.

- James Agee's *Let Us Now Praise Famous Men* looks at life in rural American during the Depression. The books by Riis and Agee combine photography and prose, and Agee's work in particular is what we now term *multigenre*, using many forms of writing to capture the people and the landscape of the Depression-era South.

- Science topics are covered in Mary Roach's hilarious *Gulp*, which explains the human digestive system, and Rebecca Skloot's *The Immortal Life of Henrietta Lacks*, which is the story of how scientists used a woman's tissue to make breakthroughs in cancer treatments and at the same time raised ethical issues about the use of human tissue.

- Disasters are a perennially favorite topic, and students can read about hurricanes (Erik Larson's *Isaac's Storm: A Man, a Time, and the Deadliest Hurricane in History*), shipwrecks (Erik Larson's *Dead Wake: The Last Crossing of the* Lusitania), whaling accidents (Nathaniel Philbrick's National Book Award–winning *In the Heart of the Sea: The Tragedy of the Whaleship* Essex), and deadly mountain climbing (Jon Krakauer's *Into Thin Air: A Personal Account of the Mt. Everest Disaster*).

- Exposés are popular nonfiction topics: Barbara Ehrenreich writes about the difficulties of working poverty in the United States in *Nickel and Dimed*, and the food industry is covered by Michael Pollan in *The Omnivore's Dilemma* and Eric Schlosser in *Fast Food Nation*.

- There are also illuminating stories of race in America (Wes Moore's *The Other Wes Moore*) as well as the account of a terrifying event from the Civil Rights movement detailed in *The Freedom Summer Murders* (by Don Mitchell).

- What is your pleasure? There are books about a legendary and unlikely racehorse (Laura Hillenbrand's *Seabiscuit*), long-distance and endurance swimming (Lynne Cox's *Swimming to Antarctica*), and the capture of assassin John Wilkes Booth (*Chasing Lincoln's Killer* by James Swanson).

- There are also biographies of figures as disparate as Wonder Woman (by Jill Lepore), Elvis (*Careless Love* and *Last Train to Memphis* by Peter Guralnick), the Wright Brothers (by David McCullough), Cleopatra (by Stacy Schiff), and Alexander Hamilton (by Ron Chernow), on which the blockbuster 2016 Tony-award-winning Broadway play is based.

- Today, memoir is experiencing resurgence, and students who might be turned off by classic fiction may well be interested in contemporary accounts of individual lives. Try young adult writer Paula Fox's *Borrowed Finery* and Frank McCourt's *Angela's Ashes*. Fox recounts her life with elegant but indifferent parents in urban New York City; McCourt's book takes place in Limerick, Ireland, and details, often with grim humor, poverty and hardship. *It Was Me All Along* by Andie Mitchell traces the story of her issues with food addiction, body image, and weight.

- In addition, there are numerous slave narratives from the nineteenth century and many excellent accounts of war—both older conflicts and more contemporary—which can be riveting to students despite their often-depressing content.

Informational Text Genres

Informational texts place a premium on clarity, accuracy—and in the best cases—reader engagement. Their primary purpose is to communicate specific material of use to particular audiences: those readers who are personally interested in the material, and those readers the informational text authors believe *should be* personally interested in the material.

And what is the range of this material? How things work, how things are built, statistics regarding weather, sales, and achievements are all the province of informational texts, and these texts often fascinate students. The broad range of informational text genres available for study in ELA classes may be less familiar to English teachers with a traditional background in literature. Informational texts include these genres:

- historical studies
- technical documents that include information displayed in graphs, charts, maps, or other visuals
- economic analyses
- directions
- forms/surveys
- articles on technical topics written for broad audiences
- applications (job, college)
- résumés

- literary analyses
- political cartoons
- infomercials
- documentary films
- manuals
- workplace/business correspondence (memos, emails, texts, tweets)
- scientific reports
- summaries
- précis

Sources for interesting informational texts abound—everything from nonfiction magazines, to *The Guinness World Records*, issued and updated every year (one of the most popular books in any school library), to nonfiction books. Orbis Pictus winner *Phineas Gage: A Gruesome but True Story About Brain Science* by John Fleischmann tells students much about an emerging scientific area of study, and George Sullivan's *Built to Last: Building America's Amazing Bridges, Dams, Tunnels, and Skyscrapers*, though geared to younger readers, offers narrative, photographs, and statistics on important structures in America. The DK (Dorling Kindersley) Eyewitness series, examples of which are often housed in reference sections in the school library, combine in oversized books beautiful photography and interesting information on topics as wide-ranging as the ocean, weapons of spies, and animals of all kinds. Again, for students who believe that the world of reading is confined to boring stories about uninteresting people who mostly live in the past, informational texts open a very different landscape.

Reading Informational Texts for Authentic Purposes

It's rare for anyone to read an informational text against his or her will. Most people in the world outside school read informational texts constantly, but they do so for specific purposes that matter to them. Instruction manuals, tax preparation and legal advice, investment strategies, directions for signing up for health insurance or government programs, rules for games, reports on the best consumer products, recipes, articles on hobbies, movie and book reviews—these are texts that are widely read but rarely assigned. People choose to consult these texts because they will help them achieve their aims. English teachers should try to approach informational texts with these authentic purposes in mind.

In our chapter on writing, we describe the power of authentic writing assignments—assignments that engage students in writing for real audiences and for real purposes. We should also assign informational text reading in a manner that engages students' authentic purposes. Educator Nell K. Duke agrees:

> [S]tudents in school usually read informational text to answer questions at the back of the chapter, to complete a test prep worksheet, or simply because the teacher said to do so. Some of these activities may be unavoidable, but we need to create classrooms in which students read informational text as often as possible for more compelling purposes. (2004)

What compelling purposes might we devise for students to read informational texts? They might research any of the following:

- archival documents from local historical societies
- local civic association documents, town hall meeting notes, school board meeting minutes

- informational sources on their own outside interests and passions to further develop their own pursuits
- books and articles about the life of a favored athlete, musician, author, inventor, business leader
- recipes, song lyrics, speeches, diaries, personal essays, and other cultural texts related to a book they are reading in class
- scientific, economic, and policy studies on environmental or humane concerns raised by a book the class is reading or to an important local issue
- studies that can allow students to find facts related to a local election or local controversy
- statistics on future employment, the best colleges for specific majors, wealth management
- research-based articles on what makes people happy.

English Journal frequently publishes articles in which teachers describe lessons that have engaged students in research and writing projects that are linked to community action. We recommend Kim-Marie Cortez-Riggio's (2011) "The Green Footprint Project," for which students conducted research, composed pamphlets, and gave presentations to engage community members in important local environmental issues, and Heidi L. Hallman's (2009) "Authentic, Dialogic Writing," in which her students (all pregnant or parenting teens) found a positive way to confront a disrespectful letter about them in their local newspaper.

TECH TALK: *Finding Authentic Informational Texts of Interest*

A great way to find interesting informational texts is to simply plug into an Internet search engine "Government Study on _____" and in the blank put a hobby or other interest of your students; for example, video game violence, soccer, car accidents, environmental activism. There's literally no end to the kinds of interesting informational reading students can do if teachers create the space for them to engage their own interests in the world around them. Common Core recognizes the value of authentic purposes in reading informational texts and encourages teachers not to shy away even from texts that might appear controversial: "The use of authentic reading material may mean that some material is emotionally charged or may use language outside of a student's particular cultural experience" (New York State Education Department 2013).

Approaching Informational Texts

Frankly, one of the concerns teachers have about students approaching informational texts is their density, dryness, and length. Unlike fiction, many informational texts are not meant to be read from beginning to end, but are rather to be skimmed. Studies, policy statements, and the like shouldn't be read the same way we read traditional literature. Rather, one should look at the title, the subtitles, and the references to get a sense of the purpose and structure of the piece and how its claims will be supported. Readers should try to detect any bias, frame, or slant that will influence the writing's value. If readers are looking for something specific within the piece, they should find that before they read the entire piece, so they know it's something they should spend their time on. Only then should readers read the entire piece from beginning to end. One of the reasons why readers should engage informational texts is so they can experience the different forms that authentic reading takes. This is somewhat different for students, and it needs to be explicitly highlighted by teachers.

On the other hand, some informational texts are written to be read like works of fiction. In his *Minds Made for Stories: How We Really Read and Write Informational and Persuasive Texts*, Thomas Newkirk challenges the notion that informational texts are not meant to be read like narratives.

> [Many claim] that with narrative texts we "enter into the world of the author," but that with informational texts we do not—primarily because nothing "happens" in these texts. We stay more outside of them; we use them, but we don't enter them. (2014, 11)

In Newkirk's aptly named chapter, "All Writing Is Narrated," he explains several ways in which informational text writers entice readers to enter their texts by "narrating" their works in the following ways: using humor, adding "surprise value," employing colloquial speech, expressing "affection" for their subject, "grounding the complex in the familiar," and practicing "strategic self disclosure" (2014, 72–84). We can help students see the power of narrative in informational texts they read and encourage them to harness it in their own writing.

Activities with Nonfiction

What else should we do with nonfiction, both informational texts and literary nonfiction? Actually, we should do similar activities to what we do with fiction: read it, discuss it, and write about it. Certainly one crucial aspect of nonfiction is point of view and how that shapes what is highlighted in research and fact: any nonfiction book or essay or article will have an undeniable slant on the topic, and asking students to discuss and discern an author's point of view or even bias is an important intellectual aspect of reading and assessing nonfiction. Although this may seem very obvious with biography and autobiography, it is also crucial in other pieces. What an author selects or fails to emphasize can shape the reader's view of any topic. For instance, in Lillian Schlissel's *Women's Diaries of the Westward Journey,* a collection of American women's writing as they trekked the Overland Trail in the mid-nineteenth century, the editor's emphasis is far different from what most historical accounts include. Schlissel highlights, for instance, the repeated mention of graves on the side of the trail, final resting places for adults and infants who did not survive the journey. This detail, which some of the women diarists consistently choose to include, is rarely mentioned in men's accounts and is part of the different point of view. As another example, *Daughters of the Samurai* by Janice P. Nimura takes an entirely different look at the recent history of Japan and details the stories of a number of Japanese young women who in the 1870s were sent to live and study in the United States and then return to Japan to "modernize" their country.

Finally, nonfiction is also an excellent vehicle for skills instruction; using any kind of nonfiction, students can take notes, locate information, summarize passages, generate questions that the text may not answer, and connect and relate ideas. Many nonfiction books use maps, drawings, charts, reproductions of period photographs and newspapers, all of which can widen students' reading ability.

Augmenting Fiction with Informational Texts

In Chapter 5 we discuss the ways in which young adult literature can serve as a bridge to more sophisticated literary texts. Informational texts can play a similar bridging role in your English class. Short, accessible informational texts can enrich complicated literature texts; for example, a short informational piece that includes statistics and theories about teen suicide can make more concrete some of the sophisticated themes in *Romeo and Juliet*. And a shorter engaging literary piece can enable students to persevere through a dense informational text; for example, Kurt Vonnegut's widely anthologized "Harrison Bergeron," about a future in which people are deliberately handicapped to ensure equality, might make a good connection to a study of *The Americans with Disabilities Act* of 1990. As Chadwick and Grassie recently put it, "The nonfiction/informational texts complement and in some cases clarify the literature. The nonfiction essays contextualize the audience, the occasion, and purpose of the literature—its aims, its passions, its styles, and its message" (2016, 48). In fact, Chadwick says she could not teach *Huckleberry Finn* without "relying on informational texts to frame the reading and exploration for twenty-first century students. As students read 'Huck,' and encounter such words/phrases such as *bill of sale* and *runaway slave notice* that to them are completely foreign, I provide illustrative information documents and notices in contemporary periodicals" (43).

Sarah Brown Wessling (2011) has developed a clever method for putting texts together in a way that both enriches and makes more accessible the complex themes and content involved in them. Her method works very well for incorporating informational texts into literature classes. Wessling selects a long, complex text that will serve as what she calls the "fulcrum text." She uses the example of *The Odyssey*. Before she has the students begin reading the fulcrum text, she has them read one or more texts, which she calls "context texts," texts that "prepare students for deeper understanding of the fulcrum text [and that are] accessible and create motivation." To give context to *The Odyssey*, Wessling selects clips from the movie *Star Wars* and excerpts from Joseph Campbell's work on the hero. Finally, Wessling selects additional texts that serve as what she calls "texture texts," which may be read with or after the fulcrum text and that complement or contradict the fulcrum text in a way that "offers nuance" to the fulcrum text and the texture texts. For texture texts in this case, Wessling picks a National Public Radio piece on war veterans and violence and a *Frontline* episode on a similar topic (2011, 26–27). The Campbell essays and the news stories are informational texts that Wessling believes will enable and enrich her students' engagement with *The Odyssey*, which is a fairly sophisticated, long work of literature.

You may treat informational texts in your classes as fulcrums, context texts, and/ or texture texts. The important thing is that you incorporate such text types into your students' reading experiences and that you help your students develop the complex reading processes that will enable them to continue to seek out and read informational texts in the future.

TECH TALK: *Use www.newsela.com to Find and Teach Informational Texts*

Many teachers have found www.newsela.com to be an extremely valuable tool for finding and teaching informational texts. The website, which includes free services and for-pay extensions, contains many engaging news stories on worldwide current events and other topics students will find interesting, such as science, sports, money, and health. Each article on Newsela is available in five levels of readability; at the click of a button readers can make the article more or less complex in terms of sentence construction and specialized vocabulary. Many articles are also available in Spanish, also leveled for readability (translated into English). Newsela also lists text sets in a variety of fields. English teachers will be particularly interested in the text sets surrounding oft-taught literary works, both classic and contemporary, young adult and adult.

James R. Carlson found an excellent way to bring literary nonfiction into dialogue with informational texts by using what he calls "song-poems" (2010). Song-poems are songs whose lyrics are about or have a very specific connection to a historical event. Connecting these songs with nonfiction texts about the event enlightens students about history and can enrich their understanding and experience with other literary texts that are set in the same historical context or approach similar themes. He talks specifically about relating Bob Dylan's song, "The Death of Emmet Till" (1963) to Chris Crowe's (2003) nonfictional *Getting Away with Murder: The True Story of the Emmett Till Case*, but he also suggests songs by Johnny Cash, Jimi Hendrix, Buffalo Springfield, and others.

Middle school English teacher Victoria Alessi describes the ways she's incorporated informational texts into her classes.

> Due to their age and their minimal exposure to a wide variety of texts, many middle school students lack the world knowledge to fully and deeply comprehend required literature such as *To Kill a Mockingbird*, *Night*, *A Raisin in the Sun*, and *The Omnivore's Dilemma*. One can argue that background knowledge is not completely necessary to appreciate the beauty of *To Kill a Mockingbird*; however, background knowledge is necessary for students to understand the complexities of the relationships between the characters, the macro, meso, and micro settings, and the issues with racism that exist to this day.
>
> Rather than inundate my students with an overwhelming amount of informational texts at the beginning of a literature unit, I took a page from Kelly Gallagher's book *Readicide*, and I assign my students an Article of the Week as a way to support our central text. My eighth graders are required to read and annotate the article as a way to show evidence of their thinking as they are reading, and then they will either write a paragraph or complete a graphic organizer that, in addition to analyzing the article for meaning, often requires the students to connect the informational text to the literature. I use the website, Newsela.com, to find many of the articles, and because Newsela.com allows the user to choose the Lexile levels, I give the students the choice of a challenge article, a grade level article, or a below grade level article. By the end of the school year, the students have read almost forty articles independently and have connected the articles to their lives and to the texts that we are reading.
>
> Because the students are slowly building their world knowledge over the course of a unit of study, they are able to make connections between historical events, current events, and literature, and they are, without being forced, reading closely and analyzing the central text for overarching themes that occur in the informational texts and in the literature.

Still having trouble thinking about what you and your students could talk about regarding informational texts? Below we suggest a number of topics to broach with students as you read informational texts together.

Logic and Logical Fallacies

Logical thinking, deductive reasoning, and otherwise consistent, fact-based analytical skills are crucially important competencies for all students to develop. Anyone who knows adolescents knows they love debating and pointing out flaws in equity or logic, unless it's their own. Informational texts on topics that students truly care about provide excellent opportunities for developing logical thinking.

In an *English Journal* issue about logic and critical thinking, Robert C. Covel outlines logical fallacies and other concepts in logic that students would enjoy engaging. Here are a few of them to discuss with your students:

- *ad hominem*—"attacking the person instead of his or her argument"
- *ad populum*—"appealing to people's emotions, prejudices"

- *post-hoc, ergo propter hoc*—"faulty cause and effect," "jumping to conclusions"
- false dilemma—"giv[ing] only two options in a situation when more are available" (for example, "You're either with us or against us"). (2010, 49)

If you'd like a more fun way to examine logical fallacies, check out Ali Almossawi's (2013) *An Illustrated Book of Bad Arguments*, which is available free online (in five languages) and which includes simple descriptions of nineteen common logical fallacies with memorable drawings.

In fact, there is a great deal more to teach beyond logic that has to do with the ways in which writers (and speakers) use rhetoric in nonfiction and informational texts. English teacher Mary R. Lamb uses précis writing and what she calls "rhetorical reading responses" to get her students to "begin recognizing the various types of nonfiction genres and to evaluate various claims and methods" (2010, 49).

A truly unique and excellent book for teaching rhetoric is *Understanding Rhetoric: A Graphic Guide to Writing* by Losh et al. (2013). This comic-book-style textbook includes chapters on "Reading Strategically," "Argument Beyond Pro and Con," "Research," and more. The scholarship and advice in the book are excellent and the writing and illustrations are truly entertaining.

Studying Technical Writing Through Informational Texts

There's an entire field of study focused on the practice of and scholarship about technical writing. Technical writers must write about complex matters in clear, unambiguous, and accessible ways. Tech writers must also be able to understand specialized content knowledge and translate it to nonspecialists. This is no easy task, but reading technical documents and incorporating them into reading and research will give students experience and practice in these important skills.

A good entrée into the world of technical writing is to discuss with students some of the most important attributes of technical documents. According to author Mike Markel, there are eight measures of excellence worth exploring:

- honesty (to help people make wise choices about how to use the information)
- clarity (use of plain language, appropriate vocabulary, accessible style)
- accuracy
- accessibility (using subheadings, for example)
- comprehensiveness (including all the necessary information)
- conciseness
- professional appearance
- correctness (quoted in Welch [2010])

Swain, Graves, and Morse (2010) suggest that studying prominent features of writing is a powerful way to engage students in close reading of technical documents. Asking students to identify any of these features in informational texts can generate valuable discussion, which can improve students' attention to their own writing and thinking.

- Elaborated details
- Metaphor
- Vivid nouns/verbs
- Striking words
- Balance and parallelism
- Sentence variety
- Narrative storytelling

- Sensory Language
- Alliteration
- Hyperbole
- Effective repetition
- Effective organization
- Transitions
- Voice

(Swain, Graves, and Morse 2010, 84–85)

Figure 6–1. Positive Features in Writing

- Usage problems
- Garble
- Redundancy
- Faulty punctuation
- Shifting point of view

- Weak structural core
- Weak organization
- List technique
- Faulty spelling

(Swain, Graves, and Morse 2010, 85)

Figure 6–2. Negative Features in Writing

If you find yourself or your students seeking out more information in the field of technical writing, check out the website of the Association of Teachers of Technical Writing. This active group produces a great many valuable publications for writing teachers.

TECH TALK: *Using Google Alerts to Find the Latest Informational Texts*

To find very current informational texts, try using Google Alerts. Find Google Alerts by pasting it into your web browser and searching. Once there, and after establishing a Google account, you may create an alert on any topic in which you are interested. A few semesters ago, Ken taught a class using informational texts on happiness and on food production and nutrition, so he created an alert for the topics. Each week, he received an email with links to related blog posts, newspaper articles, government websites, videos, and more. Google alerts allows you to select how often you want to receive the lists of links (daily or weekly), how many links you want delivered, and from what regions of the world.

Disinformation, or Should We Save the Endangered Pacific Northwest Tree Octopus?

The Pacific Northwest tree octopus is the most intelligent cephalopod known, and this shy, solitary creature inhabits only the mild rain forests of the Olympic Peninsula. Moving from branch to branch using a form of locomotion called *tentaculation* and feeding on insects and small vertebrates, the tree octopus is a brilliant example of evolutionary "arboreal adaptation." You can find these facts and a great deal more fascinating, specific information about this amazing creature on the popular and remarkably thorough website dedicated to it (Zapato 2015).

What you will not learn from that website is probably the most important fact about the Pacific Northwest tree octopus: *It is completely made up.*

Apparently no one quite knows why Zapato took such pains to create the admirably copious and very authentic-seeming site dedicated to this fantasy creature, but clever teachers have for years been using the site to clue students into the fact that they can't believe everything they read on the Internet, even if it looks really, really true, if it exhibits all the qualities of what comedian Stephen Colbert has called "truthiness."

For as long as people have been communicating, rumors, innuendo, and deliberate subterfuge have been with us. With the dramatic increase of information sharing that the World Wide Web allows, Internet hoaxes abound. It is important that we not only acquaint students with the skills of critical analysis and the ability to spot logical fallacies but also alert them to the fact that they will also encounter *disinformation*: false information that is deliberately shared to hide the truth or to influence people's thoughts and actions.

Jonathan Ostenson outlines important activities for helping students develop the healthy Internet skepticism that they'll need to survive in an age of information and disinformation. He suggests that students be taught "initial markers" of website credibility, the importance of seeking out "corroboration," and learning to detect "author bias/agenda" (2009, 55–57).

Students must learn not only to be skeptical, but also to use tools such as Snopes .com to corroborate and confirm sources before using information from the Internet for significant decisions or actions. Of course, we should also teach students how to determine if a website is from a credible source, but even that can be very tricky. If you look for it, you can find a rerecording of Lincoln's voice taken from a wax velum recording housed at the Stanford University American Heritage Fellowship. However, the first recording device wasn't invented until twelve years after Lincoln's death; so this site is another hoax, and it's got nothing to do with Stanford University.

Crowdsourcing is another contemporary concept students should learn about. There is so much information out there that sometimes it's a good idea to pool the experiences of as many people as possible. Crowdsourcing is now common in fundraising and marketing, and it's even becoming a somewhat useful tool in research. Wikipedia, the online, crowdsourced encyclopedia-like website, has actually grown from a specious, frequently outlawed source of information to a valid first step in research. Crovitz and Smoot (2009) were two of the first English teachers to recognize that Wikipedia could be and should be an option for students. Used well, Wikipedia is a way to easily find more credible sources. In fact, as Crovitz and Smoot suggest, Wikipedia is potentially more useful than other sources because with an unlimited number of contributors, the information is often more up-to-date and further reaching than other sources could be (2009, 93). Again, of course, this is only valuable as a resource if Wikipedia users are predisposed to seeking credible confirmation before acting on the information learned. Responsible research is as much about attitude as ability.

Big Data, Visual Rhetoric, and Data Visualization

Powerful computers and software have enabled unprecedented amounts of data collection and number crunching. As a result, "big data" has become an influential force across fields. English teachers are not in the position to teach the quantitative aspects of big data, but we are neither immune to nor free from the responsibility to address big data. Big data is a primary force behind the major emphasis on standardized testing in education. It allows massive amounts of data gathering and endless analyses, comparisons, and cost-effectiveness ratios, which result in influential budget, policy, and ultimately classroom implications. All fields are now to at least some significant degree driven by data, and we must help students understand the ways in which data can be communicated clearly, compellingly, effectively, and ethically. These are the ways in which big data can be taken up in English classes.

One of the fasting-growing fields right now is data visualization, the creation of compelling visuals that engage viewers in the stories that data tells. In fact, thinking of data visualization as storytelling is not only what can connect big data to ELA; it's also how many in the field of data visualization describe their work.

David McCandless' (2016) TED Talk, "The Beauty of Data Visualization," is a great place to start a unit on data visualization or to get yourself thinking about how this area of study can connect to your curriculum. In it, McCandless demonstrates how appealing visual representations of massive amounts of data can engage ordinary audiences in specialized knowledge. According to Randy Krum, author of *Cool Infographics*, data visualizations are "visual representations of numerical values . . . [that] . . . create a picture from a given set of data" (2014, 2). Data visualizations are powerful tools—such as pie charts, bar graphs, line graphs, and streamgraphs—that help readers understand complex information.

One especially powerful form of data visualization is infographics: those ubiquitous Internet posters that give specific information about a particular topic, including links for more information and usually some call to action.

Infographics: Reading and Sharing the Stories That Data Tell

Searching the Internet for "infographics" or a specific search term with infographics (such as "fast food infographics") will quickly call forth a wealth of examples. But infographics are more than just data visualizations. An infographic is a "larger graphic design that combines data, visualizations, illustrations, text, and images together into a format that *tells a complete story*" (Krum 2014, 6, emphasis added).

Good infographics, according to Krum, are designed with attention to "storytelling by combining data visualization design and graphic design. Many of the good infographics follow a simple three-part story format: introduction, key message, a conclusion" (27). In fact, "If you're not 'telling a story' with your infographics . . . then you're doing it wrong," according to Lankow, Richie, and Crooks in *Infographics: The Power of Digital Storytelling*. "People are going to want to engage an infographic that tells a story that they care to know" (2012, 132). Taking the storytelling approach to infographics even further, Nathan Yau, author of *Visualize This*, says a composer of infographics should "[t]hink character development. Every data point has a story behind it in the same way that every character in a book has a past, present, and future" (2011, 7).

But there's an even more compelling reason why data visualization and infographics work so well: the "picture superiority effect." "People remember pictures better than words, especially over long periods of time" (Krum 2014, 20). Stephanie D. H. Evergreen explains further:

> [The picture superiority] effect is what allows us to move information along the memory continuum to catch the reader's eye, focus the reader's attention, and affix in the reader's memory. (2014, 10–11)

Data visualizations and infographics are thus powerfully compelling ways to communicate complex information. Even more impressively, though infographics are short, quick reads, they operate at sophisticated levels of critical thinking. Because infographics generally bring images and text together and because they almost always contain explicit links to credible sources of information, they are highly sophisticated examples of *synthesis*, a higher-order domain in Bloom's taxonomy. Ken and several of his colleagues have written extensively about how they use infographics to engage synthesis in informational texts (see Lindblom et al. [2016]), and they reflect here on how they've continued to treat infographics as an important element in their teaching.

High school English teacher Sara Grabow finds that infographics excite her students and help them develop an important set of new, critical thinking skills.

> Students are faced with visual texts all day, every day now that we are living in a technology- and information-driven age. Engaging with infographics provides students with the opportunity to discover information through a different medium. Infographics force students to engage in different modes and methods of thinking that are outside of the norm; the need for critical thinking increases when trying to understand infographics. They provide teachers with a forum to teach students how to read a visual text. Additionally, when students are asked to create infographics, that's when the real magic begins. The students

are thrilled that they are somehow "getting out of" writing an essay, and they are also encouraged to express their knowledge in a creative and visually appealing way. What students might not realize is the amount of thought and the depth of knowledge that creating an infographic requires. It is a win-win situation: students are excited to create the infographics, and I'm excited to see student learning taking shape and being expressed in an innovative manner.

Brittany Wilson, who is currently substitute teaching in a number of different school districts, focuses even more heavily on the depth of rigor students are willing to engage in when she assigns infographics.

In order to create a sufficient Infographic students have to utilize skills and a process similar to that of writing an essay. Infographics change the way students feel about reading informational texts and even writing essays because they begin the assignment with a different mindset. Students are excited and motivated to create their infographics, which leads to obtaining more from the informational texts because they see value to actively reading and annotating the information. I have even noticed that creating Infographics boosts students' confidence in their writing ability because the task is difficult but their motivation allows them to push through new levels of success. Students love to present and view each other's final products because they take pride in their Infographics.

TECH TALK: *Creating Infographics*

There's nothing like the experience of creating infographics to help students understand how to read and understand them. There are several free programs available for composing infographics, but we especially recommend two: pikochart and easel.ly, each found with a quick Internet search. Both programs offer easy-to-use infographic templates, icons, backgrounds, and colors. Composers can download the infographics, keep them private, or make them public. Infographic technology continues to evolve and now includes the ability to add animated graphics (that change when one hovers the cursor over them) and the ability to embed videos directly within them. Try having your students compose infographics in which they link important social issues (and informational texts about them) to literary works you are reading in class. Or, compose infographic assignments for which students must relate a historical context to a literary work.

More Ideas and Resources for Teaching Nonfiction and Informational Texts

Inhabit the Text

Earlier in this chapter, we discussed Newkirk's confrontation of the idea that people "enter the world" of fictional texts, but not informational texts. A great way to encourage students to enter the world of an informational text is to stage a debate, mock trial, or other performance activity for which the students play the role of the authors they are reading. What would Thoreau and Barbara Ehrenreich say if they were to meet? What would a long elevator conversation shared by Martin Luther King Jr., Sandra Cisneros, and Louise Erdrich be like? In an even more radical sense of entering, or even inhabiting, the text, Joel M. Freedman (2009) suggests having students write from various perspectives in a news story. Freedman's fascinating idea stemmed from a disturbing newspaper article he read about a young gay man who was murdered in an area near where he taught. For the National Day of Silence that year, Freedman brought that article to class and had students write letters and statements as if they were the people—the real-life characters—in that article: the murdered young man, the accused murderer, the parents and friends of both boys, the police officers involved, and the judge who would be deciding the outcome of the trial. This method truly brings informational text to life.

Connect to Students' Future Employment

It's a common assignment to focus students on writing and reading résumés, cover letters, and other work-related documents. But infusing such lessons with contemporary statistics and projections about workplace needs and required education can energize this tired assignment. Well-known English teacher Jim Burke (2012) wrote an in-depth description of a particularly well-designed lesson for his students in which the local Rotary Club played an important role.

Engage Students in Community and Global Action

Part of being a good citizen of a democracy is knowing how to advocate responsibly and effectively for causes you believe in. Adolescents are notoriously rigorous when it comes to fairness, and they should be encouraged to find positive ways to address injustice when they find it. One *English Journal* issue dedicated to environmental issues includes descriptions of projects that engaged students in interesting ELA-related projects. Michelle Jewett (2011) used mandalas and other creative assignments to engage her students in local, environmental concerns. Miller and Nilsen (2011) describe a lesson they developed focused on academic language related to environmental sustainability. In another issue, Cuff and Statz (2010) designed a series of readings and projects on analyzing advertisements after students view the documentary *The Story of Stuff*. Finding issues students care about will motivate them to research, read, and use a variety of informational texts—and we can help them deal with such texts effectively and responsibly.

Visit Historical Archives

If you've never been to an archive, you should go—and take your students with you. Many archives are available online now, but being there in person, seeing and feeling old documents is so much more exciting. Archives collect fascinating nonfiction pieces, including personal diaries, business logs, collections of letters, photographs, out-of-print books, and more. Finding and telling the stories hidden in archival treasure chests is utterly engaging and takes serious attention. Lisa Beckelhimer exposes her students to a great variety of authentic historical documents in her English class. "History," she says,

> is not confined to books but is available in texts ranging from online archives, websites, and blogs to documentaries, videos, photographs, and editorial cartoons and from documents such as meeting minutes and government reports to personal writing such as diaries and memoirs and literary sources such as poetry and song lyrics. (2010, 55)

After working with so many real-world documents, perhaps it's no surprise that Beckelhimer's students thought the work in her class "seemed more real" (60). You can also employ students' imaginations to bring the historical contexts of literature you read to life. For example, Lori W. Kloehn (2009) worked with a social studies teacher to create details about the lives of people who might have lived during the Civil War. The students read histories, conducted research on both the Civil War and the towns where these people hailed from, and wrote imaginative biographies about them. Even more interestingly, once the students had written about their characters, they began exchanging historically accurate letters (tea-stained for effect) to each other in character.

Understanding Information

We began this chapter with wise words from Kofi Annan, "information is liberating." In truth, it's not that simple. As Paulo Freire (1972), legendary teacher and educational theorist, reminds us, "Liberating education consists in acts of cognition, not transferrals of information." Information isolated from contexts, people, and actions is worthless. But when people use good information for good purposes—when they use it to experience and create genuine acts of cognition—information can be a powerfully liberating tool.

Teach your students to prefer credible information, encourage them to develop a disposition toward rigorous research and reasoning, and help them earn the confidence to use it responsibly in the directions they wish to pursue in their lives. Standards require attention to nonfiction and informational texts for a variety of good reasons, but the best reason we know of for teaching them is because they will help your students build a better future.

For Your Journal

One of the most intriguing aspects of nonfiction and informational texts is the concept of what is unvarnished fact presented as being "true." Although fiction is often critiqued for its departure from reality, many nonfiction and informational texts also present factual information that is interpreted and shaped. Pick one or two pieces of nonfiction and/or informational text that you think your students might like to read. What is in those texts that could be clearly characterized as fact? What could be characterized as interpretation of fact? How do the two, fact and interpretation of fact, intertwine, and to what extent do you think your students need to make this distinction as they read these nonfiction and/ or informational texts?

References

Annan, Kofi. 1997. Address to World Bank Conference "Global Knowledge '97." Toronto, Canada. 22 June. www.un.org/press/en/1997/19970623.sgsm6268.html.

Beckelhimer, Lisa. 2010. "From Hitler to Hurricanes, Vietnam to Virginia Tech: Using Historical Nonfiction to Teach Rhetorical Context." *English Journal* 99 (4): 55–60.

Burke, Jim. 2012. "*EJ* in Focus: Connecting the Classroom, Community, and Curriculum." *English Journal* 101 (4): 17–28.

Carlson, James. R. 2010. "Songs That Teach: Using Song-Poems to Teach Critically." *English Journal* 99 (4): 65–71.

Chadwick, Jocelyn A., and John E. Grassie. 2016. *Teaching Literature in the Context of Literacy Instruction*. Portsmouth, NH: Heinemann.

Cortez-Riggio, Kim-Marie. 2011. "The Green Footprint Project: How Middle School Students Inspired Their Community and Raised Their Self-Worth." *English Journal* 100 (3): 39–43.

Couros, George. 2015. *The Innovator's Mindset: Empower Learning, Unleash Talent, and Lead a Culture of Creativity.* San Diego, CA: Dave Burgess Consulting.

Covel, Robert C. 2010. "The Three Rs of Teaching Logic: Revelation, Relevance, and Reinforcement." *English Journal* 99 (6): 47–50.

Crovitz, Darren, and Scott W. Smoot. 2009. "Wikipedia: Friend, Not Foe." *English Journal* 98 (3): 91–97.

Cuff, Shannon, and Heather Statz. 2010. "*The Story of Stuff*: Reading Advertisements Through Critical Eyes." *English Journal* 99 (3): 27–32.

Duke, Nell K. 2004. "The Case for Informational Text." *Educational Leadership* 61 (6): 40–44. www.ascd.org/publications/educational-leadership/mar04/vol61/num06/The-Case-for -Informational-Text.aspx.

Evergreen, Stephanie D. H. 2014. *Presenting Data Effectively: Communicating Your Findings for Maximum Impact*. Thousand Oaks, CA: Sage.

Freedman, Joel M. 2009. "Echoes of Silence: Empathy and Making Connections Through Writing Process." *English Journal* 98 (4): 92–95.

Freire, Paulo. 1972. *Pedagogy of the Oppressed*. Harmondsworth, UK: Penguin.

Gallagher, Kelly. 2009. *Readicide: How Schools Are Killing Reading and What You Can Do About It.* Portland, ME: Stenhouse.

Hallman, Heidi L. 2009. "Authentic, Dialogic Writing: The Case of a Letter to the Editor." *English Journal* 98 (5): 43–47.

Jewett, Michelle. 2011. "Between Dreams and Beasts: Four Precepts for Green English Teaching." *English Journal* 100 (3): 30–38.

Johannessen, Larry R. 2002. "When History Talks Back: Teaching Nonfiction Literature of the Vietnam War." *English Journal* 91 (4): 39–47.

Kloehn, Lori W. 2009. "Imagination and Learning: Students Living 'Real' Lives During the Civil War." *English Journal* 9 (2): 37–41.

Krum, Randy. 2014. *Cool Infographics: Effective Communication with Data Visualization and Design.* Indianapolis, IN: Wiley.

Lamb, Mary R. 2010. "Teaching Nonfiction through Rhetorical Reading." *English Journal* 99 (4): 43–49.

Lankow, Jason, Josh Ritchie, and Ross Crooks. 2012. *Infographics: The Power of Visual Storytelling.* Hoboken, NJ: Wiley.

Lindblom, Kenneth. 2005. "Teaching English in the World: The Post-9/11 English Teacher." *English Journal* 94 (4): 106–109.

Lindblom, Ken, Nicole Galante, Sara Grabow, and Brittany Wilson. 2016. "Composing Infographics to Synthesize Informational & Literary Texts." *English Journal* 105 (6): 37–45.

Losh, Elizabeth, Jonathan Alexander, Kevin Cannon, and Zander Cannon. 2013. *Understanding Rhetoric: A Graphic Guide to Writing.* New York: Bedford/St. Martin's.

Markel, Mike. 2009. *Technical Communication.* 9th ed. Boston: Bedford.

McCandless, David. 2016. "The Beauty of Data Visualization." TED. Jul 2010. Lecture. www.ted .com/talks/david_mccandless_the_beauty_of_data_visualization?language=en.

Miller, Donna L., and Alleen Pace Nilsen. 2011. "Sustainability and the Recycling of Words." *English Journal* 100 (3): 55–61.

New York State Education Department. 2013. "Selection of Authentic Texts for Common Core Instruction: Guidance and a List of Resources for Text Selection." Engage.NY. https://www .engageny.org/resource/selection-of-authentic-texts-for-common-core-instruction-guidance-and -a-list-of-resources.

Newkirk, Thomas. 2014. *Minds Made for Stories: How We Really Read and Write Informational and Persuasive Texts.* Portsmouth, NH: Heinemann.

Northeastern University. 2013. "Innovative Imperative: Enhancing Higher Education Outcomes: Public Opinion Survey Results." Northeastern University 2nd Annual Innovation Poll. www .northeastern.edu/innovationsurvey/pdfs/Northeastern_University_Innovation_Imperative_Higher _Ed_Outcomes_Poll_Deck_FINAL_Delivered.pdf.

Ostenson, Jonathan. 2009. "Skeptics on the Internet: Teaching Students to Read Critically." *English Journal* 98 (5): 54–59.

Swain, Sherry Seale, Richard L. Graves, and David T. Morse. 2010. "Prominent Feature Analysis: What It Means for the Classroom." *English Journal* 99 (4): 84–89.

Welch, Kristen Doyle. 2010. "Poetry, Visual Design, and the How-To Manual: Creativity in the Teaching of Technical Writing." *English Journal* 99 (4): 37–42.

Wessling, Sarah Brown. 2011. *Supporting Students in a Time of Core Standards: English Language Arts, Grades 9–12.* Urbana, IL: NCTE.

Yau, Nathan. 2011. *Visualize This: The Flowing Data Guide to Design, Visualization, and Statistics.* Indianapolis, IN: Wiley.

Literature Cited

Agee, James. 2000. *Let Us Now Praise Famous Men* (with photographs by Walker Evans). New York: Houghton Mifflin.

Almossawi, Ali. 2013. *An Illustrated Book of Bad Arguments.* New York: HarperCollins Publishers. https://bookofbadarguments.com/.

Americans with Disabilities Act of 1990, as Amended. 2016. www.ada.gov/pubs/adastature08.pdf.

Capote, Truman. 1994. *In Cold Blood*. New York: Vintage.

Chernow, Ron. 2005. *Alexander Hamilton*. New York: Penguin.

Cox, Lynne. 2004. *Swimming to Antarctica: Tales of a Long-Distance Swimmer*. New York: Harcourt.

Crowe, Chris. 2003. *Getting Away with Murder: The True Story of the Emmett Till Case*. New York: Dial.

Dorling Kindersley Eyewitness series. New York: Penguin.

Dylan, Bob. (1963) 1991. "The Death of Emmett Till." Special Rider Music. CD.

Ehrenreich, Barbara. 2001. *Nickel and Dimed: On (Not) Getting by in America*. New York: Henry Holt.

Fleischman, John. 2002. *Phineas Gage: A Gruesome but True Story About Brain Science*. New York: Houghton Mifflin.

Fox, Paula. 2001. *Borrowed Finery*. New York: Henry Holt.

Guinness World Records. www.guinnessworldrecords.com/.

Guralnick, Peter. 1994. *Last Train to Memphis: The Rise of Elvis Presley*. Boston: Little, Brown.

————. 1999. *Careless Love: The Unmaking of Elvis Presley*. Boston: Little, Brown.

Hansberry, Lorraine. 1958. *A Raisin in the Sun*. New York: Random House.

Hillenbrand, Laura. 2001. *Seabiscuit: An American Legend*. New York: Ballantine.

Krakauer, Jon. 1999. *Into Thin Air: A Personal Account of the Mt. Everest Disaster*. New York: Anchor Books.

Larson, Erik. 1999. *Isaac's Storm: A Man, a Time, and the Deadliest Hurricane in History*. New York: Random House.

————. 2015. *Dead Wake: The Last Crossing of the* Lusitania. New York: Crown.

Lee, Harper. 1960. *To Kill a Mockingbird*. New York: Grand Central.

Lepore, Jill. 2015. *The Secret History of Wonder Woman*. New York: Vintage.

Levy, Ariel, ed. 2015. *The Best American Essays 2015*. New York: Houghton Mifflin.

McCourt, Frank. 1996. *Angela's Ashes*. New York: Scribner's.

McCullough, David. 2015. *The Wright Brothers*. New York: Simon and Schuster.

Mitchell, Andie. 2015. *It Was Me All Along: A Memoir*. New York: Potter/Ten Speed/Harmony.

Mitchell, Don. 2014. *The Freedom Summer Murders*. New York: Scholastic.

Moore, Wes. 2010. *The Other Wes Moore: One Name, Two Fates*. New York: Random House.

Nimura, Janice P. 2015. *Daughters of the Samurai: A Journey from East to West and Back*. New York: W. W. Norton.

The 9/11 Commission Report: Final Report of the National Commission on Terrorist Attacks upon the United States. 2004. Authorized Edition. New York: W. W. Norton.

Oates, Joyce Carol, and Robert Atwan, eds. 2001. *The Best Essays of the Century*. New York: Houghton Mifflin.

Philbrick, Nathaniel. 2000. *In the Heart of the Sea: The Tragedy of the Whaleship* Essex. New York: Penguin.

Plato. 1991. *The Republic*. 2nd ed. Translated by Allan Bloom. New York: Basic Books.

Pollan, Michael. 2006. *The Omnivore's Dilemma: A Natural History of Four Meals*. New York: Penguin.

Riis, Jacob A. 1971. *How the Other Half Lives*. New York: Dover.

Roach, Mary. 2013. *Gulp: Adventures on the Alimentary Canal*. New York: W. W. Norton.

Schiff, Stacy. 2010. *Cleopatra: A Life*. Boston: Little, Brown.

Schlissel, Lillian. 2004. *Women's Diaries of the Westward Journey*. New York: Schocken.

Schlosser, Eric. 2001. *Fast Food Nation: The Dark Side of the All-American Meal*. New York: Houghton Mifflin.

Skloot, Rebecca. 2010. *The Immortal Life of Henrietta Lacks*. New York: Random House.

Skloot, Rebecca, and Tim Folger, eds. 2015. *The Best American Science and Nature Writing 2015*. New York: Houghton Mifflin Harcourt.

Sullivan, George. 2005. *Built to Last: Building America's Amazing Bridges, Dams, Tunnels, and Skyscrapers*. New York: Scholastic Nonfiction.

Swanson, James. 2009. *Chasing Lincoln's Killer*. New York: Scholastic.

Vonnegut, Kurt. 1961. "Harrison Bergeron." *The Magazine of Fantasy and Science Fiction* 1 (Jan.): 5–10.

Zapato, Lyle. 2015. *Help Save the Endangered Pacific Northwest Tree Octopus from Extinction*. 17 May. http://zapatopi.net/treeoctopus/.

7 | WORDS, WORDS, WORDS

Language, be it remember'd, is not an abstract construction of the learn'd, or of dictionary-makers, but is something arising out of the work, needs, ties, joys, affections, tastes, of long generations of humanity, and has its bases broad and low, close to the ground.

—Walt Whitman, *Slang in America*

There is perhaps no more challenging aspect of language arts than teaching language itself. As Whitman (1964) points out, language constantly changes as the needs and whims of its users (us) shift. Often we find that new teachers are most uneasy about their knowledge of English language and how they may (or should) approach it with their students. In this chapter we provide a great deal of information about the research underpinning English language and options for teaching it in your classrooms. As you will read, we're not shy about pointing out social injustices that have occurred in the teaching of English usage, nor do we neglect the importance of teaching all students how to develop their skills in what is often called Standard English. We hope you will find this chapter provocative, informative, and—most important—full of ideas for enriching your language arts classroom. It is, as the Prince of Denmark somewhat wearily noted, "words, words, words" (Shakespeare 1942, II. ii)—and it is far more.

"Just Give Us the Right Answer, Already!"

Many people would like English language to be a simple matter of right and wrong: "Just give us the rules we need to follow, and we'll follow them." Unfortunately for them, linguistics does not provide what they are looking for. For this reason, we know that many people, especially those who equate others' pronunciation or vocabulary or usage with their innate human worth, are highly frustrated by the field of linguistics. These individuals are looking for authoritative, definitive rules of right and wrong when it comes to language use and language choice. They want, essentially, prescriptive information from linguistics, rules and regulations, dos and don'ts, shoulds and oughts and musts. Such hard-and-fast rules might also make teaching language far simpler, especially for new teachers.

Linguistics, however, is anything but prescriptive. In fact, maddening to many, it does little or nothing about decreeing right and wrong; if a statement works to create the intended meaning, it works. Linguistics doesn't tell us what is right or wrong, it tells us how language works; thus linguistics is not *prescriptive* but *descriptive*. It looks at, for instance, *he don't* as a legitimate, recognizable, definable form of language. Truth be told, *he don't* is nothing more than the use of a singular pronoun and a plural form of the verb *to do*; linguistics would note that there is no diminution of meaning in *he don't*.

Edgar Schuster also makes this point in his terrific book on grammar instruction, *Breaking the Rules*: "A linguist once observed that there is not two cents worth of difference between 'I seen them yesterday' and I 'saw them yesterday'—except that the I-saw-them-people run the schools" (2003, 55).

As you know, of course, it turns out that who runs the schools and who has power actually does make a difference—and students should be taught about those differences and the disapproval they may arouse. But we can't just teach young people that deviations from Standardized English are linguistically *wrong*. In the following section, we discuss more about linguistics and why some of its specific concepts should be an important influence on your teaching. Please look at the references at the end of this chapter for further resources; this section on language is a quick excursion, not a full tour.

Prescriptive Versus Descriptive: The World of Linguistics

Linguistics, the study of and the science of language, is a very complex field with a dizzying array of areas. There is, in one branch, *psycholinguistics* (language in relation to mental processes). Psycholinguistics includes *morphology* (the shape of language), *phonology* (the sound of language), *semantics* (the meaning of language), and *syntax* (the structure of language in word and sentence patterns). Another branch of linguistics is *sociolinguistics* (language in relation to culture or behavior), and yet another is *stylistics* (the study of literary language). *Historical linguistics* considers the history of language through time, and *anthropological linguistics* looks at language as a social phenomenon, a form of behavior. *Pragmatics*, another branch of linguistics, examines how language meanings are negotiated between people in particular contexts and how those conversations are affected by the assumptions, backgrounds, and purposes of hearers and speakers in specific contexts. Linguistics looks at all aspects of language, from how very young children acquire speech to how remote indigenous tribes in South America transcribe their language to the history of a verb form. Linguists work as much in laboratories (with actual recordings of people's speech) as in classrooms (with students) as in libraries (with research studies) and with huge collections of real-world written and transcribed language (called *corpuses*); theirs is virtually a universe of study.

In a well-known and widely quoted article, "Never Mind the Trees," linguist Suzette Elgin writes that an English teacher needs to know a few basic linguistic principles. Among other concepts, Elgin urges all of us to know about grammar, dialect, register, and a little bit of the history of our language. She also notes that we as teachers should have a basic grasp of "normal" human language development, what languages do, and, crucially, how to find answers to questions about language and linguistics. We should also take our cues for what teachers should know about language from what state and national standards tell us students should know about language, as we discuss later in this chapter.

In all cases in the study of linguistics, as stated before, English language arts (ELA) teachers seeking immutable standards of correctness will not find the ammunition they may be looking for. Linguistics reminds us:

- There are no languages or forms of language that are inherently "superior" to others.

- There are no languages or forms of language that are inherently easier or harder to learn or even "prettier" to the ear.

- The association of certain usage forms with class markers—certain people from certain economic strata will use certain linguistic forms—is not only arbitrary in almost all cases but will also shift over time.

So, what then, are language principles? We assert there are two, language changes and no "bad" language, both explored in the following section.

Language Changes

The poet Pablo Neruda (1991) once wrote, "Is a dictionary a sepulcher or a sealed honeycomb?" It is a powerful question and a powerful metaphor that pinpoints the tension regarding words and language. To that end, James Stalker, former chair of the

National Council of Teachers of English (NCTE) Commission on Language, reminds us what English teachers should remember about language. Stalker tells us

- that all languages, including our own, are in a constant state of flux
- that all languages are comprised of variants, which are used for different purposes and enjoy different levels of acceptability
- that all languages and varieties of languages serve a multitude of functions
- that all languages and their varieties are orderly and therefore can be described and explained through complex structures, including syntax (sentence structure) as well as phonology (the system of sounds), morphology (word structure), semantics (meaning), discourse (structures larger than the sentence), and pragmatics (language use in context). (1987, 4)

The fact that language changes is a serious problem if we believe that our language should be (or is) stable and that changes in it should be resisted. You may recall changes you've heard others or even yourself resist: words imported from other languages, such as *emoji, jihad, manga,* and *tattoo;* new meanings for old words, such as *tweet, mouse,* and *gay;* combinations of words, such as *emoticon, 24-7;* nouns that are now used as verbs, such as *text, impact,* and *dialogue;* and other variations, such as *lite* for *light.* As Simon Winchester writes in *The Meaning of Everything,* his history of the making of the *Oxford English Dictionary,* language is ever expanding:

> Since Shakespeare—and since William Hazlitt and Jane Austen, since Wordsworth and Thackeray, the Naipauls and the Amises, and the fantasy worlds of the hobbits and Harry Potter . . . the language that we call Modern English has just grown and grown, almost exponentially. Words from every corner of the globalized world cascade in ceaselessly, daily topping up a language that is self-evidently living, breathing, changing, evolving as no other language ever has, nor is ever likely to. (2004, 17)

There Is No "Bad" Language

In addition to the concept that language never changes—because it does—is a second misperception that language can be *wrong* or *bad.* The latter ignores the fact that certain language forms provide what linguists call class markers. Thus, when a student of yours says "Me and him went to the game" rather than "He and I went to the game," there is an immediate assumption about that student's educational—and social and economic—background. Actually, though, there is little real difference between the two sentences; both convey that two people went to the game, regardless that objective pronouns (*me* and *him*) are used for the standardized nominative pronouns (*he* and *I*). This kind of "misuse" is, however, a form that is associated with those who aren't formally educated or are economically disadvantaged, and, regardless of its ability to convey information, is considered unacceptable to many speakers. This usage is, in fact, so marked that we would call that usage *stigmatized*. You can think, I'm sure, of similar constructions that in your community and your context are equally powerful class markers, which, for some hearers, reveal the speaker's supposedly lower status.

Leila's Story: Arguing About Language

Arguments about language correctness can get terribly petty, zeroing in on acceptable variations rather than on the big issues of standard and nonstandard practice. I once encountered a woman who was most interested in my work as an English teacher, and inquired intently how I pronounced the word *mauve*. My pronunciation, she said, would tell her a great deal about my education and erudition because, according to her standards, there was only one right way to pronounce the word. Of course, I failed her test: my pronunciation is from my regional heritage, *mawve*. Hers was the other variant, *mowve*, and she instructed me to change the way I pronounced the word. Although most dictionaries cite both pronunciations, this speaker found her choice the only right choice. We were both talking about the light purple color, but, for this person, it became much more than color and intelligibility; the pronunciation of *mauve* became a crucial issue. Now, if that woman had influence over me—say, if she were considering me for a teaching position—her opinion would be powerful, even though it is wrong. Luckily for me, I could simply nod politely, call her names in my head, and walk away.

Ken's Story: Language Correctness Depends on Context

Issues of language correctness can go either way. Many members of my family and their friends work as first responders in New York City. They are firefighters, EMTs, and police officers, who are brave, smart, and in many cases formally educated people. When they get together to socialize, they tend to use what I would call working-class vernacular English, including phrases such as *he don't know*, as opposed to the standardized *he doesn't know*. When I visit with this crowd, I stick out like a fire hydrant in a flower bed the minute I open my mouth. I am used to speaking standardized English because I tend to hang out with English teacher types and that's how we habitually talk. By speaking in standardized English phrases, I am immediately marked as an outsider and I usually elicit some sort of response. It doesn't bother me to be seen as an outsider, because they are still friendly with me, but the point is that my language marks me immediately as different. If they used that difference against me, it would be a problem, just as if the woman Leila met had had some power over her.

As a linguistic study without value judgments, language difference is a fascinating topic. But clearly, we don't like conversations such as these if they devolve into feelings of superiority, moral judgments, and snobbery. We find them unhelpful and unpleasant. One speaker corrects another; someone gets to feel superior; someone gets to feel wrong.

It is, of course, one thing to encounter such a dispute with a peer. It is another to encounter it in class. Ken makes this point in his book with Patricia A. Dunn, *Grammar Rants*:

> [M]any issues of language are situational, and what counts as correct depends upon the intended audience, the genre, and the content of the communication. There are rights and wrong in language use, but they are not as black and white as most grammar [sticklers] make it appear, and the moral implications, often related to race and class, are simply inappropriate. Instructors and students need to know this so they don't perpetuate these prejudices or allow the moralizing of those ignorant of (or uninterested in) the true complexities of language to beat them down. (2011, 10)

Teachers must not ignore language differences, nor should we be shy about making sure students learn all about standardized English, but we must teach students in a way that refrains from denigrating various forms of English. Yes, there are powerful people who will hold their language use against them, so they should learn to write and speak in ways that will be empowering, but at the same time students should also learn that many of the attitudes they may encounter rest on misassumption and flat-out prejudice.

Although the authors of the Common Core State Standards (CCSS; National Governors Association Center for Best Practices, Council of Chief State School Officers 2010) may not explicitly eschew using language for value judgments, they certainly seem to agree that college- and career-ready students value the kinds of difference represented in varied uses of English:

> [College- and career-ready students] come to understand other perspectives and cultures. Students appreciate that the twenty-first-century classroom and workplace are settings in which people from often widely divergent cultures and who represent diverse experiences and perspectives must learn and work together. Students actively seek to understand other perspectives and cultures through reading and listening, and they are able to communicate effectively with people of varied backgrounds. (7)

Standard English or Standardized English?

You may have noticed that we use the phrase *Standardized English* when we talk about the form of English expected in most professional and academic contexts. This version of English is also called Standard English and Well-Edited American Prose, and linguist Geneva Smitherman (1995) has called it "the language of wider communication." Using the term *standardized* makes it clear that this form of language is not inherently better than any other form. It is preferable in many professional and academic contexts because some institutions (particularly publishing houses) have taken it upon themselves to create sets of rules. But even Standardized English has different versions; for example, the Modern Language Association (MLA) and the American Psychological Association (APA) and the *Chicago Manual of Style* don't all use the same rules. Also, many publications and institutions have internal style sheets that differ on, for example, when to use commas, when to use numbers instead of spelling them out, and how to deal with sexist language.

Take an *Additive*, not a *Deficit*, Approach to Language Teaching

For some language purists, it may come as a surprise that students don't come to us broken and they don't need their language fixed. Our students have vast experience as users of language, but some of that experience is with versions of English that are not standardized or are what Vershawn Ashanti Young calls "undervalued English" (2014, 11). What English teachers should do is add Standardized English to students' linguistic toolboxes. All students should learn to use Standardized English effectively. But it's not our job to eliminate other forms of English from our students' repertoire. African American English, working-class English, Spanglish, and other forms of English are valid language and are part of our students' identities. Students can learn when to use one version of English or another or even to use more than one at once (see code-meshing near the end of this chapter). It's our work to add to, not subtract from, students' language skills and experience.

Take a *Contrastivist*, not a *Correctivist*, Approach to Student Writing and Speaking

Researcher and teacher Rebecca Wheeler (2005) suggests that to keep from making students feel like we're disrespecting them when we teach Standardized English, we should show differences between languages, not show *correct language* vs. *incorrect language*. Such an approach is *contrastive* (focuses on difference). For example, working with a group of elementary school students who are native speakers of African English, Wheeler puts the following on the board:

My goldfish name is Scaley.   My goldfish's name is Scaley.

On the left is a correct African American English sentence, and on the right is the same thought expressed in correct Standardized English. In African American English, the 's is not needed because possession is shown by proximity. In Standardized English, proximity and 's are required to show possession. It's not a matter of right vs. wrong. It's a matter of two forms of correctness (Wheeler 2005, 111).

Use Language Education to Give Students Options, not Limits

English teachers are at their best when they are offering students choices for language use. We have no idea what contexts our students will find themselves in in the future. What they need from us is knowledge of a range of options for language and practice developing all those options, so they can become expert at adapting their language to their purposes and their audiences. We should help students see language not as a set of rules to which we are subject, but rather as the fascinating set of options it offers to writers and speakers.

As indicated in other chapters, CCSS support this approach. In a section on the "Key Features of the Standards," we're told, "The Language standards include the essential 'rules' of standard written and spoken English, but they also approach language as a matter of craft and *informed choice among alternatives*" (National Governors Association Center for Best Practices, Council of Chief State School Officers 2010, 8; emphasis ours). "Informed choice" means we need to help students become aware of many ways to use language to express thoughts. The fact that *rules* appears in scare quotes in the CCSS is an acknowledgement of the dearth of hard and fast rules in English language. Later, the CCSS point out that students must "be able to choose words, syntax, and punctuation to express themselves and achieve particular functions and rhetorical effects" (51).

For Your Journal

Do any of the concepts above challenge your views or the way you have been taught to think about language? In your journal, write specific statements that you find of concern or in some conflict with your education. What further information will you need to seek out to resolve these conflicts, so you may engage your future students in language instruction that is research-based and that aligns with your thinking? If you have no conflicts with the above concepts, how will you engage your future students in these aspects of English language?

The Place of Standards in Language Instruction

The CCSS and other language standards offer valuable guidelines to help teachers think about what to focus on when they teach language. In addition to six general (or "Anchor") standards for language, the CCSS contain a useful list of eighteen specific language skills that even teachers in non-CCSS states would find useful. It lists, for example, some traditional and expected skills:

- L.6.1d. Recognize and correct vague pronouns (i.e., ones with unclear or ambiguous antecedents).

- L.6.2a. Use punctuation (commas, parentheses, dashes) to set off nonrestrictive/parenthetical elements.

- L.9–10.1a. Use parallel structure. (56)

The CCSS also include language skills that recognize the complexity and shifting standards of correctness that occur when writing for different purposes for different audiences and in different genres:

- L.4.1f. Produce complete sentences, recognizing and correcting *inappropriate* fragments and run-ons.

- L.6.1e. Recognize *variations* from standard English in their own and others' writing and speaking, and identify and use strategies to improve expression in conventional language.

- L.6.3a. Vary sentence patterns for meaning, reader/listener *interest*, and *style*.

- L.8.1d. Recognize and correct *inappropriate* shifts in verb voice and mood. (56, emphasis ours)

There are valid uses for sentence fragments (see, for example, Schuster's [2006] "A Fresh Look at Sentence Fragments"). The standards describe "variations" from, not errors in, standard English. And the standards acknowledge that reader interest and style are valid and important parts of language education. Teachers can use these guidelines to engage students in meaningful and interesting discussions of language as a palette of paints they can use to color their world. Doesn't this sound more engaging and authentic than teaching a list of rules?

The NCTE and International Reading Association (IRA) Standards for ELA (1996)—the standards written by English teachers—do not separate standards for language as neatly as the CCSS do. Instead, language skills are embedded throughout the twelve standards. However, several include special note of specific language skills:

- "knowledge of word meaning"

- "word identification strategies," including "sentence structure, context"

- ways to "adjust" language for "a variety of audiences and different purposes"

- knowledge of "language structure, language conventions (e.g., spelling and punctuation)"

- "an understanding of and respect for diversity in language use, patterns, and dialects across cultures, ethnic groups, geographic regions, and social roles."[†]

† Published jointly by NCTE and the International Reading Association (IRA) in 1996, the *Standards for the English Language Arts* is designed to complement other national, state, and local standards and contributes to ongoing discussion about English language arts classroom activities and curricula. Visit http://www.ncte.org/standards.

Usage

When we discuss "good" English, most of us rely on the language used by the most reputable of speakers. And yet, as Robert C. Pooley in *The Teaching of English Usage* reminds us, the issue is complicated:

> "[G]ood usage is the usage of the best writers and speakers" . . . is probably the expressed or implied standard of good English in almost every American schoolroom today, . . . [yet] the chief difficulty lies in the interpretation of the terms "the best writers and speakers." For example, at the same time that these definitions of "correct" English were current, nearly all grammar books listed as undesirable English the use of the split infinitive, the dangling participle or gerund, the use of the possessive case of the noun when naming inanimate objects, the objective case of the noun with the gerund, and the use of whose as a neuter relative pronoun, among many others; yet all of these uses may be found in the authors who form the very back-bone of English literature and who are "the best writers" in every sense of the words. If the standard makers defy the standards, to whom shall we turn for authority? Moreover, the use of literary models tends to ignore the canon of present usage, for by the time authors have come to be generally recognized as standard their usage is no longer "present." And among present speakers, who are best? Any careful listener who has heard a large number of the most prominent platform speakers of the day has still to hear one who does not in some manner violate the rules of the books. Are all great writers and speakers at fault, or is it possible that the rules we think we must follow are inaccurate? The way out of this perplexity about usage is to shift the search for standards away from "authorities" and traditional rules to language itself as it is spoken and written by real people today. (1974, 11–12)

 Ken's Story: A particularly dramatic moment in one of my English methods classes may bring this problem home for you. As the class and I discussed several essays that demonstrated how nonstandardized English dialects are as linguistically valid as standardized English, one student teared up. She confessed that she had always been privately ashamed of the way her Italian immigrant grandparents spoke and that she viewed her education as a means of "rising above" her ancestry. In undertaking the readings in our class, she recognized in herself a contempt for her family history that she had allowed to be instilled in her along with her ability to communicate in what she learned was "correct" English usage. The reason she cried, she explained, was that her last grandparent had recently died just before she was able to appreciate her heritage in a new light. "Why was I taught in a way that made me think my grandparents were dumb?" she asked. (For more on this student's story and Ken's reaction, see Lindblom [2006].)

Thus we turn to what is actually around us in language and from that source make determinations about "correct" and "incorrect." This is precisely how writing teacher and usage expert Bryan Garner [2009] has created his indispensable yet surprisingly little known (at least among English teachers) *Modern American Usage*. We recommend this beefy resource (it's almost a thousand pages long) as a thorough, careful, unexpectedly humorous, go-to guide for questions about usage. Should *dialogue* be used as a verb? (Probably not [2009, 251].) Should we use *until* rather than *till*? (It doesn't matter; they are equally acceptable [814].) When should we use *who* versus *whom*? (He's got three pages on this, and the jury is still somewhat out [860–862].) Is it OK to split infinitives? (Absolutely, "where they feel natural" [767].) To make his determinations, Garner—a highly respected writing teacher and lawyer, who has written over twenty books on language and the chapter on grammar and usage in the *Chicago Manual of Style*—and his expansive team have gathered and studied millions of documents published in American sources, such as local and national newspapers, government and scientific reports, informal sources, and many, many more. Having done this, Garner then makes judgments based on his principles, which include the purposes of the words, the realism of the language in question, linguistic simplicity, stage of acceptance of a change, and his own subjective preferences (xviii). His book, organized as a dictionary of contemporary words, phrases, and concepts in English (as practiced in the United States), is a list of his very educated and informed judgments, complete with many references to scholarly linguistic sources. Writers and editors love the book for its usefulness. In fact, Ken learned about it from his senior editorial associate at *English Journal*, Theresa Kay. Plus, English teachers who know it love the book for its readability and clever writing. When colleagues and friends come to you with tricky usage questions, Garner is your secret weapon!

Spelling

In *The Mother Tongue: English and How It Got That Way*, writer Bill Bryson (2001) notes that over 300 million people in the world speak English. He calls the language, which expands every year, "one of the world's great growth industries" (2001, 13) and cites the existence of over 600,000 English words. This is a very large number of words both to define and to spell correctly, especially because one aspect of "correct" language is spelling and vocabulary usage. In fact, many people outside of schools equate most of what we do as ELA teachers not only with correct grammar but also with correct spelling and appropriate use of vocabulary. Let's start with spelling.

We know of no study that shows a correlation between intelligence and correct spelling. And, as rhetoric scholars Sharon Crowley and Debra Hawhee point out:

> People have trouble spelling English words because English spelling is irregular and erratic; it is irregular and erratic because it reflects accidents of linguistic history. For example, the "gh" in words like *light* and *bright* is there because it used to be pronounced. (2009, 413)

In fact, English spelling is so confusing that a Simplified Spelling Society was established in the United States over 100 years ago to make English spelling easier and more logical. They suggested *bred* for *bread*, *paragraf* for *paragraph*, *alternativ* for *alternative*, and many more changes. Who were these radicals? The board in 1909 included Andrew Carnegie, Mark Twain, Hermann Melville, John Dewey, Isaac K. Funk, William James, and President Theodore Roosevelt (Dunn and Lindblom 2011, 52). The British organization of this society is still active (http://spellingsociety.org/).

And yet many people equate misspelled words with stupidity and ignorance. Ken and Patricia A. Dunn (2011) have written an entire chapter, "Grammar Rants on Spelling," on the ways in which many journalists, teachers, and other members of the public discriminate again people unfairly as a result of deviations from or mistakes in standardized spelling.

As a teacher you are expected to be almost perfect in your spelling—an expectation that, frankly, is often hard to fulfill. In fact, you may find that teaching middle and high school students actually impedes your own spelling ability, a result of viewing frequent spelling errors in your students' writing. Because proficient writers and readers often spell automatically via "sight words," seeing the same misspelling time and again can affect their internal list of sight words. Yet, as the teacher, you have a responsibility to spell consistently and correctly. On the other hand, spelling is really only a small part of ELA and should not take a disproportionate amount of class time.

It will help you, however, if in their language study your students learn a little bit about the history of English spelling. Bryson reminds us that we have forty sounds in English but more than 200 ways of spelling those sounds (2001, 120). Linguist Mario Pei terms the English spelling system "the world's most awesome mess" (1952, 310), and for many of our students, that description is pretty accurate. Students need to know that correct spelling was only very recently perceived as an important issue. In fact, only in the last few hundred years has the spelling of English words been at all standardized and have dictionaries entered wide use as repositories of the "correct" way to spell a word. Samuel Johnson (1819) published his *Dictionary* in 1755; spelling instruction in this country entered the classroom around that same time. We have only to look at our own nation's original documents—and the correspondence of our not-so-distant forebears—to see that literate people used a dizzying array of forms to spell the very same words.

There was a time in the history of teacher education when spelling was seen as a major issue. At the very influential Illinois State Normal University in the mid-1800s, teacher educators were so concerned with their students' spelling that all preservice teachers were required to take a twenty-five word spelling exam every morning until they could go a *full term* without missing more than one word. And even after passing this full-term spelling challenge, if a professor ever spotted a spelling mistake in a student's writing (even if the student corrected the misspelling before turning in the paper), the student was forced to return to the spelling exams for another term (Lindblom, Banks, and Quay 2007).

The history is, of course, helpful. On the other hand, the practical reality is that we want our students to spell correctly. Even with the use of spell check, students can do some individualized work to enhance their own list of challenging words, sometimes called "spelling demons." Students can improve their spelling and appreciate its diversity by

- keeping a spelling log with their own frequently misspelled words
- exploring the spell check feature of most word processors
- researching a few words and their variant spellings over the years.

In final draft writing (but not in spontaneous writing in class or journal entries, for example), we can expect students to check their spelling and conform to a standard. Of course, students with learning disabilities and English language learners (ELLs) have more than ordinary difficulty with correct spelling; for those students more patience and more time are necessary.

Vocabulary

With vocabulary, many English teachers trust they are expanding their students' language by giving them a list of vocabulary words to learn, both spelling and definition, every week or so. In many schools across the country, the words are chosen by the teacher (or the text), given to the students, and tested regularly. This is a staple of the ELA classroom, but it may surprise you to know that as it is often practiced, it is virtually useless. As educators Don and Alleen Nilsen remark wryly in an excellent book on vocabulary instruction, "except for saying, 'You might be tested on this word,'. . . most teachers [are] unable to answer . . . questions about why students should be memorizing the meaning of words they had never heard spoken, never seen in writing, and never anticipated using" (2004, vi).

As Nilsen and Nilsen are saying, the lasting effect of this practice is negligible; most students forget the words and their definitions almost immediately after the test. A student of Leila's, Laurie Messer, recalls:

The vocabulary tests [in English class] were standard tests taken from the teacher's manual, and some last minute cramming was all that was required to learning the spelling and definitions of the words for the multiple choice tests. Some teachers did try to individualize the vocabulary exercises to make them more interesting and to show us how to use the vocabulary words in "real life." . . . But generally no one really ever learned the vocabulary words, and I think the teachers hated the exercises just as much as the students.

The point is that people will expand their store of words, their language, their vocabulary, when they use the words *in context* or when they have a *need* for the words.

As language lovers and as teachers we must create vocabulary/spelling lists that have some relevance for our students, lists that come from

- reading (words they recently read that they did not know the meaning of)

- life (words that are used frequently by their family or in their neighborhood or on their after-school job that they do not think are as frequently used by those outside those contexts)

- class work (words that they have encountered in English or other classes that are new to them or that they consistently misspell or stumble over).

It is not impossible to have students working on individual lists within a class setting; a teacher can keep track of such lists by collecting them on a regular basis or having students store them on a shared electronic forum, and students, with some prior direction and organization, can demonstrate their mastery of their *individual* spelling lists by choosing a selected number of words and using them or defining them on a quiz. Leila did this with her students in English 11 when she returned to teach high school, and she found it one of the more successful activities of the semester.

At any rate, to present students isolated lists will not help them score higher on the state-mandated test or any other vocabulary or language-based measure. It will, however, encourage them to see language as nothing more complicated than the memorization of disconnected lists of words. Letting students participate in their own spelling/vocabulary lists and encouraging them to expand those lists not only gives students more control over this aspect of ELA but also shows them that they, too, live in a world of language. It is not confined to the vocabulary presented in a textbook; it is in their world and all around them.

TECH TALK: *Vocabulary.com*

Quite a few teachers we know are excited about a commercial website called Vocabulary.com that provides gamified vocabulary lists. Players answer questions about word meanings, and the site responds by raising or lowering the difficulty of the terms, repeating them as necessary till the player understands. Questions include simple multiple choice, fill-in-the-blank, and matching the term to a picture. Players earn points and badges to keep them motivated. Teachers may upload their own lists or select from thousands of vocabulary lists tied to popular topics and oft-taught literature. Teachers can follow students' progress and set up competitions. Basic features are free, but some require a school subscription.

In a 2011 *English Journal*, one English teacher announced he would no longer teach vocabulary (at least not explicitly) because he knows the students won't generally remember vocabulary traditionally taught, and he knows that language is "too slippery, especially for inexperienced readers" to be fixed in memorized lists (Heverly 2011, 100). Instead, this teacher suggests setting up a classroom that engages students in reading that they care about; then they will learn new words. Jerry Heverly lists three things students need:

1. a genuine need to know, an interest in what they are reading

2. contextual clues (e.g., pictures on the page, titles, the font and layout, the table of contents) and lots of other subtle helpers

3. prior knowledge of the subject—which often means using film or the Internet or other ways to give students enough context to enjoy their reading. (100)

The CCSS and standards modeled on them require students to learn to figure out word meanings on their own, using context clues, and they require students to develop sophisticated understandings of words with multiple and figurative meanings. Words like these aren't memorized from lists, but rather encountered and used as one reads and writes. Another important type of vocabulary is what the CCSS call "domain-specific" words. These include technical terms or terms that are very specific to genre, profession, or other contexts of written discourse. (You may also encounter these kinds of words if you complete the edTPA [formerly known as the Teacher Performance Assessment] for which you must list "language demands" along with your lesson plans.) The way to increase your students' knowledge of and ability to work with unfamiliar domain-specific words is to create a classroom in which your students have a need for and interest in developing that knowledge and ability.

For Your Journal

Make a list of words that you have difficulty spelling; write a brief statement of why you think you stumble on those words (actually, most spelling mistakes are logical!). Then go to the library or online and look up the *etymology* (origin and development) of your spelling demons in a resource such as the *Oxford English Dictionary* (1971). What are the origins of the words? What different spellings do they have? What are their different meanings?

Grammar

What do we do with grammar, or more accurately, the conventional schoolroom version of traditional grammar, what Edgar Schuster (2003) calls "Traditional School Grammar" (TSG)? Many teachers and members of the public assert that the teaching of grammar is important because they believe it improves our students' writing and speaking. Unfortunately, however, especially when done through books and worksheets and rule memorization, the teaching of grammar does not result in better—or even different—speaking and writing. Many assume that when students do not improve after years of grammar study it is either the students' fault (they just didn't get it) or the quality of instruction (the teacher did not teach it enough; the teacher did not teach it clearly enough; the teacher didn't teach it at all). It is, however, the finding of many researchers who have looked for decades at the results of formal grammar instruction on student language and composition that that is just not the case.

The most famous of these grammar researchers is probably Findley McQuade, a writing teacher who in 1980 set out to prove that his Editorial Skills course improved his students' writing abilities. An intense course in TSG, Editorial Skills students studied sentence structure, parts of speech, punctuation, spelling, and so on. To his own surprise and disappointment, McQuade found that his course had no effect on his students' standardized exam scores, and on average the students scored better on *pretests* than on posttests on their knowledge of grammar. McQuade also acknowledged that his students' essays were *worse* after his course because the students were too concerned about "honor[ing] correctness" (1980, 29).

Many studies have pointed to the ineffectuality of teaching TSG. Those interested in pursuing them further are encouraged to see the resources listed in this chapter.

The difficulty seems to lie in two areas: how grammar texts are set up and how teachers are encouraged to teach grammar.

Let's consider the issues. We acquire language messily, aurally, by mimicking patterns. The verb *acquire* is deliberate here: we don't really *learn* our native language as we learn most other things. We do, however, *acquire* it by a rather indirect process. The small child does not consciously choose verbs or adverbs or clauses or phrases; he or she produces what he or she hears and by trial and error becomes an accomplished language user. By the time that small child is ready for school, he or she actually has most of the syntax needed to produce relatively complex conversation or discourse.

We often seem to ignore this competence, though. In secondary and middle school, we ask students in traditional "grammar" classes to go back and label with abstract terms and possibly with conceptual representations (such as diagramming) what they are naturally producing. The hope is that understanding the abstract framework of what they are doing will make their language "better." But that transfer just *does not readily occur*.

Think about the abstract pattern that students study: in most classes, it proceeds from rule memorization to worksheet/example practice to actual writing. The problems lie directly in that pattern: the rules are not sufficiently inclusive or clear; the examples for practice are deliberately restricted so that they will fully conform to the rule; and unfortunately the rule and the example often do not bear a relationship to real student speaking or writing. And we expect our students to move from rule and restricted practice to the universe of their own sentences. The transition is most times just not made.

For example, consider the last time you needed to verify a grammatical construction you used in a research paper or an essay. If you went to a standard usage "handbook" (or "grammar"), you probably had a very hard time finding a direct answer to your question. The fact is, however complex they might sound, the rules in most "grammars" are presented in very simplified versions, and the illustrations of those rules are rarely comparable to the highly complex constructions even elementary school-age children are capable of producing.

To make matters worse, some of the "rules" of TSG are not even rules at all. They are what Schuster calls "mythrules," "rule[s] that some believe should be followed by educated speakers of the language, which is generally not followed by them" (2003, 55); for example, that sentences should not end with a preposition (a holdover from Latin that has no relevance to English) and that one should not use *I* in formal writing. Many of these mythrules have developed over hundreds of years of grammar handbook authors who created lists of rules to satisfy a market hungry for right answers where they really don't exist.

So what do we do? In some cases, regardless of its demonstrated lack of efficacy, we are expected to teach grammar in our classrooms. Although no research buttresses the transfer, school authorities can insist that knowledge of the rules will indeed improve our students' speech and their final drafts. Accordingly, some feel that "grammar" instruction, a familiar and traditional part of language arts, should remain part of the twenty-first-century English class and they enforce that in curricular decisions. Jim Meyer summarizes the issue:

> Public school teachers who have a strong background in linguistics and in language study find themselves in a bind. Their commitment to serious research and study, to the discipline of linguistics, and to intellectual honesty is in conflict with their responsibility to their employer and to the legally constituted education authorities. Even to obtain a license to teach they must be willing either to parrot definitions that they know to be misleading or to accept no credit for their answers. To continue as teachers they must engage in continual gymnastics, balancing contrary expectations of what is to be taught in their classrooms. (2003, 39)

But let's get down to brass tacks.

What Should We Actually Do to Teach Grammar?

According to Edgar Schuster, there are four forms of rules in grammar that we and our students should be aware of (2003, xi–xii):

1. "Bedrock rules of English syntax," rules that are hardwired into the head of every native English speaker and need not be taught. For example, no native English speaker would ever say, *I wore a shirt blue.* It simply doesn't compute.

2. Universal Agreements, such as the differences between *it's* and *its*, *affect* versus *effect* and the like.

3. Mythrules, rules that exist only in the minds of picky, pedantic purists and those who trust them.

4. Usage rules, which can vary according to region, dialect, social class, race or culture, and other social contexts. These are the rules that can be fascinating to examine and for which a text like Garner's *Modern American Usage* (2009) can be a godsend.

In an issue of *English Journal* that Leila edited some years ago, twenty teachers wrote about how grammar should and should not be taught. Although all twenty had very different approaches, the conclusions were clear. Grammar and usage, they maintained, should be taught

- in connected units of study

- in small and targeted doses

- in relation to student writing

- when there is a real need for it. (Christenbury 1996, 12)

For instance, teachers need to provide students with grammar and usage instruction in some sort of logical sequence (when students are writing their short story dialogue, they need information on quotation marks and capitalization, not necessarily on semicolons). Teachers need to spend limited amounts of time on such instruction (two solid weeks spent on clauses and phrases will not be helpful to most students). Teachers also need to look at what specific students are having difficulty with—and at what they have clearly mastered—before they drag the entire class through, as one example, subject–verb agreement. It just may be that in a class of twenty-five only five students have this as a problem area.

Teachers also need to provide students with outside audiences for their work, audiences that may give the students more of a feeling that their correct final draft writing matters. If the teacher is the only one who reads the students' work and cares about correct usage, many students will remain indifferent to surface errors.

If nothing else, we need always to remember context. We need to teach grammar not as a separate unit but as it relates to specific issues in our students' writing and in their speech. We need to make sure that the students who study an aspect of grammar have a need for it and can, in fact, use that aspect in their class work. To do otherwise is to teach a skill or a piece of knowledge that has no application at all or has application to only a very few students in our classes. Mark Lester suggests teaching grammar in a few general areas:

- grammar terminology to provide a shared vocabulary for talking about grammar and writing

- key grammatical concepts (the sentence, inflection, tense, agreement) that underlie most written error

- practical techniques for monitoring error in their own writing. (1990, 366)

Doesn't this seem logical? Why, then, do many teachers continue to use unrelated content from handbooks and employ worksheets and tests to teach grammar? If you think about it, that kind of teaching is easier as it becomes a one-size-fits-all instruction. When a teacher chooses to pay attention to what an individual student needs as opposed to delivering blanket instruction for all in a single class, then life is a bit more complicated. Yet the effort is worth it: students will respond to instruction in grammar and usage if, indeed, they need the instruction and if it bears some relation to their own writing.

Since the *English Journal* issue Leila edited, there have been several others on grammar and language that largely confirm the above findings and suggest other ways for working with students on grammar. See the resources in the next section for more information.

As far as the time spent on these subjects, linguist Constance Weaver (1996), like Nancie Atwell (2014) in *In the Middle*, advocates using minilessons for such grammar instruction, devoting no more than ten minutes or so at the beginning of class to go over what a number of students—if not all—need to know or review. Confining instruction in grammar, usage (the choices speakers make when they talk or write), and mechanics (surface conventions of spelling, punctuation, capitalization, and so on) can be very helpful to students. Asking students to generate their own rules from their reading—and their own writing—can also be very beneficial.

All of this discussion about grammar may make you relatively uneasy, especially if you feel that you do not know much about grammar and usage yourself.

There are, fortunately, many sources to which you can turn, and you should not despair if, at this point, you feel your knowledge is inadequate. You can learn, and it may be, as with many teachers, that the concepts are easier to handle now than they were when you were younger—especially if you have some good resources.

English Journal Issues on Grammar and Other Resources　R

- January 2003, "Revitalizing Grammar," edited by Virginia Monseau. Includes articles on analytical thinking and grammar; state frameworks; the semicolon; balancing content and form in writing workshops; and an article that raises questions about the value of teaching grammar in writing courses.

- May 2006, "Contexts for Teaching Grammar," edited by Louann Reid. Includes articles on teaching in the contexts of state exams the value of stylistic sentence fragments; teaching phrases and clauses to ESL/ELL writers; analyzing grammar rants; a countywide grammar initiative; and using grammar to understand adolescent literature.

- March 2011, "Beyond Grammar: The Richness of English Language," edited by Ken Lindblom. Includes an in-depth examination of one writing teacher's evolution in grammar instruction; teaching Standardized English as the language of power; using hip-hop to teach code-switching; teaching writing style; and—for the truly fearless—studying derogatory terms to engage students in etymology and social justice.

- Lynne Truss' (2004) best-seller *Eats, Shoots & Leaves* may be helpful, although her language quibbles are based on British, not American, English.

- Usage manuals such as the previously cited *Garner's Modern American Usage* and the phenomenally rich (and free!) Purdue Online Writing Lab website are also excellent resources.

- More germane to us professionally are books by teachers: Brock Haussaman and colleagues' (2003) *Grammar Alive!*, Jeff Anderson's (2005) *Mechanically Inclined*, Harry R. Noden's (2011) *Image Grammar*, Martha Kolln's *Understanding English Grammar* (1998) and *Rhetorical Grammar* (2007), and Weaver's *Teaching Grammar in Context* (1996).

- You may also find the NCTE Assembly on the Teaching of English Grammar's Facebook page to be an excellent resource.

TECH TALK: *The Internet's Effect on Grammar and Usage*

Several years ago it was still common to find teachers and others concerned about the supposedly negative ways in which Internet discourse has affected students' writing. Much of that talk has died down, as more genres of Internet writing have been invented, and standardized English remains largely intact. In fact, focusing students on the differences between styles of writing can enhance their skills as writers, including in standardized English. Instead of demanding students always write in standardized English, create a chart in which students are asked to convey the same information in a tweet, a Facebook post, an Instagram post, a PowerPoint slide, and a standardized English paragraph. Then talk about the style differences and how some features (abbreviations, emojis, images, footnotes) are appropriate in some genres, but not in others. You'll create more flexible, metacognitively aware communicators with these kinds of activities.

What Else About Language Should We Teach?

There are many concepts about and ways to teach English language. Below we offer just a few you might focus on or draw inspiration from. Again, see the resources noted previously for more ideas.

Register

An important concept for all students to master is level of formality, or register. When speaking or writing, one must match one's level of formality to the situation. Greek and Roman teachers from ancient times identified three different levels of register: grand, middle, and plain (Crowley and Hawhee 2009, 332). Grand, or high style, is reserved for very formal occasions, such as graduations, weddings, legal proceedings. Middle style is not quite ordinary language, but is less exhausting and ornate than high style.

Plain, or low style, uses day-to-day speech and focuses on clarity and generally on economy of language.

Anyone who has received or sent an inappropriately informal email to an authority figure knows the importance of register. Ken sometimes gets email inquiries about his graduate program that begin with "Hey, Ken" and continue with unpunctuated sentences all in lowercase letters—and Ken is not amused. But there are also times when ordinary language is quite appropriate, such as between friends or busy colleagues, or when one is trying to lower someone else's guard or create intimacy.

You can have fun with your students with register. For example, you could ask students to write a sentence in each register for a different purpose:

- To welcome people:
  - Grand: Students, parents, and colleagues, I bid you welcome on this most auspicious occasion of the 2017 graduation.
  - Middle: Good morning, students, and welcome to class.
  - Plain: 'Sup, Bro!

- To ask for donations:
  - Grand: I beseech you, dear brothers and sisters: Do not allow this budgetary injustice to go unanswered. Please contribute all you can to the club that sings our athletes to victory.
  - Middle: Excuse me, sir. Would you be willing to support our school's marching band with a small donation?
  - Plain: Donate before our band is disbanded.

Rhetorical Devices and Style

Whether you realize it or not, you are familiar with a boatload of rhetorical devices, and you probably use them frequently in your writing and speaking. A few popular ones are alliteration, rhetorical questions, repetition, metaphors, parenthesis, and hyperbole. You can increase students' scribbling and speech skills by offering them options for their writing and speaking, and rhetorical devices are exactly those: options. There's no right and wrong with style—that's correct: there is no right and wrong—it's more about what works and what doesn't in any particular situation. Helping your students learn about many ways of making their points (by using engaging humor, pleasant figurative language, clarifying metaphors and analogies, for example) can greatly enhance their language skills and their interest in language. They will be Martin Luther Kings and Eleanor Roosevelts in no time! Remember: It's not so important that your students know the names of rhetorical devices. What matters is that they can wield them effectively in their own writing when they wish to. Don't you agree?

By the way, how many of the rhetorical devices we mentioned can you find in the above paragraph? (We're not saying they're all brilliant—but they are all there.)

Imitation

Imitation is an ancient and still very effective way to learn to write and speak in more interesting and complex ways. Deborah Dean favors selecting novel sentences from popular young adult literature and having her students write sentences that mirror them. For example:

- To the person who expects every desert to be barren sand dunes, the Sonoran must come as a surprise (from Jerry Spinelli's novel, *Stargirl*).

- To students who have never worked with sentence imitation, the practice must seem somewhat like a puzzle. (2011, 21)

Dean also points out, rightly, that student writers must also learn when complex sentences fit in a discourse and when they don't. When one of her students used imitations of a President John F. Kennedy speech in a skateboarding essay, she and the student knew there was a problem (21).

Digitalk

Have you or your teachers ever worried about the effects of texting language and emojis on students' abilities to write formal, academic prose? You're not alone. But Kristen Hawley Turner (2010) believes that texting, blogging, social communication, and other forms of what she calls adolescents' "digitalk" do not interfere with students' writing abilities; instead, they are evidence that many students are excellent communicators. "Manipulating language so that it efficiently conveys an intended message and effectively represents the voice of the speaker requires both creativity and mastery of language for communicative purposes" (2010, 43–44). Rather than seeing digitalk as a lazy form of English, Turner suggests teachers could be more effective by embracing it in the classroom as a powerful form of adolescent literacy in its authentic environments (46).

In a later *English Journal* article, Turner (2012) offers specific ideas for English teachers to take up digitalk, drawing on code-switching methods. She suggests that students bring in real sentences from their digitalk communities and revise them for different audiences (for example, the principal of your school in your classroom, a friend in the lunchroom, and a spiritual leader in a house of worship) (2012, 41). In such a lesson, students learn to appreciate their own abilities as digitalkers and they learn to code-switch for vocabulary, register, and conventions of standardized English.

Activities for Teaching Language

Field Notes

It may seem funny to treat people as test subjects, but ethnographers of language and some linguists observe speakers in their natural habitats communicating with others, and they take notes on what they hear for later analysis. Ken has often assigned his students to quietly sit in a public area and take notes on interesting words, phrases, and sentences they hear. Students have done so in malls, cafeterias, movie theatre lines, not-so-quiet sections of libraries, grocery stores, and even where they work. All contexts in which people talk are rich ground for cultural language analysis.

Once students bring in their field notes, we look at them to examine similarities from which we can draw "rules" about conventions or identify new words or phrases that are becoming popular among specific groups (usually young people), or note pronunciations that are located in one particular geographic area. These are also great ways to get students to examine emerging oral conventions, such as "uptalk" (in which a speaker's voice inflects upward in pitch at the ends of sentences, as if they were questions) or, more recently, the phenomenon first noticed among young women but now becoming more common among young men called "vocal fry" (in which speakers vibrate their vocal cords and strike a low pitch). One can also use field notes to study differences in language use among men and women, people of different ethnic and national backgrounds, even different neighborhoods. And when students are looking closely at language use, you can also help them learn relevant concepts in grammar and usage.

Grammar Rant Analysis

Ken and his colleague Patricia A. Dunn (2011) have developed an unusual approach to studying language that actually takes advantage of the fact that some people enjoy pointing out other people's errors or deviations from standardized English grammar. In their book *Grammar Rants* (2011), they identify and study newspaper articles and blogs that attack other people's writing for what those authors believe are mistakes. Sometimes the problems they point out are errors, but other times they are simply stylistic differences that are completely legitimate. The book examines the real reasons behind grammar ranters' rants, and the results aren't pretty. Often, people who judge other people's writing and speaking don't have a linguistic leg to stand on; what they are really doing is making judgments based on their perceptions of other people's moral quality, intelligence, and cultural background. Grammar rants can bring lively debate to a high school or middle school English class on language. But if you are yourself a bit of a snob when it comes to language and correctness, get ready to be challenged.

Literacy Autobiographies

Well-written and researched stories of how people have acquired and developed their language skills can be instructive and a real joy to read. They can help to educate you about the intellectual lives of people whose backgrounds differ from yours, and they can affirm cultural knowledge you share with these authors, which may have been marginalized in mainstream education. Two highly regarded standards in the genre of literacy autobiography are Keith Gilyard's *Voices of the Self: A Study of Language Competence* and Victor Villanueva's *Bootstraps: From an American Academic of Color*.

Hunger of Memory by Richard Rodriguez and *Lives on the Boundary* by Mike Rose are both controversial but also compelling. A new and already celebrated book is Carmen Kynard's *Vernacular Insurrections: Race, Black Protest, and the New Century in Composition-Literacy Studies*. And, although it's not about his life, David Kirkland's *A Search Past Silence: The Literacy of Young Black Men* gives excellent insight into the literacy lives of a group of young men. Teachers would be well advised to read these works in their entirety, but bringing excerpts into middle and high school classes can generate valuable discussion about literacy that also improves literacy. And because they are highly complex texts—bonus!—these works offer the kind of rigor called for in the CCSS and similar standards.

At the end of this chapter, we include a journal assignment that encourages you and your students to write your own literacy autobiography. This can be a fascinating way to find insight into your own intellectual history.

Language Play and Language Games

We also need to remember the wonderful world of language play and language games. As children, all of us had some exposure to—and delight in—games with words, rhymes, riddles, puns, jokes, and stories. How sad it is that in middle and high school we seem to leave all of this richness behind in the name of being more serious and academic. We need to recapture the broad and fine idea of play—experimentation—with language.

There are many resources available that can lead you and your students to working with a number of areas of language study. *Etymology* (the origin and history of words), *semantics* (the meanings of words), *doublespeak* (deliberate deception in language, often used in politics and brilliantly described by George Orwell in a famous essay, "Politics and the English Language" [1950]), and *dialect* (the wonderful variations of both pronunciation and word choice) are just a few of the fascinating topics you can pursue.

Language is literally all around us and although it may not be immediately apparent to you, your students are adept at language play. What they play with and toy with may be wholly outside the classroom—in the cafeteria or in the parking lot or at the mall—but you can, with some encouragement, have them bring what they know and use into the classroom—and this includes your ELLs, for whom language play is also very important. The following is a sampler of activities.

Puns and plays on words are used in menus, billboards, bumper stickers, advertisements, and other aspects of daily life. A local church billboard reads, for example: "Seven days without God makes one week [weak]." Such puns and slogans are creative uses of language and can be tools not only to encourage students to explore homonyms but to look at how such homonyms are effective. (*Week*, a noun, is the direct object; *weak*, a modifier, is the predicate adjective; one is, in the first sense of the sentence, an adjective but a pronoun in the second sense of the sentence.) Another such pun or slogan is the insult terming a person "a legend in his own mind," a play on the more familiar phrase, "a legend in his own time." Both words, *mind* and *time*, are nouns used in parallel constructions that not only have a near rhyme, but also convey widely different meanings.

Bumper stickers have become wonderful examples of wordplay. A few of Leila's favorites include the following:

- I used to be indecisive; now I'm not sure.
- Eschew obfuscation.
- Anything free is worth what you pay for it.
- Editing is a rewording activity.

Advertising offers many such puns and plays on words. Some of Leila's students collected a few, taken from billboards, signs, and print advertisements:

- Yule Laugh; Yule Cry (billboard advertisement for a Christmas movie)
- Coffee Brake (sign on outside of convenience store)
- Faster Than The Speed of Fright (billboard advertisement for a roller coaster at a local amusement park).

Our friend and colleague Jim Strickland is tickled by this one:

- And Leave The Rest to Us (from a mattress company).

And, finally, from Alleen and Don Nilsen's work, "After 35 Years, We've Got the Hang of It" (advertisement for a drapery company) (2004, 20).

Darren Crovitz advocates studying "eggcorns": "mistakes that are usually the result of a quasi-logical deduction." The name is a mishearing of *acorn* (2011, 34). Here are a few of the eggcorns that Crovitz suggests:

Correct Word or Phrase	Eggcorn
Alzheimer's disease	"Old timer's disease"
Prima donna	"Pre-Madonna"
Pastime	"Past time"
For all intents and purposes	"For all intensive purposes"

Crovitz doesn't just suggest this activity for play but also to help students understand that not all errors come from ignorance or laziness; some come from a thoughtful and logical miscue. Teachers must know that "errors are not always random, that we might be able to understand why they happen, and that this knowledge might somehow give us a broader picture of language miscues without the threat of punishment" (2011, 34).

Oxymorons, contradictions in terms, are also fun and can be, within limits, wonderfully insulting. A few popular ones include: *found missing*; *jumbo shrimp*; *alone together*; *taped live*; *new classic*; *military intelligence*; *small crowd*; *plastic glasses*; *diet ice cream*; *exact estimate*.

Have students recall puns, plays on words, oxymorons, or even jokes they have seen or create new ones that make a statement, promote a product, advance an idea, or provide humor. Then have them do the following:

1. List the possible homonyms or similar sounds for the crucial word or words.

2. Label the part of speech and the sentence function of the word or words.

3. Explain, in prose, how the sentence can be read two—or more—ways.

Do know that some of these activities will be especially challenging for ELLs and, in fact, may not be appropriate unless adapted extensively. As Yu Ren Dong writes, "the complexity of understanding multiple layers of meaning" is not quickly mastered, and many second language speakers "acquire one meaning of a word, often . . . associated with concrete, sensory referents, without knowledge of other meanings or abstract and metaphorical referents" (2004, 30). When using these kinds of games in your classroom, consider each one to be sure it is appropriate (and fun) for all students.

Relative meanings/semantics The women's movement has sensitized all of us to the varying uses of language, especially when describing people's behavior. "He's assertive, she's pushy" shows how language can be used to stereotype genders. Our language also provides an array of degrees of intensity, of approval or disapproval, all of which can be conveyed by words. Look at minimal, average, and maximum as degree distinctions for color (pink, red, scarlet) or weight (slim, thin, emaciated) or any other characteristic you might want to describe. Your students can come up with a number of "families," and this kind of language play can be especially effective for vocabulary expansion for your ELLs. Use the following headings, and have students make a chart such as the one that follows:

Minimal: creek, pebble, big, unhappy, dislike

Average: stream, rock, huge, depressed, hate

Maximum: river, boulder, gargantuan, miserable, detest.

Euphemism Newspapers, magazines, and other online news sites, like most forms of the popular press, often use phrases and words that mean something relatively different from their surface meaning. Politics, too, uses euphemism all the time; think of the widely used phrase for overtopping an extant government, "regime change." As civilians flee countries where there is incessant warfare, are they "refugees" from the conflict? Are they "undocumented aliens" to be resisted? Are they "immigrants" looking for new lives in other countries? To what extent does this difference in nomenclature affect how they might be received in any new country? A candidate promises to investigate "revenue enhancement," for example, while an ad in a local newspaper touts "friendly service," and a letter to the editor discusses the "human spirit of America." In response to deadly force used by police in some communities, citizens protest that "black lives matter." What do these phrases really mean? What is gained by using such phrases? What is lost?

Look at an online or print issue of a magazine, newspaper, or news website, and find as many "doublespeak" or euphemistic words and phrases as you can. Follow these steps for each:

1. List the phrase or word.

2. Define what you assume, from context, it *really* means.

3. Suggest a more accurate replacement or defend the word or phrase as it stands.

Minidictionaries Dictionaries can be great fun and can provide not only information but also a look at what is popular, what is in, and what is out. Within a group, have students follow these steps to compile a minidictionary of words or phrases that seem indigenous to their school and its students.

1. List the words or phrases.

2. Define the words or phrases.

3. Use the words or phrases in a single sentence.

Games and activities such as these can open the world of language for our students; students can also design and enjoy their own language play.

For Your Journal

Of the activities described above, which arouse the most interest from you immediately? Do you think students would enjoy them and find them instructive? In your journal think on paper about how you might approach one of these activities in a real class and how you think your students would respond.

Code-Switching and Code-Meshing

The term *code-switching* was originally used by second language acquisition and English as a second language (ESL) scholars as a way to describe how multilingual speakers shift from the use of one language to another in their daily interactions. The term has since been expanded to encompass the ways in which speakers of so-called nonstandard dialects of English use various forms of English in various settings. You probably engage in some version of code-switching yourself. Compare an email you've written to a respected professor to an email you've written to a friend. They probably vary in tone, register, diction, and conventions. You probably do this quite naturally, and you may not even think about it. If you've ever written an email that was too informal or otherwise inappropriate to a professor or employer, you've probably felt a sting in reply. And if you've texted in complete sentences with no abbreviations to your non-English-major friends, you've probably been teased about it.

Rebecca Wheeler has adapted code-switching scholarship into a valuable method of teaching English, including standardized English, in a manner that focuses on comparing students' home English to standardized, or school English. One of Wheeler's most valuable resources is a book, *Code-Switching Lessons: Grammar Strategies for Linguistically Diverse Writers Grades 3–6*, which she authored with teacher Rachel Swords (2010). Though it is intended for students younger than readers of this book will teach, the lessons are easily adaptable for older students.

Wheeler and Swords advocate a scientific, linguistic approach to working even with very young children on language. To teach grammar, they complete the following with students: "1. Collect data (student examples) 2. Examine data 3. Seek grammar patterns 4. Describe grammar patterns (a hypothesis) 5. Test the pattern 6. Write the grammar pattern (the grammar rules)" (2010, xvii). When using data from students' own language, particularly when your class is made up largely of native speakers of nonstandardized English, your students will come to see their home language as legitimately rule-bound (not wrong, or lazy), and they will learn that standardized English is another version of English that uses different (not better) rules. Using the terms *informal* and *formal*, as opposed to *nonstandardized* and *standardized*, the authors give this example of a chart (xvi) they made with their students, who were native speakers of African American English:

Informal	Formal
"Yes, said Annie mom.	"Yes," said Annie's mom.
She shouted Judy name.	She shouted Judy's name.
My goldfish name is Scaley.	My goldfish's name is Scaley.
Toni take Jeni ex-boyfriend.	Toni took Jeni's ex-boyfriend.
Christopher family moved to Spain.	Christopher's family moved to Spain.
I want to sing in the kid choir.	I want to sing in the kids' choir.
THE PATTERN	**THE PATTERN**
Owner + owned	Owner + 's + owned

Figure 7–1. Showing Possession

Wheeler and Swords use this form of language instruction because it builds on students' home language competency and adds competency in standardized English. They draw on a great deal of research to back up their methods—and why they work—and it's clear that this respectful approach to what students already know and can do is far less likely to offend and shut students down than a red-pen correctivist approach to language will. For more on the research behind code-switching pedagogies, see Wheeler and Swords' (2006) *Code-Switching: Teaching Standard English in Urban Classrooms*, a book in NCTE's Theory & Research into Practice series.

Code-switching is not without its problems or critics. Vershawn Ashanti Young finds that code-switching inadvertently encourages a sort of "linguistic segregation" because it requires students to see their home identities as completely separate and distinct from their school identities (2014, 3). He draws on the work of sixth-grade English teacher Erin McCrossan Cassar, who found that although using code-switching methods did improve her African American students' skills in standardized English, it also, unfortunately, decreased her students' self-esteem and racial self-concept. Young prefers code-meshing to code-switching "because it requires combining rather than switching between Englishes. And since language is inherently tied to identity, code-meshing means blending home and school identities, instead of keeping them separate" (3). Young acknowledges that Wheeler and Swords' code-switching is well-intended and that it "add[s] value to the often maligned African American English by presenting it as it rightfully is—a rule-governed dialect, no better or less than any other one, even Standard English" (2014, 11). However, he asks, "Why not reduce, if not avoid, sociolinguistic and educational conflicts by allowing students and professionals to merge their Englishes, to produce the best prose from a combination of all of their language resources?" (5).

Y'Shanda Young-Rivera (2014) presents an exemplary, in-depth study of code-meshing lessons she taught in her middle school classes. She took up the concept of code-meshing with her students and debated with them the merits of teaching code-meshing in schools. She and the students drew on examples of code-meshing from rap lyrics and other popular sources and wrote their own code-meshed works, which blended standardized and other forms of English to create rhetorically powerful statements. Young-Rivera found code-meshing a very positive experience for her students because she knows that "self-confidence, self-efficacy, and success . . . go hand in hand" (2014, 117).

One of the most basic things we can aim to do in the classroom is to provide an environment that takes advantage of this relationship; an environment that meets students where they are, validates who they are, and exposes them to new experiences, which in turn enhances who they become. Judging from my time spent in the classroom, I would say code-meshing holds the promise of creating this environment. (2014, 117)

As Young-Rivera points out, respecting students' home languages is not new. In 1974, the Conference on College Composition and Communication (an organization within NCTE) adopted a resolution called *Students' Right to Their Own Language*, and the statement was modified and adopted by the full NCTE in 1995 and then reaffirmed in 2003 (NCTE 1974, 90). (We discuss *Students' Right to Their Own Language* in much greater detail in Chapter 10.) Like code-switching, code-meshing methods can be used for all students at all grade levels. For more information, see Young and Martinez's (2011) *Code-Meshing as World English*, which includes applications of code-meshing to Chinese English, white working- and middle-class English, Appalachian English, Spanish-speaking Mexican Americans, German hip-hop performances, Cajun English, Hawaiian English, and more.

Code-meshing doesn't mean that learning standardized English isn't as important as it always has been. It means that respecting students' home languages and allowing them to use their already-developed literacy skills in their writing and speaking will help them develop the kind of fluency and appreciation of language that will enable them to learn standardized English more quickly and more effectively.

Honoring students' home languages and linguistic heritage can also open our classrooms to more engaging and relevant concepts and methods in pedagogy. For example, taking hip-hop language, music, and culture seriously has led to a vibrant intellectual movement in hip-hop pedagogy. In his *Beats, Rhymes, and Classroom Life*, Marc Lamont Hill examines how hip-hop texts helped transform his urban Philadelphia high school class into a "storytelling community," which allowed for "a variety of classroom identities that created spaces for effective pedagogy [and] community-building" (2009, xix). Lauren Leigh Kelly has written two articles about how she has used hip-hop texts to inform her English classes in a suburban Long Island, New York, high school. Kelly brings hip-hop into her classroom because it addresses part of her identity, which had been largely ignored in her formal education:

> I found myself taking on a dual identity: I was hip-hop outside the classroom and student inside it. There was no space for both at once. As well-versed as I could be in the language of hip-hop, that knowledge did not provide me with any source of power or access inside academic spaces. While I saw myself in hip-hop, I did not see myself in classroom texts. Ultimately, I was only marginally involved in my own education. (2013, 52)

This is not to say hip-hop is all rubies and rainbows. Kelly acknowledges many controversial aspects of the genre, and in fact, she uses hip-hop texts as "opportunities for discussions of power and identity that provide young people, particularly adolescents, with culturally relevant tools" for analysis and addressing social injustice (2015, 2).

However you teach language, should you decide to use code-switching, code-meshing, or other methods, you should teach in a manner that honors the language heritage of the students with whom you work.

English Language Learners

Depending on where you teach, you will have either some or many students for whom English is a second language. Few communities in America today are populated entirely by native speakers, and when the children of non-English-speaking parents come to school, many of them will need a great deal of support to succeed. Researchers Wayne P. Thomas and Virginia P. Collier (2002) predict that by 2030, 40 percent of the total U.S. school population will be ELLs. Some of these students will know virtually no English at all and, depending on your school district, they may not be given many resources to learn English quickly and effectively. Preservice English teachers are learning more than they used to about ELLs, but you still may be very concerned about these students mainstreamed into your classroom and about what you can do on a daily basis to help them with their vocabulary (academic language in particular), their pronunciation, and their reading comprehension. The scope of this book is not wide enough to give you even part of what you might need to effectively serve these students, but we can sketch out for you some principles and also point you to some resources to help your ELLs make progress, stay in school, and graduate.

Let's start with some principles for teaching second language learners. The following is taken from one of Leila's favorite books, *When They Don't All Speak English* (Rigg and Allen 1989). If you read these principles carefully, you will see, much perhaps to your relief, that what is good for first language students is also good for second language ones. Pat Rigg and Virginia Allen articulate the following guidelines:

- People who are learning another language are, first of all, people. "Children's developmental stages are more important than levels of English proficiency."

- Learning a language means learning to do the things you want to do with people who speak that language. Learning a language "doesn't mean learning forms of language to use someday in some possible situation: it means using the language (however badly) today, now, to do things."

- A person's second language, like the first, develops globally, not linearly. "Talk is the 'warm bath of language' . . . the second-language learner hears and participates in conversation that is usually meaningful because the context makes the meaning clear."

- Language develops best in a variety of rich contexts. "Ideal situations are those in which the student understands what's happening and is also learning something new."

- Literacy is part of language, so writing and reading develop alongside speaking and listening. "Even students just beginning to learn English can write, as long as the writing is authentic; that is, it is the student's own composition for the student's own purposes, not a product for the teacher's evaluation." (1989, vii–xv)

What do these principles imply? They mean that you can create a positive environment for all your students, including your ELLs, by extending to them the kind of rich context you would create in your classroom anyway. But remember, also, that this is a long-term process and one where you may not see the kind of quick progress you would like. Although most ELLs will have a basic oral competence after about two years in school and quickly acquire what is needed to actually function in school and life, academic language (and this is what they will need in your class and other content classes) takes five to seven years to master. So just because an ELL is competent orally, he or she may, as Kimberly Gomez and Christina Madda tell us, "continue to need vocabulary and conceptual support in reading and writing in content-area study" (2005, 46). Modification of instruction is key, and if you don't have background in this area, do know that the kinds of individualization you would provide for any of your struggling students is also appropriate for ELLs. You will also want to keep in close contact with the ESL/ELL teachers in your school; their expertise is wonderful, and many of them are familiar with helpful programs and strategies, such as the Center for Applied Linguistics' Sheltered Instruction Observation Protocol, known as SIOP. (For more information on SIOP, see Short, Hudec, and Echevarria [2002].)

From 2009–2013, linguist and ESL teacher Margo DelliCarpini edited an *English Journal* column called "Success with ELLs" that contains excellent background and resources for mainstream English teachers. In particular, her first column, titled "Working with English Language Learners: Looking Back, Moving Forward" (2008) gives information you'll want to read when you find yourself faced with nonnative English speakers in your classes. In the column, she discusses challenges for students with interrupted formal educations and the importance of focusing on ELLs' Basic Interpersonal Communication Skills and Cognitive Academic Language Proficiency. A later column, "Authentic Assessments for ELLs in the ELA Classroom," offers valuable ways to ensure ELLs' language skills are assessed accurately, for which DelliCarpini recommends "meaningful, naturalistic, context-embedded tasks," using a "variety of assessments," "involving students in performance," and "promoting participation in non-threatening situations" (2009,118–119).

Let's turn to some specific activities you can do to help your students become more proficient in English.

Activities for ELLs (and All Students)

Danling Fu, who taught for some years in New York in Chinatown, suggests that, first and foremost, teachers "forget the grade level curriculum" (2004, 8) and literally teach students where they are. This means that if students don't have basic English skills, you need to adjust what they do as well as your expectations. It may mean that these students need something as basic as a review of the English alphabet; it may mean that they need to read different texts (such as children's books, picture books, magazines) from what other students are using in your classroom.

In addition, giving ELLs regular opportunities to speak in class is very important. English pronunciation and cadence of word clusters in sentences may be quite foreign to your ELLs; if they don't have an opportunity to read aloud—prose or poetry—or to dialogue with others, they will not progress in language mastery.

But what about writing? Certainly if a student is struggling with the alphabet and the vocabulary and the syntax of English, shouldn't we just back away? Fu says no, and advocates that teachers help students *work into writing* by, first, giving them a topic of interest, such as describing themselves and their lives, and letting students address that subject by: using drawings or photos; writing captions for the pictures; reading the caption aloud. (13)

DelliCarpini draws on SIOP research to list useful advice for creating effective activities for ELLs. Teachers should ensure that lessons

- focus on language and content and provide supports for both kinds of learning
- allow ELLs to make concrete connections to their personal lives and experience
- include both spoken and written language
- require students to interact, discuss, and clarify in small groups
- give students immediate opportunities to practice new words and concepts
- allow ELLs to use their native language to learn new content. (2008, 99–100)

Small-group and pair work, a staple of the English classroom, can also be especially effective with second language learners. Working with another student who is more proficient in English, Fu notes, can help the ELL make an easier transition; get to know other students; and, most importantly, use English more effectively by talking with peers.

Finally, remember that ELLs may not have mastered English vocabulary or pronunciation, but that does not mean that they do not come to your classroom without intelligence, background, and skills. Although it may be difficult to individualize, try to study your ELLs and make real adaptations for them. Many ELLs are highly motivated, and with encouragement from you and a positive classroom atmosphere, they can make remarkable progress. It's rare that we have the opportunity to see such rapid growth in our students, so enjoy these opportunities to make a real, lasting, and swift difference!

The code-switching and code-meshing methodologies we spoke of earlier can be very effective with ELLs. Allowing students the opportunity to play and take safe risks with their native language and with English will allow them to develop fluency, engagement, and persistence in their writing. It will also help avoid developing risk-aversion in ELLs, which can come from too heavy a focus on mistakes and will significantly slow students' second language acquisition.

Remember also that assessing the proficiency of ELLs can be very tricky. One of Leila's graduate students, who was also a teacher, had an illustrative experience in what can go wrong. In this case, one of the teacher's students, new to this country from Central America and with little English background, was given a basic school screening test and subsequently labeled as having an intellectual disability, a diagnosis that did not seem consistent with what the teacher had briefly observed in class. When, however, the teacher talked with the tester about the student's results, she understood the incorrect diagnosis immediately. One of the major parts of the test had been to ask the student, using pictures, to put in order the steps for baking a traditional layer cake. The student had hopelessly confused the order of the task, and the sad conclusion was that she underperformed cognitively. The teacher, though, knew enough about the student's rural background and country to understand what had happened: this student had never seen a layer cake, much less baked one. In her country, she knew cooking sequences of a different sort, and if she had been presented pictures regarding the steps to kill, pluck, and bake a chicken, she would have scored 100. When this fact was presented to the school, the student's diagnosis was changed.

Indeed, we need to be open to our ELLs and ready to adapt, modify, and, of course, enjoy what they bring to enrich our classes.

The Language of Hate

This chapter has discussed language change and that there is actually no "bad" language, but what about the language of hate, language used to demean, exclude, shock, or hurt? All of us, some perhaps more frequently than others, have been the target (possibly the originator?) of language that was designed to wound. And schools and classrooms are places where such language can crop up and be an issue both for teachers and their students.

We must acknowledge that language is a two-edged sword and although in this book we concentrate on the positive power of words, we would be naïve if we did not recognize that language can also be used as a potent weapon. As teachers, one way we can blunt such language is to demystify it and to examine it rationally. It is not inconceivable to place the insult of the week or even the obscenity of the month on the board and to bring it directly into our lesson plan, but one must be sure the students treat such lessons responsibly. In his first year of teaching, Ken taught a lesson in which a number of terms of hate were put on the board and were used by one student to quietly bully another student, unbeknownst to their new and not-yet-classroom-savvy teacher. But when such language is approached well, we can briefly discuss its origin and meaning and use and, yes, examine with our students why derogatory words are so powerful and so repugnant. There may be some snickers and some inappropriate comments at first, but looking directly at the language of hate can defuse it and can help raise your students' levels of maturity. Many students appreciate the respect shown to them when a teacher takes an age-appropriate yet direct approach to adult-themed content, and students generally rise to the occasion.

Karen Keely took this method even further by having her high school students choose especially derogatory terms and study their origins, cultural histories, contemporary uses and make determinations as to whether the words were ultimately harmful or empowering for particular groups of people. Keely's admirable and academically rigorous Dangerous Words Assignment is only for the fearless, and she (and we) recommend getting the approval of your department chair and building principal before adapting it for your class (2011, 55).

Talking about such language and bringing it into our classroom is one way to deal with it. Although we can forbid its use within our classroom walls, forbid it being used against us as teachers or against students by students, we cannot, realistically, wipe the halls or the cafeteria or our communities or social media or the printed lyrics of popular songs of certain words or phrases or language used to demean. Taking the power of language—its negative power, and the power groups can take when they reclaim a derogatory term that has been used against them—into account may be one of the more potent aspects of language we can bring into our classroom. For more on the language of hate, see our chapter on social justice.

The Glory and Richness of English Language

In all cases it is good to remember that although we may want students to know and be able to use "correct" or "standard" English—the language of those who approve loans, give diplomas, and hire employees—we need to remember two things.

First, we need to understand that "standard" language is arbitrary, and second, that "correct" language has changed and will continue to change. We have an obligation to make our students' options broad, to help them—and invite them—to learn "standard" and "correct" English, but we need to place the issue in perspective and to acknowledge that those two terms get placed within quotation marks for a reason. And that reason is that there is just no immutable, definable, *standard* English and no immutable *correct* English.

The English teacher as language cop is a sad picture, but you know very well that most people associate your role in the classroom with the primary task of correcting and reshaping speech. Even for many of your students for whom such school experiences were painful—or futile—there is the expectation that you, new ELA teacher, will do it right, do it effectively, and do it a whole lot.

Knowledge is your armor. Language shifts. Differences in language are not to be condemned or squelched. Yes, by all means students should learn to communicate effectively in all manners of English that matter to them, including standardized English. Mechanics and usage have a place in final draft writing. Without them we would have a difficult time understanding meaning; our students need to be able to present finished prose that is clear. (For instance, we can't tell you how many times we and our editors at Heinemann have proofread this very text. And any leftover errors are obviously Ken's! [They are *not*!]) On the other hand, we are about larger things than teaching students to memorize the functions of the semicolon and to fear the split infinitive and, regardless of the circumstances, rarely to use slang or colloquialisms. As difficult as it may be, we need to balance our obligation to teach correctness with an ethical mandate to respect our students and the language they bring to us, and to honor meaning before form.

When students walk into our classroom self-conscious about their speech, worried about how they talk, afraid to express what they know—or don't know—we are in a territory of pain and difficulty. Many of our students don't have an academic vocabulary; some have variations of speech that are unfamiliar even to some of their peers; some use, almost exclusively, a lot of slang. Your students may seem confident, brash, even display a certain linguistic bravado. But underneath that may be a fair amount of insecurity. It is your job to create a lively, positive, language room: there is a place for all kinds of talk in our classes, just as there is a place for all of our students. To do any less is to silence them; and that is the one thing we simply cannot, in all conscience, do.

Our goal as teachers is to enhance, not erode, the language skills students bring with them to our classes, as Deborah Dean advises:

> Teaching for today and tomorrow requires a more increased awareness of language use and language options in the world around us than was probably suggested by the training most English teachers received in the past. If we really want to help students see language as important to them . . . teachers will need to develop this broader perspective, this greater awareness of language and its uses in a wider variety of situations. (2011, 25)

Language is a fascinating, living thing. As we teach students about language, grammar, usage, rhetorical style, and power, we should also revel in language with our students and teach them to wield it effectively for the purposes they have now and will have in their future. When we teach language as only a set of rules to follow, we end up with students who see language as their master, when it should be their servant. If we help students understand and enjoy language as a tool for their interests and desires, language as a way to express themselves and interpret their lives, our students will be both more successful in all their endeavors and, most likely, happier human beings. This is a worthy outcome, we think, and certainly something that we as teachers can strive to achieve.

For Your Journal

Writing a Linguistic Autobiography

Writing your literacy history can be very illuminating about *your* own language background and, of course, linguistic autobiographies are also appropriate for your students. Mark A. Christiansen (1987) writes that to write linguistic autobiographies, students need some data about themselves. The following are excerpts of some of the questions he suggests that students consider for their final paper.

Family Background

1. What is your racial or ethnic background?
2. To what extent have members of your immediate family affected your language? (Remember that your mother was probably your first English teacher.)
3. Have any elderly relatives influenced your language growth? How?
4. Does anyone among your relatives speak a foreign language? As a result, have you looked upon the English language differently?
5. What are your father's and/or mother's occupations? Are there specific words associated with their jobs?

Leisure Time Activities

1. What is your favorite hobby/sport? Are there words associated with it that you have learned?
2. How much recreational reading do you do? Has your vocabulary been expanded because of this reading?
3. Have you traveled much? When you have been away from home, have any people ever called attention to certain expressions you use? Have people ever made fun of your dialect? If so, how did their cajoling make you feel?
4. Have your peers had any effect on your pronunciation or vocabulary? Do you use much slang? Are there certain idioms that you use with your friends or in a social group that you do not use with your parents?
5. Do you work after school or during the summer? Has your vocabulary been affected as a result of this employment?

Formal Education

1. What is (are) your favorite subject(s) in school? Have you encountered any new words from studying this subject?
2. Have you studied a foreign language? Do you use any terms from that language?
3. Have you made any attempt to change your grammatical constructions or usage? If so, what specifically have you altered?

4. When you speak, are you conscious of using certain gestures, facial grimaces, and vocal inflections? If so, how do they support what you say?

5. Do you have more difficulty expressing yourself in writing than in speaking? If so, why?

Residence

1. To what extent has the urban, suburban, or rural area in which you live affected your speech?

2. Do you watch or stream much television or YouTube? Have you adopted certain expressions used by your favorite performers?

3. Have you moved from one residence to another? If so, how have the neighborhoods been different? Has the neighborhood in which you now live affected your speech? (Christiansen 1987, 119–21)

References

Anderson, Jeff. 2005. *Mechanically Inclined: Building Grammar, Usage, and Style into Writer's Workshop*. Portland, ME: Stenhouse.

Atwell, Nancie. 2014. *In the Middle: New Understandings About Writing, Reading, and Learning*. 3rd ed. Portsmouth, NH: Heinemann.

Bryson, Bill. 2001. *The Mother Tongue: English and How It Got That Way*. New York: Perennial.

Christenbury, Leila. 1996. "From the Editor." *English Journal* 85 (7): 11–12.

Christiansen, Mark A. 1987. "Writing a Linguistic Autobiography." *Virginia English Bulletin* 37 (Spring): 119–21.

Crovitz, Darren. 2011. "Sudden Possibilities: Porpoises, Eggcorns, and Error." *English Journal* 100 (4): 31–38.

Crowley, Sharon, and Debra Hawhee. 2009. *Ancient Rhetorics for Contemporary Students*. 4th ed. New York: Pearson.

Dean, Deborah. 2011. "Shifting Perspectives About Grammar: Changing What and How We Teach." *English Journal* 100 (4): 20–26.

DelliCarpini, Margo. 2008. "Working with English Language Learners: Looking Back, Moving Forward." Success with ELLs. *English Journal* 98 (1): 98–101.

———. 2009. "Authentic Assessment for ELLs in the ELA Classroom." Success with ELLs. *English Journal* 98 (5): 116–19.

Dong, Yu Ren. 2004. "Don't Keep Them in the Dark! Teaching Metaphors to English Language Learners." *English Journal* 93 (4): 29–35.

Dunn, Patricia A., and Ken Lindblom. 2011. *Grammar Rants: How a Backstage Tour of Writing Complaints Can Help Students Make Informed, Savvy Choices About Their Writing*. Portsmouth, NH: Boynton/Cook.

Elgin, Suzette Haden. n.d. "Never Mind the Trees: What an English Teacher Really Needs to Know About Linguistics." National Writing Project: Occasional Paper No. 2, 1–15.

Fu, Danling. 2004. "Teaching ELL Students in Regular Classrooms at the Secondary Level." *Voices from the Middle* 11 (May): 8–15.

Garner, Bryan. 2009. *Garner's Modern American Usage: The Authority on Grammar, Usage, and Style*. 3rd ed. New York: Oxford University Press.

Gilyard, Keith. 1991. *Voices of the Self: A Study of Language Competence*. Detroit, MI: Wayne State University Press.

Gomez, Kimberley, and Christina Madda. 2005. "Vocabulary Instruction for ELL Latino Students in the Middle School Science Classroom." *Voices from the Middle* 13 (September): 42–47.

Haussaman, Brock, with Amy Benjamin, Martha Kolln, Rebecca S. Wheeler, and members of NCTE's Association for the Teaching of English Grammar. 2003. *Grammar Alive!* Urbana, IL: NCTE.

Heverly, Jerry. 2011. "Why I No Longer Teach Vocabulary." *English Journal* 110 (4): 98–100.

Hill, Marc Lamont. 2009. *Beats, Rhymes, and Classroom Life: Hip-Hop Pedagogy and the Politics of Identity*. New York: Teachers College Press.

Johnson, Samuel. 1819. *Dictionary*. Philadelphia: J. Maxwell.

Keely, Karen A. 2011. "Dangerous Words: Recognizing the Power of Language by Researching Derogatory Terms." *English Journal* 100 (4): 55–60.

Kelly, Lauren Leigh. 2013. "Hip-Hop Literature: The Politics, Poetics, and Power of Hip-Hop in the English Classroom." *English Journal* 102 (5): 51–56.

———. 2015. "'You Don't Have to Claim Her': Reconstructing Black Femininity Through Critical Hip-Hop Literacy." *Journal of Adolescent & Adult Literacy* 47 (1): 1–10.

Kirkland, David E. 2013. *A Search Past Silence: The Literacy of Young Black Men*. New York: Teachers College Press.

Kolln, Martha. 1998. *Understanding English Grammar*. 5th ed. Boston: Allyn & Bacon.

———. 2007. *Rhetorical Grammar: Grammatical Choices, Rhetorical Effects*. 5th ed. New York: Pearson.

Kynard, Carmen. 2013. *Vernacular Insurrections: Race, Black Protest, and the New Century in Composition-Literacies Studies*. Albany: SUNY Press.

Lester, Mark. 1990. *Grammar in the Classroom*. New York: Macmillan.

Lindblom, Kenneth. 2006. "Unintelligent Design: Where Does the Obsession with Correct Grammar Come From?" *English Journal* 95 (5): 93–96.

Lindblom, Kenneth, Will Banks, and Rise Quay. 2007. "Mid-Nineteenth-Century Writing Instruction at Illinois State Normal University: Credentials, Correctness and the Rise of a Teaching Class." In *Local Histories: Reading the Archives of Composition,* edited by Patricia Donahue and Gretchen Flesher Moon, 94–114. Pittsburgh: University of Pittsburgh Press.

McQuade, Findley. 1980. "Examining a Grammar Course: The Rationale and the Result." *English Journal* 69 (7) 26–30.

Meyer, Jim. 2003. "Living with Competing Goals: State Frameworks vs. Understanding of Linguistics." *English Journal* 92 (3): 38–42.

National Governors Association Center for Best Practices, Council of Chief State School Officers. 2010. *Common Core State Standards for English Language Arts & Literacy in History/Social Studies, Science, and Technical Subjects*. Washington, DC: National Governors Association Center for Best Practices, Council of Chief State School.

NCTE. 1974. *Students' Right to Their Own Language*. Urbana, IL: NCTE.

NCTE and IRA. 1996. *Standards for the English Language Arts*. Urbana, IL: NCTE. www.ncte.org /standards/ncte-ira.

Neruda, Pablo. 1991. "# LXVII." In *The Book of Questions*. Translated by William O'Daly. Port Townsend, WA: Copper Canyon Press.

Nilsen, Alleen Pace, and Don F. Nilsen. 2004. *Vocabulary Plus High School and Up: A Source-Based Approach*. Boston: Pearson.

Noden, Harry R. 2011. *Image Grammar: Using Grammatical Structures to Teach Writing*. 2nd ed. Portsmouth, NH: Heinemann.

Orwell, George. 1950. "Politics and the English Language." In *Shooting an Elephant and Other Essays*. New York: Harcourt, Brace.

Oxford English Dictionary. 1971. New York: Oxford University Press.

Pei, Mario. 1952. *The Story of English*. Philadelphia: J. B. Lippincott.

Pooley, Robert C. 1974. *The Teaching of English Usage*. Urbana, IL: NCTE.

Rodriguez, Richard. 1982. *Hunger of Memory: The Education of Richard Rodriguez*. Boston: David R. Godine.

Rose, Mike. 2005. *Lives on the Boundary: A Moving Account of the Struggles and Achievements of America's Educationally Underprepared*. New York: Penguin.

Rigg, Pat, and Virginia G. Allen, eds. 1989. *When They Don't All Speak English: Integrating the ESL Student into the Regular Classroom*. Urbana, IL: NCTE.

Schuster, Edgar H. 2003. *Breaking the Rules: Liberating Writers Through Innovative Grammar Instruction*. Portsmouth, NH: Heinemann.

———. 2006. "A Fresh Look at Sentence Fragments." *English Journal* 95 (5): 78–83.

Shakespeare, William. 1942. *Complete Plays and Poems of William Shakespeare*, edited by William Allan Neilson and Charles Jarvis Hill. Boston: Houghton Mifflin.

Short, Deborah, J. Hudec, and J. Echevarria. 2002. *Using the SIOP Model: Professional Development Manual of Sheltered Instruction*. Washington, DC: Center for Applied Linguistics.

Smitherman, Geneva. 1995. "'Students' Right to Their Own Language': A Retrospective." *English Journal* 84 (1): 21–27.

Spinelli, Jerry. 2000. *Stargirl*. New York: Random House.

Stalker, James C. 1987. "What Should English Teachers Know About Language?" *Virginia English Bulletin* 37 (Spring): 323.

Thomas, Wayne P., and Virginia P. Collier. 2002. "A National Study of School Effectiveness for Language Minority Students' Long-Term Academic Achievement." Santa Cruz: University of California, Center for Research on Education, Diversity and Excellence. www.usc.edu/dept/education/CMMR/CollierThomasComplete.pdf.

Truss, Lynne. 2004. *Eats, Shoots and Leaves: The Zero Tolerance Approach to Punctuation*. New York: Gotham.

Turner, Kristen Hawley. 2010. "Digitalk: A New Literacy for a Digital Generation." *Kappan* 92 (1): 41–46. http://late-dpedago.urv.cat/site_media/papers/Digitalk_A_New_Literacy_for_a_Digital_Generation.pdf.

———. 2012. "Digitalk as Community." *English Journal* 101 (4): 37–42.

Villanueva, Victor, Jr. 1993. *Bootstraps: From an American Academic of Color*. Urbana, IL: NCTE.

Weaver, Constance. 1996. *Teaching Grammar in Context*. Portsmouth, NH: Boynton/Cook.

Wheeler, Rebecca S. 2005. "Code-Switch to Teach Standard English." *English Journal* 94 (5): 108–12.

Wheeler, Rebecca, and Rachel Swords. 2006. *Code-Switching: Teaching Standard English in Urban Classrooms*. Urbana, IL: NCTE.

———. 2010. *Code-Switching Lessons: Grammar Strategies for Linguistically Diverse Writers Grades 3–6*. Portsmouth, NH: Heinemann.

Whitman, Walt. 1964. "Slang in America." *Walt Whitman Prose Works 1892*. Vol. 2, edited by Floyd Stovall, 573. New York: New York University Press.

Winchester, Simon. 2004. *The Meaning of Everything*. Oxford, UK: Oxford University Press.

Young, Vershawn Ashanti. 2014. "Introduction: Are You a Part of the Conversation?" In *Other People's English: Code-Meshing, Code-Switching, and African American Literacy,* edited by Vershawn Ashanti Young, Rusty Barrett, Y'Shanda Young-Rivera, and Kim Brian Lovejoy. New York: Teachers College Press.

Young, Vershawn Ashanti, and Aja Y. Martinez, eds. 2011. *Code-Meshing as World English: Pedagogy, Policy, Performance*. Urbana, IL: NCTE.

Young-Rivera, Y'Shanda. 2014. "Code-Meshing and Responsible Education in Two Middle School Classrooms." In *Other People's English: Code-Meshing, Code-Switching, and African American Literacy,* edited by Vershawn Ashanti Young, Rusty Barrett, Y'Shanda Young-Rivera, and Kim Brian Lovejoy. New York: Teachers College Press.

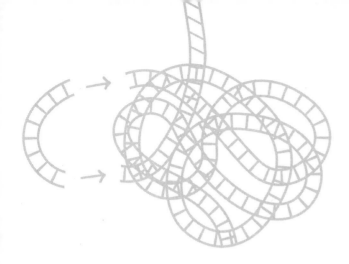

8 | WRITING, REVISING, AND PUBLISHING

Experience has shown me that there are no miracles in writing. The only thing that produces good writing is hard work.

—Isaac Bashevis Singer

Teaching Writing

Most English teachers enjoy and feel more comfortable with literature than with writing. This is also true of most of our students. For us, our love of literature has sparked a desire to teach others to love literature as well. Writing, for many, is secondary.

This preference for literature makes historical sense. In the American classroom of the mid-nineteenth century, classwork was done orally, through recitation. Writing developed as a major component of classroom teaching only when class sizes became so big that there wasn't enough time for a teacher to quiz each student orally in every class, and as paper became affordable. Thus, writing was seen purely as a conduit for communication, as a technology (a means) more than even a skill or ability. As a purely communicative technology, the most important aspect of writing was that it was correct, and thus the use of writing became most focused on correctness, rather than as a creative means of thinking and problem solving. The five-paragraph essay, Sheridan Baker's (1951) invention in *The Practical Stylist*, became the accepted formula for composing a piece of classroom writing—and that formula continues to have tremendous influence today.

Arguably, it wasn't until a group of British and American teachers met during the celebrated Dartmouth Conference in 1966 that the teaching of writing grew into the rich, multimodal, creative discipline it is today. The ensuing evolution of the modern field of college composition and the founding of the revolutionary National Writing Project have increased the rigor and depth with which writing teachers think about the field. Since then, more and more teachers have come to understand the teaching of writing as an important and fascinating part of English language arts.

Still, most of us, veteran and beginning English teachers, identify more as true readers than as true writers. We believe this is primarily because most English teachers have far more experience as authentic readers than they do as authentic writers. Think about it. You've probably been a reader for as long as you can remember, and you probably read books both for assignments and pleasure. You enjoyed what you read and could probably list favorite authors and works very easily. But, how about your favorite writings? Have you written many pieces that were not intended only for the eyes of a teacher and for the purposes of a grade? If you have, great—but know you are definitely in the minority. Real writing, *authentic* writing, is writing one does for a particular purpose, for a particular audience, and in a particular context. Authentic writing is not written for a teacher in a classroom, but for real people to whom a writer wishes to communicate something important and gain something in return: a specific action, respect for a position, understanding of a situation, laughs, a poignant response. Real writing has no formula, no simple one-size-fits-all strategy. Instead real writing is—as Singer points out in our opening quote—hard work. And to teach real writing, teachers need to experience *being* real writers.

Christina Berchini (2015), a Wisconsin writing teacher, put the matter in unique and accurate terms in an essay subtitled, "To Teach Writing, You Too Must Get Your Ass Kicked." Berchini explains that she is able to give credible responses to her students' writing because she also submits her own writing frequently to publications, and the responses she receives are just as tough and hard to take as a teacher's comments can be on student writing. She says, "I'm always on a mission to make a painful process [writing] a bit more palatable, and I think that the simple knowledge that I put myself on the line for others to consume . . . was [something] that a couple of my students needed to hear" (2015, 134).

Berchini is right not just because her students will better appreciate her responses to their writing because she too allows herself to be vulnerable to the responses of others—in her case, journal editors and blog readers—but also because her experience as a publishing author gives her a great deal of experience to draw from as she gives feedback and advice to her students.

We are also published authors and veteran writing teachers at the secondary and college levels. We use this chapter to share our experiences to help you develop your own style as a writing teacher, regardless of how much experience you have as an authentic writer. We will help you understand best practices for creating writing assignments and for helping students come up with ideas, develop their drafts, edit their writing, and publish their writing in meaningful ways. We will discuss the kinds of skills students must have to succeed in on-demand writing situations (such as timed writing in standardized exams). We'll also offer strategies for responding to student writing and give background to help you understand more fully the complex and fascinating world of writing, which we all want our students to enter.

A Contemporary Model of Teaching Writing: Writing Process and POWER-P

Today, many English language arts teachers use what is termed a "process" model for teaching writing, a model that is not so much based on an ideal of how writing *should* proceed but on how studies of the behaviors of real writers show that it actually proceeds. This model of teaching writing is more closely based on what we know real writers do. Although this movement probably has its origins in the 1950s, the work of composition teacher Janet Emig (1971) in the 1970s triggered a reconsideration of the traditional way of teaching writing when she focused her research on the actual behavior of student writers as they wrote rather than an idealized conceptual schema of writing.

What was Emig's research? Emig observed students as they drafted and revised and asked them questions, to which they responded, during their actual writing. What she found—again, based not on theory but on observation of behavior—was far removed from the "ideal" writing procedure that had governed writing instruction. Students did not appear to get their ideas, outline them, write, and then revise—but seemed to jump among activities, writing not in a linear step-by-step manner but in more of a recursive pattern. Students Emig studied got their ideas as they wrote, and they revised their writing not at the end but throughout the entire writing. As composition researcher Frank Smith describes it, "Writing is not a matter of taking dictation from yourself; it is more like a conversation with a highly responsive and reflective other person" (1990, 27). This insight into writing behavior, accompanied by an understanding of the importance of invention—that writers need to use techniques more like artists in their creative processes to find ideas—became the centerpiece of writing best practice and the process model of teaching writing. In essence, how students *got there* was far more important than what they produced at the end. More important to teachers, however, Emig's research also showed that how students got there was not consonant with much of the direction they were then receiving from their writing teachers.

It's important for students to understand that the skill of "writing" is actually a collection of various abilities and attitudes. Writing successfully takes creativity, organization, strategic planning, discipline, confidence, enthusiasm, skill with language, and a thick skin—among other qualities. We can't really teach all these qualities; however, we can design authentic writing experiences that will allow students to develop these qualities over time. Ken uses the "POWER-P" acronym to describe the authentic writing processes he engages his students in. POWER-P stands for the following:

- **P**rewriting
- **O**rganization
- **W**riting
- **E**valuating
- **R**evising
- **P**ublishing.

POWER-P is one manifestation of what most English teachers call the "writing process," but we must be careful not to treat writing process as a fixed set of steps that writers complete to compose. Real writers go back and forth through the many aspects of writing process and, in fact, different writers have different processes at different times. Thus, there is no such thing as *the* writing process; rather, there are many processes that writers may use to compose. Teaching students about the many options they have for composing is a writing process approach, and one that we recommend.

POWER-P outlines the various activities in writing, and writers may go back and forth between them. Here are brief descriptions of each activity; we explain what may be new terms to you later in the chapter:

Prewriting: Also known as the rhetorical concept of "invention," prewriting is when writers are coming up with the ideas they can write about. There are many strategies you can teach students for prewriting, including webbing, brainstorming, drawing, talking with peers, using various graphic organizers, free writing, reading mentor texts. The more time students spend thinking about how they can approach their topic and what kinds of evidence, rhetorical appeals, sources, stories, and other elements they can use in their writing, the more likely they are to be invested in the writing and successful in their final product.

Organizing: Organizing is when a writer begins to decide how the piece of writing will be structured. What parts will come first, second, and so on? When will different forms of evidence or anecdotes be used? How will it end? Strategies for organizing include outlines, cutting out printed free-written paragraphs and sentences and moving them around, making a list, following the structure of a mentor text.

Writing: This is when writers begin to write a complete first draft. They take notes, sketches, phrases, planned outlines, and whatever else they've so far created and write them up into a draft that takes whatever shape is appropriate for the assignment.

Evaluating: Once a draft is written, as you well know, much of the work is still ahead. Successful writers work hard to reflect carefully on how effective their drafts are and to find areas that could be improved. To evaluate their writing, writers can read carefully, ask peers or writing tutors to read their drafts and make suggestions, read their drafts out loud to themselves (or have a computer read it to them), run the draft past a test audience to see if the draft does what the writer intends it to do, and so on. This is a crucial area that is often underattended to in English classes. Let the name of this stage remind you why you should take it seriously: e-VALU-ating.

Revising: Once writers make decisions about what's working well and what could use improvement in their drafts, they make revisions to improve them. Those revisions will often include major organizational shifts, deleting and replacing whole paragraphs, and other changes. Further revisions will include surface corrections and minor tweaks that would be properly called copyediting. Note that it doesn't make sense to do any copyediting until the major revisions have been made.

Publishing: Finally, the writing is published. Real writing is always *published* in some form for some genuine audience, and there are many, many forms of publication writing may take. In a traditional classroom, publishing is turning in a final paper for a grade. This is the weakest, least engaging, and most artificial form of publication and feedback writing can take. Unfortunately, it is also the form that is most common in English classes. Instead, consider these publication ideas:

- Publish writing in a school newspaper, national journal, trade magazine, or some other print forum read by an audience outside the class.

- Post writing online on a personal, school-sponsored, or professional blog or website; tweet out to followers or send to friends on Facebook, Instagram, Tumblr, and so on.

- Read writing out loud to a real audience (that audience can be the whole class, a group of peers, or a school event to which the whole neighborhood has been invited).

Principles of Process Writing Instruction

There are, of course, parts and procedures in writing, just as outlined in POWER-P, but there are also some limitations. The implications of a writing process approach for us as teachers are serious: we cannot spend Monday getting ideas, Tuesday writing, Wednesday revising, and Thursday copyediting. If we put students on such a schedule, even in the name of process writing, we are not truly letting students explore or use their recursive process.

We need to help students get started and then give them time to use and develop their own patterns for working through drafting to a final (or somewhat final) version. They may be getting ideas on Wednesday and Thursday, writing on Friday and Sunday, and getting more ideas on Monday. If we believe writing is truly recursive, we create a schedule that allows for that recursiveness. This does not mean we abandon our students and give them three days to figure it out for themselves; we need to help them during this time by using a workshop format, in which students are given time in class to think about, draft, get feedback from peers, and revise their writing. In a process model, however, you cannot completely confine writing behaviors to certain blocks of time—because it doesn't work that way. Teachers who try to schedule writing process are actually abusing the term and not really helping their students. Giving students time over a period of days to write and prewrite and revise is more helpful than pre-determining which writing "step" a group will be involved in on any given day.

For Your Journal

Think about the last writing assignment you did for a class. Try to remember how you actually got ready to write, how the writing itself went, how much time it took, and what kind of revision or rewriting you did. Did you show the draft to a friend? Did you read the words aloud to yourself? Was it important that you use a pen, a pencil, a computer? What, in short, was your *writing process* for this last assignment you did?

Teaching with Authentic Writing

Teaching within a writing process model works best when a teacher uses authentic writing assignments—assignments that have real purposes, real audiences, real contexts, and real consequences. When writing assignments are simply teacher-designed and teacher-graded, the teacher becomes an artificially overempowered audience, and all aspects of the writing become the domain of the teacher's opinion. Authentic writing assignments, on the other hand, require students to develop the kinds of critical skills and attitudes about writing that will help them in the world beyond school.

In a landmark article on the teaching of writing, education guru Grant Wiggins (2009) calls authentic writing "Writing Reality Therapy." Writing instruction is either based on reality or it's some artificial laboratory type of writing that doesn't have any real-world relevance. Wiggins boils down the idea of authenticity in writing instruction into two questions, one about purpose and one about audience:

1. Is the student regularly required to achieve a real-world result, appropriate to context, as a consequence of writing, and learn from the result/feedback?

2. Is the student regularly required to write for specific and varied audiences, so that studying and coming to empathize with that audience is a part of the assignment? (2009, 33)

Asking Wiggins' questions about the writing instruction you witness and that you develop yourself can be a good test of whether or not your writing instruction is authentic and reality based.

So what makes writing authentic? Ken wrote an *English Journal* column on exactly this question. Authentic writing has a real purpose, designed by the author and intended for a real audience that will actually read and respond to the writing. Authentic assignments encourage writers to use many resources to help their writing (including peer responses), and those pieces of writing are assessed in ways that take into account the genuine feedback of a real audience. In addition, the rules of correctness for authentic writing must come from the actual forum in which the writing will be published. For example, if the writing is for the *Washington Post*, then the rules for correctness should be the official style guide of the *Washington Post* (Lindblom 2004, 106–107). If we want all students to learn to write to the best of their ability, we must design writing assignments that allow students to select topics that they are interested in and that allow them to write to real audiences that they truly want to speak to. *This* is authentic writing.

Some readers may worry that focusing on authentic writing, as opposed to test-prep writing, may give students a disadvantage on exams. We'll let Grant Wiggins address those concerns:

> The better you teach students to write, the more their scores will improve. That is, of course, how test validity works. You need only look at the samples of student writing released from state and national tests to see this. The papers that get the highest scores are more fun to read than the low-scoring ones. (2009, 36)

TECH TALK: *A Peer-Reviewed Blog on Authentic Writing*

For additional information on authentic writing instruction, readers are encouraged to visit the blog *Teachers, Parents, Profs: Writers Who Care*. This blog, peer reviewed by members of the Commission on Writing Teacher Education of the Conference on English Education, offers commentary, examples, research, and advice about best practices in authentic writing instruction. The blog posts are written for nonspecialists and are also great resources for communicating with students, parents, and administrators about the value of authentic writing instruction.

Traditional Writing Instruction Versus Authentic Writing Instruction

You may not have been taught in a manner consistent with process writing and authentic writing principles; thus, it might be helpful for us to lay out some of the differences between the two approaches. The chart on the next page summarizes the two models. Use it as a way to think back to your own instruction in writing and to assess whether the way you see your teaching in the future is consistent with authentic writing instruction.

	Traditional Model	Authentic Writing
Topic	Teacher determined	Teacher and student or student determined
Prewriting	Limited or none	Extensive
Time	Limited	Extensive
Help/Collaboration	None	Extensive
Response	From teacher only	From teacher and peers and audience
Response	Summative	Formative and summative
Revision	Limited	Extensive
Audience	Teacher only	Teacher and others, including audiences outside class
Structure	Provided by teacher	Provided by student and determined by nature of project
Genre	Primarily academic essay	Varies widely

Helping Students Get Writing Ideas: Structuring Choice

Students often resent teachers who consistently tell them what they are to write about, when, and how. It is also, paradoxically, no solution to tell students to "write about anything you want." In fact, few students will take that freedom and do much with it other than become frustrated and anxious. As teachers, we can help strike a balance: we can present our students with a general direction in which they can go and yet also allow them to be creative and inventive. How can we do this? By adhering to three principles of successful—and authentic—writing assignments. These assignments

- must be interesting to the student
- must be both specific and general
- outside of research projects, must be within the student's area of expertise.

Let's look at each of these in turn.

The first principle for any successful writing assignment is that it must be *interesting* to the student; it must, in essence, be perceived by the student as worth doing. Many times, ideas that are immediate and important to us as adults—such as municipal regulations in apartment buildings or legal requirements for day care centers or what will happen to social security, issues which may be affecting *us* right now—are often of little concern to our students. We need to think of topics with which they, not just we, can have some intellectual and emotional engagement. Linking the granting of a driver's license to school grades, for instance, or providing tuition support to college students whose parents are not American citizens may be of far more import to your students than the issue of the price of prescription drugs. Are there school issues or community issues that concern your students? Try to present students with topics that appeal to them.

The second principle for a successful writing assignment is that it must be *both specific and general:* Although this seems like a contradiction, it really isn't. Building choice for students is vital so that while satisfying, for instance, the need (or the curricular mandate) to have students write an "argument" paper (taking a stand on an issue and presenting a case), we can let students determine what specific issue they will pursue.

One example of this kind of assignment is "Scars," a personal narrative and exposition with which Leila has had some success. In "Scars," students write about a physical scar they have: where it came from, when they acquired it, who was involved, why it happened, and what (if anything) the scar means to them now. Students have boundaries regarding this assignment—it is a narrative and exposition with a structure—but they and they alone determine the specifics.

The third principle for a successful writing assignment is that it must, somehow, be *within the area of the student's expertise.* Although research papers are legitimate places for students to learn about new topics, essay-writing assignments are rarely successful if they require students to take a stand on comparatively unfamiliar issues. Thus, if students have no specific background regarding the tax code or child slave labor or even climate change, why ask them to research and write about the topic? Letting students select an area about which they have knowledge—and you may be surprised at what they know—can yield a far more successful essay.

There are countless sources of "ideas" for writing (one such is the use of "mentor" or exemplary texts—see Marchetti and O'Dell [2015] for a terrific book on this topic) and, naturally, asking students about what they are interested in can result in excellent suggestions. Think also of the following:

- **Quotations:** Have students bring in a quotation (with attribution and source) and write about why they chose that quotation, what it appears to mean, and how the quotation might relate to their lives. Students can write about their own quotations or even each other's; students can make a "bank" of quotations for the use of other students and other classes.

- **Childhood memories:** Ask students to select a childhood experience (that occurred at age twelve or younger) and write about it. Topics can include finding something valuable, doing something forbidden, trying not to cry, getting an unexpected present, mastering a task, being somewhere you weren't supposed to be and getting caught, making an important friend, being laughed at and not knowing why (Tanner 1997).

- **The daily news:** Have students pick a single news article from the day's news feed and write about what it *doesn't* say: What facts appear to be left out? Why? What more would a reader want to know? What can you speculate will be the implications of this event on individuals? The community? To what extent do you think this is news important enough to include in a paper or as a segment on YouTube? Why or why not? In an audacious twist on this assignment, high school teacher Joel M. Freedman (2009) suggests having students play the various roles involved in complicated news stories. In his example, an article about a hate crime committed against a young gay man, students are asked to write their thoughts on the event from the perspectives of the perpetrators, the victim, their parents, the police officers, the judge, and the head of a community group that favors or opposes gay rights legislation.

- **Letter to self:** As the first writing assignment of a new school year, students write a letter to themselves with five parts (me, now; my world; what I do; people in my life; my future). The letter deals "with the things that are important and real" in the students' lives and can be returned to students at the end of the school year. Students can include with this letter a supplementary packet including photographs, maps, videotapes, montages, or other information that they feel will illumine who they are (Burkhardt 2003, 270, 273).

- **Local issues:** In an award-winning *English Journal* article, Lauren Esposito (2012) describes how she engaged her students in urban areas of Long Island to script and compose public service announcement videos related to local issues with which they were concerned. Videos are a specialized form of communication that are not themselves comprised of traditional writing, but traditional writing (scripts, texts in the videos, and companion assignments) is embedded in their development.

- **Observing nature:** In Fran Claggett, Louann Reid, and Ruth Vinz's (1996) *Learning the Landscape*, the authors set up a wonderful writing assignment for which students pick an animal, plant, or natural object and observe it over a period of days, taking focused field notes and writing. And you don't need to live in the country or the suburbs to do this—students can also observe a rock or a star or a houseplant. The assignment requires multiple defined journal entries, a drawing, and, more important, a conclusion, and it culminates in a finished piece of writing.

- **Multigenre paper:** Another interesting avenue is the multigenre paper, in which students combine letters, news articles, cartoons, prose, poetry, and other media (including art and different type styles and sizes) in one paper. James Agee's (2000) *Let Us Now Praise Famous Men* used this format almost eighty years ago; Agee, writing about the Depression-era South, made lists and used dialogue, prose, and Walker Evans's photography to paint his portrait. Similarly, students can break the boundaries of traditional papers by using a multigenre format and, through that perspective, present more than one perspective of an event or topic. Although teacher W. David LeNoir issues teachers a "multigenre warning label" (2002, 99) regarding unity—the papers need not just be multigenre but must be coherent in what they say—this is an interesting and promising format. In Nancy Mack's *Multigenre Research Projects: Multifaceted, Multipurpose Writing Assignments*, she points out that "a genre-analysis approach better prepares writers for a future that will include new genres that can hardly be imagined today" (2015, 11). With chapters on conducting interviews, researching nonfiction, narrating events, creating poetry, reporting information, writing academic arguments, using graphics, getting feedback, and writing for real audiences, readers will find the book to be amazingly comprehensive and filled with good advice about teaching writing. For more information still, check out Tom Romano's (2000) foundational *Blending Genre, Altering Style*.

In her *Talking, Sketching, Moving: Multiple Literacies in the Teaching of Writing*, Patricia A. Dunn (2001) describes many ways of helping students to generate and organize text using unusual methods. She has students sketch out their ideas (using images, few if any words) to try to flesh them out in more detail; she has students share "oral outlines" with each other; and she offers a number of strategies for cutting up printed-out drafts and moving them around to see opportunities for revision. Writing classrooms that engage students in topics they care about can become even more dynamic with creative methods such as those Dunn suggests.

But What About Timed Writing on Standardized Tests?

This discussion of authentic writing and student-determined writing is most likely helpful for you in your classroom. On the other hand, timed writing tests are part of the current educational landscape, and as much as we want to think about student writing that is expressive and individual, based on student interest and expertise, workshopped in writing groups, and open to revision, such is not always the case. Many state and national tests—in particular the SAT, ACT, and AP tests—use writing on demand, giving students predetermined topics or prompts and a narrow window of time in which to respond. It would seem, at first blush, that such writing is completely antithetical to everything outlined in this chapter. This kind of writing is a genre in itself, and the good work that we do in our writing classrooms need not be abandoned when we prepare our students for timed writing tests. When students are comfortable getting writing ideas, drafting, and revising, when they read perceptively and can understand what a prompt is asking them to do, they can indeed perform well in a timed writing situation. Although the scope of this book does not allow for a long discussion regarding the genre of writing on demand, it may be helpful to consider two issues of importance. Based on Leila's coauthored *Writing on Demand: Best Practices and Strategies for Success* (Gere, Christenbury, and Sassi 2004), the two issues regarding this kind of specialized writing are negotiating a predetermined topic or prompt and dealing with time.

Negotiating a Prompt

Let's imagine your students are in a timed writing situation and are confronted with the following prompt:

> Sophocles wrote, "The greatest griefs are those we cause ourselves." What do you think of the view that the worst sorrows are those for which we are responsible?

There are, in essence, a number of things that students need to consider regarding the prompt and their role as a writer. The following Prompt Analysis Questions (or PAQs) can help students approach any prompt, including the previous one:

1. What is the *central claim/topic* called for?

   Do I have choices to make with regard to this claim/topic? Will I need to focus the claim/topic to write a good essay? What arguments can I make for this claim? What do I know about this topic?

2. Who is the intended *audience*?

   If named specifically, what do I know about this particular audience? If the audience is implied or not identified, what can I infer about it or them? In either event, how might the expectations of this audience affect my choices as a writer?

3. What is the *purpose/mode* for the writing task?

   Is the purpose stated or must it be inferred? What is this writing supposed to accomplish (besides fulfilling the demands of the prompt/assignment)? What does the goal of this writing suggest about the mode (narration, exposition, description, argument) or combination of modes that I should consider in responding?

4. What *strategies* will be most effective?

   What does the purpose/mode suggest about possible strategies? Of the strategies I am comfortable using—strategies like examples, definitions, analysis, classification, cause and effect, compare and contrast—which will be most effective here? Are there any strategies—such as number of examples or type of support—that are specified as required?

5. What is my *role* as a writer in achieving the purpose?

   Have I been assigned a specific role like *applicant* or *representative*? If I have not been assigned a specific role, what does the prompt or assignment tell me about the level of expertise I should demonstrate, the stance I should assume, or the approach I should take? (Gere, Christenbury, and Sassi 2004, 67)

With this prompt, the *claim* is Sophocles' comment about grief, and it appears open to debate or discussion; there is nothing in the prompt that seems to suggest what kind of attitude the writer is to take. The *audience* is not specified—the writer is not asked to make an argument to a specific figure, so we can assume the audience is the reader or scorer of this writing. The *purpose or mode* is the presentation of a point of view (*what do you think* is how the prompt reads). *Strategies* are open and not specified in the prompt. Writers could tell a story, give hypothetical examples, or just express an opinion, but it is good to look at the pronoun *we*, which implies a personal approach to this prompt, not a distanced one. As for *role*, the writer is to tell what he or she thinks—to express a point of view—regarding Sophocles' comment.

Students can use the PAQs with a number of prompts; the time they take to assess the prompt itself is well worth it and can help them produce a solid piece of writing in a brief period.

Dealing with Time

Using time in a writing test is something that is far different from writing in a regular classroom environment. Students need to understand that they will, once they get their writing ideas in place, have to produce very quickly. As a first step, students need to know how long they have to write and then, as suggested in *Writing on Demand* (Gere, Christenbury, and Sassi 2004), they need to practice the following procedure:

- Look at the clock and write the following on a piece of paper:
  - time writing test begins
  - time that marks one quarter of the available minutes
  - five minutes before test must be completed.

- Use the first quarter of available time to plan your writing. This includes reading the prompt and instructions, prewriting, and developing a thesis or main point.

- When the clock indicates that a quarter of the time has elapsed, consider where you are in the planning process. If necessary, you can take a few more minutes to finalize your thoughts.

- Start writing your response after no more than half of the available time has elapsed.

- As you write, glance at the clock occasionally and keep looking at your thesis and prewriting to keep them in the forefront of your mind.

- Five minutes before the end of the test, draw your writing to a close.

- In the last few minutes, reread and proofread your writing, making corrections, inserting missing words, or deleting unnecessary ones. Changes that are inserted or deleted neatly are acceptable—in most cases you will not have a lot of extra time, so do not try to recopy the entire selection. (143)

Giving students practice with prompts and timed situations can help them feel more comfortable with the specific requirements of writing on demand. It's only part of the writing picture, but it is one that we cannot ignore—and working with students before the test can help them feel more confident.

For Your Journal

Think about your own writing history in school—how you "learned" to write. How did you get your ideas? What kind of computer or writing instrument did you use? Did you have a special place or time of day to write? Did you share your writing with a parent? A friend? Did you make notes before you wrote? Talk to yourself? Draw? How was your writing received in school? What help did you get to improve? What about your experiences with timed writing: Did you find this kind of writing easy or was it more difficult than the writing you had done before? What happened when you went to college and wrote? Was it different? Why? Why not?

Peer-Response Groups: Questions, Answers, and Reasons

Whether in a timed situation or in our classroom, using teacher-defined topics or student-determined ones, helping students with their writing is one of our tasks as teachers. One way to do that is by using peer-response groups that both capitalize on the collaborative aspects of writing and help students see their work as broader than just between themselves and the teacher. Sure, the very idea of peer-response groups scares some teachers. There is, of course, the fear that students will get out of control in the groups, using them for everything *but* writing response, but an even greater fear is that students don't know what to do and will do nothing in their groups but share their own ignorance about writing. It is, after all, the teacher's job, isn't it, to be the determiner of what is good writing?

These fears need not be realities. When students are told what a peer-response group is for; when the tasks and procedures are carefully planned, outlined, and consistently reinforced; and when the teacher provides adequate student supports, or scaffolds, there is little real chance that a peer-response group will get either out of control or lost. Students need to be introduced to peer-response groups; they need to model the behavior in a "fishbowl" kind of exercise (discussed later in this chapter); and they need an accountability structure for what they do in their groups. Some groups will be able to talk about drafts and take notes on their copies productively. Other groups will need checklists and worksheets that they turn in with their drafts to encourage them to stay on task. Regardless, peer-response groups can work very effectively in middle and high school.

TECH TALK: *A Method for Peer Review*

Readwritethink.org, a massive database of lesson plans, includes a helpful lesson on using a format called "PQP" for in-class peer review. "Praise—Question—Polish" is a simple format for structuring a peer-response session. Search on the site for the lesson entitled "Peer Review: Narrative," and you'll find a well-devised form that helps middle school students (grades 6–8) answer questions about one another's writing. Reviewers begin by pointing out what they like about a colleague's essay, then they ask about sections that confuse them, and they end by offering advice for improvement. The form can be adapted for other genres of writing and for other grades of students.

Don't Peer-Response Groups "Do" the Teacher's Job?

But what about the concern that response to writing is the teacher's job and that students in a writing group are doing nothing more than sharing their ignorance?

The utility of the peer-response group is that it exposes students to the writing of others. Gone is the isolation of one person writing his or her draft and never hearing or seeing what other students are doing. The writing of other students teaches; a draft presented in a writing group may be significantly better or significantly worse than the work of the other members of the group. Nevertheless, in a peer-response group students get to read and consider a range of writing—one another's drafts. They also get to "test out" their writing on an audience, which is something professional writers do all the time. Often we wonder what effect it has on students to read and see only the polished, analyzed, credentialed work of the great, whom we know can write: Annie Dillard, Ta-Nehisi Coates, Lewis Thomas, Henry David Thoreau, Martin Luther King, Jr. Letting students see and work with the writing of those who like themselves are learning to write can be a heartening experience. There is some fascinating work in manuscript studies that examines the drafting and revising practices of celebrated writers, and, if you choose to find these examples and share them with your students, such work can truly energize English classes.

Peer-response groups also tap into the collaborative, *each one teach one*, aspect of learning. If a student gets lost reading another student's draft, if the point just seems to disappear, that student—the reader, not the writer—will need to figure out why and articulate it. By trying to help a peer, the person will have to put a name on the problem area and give some sort of advice about what to do. It makes all students in the group consider and grapple with issues of writing in an immediate way, which is far more active than responding in a large group to whatever the teacher asks students to look for and discuss. Students can become more independent, and there is a double learning that can take place. For Ellen to help Mark with his writing, Ellen has to figure out what the issue is; by helping Mark, Ellen is helping herself.

The Numbers Game: Managing the Paper Load

We need also to think about the sheer impossibility of the teacher's task in the area of writing. It is an overwhelming job: the numbers, ladies and gentlemen, are just not in our favor and will not be in the near future, unless there is a major overhaul of the educational system. In fact, if a teacher is able to respond to every piece of writing his or her students write, then that teacher is possibly not assigning enough writing. To be effective writing teachers, we must enlist others to respond to student writing.

In a famous article in the very first issue of *English Journal* (Vol. 1, No. 1, 1912), Edwin M. Hopkins asked, "Can Good Composition Teaching Be Done Under Present Conditions?" The article lamented the number of students in the average English teacher's class and noted that with the time it took to teach and respond to writing, it seemed an impossible situation. Little has changed between 1912 and today; in fact, class sizes have risen in recent years. Most English language arts teachers see a large number of students every day; Leila had a student teacher who, in a burgeoning suburban school, saw 167 students a day. What, practically, does this mean?

Let's look at the numbers. Let's imagine that you give *one class a week* a writing assignment. They are taking their writing seriously, and you want to give them a response to their drafts before they do a final version. You are not using peer-response groups; you want to make all the comments and suggestions yourself.

Let's say you spend a moderate amount of time—*ten minutes per draft*—for this one class of twenty-five to thirty students. That's anywhere from 250 to 300 minutes—between four and five hours—just to give students an intermediate response to a draft. When you receive final versions, of course, you will spend another ten minutes or so per paper—and that's another four to five hours. This is for *one class* to do a single piece of writing to which you respond and then evaluate and grade; it has worked out to about eight to ten hours of your time outside of teaching and preparation.

This eight to ten hours is, by the way, in addition to work for your other three or four classes and outside whatever else you are having this same writing class do. Is it any wonder English language arts teachers avoid giving writing assignments and, if they do, work only with final drafts?

Well-planned peer-response groups can help a teacher handle some of the paper load. He or she can circulate among the groups and feel confident that with proper preparation students can share what they are working on and get feedback from other readers, not just the teacher. It's a practical solution that not only has a sound pedagogical basis but that also may help to save a committed writing teacher's sanity.

In her excellent *Write Beside Them: Risk, Voice, and Clarity in High School Writing*, English language arts teacher Penny Kittle describes well why peer-response groups are essential components of her writing class:

> I keep one group of students together for several weeks and usually at least two full units so that students become comfortable with each other and begin to learn from each other. . . . I am always seeking bridges between students in my room so that

they can learn to depend on each other for response. Writers need lots of readers; it broadens perspective. Plus, I can't read and reread each student's work as much as they need me to. If I don't create a group of good responders, students will learn less. (2008, 91)

And we are agreed.

Procedures for Implementing a Peer-Response Group

The composition of a peer-response group can be heterogeneous or homogenous; in other words, you can either mix writing ability or keep writers of the same ability in a single group. We have had most success with a heterogeneous group of three or four members; we usually mix males and females and members of majority and minority racial or ethnic groups. Diversity works well, and we prefer to use it in classes.

As a first step, ask students for an ungraded writing sample a few days before they get into writing groups. Do some prewriting together, and, for instance, have students write about a personality characteristic of theirs or something that they are good at outside of school. It's an assignment that allows students to talk about something they know about and are interested in—themselves. Read these writing samples, looking at them with an overall general eye; it is holistic grading. Although you respond to what students have written, don't yet give the papers a letter grade. Then place the papers in stacks; one stack for the strong writers (1s); one stack for the middling writers (2s); and one stack for the writers who, at this point at least and within the context of this group, look like they will need work and help (3s). Whereas one writing sample is no sure indicator of writing ability, and this sort of 1 to 3 holistic scoring has limitations, the procedure gives you a handle on where each student might be at that moment. Using this quick diagnosis, you can construct the peer-response groups, mixing the 1s, 2s, and 3s as well as the males, females, and ethnic groups. So, for example, a single group of four might have, in ability, one 1, one 3, two 2s; in gender, two females, two males; in an ethnic mix, three Latinos, one Caucasian. It's important, by the way, not to share the numerical designations of students' writing samples.

This is an initial diagnosis, based on a single piece of writing, and its function is only to allow a teacher to create intermediate groupings.

It's valuable to talk with students about why peer-response groups are important, giving them much the same argument we have outlined here. Assure them you will be circulating among the groups as they work, and that the groups will change over time. Then give them the following handout, and go over it:

Peer-Response Groups

In groups of three or four, you will have about an hour to share one another's papers, suggest changes, and reinforce what you feel are the strongest parts of the shared papers. Every member of the group must participate in the revision and should, while being respectful of the others' writing, make a conscientious effort to help the others improve their drafts.

Time

Group of three, 15 minutes apiece

Group of four, 10–12 minutes apiece

Procedure

1. One person should give copies of his or her rough draft to the members of the group.

2. The writer of the draft should then read the draft aloud to the group—there should also be no preliminary apologies or explanations, just the reading.

3. The writer should then pause for a few minutes to allow the group to consider, look over the draft, make marks, make notes.

4. The discussion of the draft should then start and include both negative and positive remarks. In all instances, the group should try to be specific about the paper. Comments such as "I don't like this paragraph" are not helpful; comments such as "In this sentence, this word seems too strong" or "This section seems out of place—could you move it more to the beginning of the paper?" are more useful and will help an author in changing and revising a draft to make better sense.

5. Ultimately, the paper belongs to the writer, not the group. It is conceivable that the writer will listen to suggestions and hints and decide to accept only some of them in revision. This is crucial because writers must develop and retain authority over their own writing. Even that word indicates its importance: *author-ity*.

Questions for Peer-Response Groups to Consider[†]

- Ideas and Content: To what extent is the draft clear? Interesting? Convincing? Are details used well? Are main and secondary ideas balanced?

- Organization: Can a reader follow where the draft is going? Are there helpful transitions? Where can points be made clearer?

- Voice: Does this draft read as if it were written by a real person? Can you "hear" the voice of the writer? Is there flavor, honesty, humor here?

- Word Choice: Are the words used fresh? Striking? Appropriate for the content?

- Sentence Fluency: To what extent does the writing move the reader along? Are the sentences varied or do they all sound the same?

- Conventions: Are there areas where the writer needs to check spelling? Punctuation? Paragraphing? Capitalization? Do any of these errors interfere with the meaning of the draft?

[†] Questions for Peer-Response Groups to Consider are adapted from *Creating Writers* by Vicki Spandel and Richard J. Stiggins (1997).

Using a Fishbowl Discussion to Model the Process

To help students understand how a peer-response group works, we use a duplicated copy of an anonymous student draft and ask students to enact a "fishbowl" writing group and role-play.

Four student volunteers sit at the front or in the center of the room and pretend they are the group discussing this draft; one student volunteers to be the author, and the others are members of the peer-response group. The group follows the procedures outlined in the handout. The "author" begins by reading the draft aloud. The discussion then proceeds. The rest of us watch in silence, noting not so much what is said about the draft but what kinds of remarks are made and by whom: who talks, who doesn't, how it goes. After about ten minutes of observation, we stop the role-play and talk about what we saw.

Then four different student volunteers do the fishbowl again. Not surprisingly, you'll find the second group is always different from the first; they have the benefit of having watched the first fishbowl, and they usually have different ideas of their own and different ways of interacting. Again, discuss how the group went.

It is only after taking a writing sample, grouping students, explaining the purpose and intent of a peer-response group, giving students some written instructions, and doing a number of fishbowl exercises that students are comfortable beginning work in a peer-response group. Even then, checklists—that teacher and students discuss and briefly review—as well as teacher circulation among the groups may be necessary to keep students on task. Groups can take a bit of time to bond, and they may have questions that need to be answered. To have students just "get in groups and talk about one another's drafts" is not effective for most; if we care about the process, we need to take these actions:

1. Model the process, step by step.

2. Reinforce the process.

3. Monitor the process.

When students are asked to take on roles they do not understand and for which they are not prepared, chaos and anxiety can ensue.

As noted by Penny Kittle (2008) and discussed earlier, we agree that how often groups are reformed is a context issue; some teachers prefer groups that last for a semester at least, but you may want to change your groups more frequently. Personality conflicts between students, discipline issues, students whose writing skill changes so drastically that they would benefit from other peers, groups that for whatever reason are not productive or harmonious are additional reasons to reconfigure peer-response groups. As you circulate among groups you will be able to sense who is working well and who is not; use your judgment to determine when and if a peer-response group needs change.

Encouraging Feedback from Peer-Response Groups

Sometimes with student-response groups, simple directions are powerful. Donald Daiker (1989) suggests two short sentence stems that can help students develop interesting discussions about each other's writing and keep the discussion positive:

- I like the way you . . .
- I'd like to learn more about . . .

You might also find assignment-specific questions to be very helpful, and it's also important to target the questions to the stage of your students' drafts. If students are in the early stages of a long project, be sure to focus peer-response groups on the quality of ideas, the number or impact of details, and the overall tone and structure of the piece. In later drafts, organization of evidence, structure of individual sentences, phrases, and words, and adherence to surface conventions become important.

The Work of a Peer-Response Group: Revision, Editing, and Proofreading

As the title of this chapter indicates, writing is also revision, and the most important work of a peer-response group can be to help with that vital function. A note, however: most students confuse revision with editing and proofreading. The three are not interchangeable. Revision, editing, and proofreading are different and represent very different levels of activity during the final draft of writing. Many students, in fact, believe that the alteration of a single word or the correction of capitalization and punctuation is revision, but such is not the case. Students must look at the whole writing, not just at the word or sentence level. Revision is the major work of changing, shaping, and improving the ideas and their expression in writing; editing and proofreading are last-stage polishing activities.

To briefly recap: *revision* is best thought of as re-vision, relooking, reworking of a piece of writing. It can occur at all stages of writing process to clarify and improve a draft or to completely rework a draft and start over. Revision activities may include changing significant portions of the writing, such as rearranging and rewriting sentences, rearranging sections, deleting sections, adding sections, rewriting openings and closings, or even refocusing the entire piece. Revision can transform a piece of writing, and the advice of writing groups can be invaluable.

Editing, on the other hand, is a look at a revised piece of writing. It is ongoing and also used during the later composing stages. During editing—and peer-response groups are helpful here—a writer reviews and changes word order, alters or fixes sentence structure, and checks usage issues (such as pronoun references, subject–verb agreement). At this stage, major changes in the writing have been established; the changes made in editing are less intrusive and far less significant to the meaning of a final piece of writing.

Proofreading is a last look at a revised, edited piece, and occurs at the very end of the writing and just before submission or publication. Activities during proofreading include verification that all minor details of usage are addressed (such as capitalization, indentation of paragraphs, sufficient spaces between title and body, and so on). It is a final polishing and can be done outside a peer-response group setting.

Most students who find writing difficult from the onset resist revision and hope that proofreading and some minor editing will be all that is needed to improve their hard-won first draft. For most students, however, revision is a vital activity to learn and practice—and one of the most powerful ways to encourage students to revise their work is to use peer-response groups.

One final caution about using a peer-response group for editing and proofreading: we have found that editing and proofreading for surface corrections are very complex skills, and learning these skills and how to communicate the results tactfully to others is challenging for all writers. We know of many writing teachers who have tried using peer-*editing* groups prematurely and found them to be ineffective at helping students write with fewer errors. The groups tend not to cohere as well because the students are by necessity focused on each other's writing *problems*. We suggest you focus on peer-*response* groups first, and that you save peer-*editing* and peer-*proofreading* groups until you and your students have formed a truly collaborative community of writers.

Conferencing with Students

Besides peer-response groups, another activity that is helpful to students is the brief but powerful writing conference. It may seem impossible to talk about a draft individually with each student in a class of thirty, but you can do it if the conferences are kept brief and are conducted while other writing/reading activities are going on. Let's imagine that students are working on their writing and you are available at your desk for five-minute conferences with people who want to talk. You could, conceivably, confer with seven or eight students and still have some time to circulate among the class or do some large-group instruction. Many students appreciate the privacy—and the reassurance—of a conference.

In *Learning by Teaching*, Donald M. Murray notes that writing conferences should be short and frequent and limited to one concern at a time. He also offers conference guidelines for teachers:

- The student responds to the text or to the experience of producing it.
- The teacher listens to the student's response to the text and watches how it is presented.
- The teacher reads or listens to the text from the student's perspective.
- The teacher responds to the student's response. (1982, 163–64)

Practically, what does this mean? It might mean that a conference would start with questions, such as the following, that ask the writer how he or she views the draft:

- What do you think of what you have written?
- What do you want to work on?
- Where are the draft's strengths? Weaknesses?
- What do you think will be the hardest part of your paper for your audience to follow?
- Where do you think you should add more detail?
- How can I help you make your paper better?

Notice that all of these questions, and the whole tenor of the conference itself, are focused not on the teacher's making the draft better—or correcting it or improving it or criticizing it—but on making the writer look at his or her own work and selecting what he or she sees—or doesn't see—as an issue. This kind of indirection may make you worry that you are not doing your teacherly job; after all, aren't we supposed to mark up and evaluate and determine what is good writing and not good writing? No. A conference that allows students to focus on selected aspects of their writing will ultimately produce more *learning* than a list of "corrections" we might hand a student in a conference setting. Ensuring that students maintain the *authority* in a writing conference helps students develop the self-concept all writers need to be effective. Far, far more important than improving the quality of any one draft is getting students to think of themselves as legitimate writers.

The Place of Correctness and Grammar in Its Place

Correctness is important. The key, though, is where and when. Correctness is important in a final draft. We need to school ourselves as teachers not to expect students—and not to ask students—to be concerned about spelling or grammar or surface issues while they are "getting it down," as Dawn Kirby and her coauthors (2013, 14 ff.) write in *Inside Out*. Getting it down is first. Getting it right is second. If we ask students to do both simultaneously, we can cripple them and their writing. They need to draft and cross out and struggle first, and then they need to go back to consider correctness. Asking students to do it all at the same time is asking for something that real writers don't practice at all; correctness has a place, but that place is firmly at the end of a writer's process.

Leila's Approach: When I work with student drafts, if it is near the end of the process I will note that students should edit and proofread, look up certain words or check for punctuation, or rework certain constructions that are either not standard or not conveying clearly what the writer means. Sometimes I will place a mark by every line of a draft where something needs to be reconsidered; students can ask one another, their group members, or they can consult their usage handbooks or dictionaries. They can, of course, also ask me, but I try to get them to pursue other sources—and thus learn to be more independent of me—as much as possible.

Ken's Approach: Like Leila, I don't focus on issues of correctness, or surface conventions, until toward the end of a student's writing process. I also try to incorporate the use of style manuals into students' editing processes. I like *A Pocket Style Manual* by Hacker and Sommers (2012), because it's small and easy to use, but the Purdue OWL (Online Writing Lab) website is an excellent free resource. It's important that students learn how to use style manuals in their final editing and proofreading. No one has all writing conventions in their heads. We should help students write the way real writers do, using all the resources available.

The point, of course, is not that correctness should be valued in and of itself but that our students need to see that correctness serves meaning. When surface errors interfere with reading, they are serious impediments. Preservice teacher Julie Morrison comments on this in her journal:

> If teachers can make their students actually see how grammatical mistakes rob their papers of the meaning intended, then they will see the importance of "correctness," not for a good grade or just to appease the teacher, but because they deserve to be taken seriously. Their ideas warrant the reader's attention, not the grammatical errors. So if students realize that their misspelled words or subject-verb disagreement trips the reader and distracts his attention, then maybe they will see worth in writing correctly.

Correctness is important, but *what* students say is paramount. Too many people associate writing only with spelling, English language arts class only with using "correct" grammar. We read that the public worries about declining standards in language, but most of those worries seem to refer only to the most surface of surface errors! Would that the public criticize recent graduates of high school because they are writing lifeless stuff, not because that lifeless stuff is misspelled. We need, as with literature, to remember why we are in the classroom: it is not to point out errors; it is to get students, in their writing, to grapple with ideas and then, only then, to present those ideas in a correct form.

Getting down to brass tacks, what can we actually do to help students with grammar in their writing? We already know that if teachers simply edit their students' writing—pointing out every error, marking up their papers till they run bloody with red pen strokes—it has only one chief effect: students will write fewer and shorter sentences, and they will not use any words they are not positive they are using and spelling correctly.

As argued in Chapter 7, "Words, Words, Words," you can teach the definition of a part of speech and test it. You can have students label participles in sentences and mark if the choices are right or wrong. You can put a fault-ridden sentence on the board and have students pick out the errors. It's testable, gradable, and can be put in fill-in-the-blank or multiple-choice format. It's harder, on the other hand, to gauge whether an opening to an essay is "effective" or not; it gets difficult putting into words why one description says more, is more evocative, than another.

What we need to do is integrate the terms, the description of the language, with the actual production of language in writing. Grammar study *before* writing will not improve writing; no studies confirm that cause-and-effect relationship, although most people assume it has just got to exist. Grammar study *with* writing or with revision is useful.

Imagine you have a student who keeps writing the same sentence patterns, subject–verb, subject–verb, subject–verb: "He drove down the lane. He saw it. He had been looking for it." You want the student to break out, vary what he is writing. Now would be the time to look at sentence patterns, at inverted verbs, introductory participial phrases, adverb clauses, periodic sentences. Maybe the student does not need to look at all of these; maybe the student doesn't need all of the nomenclature or terminology to know that you can start a sentence off with something describing something, and then complete the sentence as usual ("Driving down the lane, he saw what he was looking for"; "What he was looking for was down the lane"; and so on).

Imagine you have a student who cannot get straight where to use commas as opposed to semicolons to separate parts of sentences. The student writes, "Natural disasters such as Hurricane Katrina bring out the best and worst in people, this is obvious from news reports." Now is the time to learn how to identify complete sentences and to learn the term *conjunction*. If the student understands that she has written two complete sentences (*disasters bring/this is*) and not used a conjunction, she can use a semicolon and not a comma (*disasters bring; this is*). If the student adds a conjunction (*and* would be logical here; *disasters bring, and this is*), she can keep her comma. At this point, this student needs not only to be able to identify complete sentences but also how conjunctions work with commas and semicolons.

Memorizing the usage handbook's definitions, making lists of pronouns or adverbs, identifying items on tests, rewriting or identifying someone else's usage mistakes are contextless acts that rarely relate to real students' problems and questions in their own writing. These kinds of activities, although still frequent in many English language arts classrooms, are not, we think, worth our time. They may give us marks for our grade book and they may lull us into thinking that we are being conscientious teachers, but the fact is these kinds of isolated activities just do not do what we want—which is to improve student writing. Instead, try a more constructive approach:

- Use "error analysis" to diagnose a student's paper while reading it. Don't mark every error. But if you see an error that recurs at least twice, then you have identified pattern of error. At this point, you may point out the error and ask the student to look up more about that feature of writing. If you notice a classwide pattern, you may plan a minilesson to address it.

- Plan "focus correction." Tell students you are focusing on only one form of error in your response, and then stick to that error. Focus your other comments on other aspects of the students' writing.

- Point out when students use a complex surface feature correctly, and even have a lesson in which students show and tell each other about their successful risks in their writing. Students—all people, in fact—learn more from having their successes pointed out than having their failures pointed out. You can see it in a student's body language. Start a comment in a writing conference by saying, "Do you know what you did really well?" The student will straighten up, lean closer to listen, and often won't be able to hide a smile. That's a student who is truly ready to hear and learn from what you are about to say. Start with, "Do you know what you did wrong?" and you'll see the opposite reaction.

- If you're going to mark students' errors, make really sure you know what you're talking about. We've grown weary of seeing student writing in which teachers have labeled legitimate stylistic choices as errors—or worse—simply made incorrect claims about grammar on students' papers. When responding to student papers, the medical doctor's Hippocratic oath is apropos: "First, do no harm."

Now They've Written It—What Do You Do with It? Responding to Student Writing

There are a number of activities you can perform with the final versions of student writing. In general, the major activities are response, evaluation, and grading, and each one of these can have a clear relationship to the assignment rubric that you will create (more on that later).

The three activities are not necessarily mutually exclusive, but each differs somewhat from the others. When we *respond* to students, we make an effort to talk to them, writer to writer, reader to writer; the issues of quality, good–better–best, are not of primary importance. When we respond to a student paper, we try to do three things:

1. **Link something the student has written to us personally**. Yes, we had a similar experience; that would anger us, too. That happened to a friend of mine.

2. **We tell the student what we like about what he or she has written**. We pick one or two things the student does well and ask the student to think about it. Your introduction really grabs me—do you have any idea why that opening image is so powerful? You are using parallel construction effectively here—do you see how?

3. **We ask the student questions about the draft**. Look at your title—is that what this paper is really about? If not, what is it about? Where might you break this long section into two paragraphs? What effect do you think this word has on what you are trying to say in this paragraph?

When we *evaluate* a paper, we put more emphasis on how well we think the paper is doing what it is trying to do. That may mean more emphasis on number 2 and more direction on number 3. (You might say, I am lost in this section; what is it about? Your paragraphs are long and combine a number of points; how can you break the section on page 2 into two—or three—paragraphs?)

This kind of response is called a *facilitative* response, because it helps to facilitate students' thinking about their own writing. It gives them feedback that helps them think and grow as a writer. The opposite kind of feedback is called *directive,* and you've probably seen many examples of it: "sentence fragment," "use better evidence here," "needs a topic sentence," "watch your spelling," "awkward." Directive comments tell a writer what to do, essentially turning the writer into the teacher's writing assistant.

As we noted previously, pointing out to students what they do well is one of the most challenging—and underdiscussed—aspects of teaching writing. We are convinced that teachers tend to pounce on error, because, frankly, many often don't know what else to do with student writing. As an English teacher, however, you are an expert close reader. Use those skills to identify what a student is doing well in piece of writing, and help that writer do it more often. Have your students share in class what they have done well in their writing and teach it to each other. Have students read writing that does something well and have them use it as a mentor text and compose their own writing that models it. Focusing students on positive learning (instead of correction) is so much more effective—and pleasant.

We should remember the eight habits of mind crucial for college success spelled out in the *Framework for Success in Postsecondary Writing,* coauthored by the Council of Writing Program Administrators, the National Council of Teachers of English, and the National Writing Project (2011). As you respond to student writing, use facilitative responses to build the following attributes: curiosity, openness, engagement, creativity, persistence, responsibility, flexibility, and metacognition (reflection).

And we must point out again that in *authentic writing assignments*—those for which students have real purposes, real audiences, real contexts, and real consequences all outside the classroom—facilitative teacher response is much easier. Those purposes, contexts, consequences, and audience reactions give teachers a great deal of real-world matter to respond to. It's far harder to give a useful, nondirective response when the teacher really is the sole judge and jury of a piece of writing.

To *grade* a paper requires a letter or numerical designation *and* some sort of final evaluative comment. We use single letter grades and have never found the "split" grade of one letter for content and one for form to be successful. Some teachers like the split grade, as it seems to make a distinction between content and conventions (surface errors), but we have a hard time accepting that distinction anymore. If surface errors diminish meaning—and they can—then content is really intertwined with form. How can we separate them?

And this leads us to constructing rubrics.

Creating and Using Rubrics

Whether it is for a timed writing test or for an assignment you have created, rubrics are invaluable instruments to assess students fairly and, when shared with students beforehand, help them understand what they should emphasize or concentrate on in their writing. Traditionally, rubrics involve five or six standard items or traits—*ideas, organization, word choice, voice, sentence fluency,* and *conventions* are typical—although the "weight" or emphasis on each one of these can appropriately vary. This is important. It may seem tempting to use the same rubric for all your writing assignments and make all of the traits of equal importance, but it's not a good idea. You need to adapt your rubrics so that they credit what the assignment itself emphasizes. There is, accordingly, no "perfect" or template rubric that is appropriate for all assignments. Likewise, although there are many good rubrics available on the Internet, you should treat these as generic rubrics and tailor them appropriately to your assignment.

For example, a traditional paper that emphasizes a logical argument would probably want to account for ideas and organization and perhaps make each of those items worth more points. For a narrative that tells a personal story, you might want to give emphasis and significant point credit for organization and voice. If the assignment involved description, word choice might be truly important and thus weighted more heavily in the rubric more than other aspects. At any rate, the assignment itself and the rubric should be clearly related: if you ask students, for instance, to cite three examples to buttress their point, the rubric should pay attention to the presence—or absence—of three examples.

There are two forms of rubric: (1) an *informational rubric*, which is given to students early in their writing process to help them make sure they are composing an effective piece of writing; (2) a *scoring rubric*, which helps teachers give specific feedback on student writing and gives students an explanation of their grade. A blank scoring rubric may be given along with the assignment or held back until the assignment is graded, depending upon the teacher's goals.

Leila on Rubrics: Let's take a look at two documents, an abbreviated assignment sheet for a writing that my students and I often enjoy, the epiphany paper, and the rubric I used to grade it. Students had both of these before they wrote. Can you see how the two are related?

Epiphany Paper

Purpose: To describe convincingly a significant incident in your life

Audience: A fellow or sister writer

Function: Narrative description

Length Suggestion: Three to four pages, typed, double spaced

Discussion: An epiphany is a manifestation or, literally, a showing.

Christian theology designates the visit of the Magi, the three wise men, as the epiphany of Christ to the world, and many other religions and also mythological tales feature epiphanies. In our own lives, all of us have experienced incidents that operate as a moment or revelation or insight, some of which last for many years, if not a lifetime. These incidents—and there can be many depending on the individual—serve as emotional, psychological, even spiritual touchstones in our lives.

- Think, in your life, of such an incident or epiphany. Questions to consider:
- What was the nature of the epiphany?
- Who, if anyone, was involved in the event?
- How did anyone inside or outside the event help you assess its significance?
- What did you think you learned at the time? Now?
- What happened in what sequence?

If moments of epiphany in your own life are far too personal to write about, consider such an event in the life of a close friend or relative. Do understand that being highly revelatory is *not* expected as part of this assignment, and it is not anticipated that you will share in this essay—which your peer-response group will see and which is for credit and a grade—something that for you is intensely private and sensitive. If you can select an incident that is not supercharged, do. Otherwise, focus on another person's epiphany.

What kind of rubric would be useful for this assignment? In this case, I followed the traditional ideas–organization–word choice, and so on. Notice, though, how I made a 30-point rubric that reflected, at least in some sections, the specific assignment requirements itself. As constructed, the rubric also rewards what was most important about this memoir, ideas, and organization, and, because of the personal nature of the assignment, voice.

Epiphany Paper Rubric

Ideas	7 6 5 4 3 2 1

What was the nature of the epiphany?
Who, if anyone, was involved in the event?
How did anyone inside or outside the event help you assess its significance?

Organization	7 6 5 4 3 2 1

Who, if anyone, was involved in the event?
How did anyone inside or outside the event help you assess its significance?
What did you think you learned at the time? Now?
What happened in what sequence?

Voice	7 6 5 4 3 2 1

What did you think you learned at the time? Now?

Word Choice	3 2 1

Sentence Fluency	3 2 1

Conventions	3 2 1

Three to four pages
Typed, double spaced

TOTAL SCORE _____

Key:
30–25: A
24–19: B
18–13: C
12 or below: D

Ken on Rubrics: I favor a table-style rubric that allows me to type comments into a grid to give students specific feedback on different aspects of their writing. The rubric that follows is what I use to respond to preservice teachers' field experience blogs:

Field Experience Blog I Rubric

	Very Strong (4pts)	Strong (3 pts)	Fair (2 pts)	Needs Improvement (1 point)
Uses creative license/is fun to read (and was hopefully fun to write)				
Explores reasons for claims (explains and analyzes)				

	Very Strong (4pts)	Strong (3 pts)	Fair (2 pts)	Needs Improvement (1 point)
Uses education terminology on a professional level				
Incorporates readings and concepts from class discussion				
Shows progress in thinking and experience since previous response				
Follows word length guidelines (400–750 words), is edited appropriately, and follows other blog conventions				
Makes effective use of images, links, video, and so on. ("Very Strong" not only includes these features, but uses them creatively.)				

Total Score: _____ /28

Additional Comments:

I created a template file, so it's easy to click open a blank rubric for each student. Then I fill it out with comments in each area and save it by the student's name. When I'm done, I email it and the student has a record of my comments. This is especially useful when the students write additional blog posts. They can refer back to this rubric to see how to improve their score next time.

Even if I don't have time to write up comments, I still use a rubric as a checklist. I'll use smaller boxes in the grid, and I'll simply check where the level of quality of the student's writing falls. Comments are better, but at least a set of checks showing the gradations of quality in a student's work is better than something like an overall check-minus, check, check-plus response that gives no specific information.

Rubrics keep our writing evaluation and grading on target and also tell students what is expected in a writing assignment. This is a win-win situation for both teacher and students and a real incentive to use rubrics with all graded writing assignments.

Rubrics are also very useful for purely practical reasons (i.e., justifying a grade). When students—or their parents—want to know why a particular paper received a specific grade, a rubric is a handy thing to have ready. Let's face it: a great deal about writing (about much of language arts, for that matter) is unavoidably subjective. A good rubric can ensure that you are using your professional judgment responsibly and fairly. A good rubric also "demystifies" grades. How many times have you gotten a single letter grade with a comment such as, "Nice work," but you really didn't know what the grade was based on—or, what made your work so nice? A rubric is a way for a teacher to give more specific feedback without spending inordinate amounts of time.

Finally, don't assume that as the teacher you should be the only one developing rubrics. We often coconstruct rubrics *with* students. We give out an assignment to students, and then ask them about what an excellent version of the assignment should include. We (or a student) scribe the suggested criteria on the board. Of course, we also add our own thoughts and encourage the students to tweak the ideas as we go along. When we have a full list, we work together to combine repetitive or similar criteria, and we eliminate some that don't really work. Sometimes we even slightly revise the assignment if something in our rubric discussion inspires it. In the end, we insert the results into a formal rubric, and we discuss it again in the next class. What is the result? You would be amazed at how students are much more invested in and understanding of a rubric when they have had an equal hand in creating it. You can also have students work in small groups to create rubric criteria and work from those suggestions. The point is to involve students in every aspect of writing from assignment design to assessment.

All our enthusiasm and praise for rubrics notwithstanding, they should be used carefully. Not everyone is enthralled with rubrics, and with good reason. In his aptly titled "The Trouble with Rubrics," education critic Alfie Kohn expresses concern that rubrics focus teachers—and especially students—too much on external evaluation:

> Any form of assessment that encourages students to keep asking, "How am I doing?" is likely to change how they look at themselves and at what they're learning, usually for the worse. (2006, 14)

Kohn's compatriot, Maja Wilson, agrees, claiming that any feedback that comes from a rubric is always "prepackaged and processed," and that it doesn't truly come from a student's writing (2007, 63). In an article written a few years later, Wilson proposes an alternative by taking us on a tour of her process for responding to student writing more individually by, as her subtitle says, "Following Students Under the Kitchen Table," that is, wherever the student wants the writing to go (2010, 50).

We still find rubrics powerful and positive elements in writing classes, but we take Kohn's and Wilson's concerns to heart, and we do all we can to keep rubrics from becoming predeterminers of all aspects of student writing. They are guidelines, not commandments.

Other Forms of Teacher and Student Response

Everyone knows a teacher may handwrite comments on a draft or type out a rubric. But there are other ways of responding to student papers that you—and your students—should try:

- Using Track Changes and Comments in Microsoft Word or Suggestions and Comments on Google Docs is a great way to interact directly with student writing. If you use Google Docs, you'll find that an entire writing group can make suggestions and comment on a single document at once. It takes some getting used to, but more and more professional writing is being done this way.

- Many software programs have the ability to insert oral comments on a written draft. Try that.

- Blog comments: If you assign a blog post to your students, you can ask them to enable the comment function so other students in the class may respond to them online. In fact, if the students simply choose to make their writing public, anyone can comment on their writing. (That raises additional challenges and opportunities, of course.) WordPress is a good blog website to check out.

- A great low-tech way to respond to student writing is simply to talk with a student after you've read his or her writing. You can give your responses and have an honest-to-goodness conversation about the student's writing. This conversation will reinforce that the student is a real writer whose work is worth the time to talk about.

- Also, there is now some very powerful dictation software that allows teachers and students to turn their voices to text. You can speak your comments onto a written draft, and students can even compose this way. Smart technology has turned phones into typewriters!

 TECH TALK: *Responding to Papers via Jing*

Jing is an easy, and free, program to use that will allow you to capture and record a video of you writing on, highlighting, and talking about a piece of student writing on your computer for up to five minutes. Students can listen repeatedly to your response, and they say it feels more dynamic than written comments. It's abstract in theory, so here's a genuine example from one of Ken's methods classes: http://bit.ly/1o7cGVN. A word of caution: Negative comments come across especially harshly on audio. Our advice is to focus on affirming responses and recast criticism into positive terms whenever possible.

Ask a friend who teaches in a secondary or middle school to lend you a copy of a student's draft (with the student's permission and with his or her name removed) or get a draft from a peer. Imagine you are the teacher and need to *respond* to the draft. Write one paragraph that you feel gives the student feedback and that offers formative comments and then write a paragraph that *evaluates* the paper with summative remarks. Next, place a *grade* on the paper as if it were a final draft. Look over what you have done: How helpful do you think your response and evaluation are? Finally, write a paragraph about how you felt doing this exercise.

The Journal or Writer's Notebook

If we believe that people learn to write by writing and that practice helps with fluency—we are right. However, how does even a highly conscientious teacher deal with a lot of writing in a number of classes? The answer for us is the journal or the writer's notebook, a great tool that can be used in a variety of ways.

Leila likes to start classes with ten minutes of writing; in a *class journal*, the topic relates to the class discussion, the readings we have done for homework, the activity we just finished. Typical topics might include these: In last night's reading, what two things did you notice? What surprised you? List three questions you have.

Another journal is the *personal journal*, which allows students to keep more private and introspective thoughts. It gives students an outlet for their ideas and emotions, and it capitalizes on a powerful subject, themselves. Although there are always issues of confidentiality (students may want to write in this journal but not share every page with you or others), this type of writing can be very effective. Typical entries might address these topics: What is the best thing that happened to you this week? Imagine you are going on a long trip and can take only one personal item with you—what would it be? Ken uses such journals during class time. Students are always required to have their journals at arm's reach, and on those occasions when Ken yells, "One hundred word dash!," students grab their journals and write one hundred words. Whoever finishes first raises a hand and "wins." As a follow-up, if they wish to, students then talk to each other about what they wrote. Games like this are fun, reinforce the power of journal writing, and help students develop writing fluency, an antidote to "staring-at-the-blank-page" syndrome.

A *writer's notebook* can be a place where a student keeps notes, records dreams, writes out phrases and story fragments, or preserves other prose or poetry he or she has read, all with the idea of using the journal as a basis for future or current writing. Many artists, inventors, and scientists keep notebooks of this sort—writers need them, too. Typical topics might include lists of interesting words, opening lines, or snatches of dialogue that could be used in any piece of writing.

Dialogue journals are written on one side of the page with space for someone else—another writer, the teacher, other students—to write back in response; the subject of a dialogue journal can be quite varied, but its strength lies in the fact that one writer writes to another and in the immediacy that this format captures. Typical entries might address these topics: What two things does this class really need? What did you think of the last assembly? What is one question you've always wanted to ask an adult?

Whatever their type, journals or notebooks need to be written in consistently, taken up on a regular schedule, and responded to in a nonthreatening manner. Surface correctness and even neatness are nonissues in journals—although the writing should be legible so that it can be read. Letter grades that absolutely judge quality are more than likely inappropriate for journals; some teachers assess journals on completion or on number of pages written. A teacher can put a check at the top of each page read or skimmed and write a comment at the end responding to what the student has written.

Journals and notebooks benefit both the teacher and the students. They are a direct answer to the paper-load issue. And, when students write regularly in a journal, they are working on their writing, and the sheer volume of writing can positively affect their writing fluency. It is hard to stay afraid of writing—to have what is known as *writing apprehension*—when you have to write regularly. Students also learn a few other things through using a journal: they can "work out" intellectual and personal issues through their own writing; not all writing needs to be perfect; not all writing needs to be graded. The wonderful and varied journal or notebook can be a powerful part of your classroom.

The Research Paper and Encouraging Academic Honesty

It is, as student Beth Hagy notes, "the research paper, commonly known as going to the [web] and expanding" that strikes fear in the hearts of both teachers and students. Most students hate this assignment; most teachers dread not just the difficulty of getting students through the process but the lifeless results of what seem to be hours of preparation. Further, Internet plagiarism is now a serious issue in the research paper.

What advice do we have about encouraging academic honesty and combating plagiarism? It's actually pretty simple: Give students an opportunity to write about something in which they are interested. Years ago teacher Ken Macrorie (1988) wrote about the "I-Search" paper, a paper that encouraged students to pursue in their research something they want to search out. We need to remember that primary and secondary research can be done on an amazing range of subjects. It is not just the Romantic Movement in England in the early 1800s or the use of fire imagery in a novel that should be the sole subject of student investigation. Certainly there are students in your English language arts class who may want to research Edgar Allan Poe's short stories or Toni Morrison's metaphors. But there are those who can also do an excellent job researching the history of their neighborhood, the latest innovations in SUV technology, the newest theories on global warming and the high incidence of hurricanes, or the influence of the Internet on just about everything.

We know this is *English* class. But we also know that when we talk about research, we need to broaden that definition and not insist that our students mimic what we did in our college Victorian poetry class or American novel course. Getting students to read and write and ferret out information is the purpose, we think, of a research paper. And, as noted in other chapters, if you insist that students write only on classic pieces of literature, you are opening the door to your students' going to a website to cut and paste (Jeffrey Klausman [1999] calls this "patchwork plagiarism"), download and present others' writing as original work. When you allow students to choose unusual topics you can foster academic honesty and minimize plagiarism. You are also getting closer to the real purposes of writing. Barry Gilmore makes this point in an essay on writing and plagiarism: "[A teacher's] ultimate goal should not be to create a prompt that produces original writing but to create an environment that leads students to devise prompts and arguments of their own" (2008b, 103).

Using his experience with the research paper, teacher Henry Kiernan offers teachers eight points about research papers and students. His advice is worth reproducing:

1. Spend instructional time teaching students to develop and frame questions, using notebooks, journals, and logs to help them define what they are pursuing.

2. Use interdisciplinary ideas that reach across a number of subject areas and that can "transcend" the English classroom and also connect it to other disciplines (in his English class, Kiernan uses the environment as the general topic area for research papers).

3. Think about organizing research in small teams, not just individually. (Kiernan suggests local history projects and community and state issues as two areas that lend themselves well to research in project teams.)

4. Have students construct and use interviews, surveys, questionnaires. Traditional databases and literature searches do not always yield what students need in their research.

5. If students do research on literature, have them pick a novel that may lead them to other interdisciplinary questions (for instance, Tim O'Brien's [2009] *The Things They Carried* could inspire a research project on aspects of the Vietnam War).

6. Get students to write letters to a number of institutions and people (government offices, businesses, individual professionals) so that they learn how to request information and also how to evaluate responses.

7. Have students share and discuss the final papers in a forum atmosphere.

8. Publish the best papers for student models in the future. (Kiernan 1990, 7)

If teachers follow these kinds of guidelines, students can broaden the idea of what research actually means, concluding that research sources can come from many areas. It is not just journal articles, books, and even information from Internet searches that can constitute quotable and useable research sources. Also, when we give students a platform to display their findings—such as in a discussion forum and through publication—we reinforce the fact that research is more about finding answers and pursuing ideas than fulfilling some kind of disembodied English teacher assignment.

Beyond Plagiarism: The Purposes for Research Documentation

It's also important to help students understand the purposes for research documentation. As researchers, we are contributing to a larger conversation, one to which many others have already contributed. Using and documenting the work of others helps a writer place his or her thoughts among those of other thinkers, and the documentation helps future thinkers follow in their tracks. Of course, few people think of young students as writing "real research." That is the biggest problem we have to solve. Again, an authentic writing assignment, in which students are engaged in a real project with a real purpose that they truly care about, makes students real writers.

A survey reported by NCTE's *Council Chronicle* (NCTE 2005) revealed that when teachers talked to their students about copying work from the Internet, it actually seemed to make a difference. The survey involved almost 170,000 students, K–12, and it found that students whose teachers did *not* discuss plagiarism and copying work from the Internet were less likely to feel that it was wrong. Conversely, students whose teachers did discuss copying from the Internet understood it was cheating. We need to take a proactive approach with students and discuss citation and paraphrase; prevention, not detection, is the issue. If we rely on Google to detect plagiarism (by entering phrases from the suspicious paper) or for-fee websites such as Turnitin.com to scan an entire paper, we have taught students little. (If you're going to use something like Turnitin.com, allow your students to use it to detect their mistakes in documentation and address them *before* they submit their papers to you. That's educating rather than policing.) Michael Freedman's recipe is "avoiding generic assignments and topics that rely on recounting information, developing writing [assignments] . . . that make plagiarism difficult, and teaching our students how and when to document their sources of information" (2004, 548). It couldn't be clearer. When a teacher concentrates primarily on detecting plagiarism, becoming a "source detective," that teacher "has already lost an education battle" (Gilmore 2008a, 5), devoting time to catching academically dishonest students instead of focusing on helping students become engaged researchers.

Leila's Assignment: One assignment with which I have had a great deal of success is asking students to research the day of their birth. Students have to read the newspapers—one national, one from the community in which they were born—for the events of the day. They have to interview family members, in particular their parents, about recollections of the momentous date and use personal material such as their own baby book. Students can then concentrate on any aspect of the day: the international scene, the movies playing, the cost of any goods or items, the weather, the sports scores, the car ads. How they weave this together is an individual choice, and I give them guidance on writing this personal yet scholarly account of a day in history.

This assignment gives students a sense of history; it gives them a sense of themselves within and as a part of history. It makes them turn to primary, not just secondary, sources; it gives them an opportunity not only to interview but to use and interpret those interviews; it asks students to choose what is most important to them; it capitalizes, again, upon that undeniable interest all of us have in that ever-fascinating subject, ourselves. I have never had, I might add, a student plagiarize this assignment or fail to turn it in. There are few activities I can say this about, but "The Day I Was Born" is a relatively surefire assignment.

One caveat we would add to these ideas about research projects is that it is a teacher's responsibility, if there are multiple parts to a research paper assignment, to set up an incremental system so that students can not only keep track of what they are doing but also garner points (or even digital badges) along the way. Thus, you might give students an assignment sheet with deadlines and progressive credit. Both of these, the deadlines and the point credit, will help keep students on target and give them a sense of progress in their project and in their final grade. What kind of steps will students need to take as they do their research? The deadlines and the points for each step will be ones that you want to establish, but the following topics should probably be included:

preliminary topic (discussion and tentative outline)

final topic (submission and teacher approval)

research source list (submitted and approved)

research source notes (submitted and approved)

optional conference with teacher

draft 1 (submitted to revision group and revised)

draft 2 (submitted to revision group and/or teacher and revised)

final draft.

Finally, it is a good idea to add one more performance assessment to students' research papers. Ask students to present their work to an audience or to create a recorded PowerPoint or Prezi presentation to post to a website. Ask the students to create a blog version of their research or to write an op-ed column or give a guest lecture to another class about it. Encouraging students to create research they are excited about and to experience an audience's reaction to their work is sharing the joy of scholarship. All students have thoughts and perspectives worth sharing; it's our job to help students believe and experience that truth.

What We Are About as Teachers of Writing

Every summer for eight years Leila worked with classroom teachers in her local site of the National Writing Project, one of many sites across the country. The National Writing Project insists that teachers of writing need to write themselves. This principle is the major point of the over forty-year-old program, and it has done a great deal to change what is practiced in the classroom. Every summer teachers of all subject matters and all grade levels meet to consider issues of writing. The core of the program is an opportunity to research and share ideas about writing, but it is also about giving teachers an opportunity to write themselves.

Teachers of writing should write. Yes, that is you, too. Whether you keep a journal at home, prewrite with your students in class, contribute an article to your local education or language arts newsletter, dash off a poem or so every month, you need to write—and you need to share your writing with others. We suspect that one reason English language arts teachers often do such artificial stuff with writing is that they are not writing themselves and have forgotten what it took, what they needed as writers.

And, yes, we write with our students. It's not that we do every assignment with them from beginning to end, but we write with them frequently. When Leila went back to teach high school a few years ago, she and her students wrote in their journals together for ten minutes at the beginning of every class. The students shared their writing aloud, and Leila shared hers, too. She also, though less frequently, freewrote drafts on the board or the overhead while students wrote at their desks. And over the years, in the classes we have taught, both of us have occasionally shown students the revision difficulties we go through to produce our own final draft writing for publication.

Leila's Writing: All of my writing agonies seem to cheer students up immensely: my journal entries are not always profound; they often ramble, and sometimes I can't read my own handwriting. Students whisper and chuckle a bit over the drafting I do in front of them, and once they get to know me, they do ask, looking at my revisions, why I don't get it right the first time when it's clear (hey, it's right here in this section) that the whole point was in that fifth paragraph of the second draft. After all, I'm the teacher. But then again, maybe all writers are like that, huh?

Ken's Writing: I'm always amazed at how interested students are in my writing, especially when I start with a published product and then show them some of the unbelievably messy, disorganized drafts that led to it. Students like knowing that I struggle with revision, that I am desperate without spellcheck (in fact, spellcheck just saved me from writing *desparate*), that I get detailed responses on my writing from peers and sometimes I really don't like what I hear, and that I sometimes procrastinate. I also learn a lot by completing my own writing assignments. Sometimes the directions aren't specific enough, and sometimes the work involved is more time-consuming than I'd realized. I revise my assignments when I find these problems—and I share those revisions with the students, too.

Yes, we struggle with writing—and that's the point. We think you can do that, too. The power of writing with your students makes you a writer alongside them, not a game master giving them another assignment from which you are completely removed. As Isaac Bashevis Singer tells us in the opening of this chapter, there are few miracles in writing; it is consistent and hard work, it is writing and rewriting, and it is work that we, as teachers, can do with our students. Although not completely devastating, the picture Connie Chantelau sketches does *not*, we think, describe how we can help our students become confident writers:

I don't remember ever using peer groups or having individual conferences about my writing; I recall no encouragement to experiment with writing beyond the standard forms; I recall no personal engagement with literature encouraged in writing. I learned how to edit, not revise. I learned to view writing as a product to be written in fifty minutes and graded based on content and grammar. I had no notion of audience other than the teacher and some faceless college examination board. I was trained, however inadvertently, to stay well within the confines of certain forms and language when I wrote, and I never learned how to handle criticism constructively. In high school I wrote safe, well-organized and entirely correct essays with no spunk, no pizzazz, no chutzpa. I was afraid to expand, to try anything different, and none of my English teachers encouraged me to. I never saw my English teachers write; I never heard them read anything they had written. While we wrote, they sat behind their desks, watching, reading, and grading.

What do we want in our classes when we teach writing, when we have our students write? It may be the vision that Julie Morrison describes:

Students need to write for the sake of writing and not to show that they've read a book or mastered the basic punctuation skills. I want my students to be challenged with their writing and value it as much as they do their own speaking voice. This will take time and lots of practice. We'll need to work together, and learn together. And when my students learn to value what they can say on paper, they will value how they say it, and mechanics will find its place and finally be of some use.

We can't say it any better.

References

Agee, James. 2000. *Let Us Now Praise Famous Men* (with photographs by Walker Evans). New York: Houghton Mifflin.

Baker, Sheridan. (1951) 1997. *The Practical Stylist.* New York: Longman.

Berchini, Christina. 2015. "Speaking My Mind: To Teach Writing, You Too Must Get Your Ass Kicked." *English Journal* 105 (2): 133–35.

Burkhardt, Ross M. 2003. *Writing for Real: Strategies for Engaging Adolescent Writers.* Portland, ME: Stenhouse.

Claggett, Fran, Louann Reid, and Ruth Vinz. 1996. *Learning the Landscape: Inquiry-Based Activities for Comprehending and Composing.* Portsmouth, NH: Boynton/Cook.

Commission on Writing Teacher Education. 2015. *Teachers, Profs, Parents: Writers Who Care.* Conference on English Education, NCTE. https://writerswhocare.wordpress.com/.

Council of Writing Program Administrators, National Council of Teachers of English, National Writing Project. 2011. *Framework for Success in Postsecondary Writing.* CWPA, NCTE, and NWP. http://wpacouncil.org/framework.

Daiker, Donald A. 1989. "Learning to Praise." In *Writing and Response: Theory, Practice, and Research,* edited by Chris M. Anson, 103–13. Urbana, IL: NCTE.

Dunn, Patricia A. 2001. *Talking, Sketching, Moving: Multiple Literacies and the Teaching of Writing.* Portsmouth, NH: Heinemann.

Emig, Janet. 1971. "The Composing Process of Twelfth Graders." *NCTE Research Report No. 13.* Urbana, IL: NCTE.

Esposito, Lauren. 2012. "Where to Begin? Using Place-Based Writing to Connect Students with Their Local Communities." *English Journal* 101 (4): 70–76.

Freedman, Joel M. 2009. "Echoes of Silence: Empathy and Making Connections Through Writing Process." *English Journal* 98 (4): 92–95.

Freedman, Michael. 2004. "A Tale of Plagiarism and a New Paradigm." *Phi Delta Kappan* 85 (March): 545–48.

Gere, Anne Ruggles, Leila Christenbury, and Kelly Sassi. 2004. *Writing on Demand: Best Practices and Strategies for Success.* Portsmouth, NH: Heinemann.

Gilmore, Barry. 2008a. *Plagiarism: Why It Happens and How to Prevent It.* Portsmouth, NH: Heinemann.

———. 2008b. "Prompt Attention: What I Learned from the Plagiarists." *English Journal* 98 (2): 102–104.

Hacker, Diane, and Nancy Sommers. 2012. *A Pocket Style Manual*. 6th ed. Boston: Bedford/ St. Martin's.

Hopkins, Edwin M. 1912. "Can Good Composition Teaching Be Done Under Present Conditions?" *English Journal* 1 (1): 1–8.

Kiernan, Henry. 1990. "The Research Paper Redux." *CSSEDC Quarterly* 12 (May): 7.

Kirby, Dawn Latta, and Darren Crovitz. 2013. *Inside Out: Strategies for Teaching Writing*. 4th ed. Portsmouth, NH: Heinemann.

Kittle, Penny. 2008. *Write Beside Them: Risk, Voice, and Clarity in High School Writing*. Portsmouth, NH: Heinemann.

Klausman, Jeffrey. 1999. "Teaching About Plagiarism in the Age of the Internet." *Teaching English in the Two Year College* 27 (December): 209–12.

Kohn, Alfie. 2006. "The Trouble with Rubrics." *English Journal* 95 (4): 12–15.

LeNoir, W. David. 2002. "The Multigenre Warning Label." *English Journal* 92 (2): 99–101.

Lindblom, Kenneth. 2004. "Writing for Real." *English Journal* 94 (1): 104–108.

Mack, Nancy. 2015. *Multigenre Research Projects: Multifaceted, Multipurpose Writing Assignments*. New York: Teachers College Press.

Macrorie, Ken. 1988. *The I-Search Paper*. Portsmouth, NH: Heinemann.

Marchetti, Allison, and Rebekah O'Dell. 2015. *Writing with Mentors: How to Reach Every Writer in the Room Using Current, Engaging Mentor Texts*. Portsmouth, NH: Heinemann.

Murray, Donald M. 1982. *Learning by Teaching: Selected Articles on Writing and Teaching*. Portsmouth, NH: Boynton/Cook.

NCTE. 2005. "Teachers Shape Student Attitudes Toward Online Cheating." *The Council Chronicle* 15 (September): 1.8.

O'Brien, Tim. 2009. *The Things They Carried*. New York: Mariner Books.

Romano, Tom. 2000. *Blending Genre, Altering Style*. Portsmouth, NH: Boynton/Cook.

Smith, Frank. 1990. "Myths of Writing." In *Rhetoric and Composition: A Sourcebook for Teachers and Writers*, 3rd ed., edited by Richard L. Graves. Portsmouth, NH: Heinemann.

Spandel, Vicki, and Richard J. Stiggins. 1997. *Creating Writers: Linking Assessment and Writing Instruction*. 2nd ed. New York: Longman.

Tanner, Marcia. 1997. "Writing and Richard Wright." NCTE Talk. October 9. To access, email: NCTE-Talk@listproc.org.

Wiggins, Grant. 2009. "Real-World Writing: Making Purpose and Audience Matter." *English Journal* 98 (5): 29–37.

Wilson, Maja. 2007. "Why I Won't Be Using Rubrics to Respond to Students' Writing." *English Journal* 96 (4): 62–66.

———. 2010. "Rethinking a Writing Teacher's Expertise: Following Students Under the Kitchen Table." *English Journal* 99 (3): 50–56.

9 | THE CRAFT OF QUESTIONING

How do I know what I think until I hear what I say?[†]

The Power of Talk

The power of talk is one of the English teacher's great resources. Our classrooms can be lively arenas of conversation where students argue, question, challenge, comment, and observe. And in frequent instances, we and our students can find out what we think or believe through our own conversation—discovering, as the chapter epigraph describes, "what we know" when we have the opportunity to talk and "hear what we say." Even though some of us would like for students to practice that art of discussion a bit more courteously or calmly or maturely, what we do in class is largely talk.

You as the teacher will mostly initiate and, yes, somewhat control that talk, and one of the most frequent activities in the English language arts classroom is the asking and answering of questions. It can be a highly adaptable, malleable activity when it comes to the consideration of language, literature, and our students' writing. In fact, most teachers are not aware of just how much they do use questions in their classrooms: numerous research studies of actual teaching confirm that teachers who think they are asking only a moderate number of questions—around twenty—in any given class were

---

[†] This quotation is variously attributed and variously written; although some give the twentieth-century British novelist E. M. Forster credit, others do not. But it's a great quotation whoever said it.

actually asking as many as four to eight times that amount—up to 150 questions a class. One study we read claimed that teachers ask 400 questions a day, up to 70,000 a year, and once you think about it, that estimate may be very accurate.

Talking and answering and asking questions can help clarify our own ideas, not only to others but also to ourselves. In its proper context, the craft of asking and answering questions can be the heart of a vibrant and learning class. And there is further impetus to pay close attention to questioning: as you may already know, college- and career-ready standards encourage teachers to ask complex, critical questions and then allow students the time and space to fully answer them.

When we think about the many discussions we have had with classes and students, we remember how awkward it was in the beginning of our teaching careers to initiate and maintain a discussion. But we did have some successes, one of which is Leila's story about one class in particular.

Leila's Story: What Discussion Can Do

I remember a class with which I never felt I had much rapport, and I remember the day that that class, more than any other, showed me what a discussion could actually achieve. We had been talking about a poem and the speaker's choices and how—or if—those choices could relate to our own lives. Learning to question, to talk with these students, I had had a hard time creating an environment where anyone *wanted* to talk. I had taken some advice and tried to slow down, tried to open up spaces in the conversation, tried not to follow my "list" of questions so precisely. My new mode, and I had instituted it for only a week or so, was a bit more comfortable to me. There was for the first time some silence in the classroom, silence that I thought was positive in that it gave students some space to think and to consider. I had, I felt, finally allowed for breathing room.

It only happened once quite this way with this class, but in the space of forty minutes we moved from the poem and its relation to any real person's choices into an area of great interest to my students: drugs. In that conversation, we moved beyond the platitudes about buying and selling and doing drugs and into the realities of the issue. Cassandra, as I recall, got teary in this class talking about how difficult it was for her to curb her own interest in drugs when her stepfather used *and* dealt. James insisted she should be stronger, said he would be in a similar situation; Maurice chimed in with a companion story and a happier ending. Towanda snorted her disapproval of the entire issue and told everyone they were fools. That made Michael laugh, but then he gave his opinion, too.

This was not in my lesson plan and, frankly, some of the details of some of this class conversation alarmed me. In a way, we were all learning names and specifics and incidents and there were, of course, ethical ramifications to what was being revealed, however tentatively, in this class. But the students wanted to talk about this, wanted actually to talk to *one another* about this, and the poem and my classroom structure had seemed to provide the space to do so.

When the bell rang and the students left (and we had, by the way, agreed not to share this conversation with others outside the class), I was both unsettled by what had happened and profoundly satisfied. The class' environment had changed; the students had talked, for the first time in my presence, about something that was truly important to them, about something that was not purely *school*. The students had, further, connected that real thing to what we were reading. What had happened was spontaneous and appropriate; although I would not expect or demand students to reveal so much about their personal lives, to talk, as in this case, of their own experiences with drugs, in this class the sharing was student initiated and treated confidentially. It was, despite the disturbing nature of the subject, a glimpse of teacher heaven.

Why Do We Ask Questions?

We think most of us want such solid and worthwhile experiences when we ask and answer questions in our classrooms. Indeed, we ask questions not only to prompt personal sharing from our students about their relationship to literature but for a number of other reasons:

- **Provide students with an opportunity to find out what they think by hearing what they say.** In responding to questions about literature or ideas, students often discover their opinions or reactions. In responding to questions about writing, students discover their ideas in prewriting or clarify their ideas in revision.
- **Allow students to explore topics and argue points of view.** Through questioning, students can pursue an aspect of a topic that appeals to them or can logically defend a theory or belief that they hold, sharpening not only oral but also thinking skills.
- **Let students function as experts.** Through questioning, students as well as teachers can probe, explore, and move a discussion into a number of areas.
- **Present students with the opportunity to interact among themselves.** Given the proper setting and environment, students can—and will—argue and debate with one another. Student talk is very important, and it can not only be a stimulus for learning but also lead students to explore topics further or to pursue new topics.
- **Give the teacher immediate information about student comprehension and learning.** Through questioning, particularly through paying attention to answers, teachers can check for comprehension and mastery. Questioning can serve as a diagnostic tool.
- **Enhance the close reading of texts.** By asking students to expand their answers by actually looking at the text and citing instances, quotations, inferences, and examples, we help students justify their answers with real evidence and real specificity. This does not need to become a court of law, but students need evidence for their assertions; this is the heart of close reading.

What follows may help you with your use of questioning in your classroom. Certainly, as a recent study of beginning teachers indicates, many "novices reported feeling uncertain about how to enact strategies of facilitating [discussion and were] unsure about the degree to which teachers should govern the discussion activities that they develop" (Williamson 2013, 62). This is not surprising as questioning and discussion are actually overlooked and at times misunderstood resources. For instance, one otherwise helpful resource on questioning warns of "unbridled talk" (Walsh and Sattes 2015b) in the classroom, as if students will totally run amuck if they are asked questions. Researcher Larry Cuban found this in his observation of thirty-two classes and sixteen teachers in two California high schools. The classes he observed were on task and productive, but the questioning was unimaginative and more of a control mechanism than a learning tool:

> Of the 26 teachers who engaged students in question-and-answer for a portion of the period, all but 6 (74%) depended largely upon factual recall questions from the text, worksheet, homework, or previous lecture. Seldom did a student in these classes (whether college-bound or non-college-bound) recite answers more than a few words in length. The 6 teachers who probed student answers by asking for explanations, elaboration, or evidence to support statements did so [only occasionally] with the whole class. (1993, 207)

More recent studies funded by the Gates Foundation and one conducted by the Consortium on Chicago School Research found that the teachers studied struggled with large-group discussion and with making it part of their classroom repertoire (Walsh and Sattes 2015b, 6–7).

So how can your class be different?

Questions That Teachers Ask

The Issue of Questioning Hierarchies

Confronted with something—anything—to talk about in a classroom, most beginning teachers make an effort to write out the questions they think might be useful and put them in a lesson plan. Certainly for the class Leila previously described, she had questions prepared on the poem for class discussion. Many times, especially with literature, teachers will use questioning hierarchies, scales of importance, or categories of schemata that classify question types. Within these schemata or hierarchies, the assumption is that certain kinds of knowledge—and the answers to certain kinds of questions—are considered superior to, more sophisticated than, or requiring higher cognitive skills than certain others.

Following this belief, most creators of questioning hierarchies suggest that teachers ask questions at the lowest level of the scale and then move up, spending the majority of questioning time in the upper reaches of the questioning hierarchy. The logical assumption is that spending all questioning time on "lower-level," or purely factual, questions (What was the main character's name? Who wrote this and when? Who is the protagonist's enemy?) is not as productive as spending time on "higher-level," or more sophisticated, questions (To what extent is this novel realistic? How does this incident relate to the opening of the short story? What do you think you would do if a similar incident happened to you?). Further, we know that students in lower-tracked classes are often asked *nothing* but factual or recall questions and are never or rarely asked to consider *why*, *how*, or *what if*. For sure, avoiding sophisticated questions is an excellent way to keep students completely uninterested. A number of sequential (ordered and hierarchical) and nonsequential (nonordered and nonhierarchical) questioning schemata are depicted in the graphic that follows.

Sequential Questioning Schemata[†]

Benjamin Bloom
- To evaluate
- To synthesize
- To analyze
- To apply
- To comprehend
- To know

Norris M. Sanders
- Evaluation
- Synthesis
- Analysis
- Application
- Interpretation
- Translation
- Memory

Hilda Taba
- Apply concept
- Interpret concept
- Form concept

Harold L. Herber
- Applied comprehension
- Interpretive comprehension
- Literal comprehension

Nonsequential Questioning Schemata[†]

Arthur Kaiser: Open ——— Closed ——— Suggestive ——— Rhetorical

Richard Smith: Convergent ——————————————— Divergent

Ronald T. Hyman: Empirical —— Definitional —— Evaluative —— Metaphysical

---

[†]Adapted from Christenbury and Kelly (1983, 4).

Each of the schemata represents a type of question or conceptual activity. The sequential schemata imply that certain questions require higher thinking skills than others and probably should be attempted in a set order. Look, for instance, at the Sanders: memory is lower on the scale, literally and figuratively, than analysis, and memory should, according to the schema, precede analysis. Some of the schemata, however, simply name different activities without giving them a value or order. Look at the Hyman schema where there is no valuative difference between definitional and evaluative and no assumption that one should precede or follow the other.

If the workings of the human mind were as orderly as some of the questioning schemata suggest, there would be no problem using such hierarchies when we plan for questioning in our classroom. We know, however, that the studies of real classrooms do not confirm such clean divisions regarding what actually happens when people talk and when they ask and answer questions. Although questioning hierarchies can be a useful starting point, researchers recording classrooms and classroom talk confirm that schemata are not that accurate a picture of conversation and that their use does not always yield what we think it might. For instance, here's what we know about questioning hierarchies:

- Few people—students and teachers—actually approach knowledge in an orderly, paced way, moving smoothly, as the sequential hierarchies would imply, up from one level to another.

- The categories of most questioning hierarchies are not only arbitrary but often overlap, leading to difficulty in actually constructing questions (for example, a question in the Bloom schema that features *analysis* as opposed to *evaluation*).

- The categories of most questioning hierarchies also imply that more superior cognitive sophistication is required for certain operations than for *others* (for example, the act of *synthesis*, in the Sanders schema, is superior to *application*).

In addition, the absolute, consistent benefit of asking "higher-order" questions is also debatable for these reasons:

- Most research studies are unsuccessful in classifying higher-level questioning in actual classroom discussions.

- Research studies are similarly mixed regarding higher-level questions resulting in greater student achievement.

- Not all students prefer or are comfortable with answering higher-level questions, especially if those questions are not matched by corresponding higher-level questions on tests.

Certainly some order of questioning is necessary and a mixture of question types, however defined, is essential. It seems, though, that discussion and questioning in the language arts classroom need not be so rigidly organized as some theorists and practitioners would imply. And although many of the creators of questioning schemata would be the first to caution against using them inflexibly, many lists similar to those we have included have been abused. They have become prescriptions rather than suggestions or guidelines, and further, they have given an unrealistic picture of human discussion.

Leila's Story: Questioning and Walter O'Brien

I learned about that unrealistic picture in my first year of teaching. My eighth graders, spurred on by one of my more memorable students, Walter O'Brien, taught me.

I had assigned a short story from the literature anthology and, for my afternoon eighth-grade class, had to the best of my fledgling abilities prepared a lesson plan for a large-group discussion. I had questions written out and notes in the margin of my copy of the story; I was ready to start; my materials were arranged on my desk, and on the board behind me were written the date, the title of the story, and the notation *Discussion*. I was organized and ready. But I really hadn't counted on my students, specifically on Walter: what I was organized for was not what happened.

The bell rang, and I moved into the hall to await my lively eighth graders. They had some three minutes to change books and classes, and they came toward me, as was customary, laughing, shoving, talking, arguing, bringing all that energy and craziness and bright-eyedness into the classroom. They were energetic and even silly and boisterous at times (the class was right after lunch), but I was coming to like this group caught somewhere between the hilarity of late childhood and the seriousness of teenhood.

Depending on their mood and personality, they entered the class, threw their books on the desk, catcalled across the room, made faces at each other, flirted, hurled insults, yawned, told jokes, smiled shyly, twirled around, stretched, pushed each other, checked hair or makeup in mirrors, and, after their fashion, got ready for the beginning of class.

The second or late bell was ready to ring, and I moved to the center of the class to begin. And then, in the midst of the din and the hubbub, Walter, who with his glasses and careful clothes looked even at thirteen like a young physician or lawyer in training, called out, "Mrs. C., Mrs. C., just tell me, *why did he do that to her?*"

Why did he do that to her? We all knew that Walter's question was about the reading, and I knew that his question was, essentially, the heart of the short story. But I was disconcerted: I had not called roll and started the class; *I* was not ready to begin the discussion I had planned; further, the issue of *why he had done that*, that question and the answer to it, was way down on my lesson plan for this class discussion.

But it was, I found, what the class was going to start with. People started talking to Walter, started talking to me, started answering and arguing and looking around to see others' reaction to their answers. In the space of my confusion and Walter's loud voice, the late bell rang, the students got into their seats and, virtually without me, continued arguing with one another as to just *why he had done that*. And we were off.

I think, to this day, my students thought I had somehow planned all this. They were a generous group of people and seemed to always give me the benefit of the doubt, believing implicitly that most good things that happened in the classroom were somehow my doing. But I hadn't planned this at all. I did, however, have the good sense to follow their lead, to seize the moment, to start calling on people and refereeing the discussion, to allow the chemistry to work.

Sure enough, by the end of the class, we had "covered" all the introductory questions I had in my lesson plan. We had also come to some consensus on the overall meaning of the story. We had not started where I had planned; we had not begun as I had envisioned; we had, however, started not only where the students wanted to start but with the most important question. In the middle of the discussion some students had asked about factual details—we dealt with those facts then returned to *why he had done that*. It was wholly out of "order": it also was very effective.

I chewed over that particular class again and again in my mind. Although I don't recall if that exact level of excitement ever occurred again—or even in a similar pattern—I knew then that Walter O'Brien and his classmates had taught me something about questioning. In hindsight, here's what I think they taught me:

- Follow your students' lead—if they want to talk about something that is not in your order or on your list, let them.
- Be flexible with your questions: let a discussion have its own evolution. You don't necessarily have to start with the basic, the recall, questions.
- Don't always play it safe: students can lead a class into exciting territory, and giving them that opportunity can be one of the more valuable instructional decisions you make.
- Know well the subject matter you are teaching: if you are fully prepared, you can let your students take the lead without being fearful of deviating from your lesson plan. Planning well means you are prepared for the unexpected. You're not just winging it.

Your classes, like most classes, will be filled with such opportunities. Your job is to tune your teacher antenna and, when it is appropriate, seize the moment.

The Questioning Circle

In a book Leila wrote some years ago with a friend and colleague, she explored questioning hierarchies and how they often do not serve teachers or students well. On the other hand, because questioning effectively is actually quite a complex skill, beginning teachers needed a place to start when they construct questions to ask in the classroom. In *Questioning: A Path to Critical Thinking* (Christenbury and Kelly 1983), there is an alternative questioning schema, "the questioning circle." It is nonsequential and nonhierarchical, offers a logical yet flexible format for questioning, and can guide teachers in constructing questions.

The schema is made of three areas, or circles: the matter, personal reality, and external reality. The first area, the matter, represents the subject of discussion or of the questioning. The second area, personal reality, represents the individual's experiences, values, and ideas. The third circle, external reality, is actually "the world": the experience, history, and concepts of other peoples and cultures.

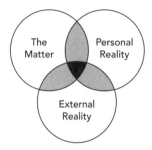

These areas overlap—as does knowledge—and are not ordered (see the shaded areas in the diagram). In addition, there is one place where *all* the circles or areas intersect—the union of the subject, the personal experience of the individual, and the experience of others. This dense area (the black area in the diagram) contains the most significant questions, those that others might term "higher ordered," but it is absolutely open as to how and when anyone arrives at the answers that reflect that intersection.

How would a teacher use the questioning circle?

We think that any discussion should contain questions not only from the three separate circles but also from where any two circles intersect (the three shaded areas) and from where the three circles intersect (the black area).

Let's look at the questioning circle as applied to a piece of literature. "Cold Snap" by American poet James Hearst (2001, 147) is a brief, image-filled piece about love and loss. Students have little problem picking up on the cold and winter imagery, and they use the outline of the poem as a springboard for discussion: Who of us, by thirteen or so, has not experienced a difficult personal relationship, romantic or otherwise?

Cold Snap

The winter night in your face
darkened, and sparkling stars of frost
enameled your eyes. My words
caught on a splinter of ice
and bled to death. As their last heartbeat
sang to the music of the band
my ears felt empty and now
I can't dance with anyone else
with my blood frozen by your white hands.

—James Hearst, *A Single Focus*

Preparing to teach the poem using the questioning circle, and considering a relationship of imagery to reality, a teacher could generate the following:

White Questions

Matter: What central image reveals how the speaker's words are received?

Personal Reality: How would *you* define a difficult personal relationship?

External Reality: What part does lack of communication play in relationships?

Shaded Questions

Matter and Personal Reality: In what ways are the poem's images appropriate for describing a broken relationship?

Personal Reality and External Reality: Are your experiences with difficult personal relationships similar to or different from those of your friends? How?

Matter and External Reality: How are the poem's images describing a specific incident applicable to a variety of personal relationships?

Dense Question

Matter, Personal Reality, External Reality: Which image in this poem do you think best expresses the complexity of difficult personal relationships?

Developing questions for other works of literature is not difficult. Although you may choose to write questions for each area—white, shaded, and dense—and thus draw ideas together, the dense question, the intersection of all three, is the focal point of the discussion. In fact, asking the dense question early in the discussion allows students to respond from a variety of perspectives: the text, their personal experience as a reader, and the external reality of the world and other literature. Even if it is entirely personal, students have a basis for responding, and the discussion can build on a variety of perspectives.

Using a dense question early in a discussion can also circumvent the usual, lower-order-to-higher-order movement of a hierarchical questioning schema. The central point, the focal or dense question, need not come toward the end of a conversation at all; you can enter it early and return as the conversation extends and moves and shifts. In fact, varying your approach from lesson to lesson will help keep students engaged.

You may also want to look at material that discusses the use of what is known in the field as "essential questions," those that, very much like dense questions, are "open ended; thought provoking and intellectually engaging; demand higher order thinking; highlight important transferable ideas; raise additional questions . . . and recur over time" (Lillydahl 2015, 36). The essential question framework is very similar to that of the questioning circle, and if you are interested in more information, also check work by Jim Burke (2010) and Jay McTighe and Grant Wiggins (2013).

Beyond Hierarchies: Questions You Don't Want to Ask

Whether you use the questioning circle or another questioning schema, there are a few general principles to keep in mind when you construct questions. You need to be aware of some questions that because of the way they are phrased will not encourage students to answer fully or even clearly. Questions you *do not* want to ask include:

- **Yes-or-no questions**: Questions that can be answered by one word are often not interesting to answer. Further, if the answer is that "easily" delivered, maybe the question itself is rather one-dimensional. Yes-or-no questions also require follow-up questions that can, possibly, make your classroom seem like an interrogation, not a discussion. Consider changing a question such as:

  Is this characterization effective?

  to something more subtle, more complex, and, actually, more worth answering:

  To what extent is this characterization effective?

  Use phrases that enrich and expand the question (why, how, to what extent) and keep out of the territory of yes or no.

- **Fill-in-the-blank questions**: At any given time many teachers ask these, but it is not best practice. In the heat of a discussion, trying to get students to see one thing or one idea, you can find yourself saying,

  The way to describe this passage is _____?

  and pausing at the end of the question while you wait for students to come up with the answer. We have also heard—and generated—this lovely version:

  The way to describe this passage is what?

What you are asking students to do is to come up with one word (your word, by the way) to fill in that blank. Not only are such questions difficult to understand, they also require that the students find that one exact word or phrase. That is not what we are about with questioning and discussing, and you want to change such a question to a more straightforward interrogative:

What do you think is a way to describe this passage?

You have a better chance of getting a multiplicity of answers—and, yes, perhaps not the answer you were looking for. The latter possibility, by the way, can be very exciting in a classroom.

- **Double questions**: It is hard enough to answer one question, much less two in the same sentence. It's confusing, there is too much to consider at one time, and students often don't know—or, confronted with such a question, don't care—how to answer two questions at one time. Don't let yourself ask a question such as this one:

What are the reasons Anna did not wish Julio to speak, and why did Julio fail to take her advice?

Separating those two good and useful questions will be helpful and less confusing to you and your students. First, you would ask:

What are the reasons why Anna did not wish Julio to speak?

and then you would proceed to ask:

Why did Julio fail to take her advice?

Further, it may well be that the answer your students come up with for Anna's motivation does not lead into the question about Julio. By not "stacking and storing" your questions, you will perhaps be more open to adjusting to what you and your students discuss.

- **Vague questions**: We all ask them, and in your first years of teaching, regardless of your care and planning, you will ask some truly unfocused questions. It happens, but it is also something to work on. Don't let yourself ask your class:

What did Hester Prynne do?

The context is just not clear, and you need to give students guidance about what the question is addressing. Give enough pointers to lead your students into the possibility of answering and discussing. Ask when, where, at this juncture, anything that will open the specifics. Change the question to:

At this point in the novel, what did Hester Prynne do?

With such a specific context, students have a better chance of answering your question.

- **Loaded questions**: English language arts teachers are infamous for these. They are questions that tell students that their answers, their discussion, are really not necessary because there is a set path to follow. Loaded questions include gems such as these:

  ○ *Why is suspense necessary in fiction?*

  ○ *Why do you think Arthur Miller is such a famous playwright?*

  ○ *Is this book average or a classic?*

  Although you may really believe all of what is listed—that suspense is necessary in all fiction, that Miller is indeed famous and justly so, that the book you are discussing deserves to be a classic—those are your assumptions, not your students'. By asking questions like these, you rob your classes of the opportunity to argue, to dispute, to determine, to explore. You have set what they are to discuss, and in a way you have also set how they are to discuss it. In addition, be aware that either/or questions, such as *Is this book average or a classic?* are biased toward the latter choice. It would be a rare student who would choose average when the question is phrased in that manner.

  Surprise can rarely operate in a classroom conversation that features questions like these. Change such questions to:

  What do you think is the function of suspense in fiction?

  Arthur Miller is a famous playwright; to what extent you think he deserves that fame?

  What is your—or others'—definition of a classic?

  By that definition, how closely does this book fit that category?

- **Questions you know the answers to**: It may be necessary to ask a few questions to ensure students have the groundwork needed for a more substantial discussion; however, once you have reached that assurance, only ask questions to which you do not know *the single, immutable* answer. Giving students the opportunity to generate original ideas about a work of literature helps them develop their critical thinking skills and think of themselves as real readers and thinkers (which they are). It also makes for a far more interesting class to teach.

For Your Journal

For fun, let's take a Bad Questions Quiz.

Look at the following awful questions and match them with the characteristics they exemplify.

Bad Questions Quiz

Directions: Read the following awful questions and decide what is wrong with them. Place the letter of the characteristic you choose in the blank to the left of the question.

a. yes-or-no question
b. fill-in-the-blank question
c. double question

d. vague question
e. loaded question

____ 1. Does the short story we have just read have a climax?
____ 2. How is foreshadowing used effectively in *Oedipus Rex*?
____ 3. Why is the study of dialect important?
____ 4. The purpose of figurative language is _____.
____ 5. How does this image work?
____ 6. Can you tell me his name?
____ 7. What is happening in this paragraph and why do you think it is occurring *now*?
____ 8. Is the main character murderous?
____ 9. What are the central issues and how do they relate to the piece as a whole?
____ 10. The best word to describe this section is what?

Answer Key

1. a.	6. a.
2. e.	7. c.
3. e.	8. a.
4. b.	9. c.
5. d or e	10. b.

Scoring:

If you scored 80 to 100 percent, you are ready to question effectively. Go to the head of the class!

If you scored 50 to 70 percent, you need to get back to work. Study and try again!

If you scored below 50 percent, review this section before you talk with your students!

Questioning Behaviors

Control is an important issue in the classroom, but it is often the death of questioning. When the asking and answering of questions becomes an inquisition, a challenge, a discipline measure, or just a terrifying event where one is asked to speak aloud, it is virtually impossible to move into real, productive conversation. If you have students who, for whatever reasons, cannot or do not wish to participate in a discussion, don't plan for one until they are ready. You would be setting up both yourself and them for failure. Try intermediate steps, such as having students work in pairs or in small groups until you think they would be comfortable in an all-class discussion.

If, however, you do think your students could benefit from discussion, there are some behaviors and some classroom structures of which you need to be aware.

Arrange your class so that students can see each other If your students sit in rows so that they cannot see other students' faces, it will be difficult to maintain a large-group discussion. Rearrange your room so that the discussion, the conversation, allows the speakers to see one another's faces, not just the teacher's face. If the desks are moveable, you can place them in a square, rectangle, or circle or even in facing rows.

Learn about wait time and practice it Wait time refers to the length of time between the asking of a question and an answer or the time between the asking of a first and then a second question. What most of you as beginning teachers fear—what you probably have in the back of your mind when you think of the difficulties of questioning—is the quiet after you ask a question. Because even experienced teachers can fear that silence (one researcher calls it "our learned discomfort with silence" [Keene 2014, 68]), the tendency is to ask, ask, ask—and sometimes even just answer our own questions. Remember the statistic cited in the beginning of this chapter about the number of questions teachers *thought* they asked compared with what they *actually* asked? Teachers in that study, who assumed they asked as few as twelve questions in a class, asked as many as 150. Imagine, if you can, a fifty-minute period and 150 questions: it works out to about three questions a minute, a question every twenty seconds. It is a pattern that might not be unbearable for part of a period but that could certainly be tiring if continued for almost an hour. The work of J. T. Dillon (1994) regarding teachers and questioning in the classroom is well worth your time if you are interested in pursuing this topic, and in an article from some decades ago, Dillon articulated it well:

> Certain studies report undesirable effects [to teacher questioning]. For example, high rates of questioning may yield negative affective outcomes, encourage student passivity and dependence and make the class appear as if it were an inquisition rather than a reasonable conversation. (1979, 217)

Researcher Elizabeth A. City invites us to speculate "What if silence [in a class discussion] means that people are thinking, not that they are waiting for you to rescue them?" She urges teachers to keep themselves "out of the discussion" (2014, 15), sound advice if your focus is on getting your students to talk.

Give students time with their own answers Rushing students with their answers (Yes? And then what?), either by adding too many encouraging comments or by conveying that the class and the discussion need to move on, can inhibit a conversation. Conveying calmness and establishing an unpressured environment gives students an opportunity to think and answer and encourages successful questioning. Although some students come from backgrounds in which rapidity of speech and response is a sure sign of a successful conversation, not all students share that experience, and too much overlapping talk too quickly can silence them. Ken, who grew up in New York City and then taught in upstate New York and central Illinois, can certainly attest to the differences in conversational speeds and acceptance of interruption in different regions.

In fact, two teacher researchers, Walsh and Sattes (2015a, 46), call this "Wait Time 1" ("after a question is posed but before a student is called on to answer") and "Wait Time 2" ("directly following that student's response"). In both cases, strategic classroom silence is needed for students not only to understand and consider the question (Wait Time 1) but also to allow breathing time so that their answers can receive attention by both teachers and peers (Wait Time 2).

Give students your attention when they answer Maintaining a certain level of eye contact with students lets them know that they have the attention of their listener. (Extensive, unbroken eye contact can be seen by some students as hostile and challenging, so you will need to adjust the degree of eye contact according to the cultural dictates of your school community.) Head nods and smiles encourage response, whereas head shakes and frowns generally do not. Turning away from students— even to write their response on the board or overhead—can break the flow of words. Turning toward students and keeping the upper body free of crossed arms (which can be seen as a defensive or negative gesture) can encourage a student to keep talking.

Have students talk to each other, not just to you One way to let students know that their answers are not solely directed to the teacher is to remind students they are telling the entire class, not just you. That reminder, which should be made in a friendly manner, can be reinforced by alternating eye contact from the student speaker to the class as a whole. The speaker will usually begin, especially if he or she can see other students' faces, to talk to the whole group, not just you, the teacher. In addition, you can move to the side or back of the classroom, taking the visual focus off you and putting it on the students. You are still the teacher, but you are not in front of the classroom. And if you are near a student who is contributing to class discussion, back away from the students to encourage him or her to speak up and to include the entire class. If the class is discussing something—such as a list or a chart—that is on the board or an overhead, it is *doubly* sensible for you to move to the side of the room. Students can then consider the material and talk without your being between them and the material.

Exhibit a pleasant facial expression and attentive body posture As we have mentioned, frowns, crossed arms, virtually no eye contact, and a turned back will usually make even the most determined student abbreviate his or her answer or perhaps not answer at all. Be pleasant and encouraging with your face and posture.

Be aware of the consequences of praise Praise that is too strong can, oddly enough, be inhibiting. Most students, when told their observations are brilliant, will rarely attempt a second one; they stop while they are ahead. In addition, as odd as it may seem, continued praise from you the teacher can make a conversation a game to get teacher points. Over-the-top and frequent praise can inadvertently engender resentment of the praised students. At its extreme, it can even encourage bullying. You can respond positively to comments without resorting to effusive praise.

Use student answers to extend or focus the discussion As a section in this chapter will reinforce, using student answers in a conversation is the most powerful demonstration of the value you place on student answers. Asking a student how he or she responds to or relates to a peer's observation tells the students that their comments are valued, are important, and can focus a discussion. When students disagree, encouraging them to explore their alternative views and inviting other students to comment on each other's observations can be helpful and interesting.

Let students repeat their own answers Related to the previous point is the issue of repeating comments that get lost in the occasional noise of a discussion. When a teacher repeats those comments, he or she takes them over. If a student wants a comment repeated, let the maker of the comment do the repetition. The more student voices—and the fewer teacher comments—are heard in a classroom discussion, the more student thinking and engagement is present. Although many beginning teachers think they are actually doing students a favor by repeating their comments, it's just not so: letting students "own" their comments gives strong reinforcement to the importance of students in classroom conversation. It's also important that students learn to speak loudly enough for a roomful of people to hear them; repeating questions discourages students—especially shy students—from developing that skill.

Watch student body language and behavior Some of the keys to getting students to respond to one another is tuning in to their reaction during a discussion. Body language is an important key, and head nods, shakes, smiles, frowns, and shifts of position can all indicate agreement or disagreement. Using that body language to invite students to respond can be nonthreatening and also very accurate: asking Marjorie if that frown meant she had something to say, observing to Ricardo that he just nodded, did he want to comment, can work wonders in a discussion.

Make it a goal to call on every student in the class It is only too easy to let the verbally assertive students respond to most or all of the questions asked in a classroom. Either use your class roll or keep it in your head, but, in a large-group discussion, make it a general goal to have asked *every* student to respond in some way. Inadvertently, many teachers call predominantly on a handful of students, sometimes based on eagerness, sometimes based on gender. You need to make sure that you open up your discussion and issue regular invitations to talk to *all*. You may be surprised by what you get back; even if students decline to respond or talk, they know that you are interested in their participation and are not willing to let them coast through or hide in a discussion.

Use writing to encourage all students to contribute to class discussion If you are asking a complicated question, try giving students one or two minutes to write answers in their notebooks and then call on them. Alternatively, you might give students a minute or two to discuss answers with a student next to them. You'll be amazed at how many more students will participate if they have a little time to prepare. There is also an undeniable comfort in having something written down from which to speak.

For Your Journal

Sit in the back of a class where a large-group discussion is going on and watch for behaviors we just mentioned. How many students (keep track and count them) in the class participate? How many comments (count them) are in response to teacher questions? In response to other students' comments? How long (use the class clock or count slowly in your head to measure the seconds) are student answers? How consistent (note this after each question asked) is the teacher's wait time? In general, how would you characterize the teacher's body language and facial expression? Finally, looking at your data and assessing the discussion more generally, write about whether this is a class you would have liked to participate in; why or why not?

When Questions Don't Work

Do remember that questioning is not always the best tool to use in a classroom. Some groups of students may need practice and help before they can function in a relatively orderly manner asking and answering questions. In addition, questions are not appropriate when students

- do not have sufficient background or information to respond or to respond well
- are not comfortable talking out loud in a large group or even arguing a point in a group
- are not at ease in your class or with each other.

Questioning can actually be threatening to some students, and you need to remember your classroom context as an important determiner of the appropriateness of asking questions. It is not appropriate to simply allow students to opt out of class discussion; it is our job as teachers to scaffold our students' abilities. Easing shy students into becoming more comfortable in class discussion is a challenging but very rewarding part of our work.

Sometimes, however, you may judge that questioning *is* appropriate with a specific class and that your questioning behavior is also appropriate, and yet the students still do not rise to the occasion of discussion. Here are some strategies you might use.

When Students Can't/Don't/Won't Answer Questions

When students *cannot* answer a question, it may be because what you asked is just not clear or because what you asked is too advanced. First, do think about making your questions as answerable as you can for your students. Second, be sensitive to students' preparation for the level of your question. Third, remember that not all students are comfortable with the interchange of questioning and answering; these are your quiet students who may be very on task otherwise but not active in discussion.

Regarding students who could be characterized as introverts, Susan Cain reminds us not to "think of introversion as something that needs to be cured" (2012, 255) but to provide for these students' collaborative classroom activities in small groups. This kind of teaching adjustment for your less extroverted students may be more successful for the student who does not—and will not—feel comfortable speaking out in a large group.

Besides the three caveats, however, unless there is a negative chemistry working in a classroom or individual problems with a class, students' general inability to answer a question usually lies in the question or the level of the question.

When students *do not* answer questions, it is possible they did not hear the question.

It is also possible they did not understand it. Using your wait time, you may want to rephrase a question as well as make sure you are audible. If you are not allowing appropriate wait time, students may not be answering questions because they are not given time to do so. Pay particular attention to the rhythm of your questioning if students are not answering.

When students *will not* answer questions, it may be that their silence is directed toward the subject or, again, toward the act of answering questions. When questioning is not an opportunity to explore but an occasion of tension and anxiety for your students, you should change your approach and avoid direct questioning. When students are more comfortable talking in the class, they will answer questions.

When Students Give Short Answers or Wrong Answers to Questions

Short answers are relatively easy to deal with. First of all, make sure you are not asking questions that call for one-word answers; if you are asking for a single piece of information, you are likely to get just that information. On the other hand, questions that ask for extensive information usually get extensive answers. If you are asking questions that should elicit more than one word but students are still giving short answers, address (to the same student) follow-up questions such as these:

- Why do you think that?
- How is that true?
- Could you give us an example that illustrates that?
- How would you compare your answer with John's (or Felicia's or any other student's)?

And, again, make sure that your questioning behavior encourages extensive answers. You may unconsciously be hurrying students along or even cutting them off by your own behavior.

Wrong answers are, frankly, tough to deal with. When students try to discuss and attempt an answer, we as teachers are often very distressed to tell students that their answer is incorrect. An obvious solution is not to ask questions that have right or wrong answers. That solution, however, is not foolproof, because even opinion and judgment involve fact and detail. We can, however, make a more concerted effort to ask students to explore options and weigh opinions rather than to determine right and wrong.

When students are incorrect in their answers, honesty is the best policy. If you give the outward impression that every student answer is right in varying degrees, you are not being fair. "No, I don't think so" or "I'm not sure" are gentle ways of telling students they are in error. Also, when a student response is misguided or mistaken, there is often alternative evidence available. If, for example, a student feels that a minor character is actually the hero of the play, it is better to point out a specific passage challenging the contention and ask the student how the passage relates to his or her point than to tell the student, "No, you're wrong." This kind of attention to detail—the craft of close reading—is essential. Further, allowing students off the hook because they retreat behind "well, it's my opinion," may be tempting, but it is not appropriate. When students are just out and out wrong, a teacher, like Lauren Dean, has to indicate such:

> There are times . . . when opinions have high value [but I also] enforce the idea that students need to anchor their arguments in facts, quotes, statistics, etc. [Some of my students, though] do not understand the idea that they may simply be wrong. When comparing the Globe to the Dionysian Theater, I had one student say that the Globe had a small stage, was indoors and only attended by poor people—despite the extensive reading on the Globe and my personal testimony about studying there! When I [refuted this] . . . the student claimed that that was his opinion! Another student questioned a definition I [indicated was wrong]. She said, "Well that is what I studied." I responded that I am sorry she studied only part of the definition, but that satire did not mean "human weakness," but it is writing that ridicules human weakness, vice or folly to bring about social reform. She looked at me as if I had insulted her.

Finally, moving without comment from a student's wrong answer to another student whom you think will supply a correct answer can create problems. Such an abrupt shift may make the first student feel ignored and may in essence place the student providing the "correct" answer in an awkward position. You may want to ask someone else the same question a student has answered incorrectly, but you owe the first student a response and an acknowledgment.

Questions That Students Ask

If the teacher is the only one to ask questions, the process of questioning can be seen as a measure of teacher dominance, inhibiting any student-centered learning environment and encouraging student passivity. The teacher as the only questioner then becomes the arbiter of all answers and classroom concerns, a role that is not only tiring but also does not foster student learning.

Many teachers would like students to generate questions, but teachers need to help the process along. Consider the following techniques:

- Asking students to write questions for discussion and then using those questions can help students take charge of their learning.

- Asking students to write questions for study, for quizzes, or for tests and then using those questions can also help students take charge of their learning.

- Turning student comments into questions for other students can be a powerful indicator that you, the teacher, consider student questions important. It also makes the student question the focus.

- Encouraging students to question by making an absurd or contradictory statement can also stimulate student questions.

- A pair of related Teacher Channel videos demonstrates an excellent activity in which a middle school teacher encourages students to compose questions for each other about the text they are reading. Thristene Edwards Francisco (2015a, 2015b) gives students a choice of several questioning frames as guides for question composition, and the students' questions lead to a very engaged conversation.

- Using questioning games such as Solve the Situation, What's the Question?, Picture Perfect, or Twenty Questions can help stimulate student questions (see Christenbury and Kelly [1983, 28–33]).

- Instituting a more formal questioning procedure such as Socratic circles automatically generates more questions from students (see Copeland [2005] for more information).

When students start asking questions in your classroom, it is powerful and useful; breaking their silence and encouraging them to ask questions is one of the more valuable things we can do in the classroom.

Teacher Questioning and Student Teacher Assessment: edTPA and Other Tasks

College- and career-ready standards, including the Common Core, encourage teachers to focus on their students' abilities to ask and answer their own questions using text-based evidence. If you teach in a state that uses the edTPA (formerly known as the Teacher Performance Assessment) or a similar device to assess student teaching, you will not be surprised that asking effective, critical questions is one of the most important skills examined. For the past several years, Ken's students in New York

State have been required to pass the edTPA to earn teacher certification, and Ken has learned from his successful students some of what helped them.

For your edTPA—and similar assessments—you will be expected to include specific questions to generate critical class discussion. To earn a passing score, be sure your lesson plans include clearly stated questions and that you point out in the Instructional Tasks section how you will use these questions to encourage your students to engage in critical discussion.

There is also a requirement to submit ten- to fifteen-minute videos as part of the edTPA, and one of these videos must focus specifically on a discussion you have with at least three students in which you scaffold and assess students' abilities to form interpretations of text. Your questioning technique and, more important, how effectively your students demonstrate their abilities as a result of your questions, is paramount here.

In all your edTPA commentaries, you'll also want to make sure you include explicit descriptions of how and why you constructed the questions you ask. It's important that you not only demonstrate these skills but also show that you are very mindful in your approach to them.

Even if you never need to compose or submit an edTPA or similar battery of tasks, you will make tremendous use of thoughtful, critical questions in your teaching. We hope this chapter comes in handy for you and your students for years to come.

Becoming Mrs. Ramsey

Virginia Woolf's novel *To the Lighthouse* contains an image Leila thinks of when talking with a class. It is the dining room scene (1927, 125 ff.) in which the intelligent and sensitive Mrs. Ramsey, unobtrusively presiding over the table, watches and orchestrates and brings out all the disparate members gathered in her house, some of whom are her children and relatives, some of whom are her guests. There is some tension and conflict in the room; the group is not a homogeneous or even harmonious one. Mrs. Ramsey knows, as the dinner begins, that some individuals feel ignored or marginalized or unimportant. But with a glance here, a question there, an encouraging smile when appropriate, Mrs. Ramsey watches over the group, gradually getting them to talk with one another and respond to one another, allowing each his or her turn. Using voice and eyes and words, somewhat as we do as teachers, she creates the ground for conversation, "the whole of the effort of merging and flowing and creating rested on her" (126). And as we do as teachers, Mrs. Ramsey asks the questions, gets others to answer, notices, encourages, bides her time. All teachers, both male and female, are Mrs. Ramsey; we watch over the dining room table of our classrooms. And the talk that we encourage there can be the stuff of life.

For Your Journal

Think about your school history and the asking and answering of questions. Can you describe any questions you wanted to ask in class but didn't? Couldn't? Why did you hesitate? Can you describe times when you asked a question that surprised even you? In your classroom as an English language arts teacher, what will your policy be on the asking and answering of questions? How orderly do you want the process to be? How unorderly? Why? What are the kinds of behaviors or remarks that would tend to make you want to terminate a large-group discussion? Why? What behaviors or remarks would tend to make you think the large-group discussion is successful? Why?

References

Burke, Jim. 2010. *What's the Big Idea? Question-Driven Units to Motivate Reading, Writing, and Thinking*. Portsmouth, NH: Heinemann.

Cain, Susan. 2012. *Quiet*. New York: Broadway.

Christenbury, Leila, and Patricia P. Kelly. 1983. *Questioning: A Path to Critical Thinking*. Urbana, IL: NCTE.

City, Elizabeth A. 2014. "Talking to Learn." *Educational Leadership* 72 (November): 11–16.

Copeland, Matt. 2005. *Socratic Circles: Fostering Critical and Creative Thinking in Middle and High School*. Portland, ME: Stenhouse.

Cuban, Larry. 1993. *How Teachers Taught: Constancy and Change in American Classrooms 1880–1900*. 2nd ed. New York: Teachers College Press.

Dillon, J. T. 1979. "Alternatives to Questioning." *High School Journal* 62 (February): 217–22.

———. 1994. *Using Discussion in Classrooms*. Philadelphia: Open University Press.

Francisco, Thristene Edwards. 2015a. "Higher Order Questions: A Path to Deeper Learning." Teacher Channel video. November 27. https://www.teachingchannel.org/videos/teaching-higher order-thinking-skills?fd=1.

———. 2015b. "Writing Higher Order Questions." Teacher Channel video. November 27. https://www.teachingchannel.org/videos/developing-better-questions.

Hearst, James. 2001. "Cold Snap." In *The Complete Poetry of James Hearst*, edited by Scott Cawelti. Iowa City: University of Iowa Press.

Keene, Ellin Oliver. 2014. "All the Time They Need." *Educational Leadership* 72 (November): 66–71.

Lillydahl, Doug. 2015. "Questioning Questioning: Essential Questions in English Classrooms." *English Journal* 104 (6): 36–39.

McTighe, Jay, and Grant P. Wiggins. 2013. *Essential Questions: Opening Doors to Student Understanding*. Alexandria, VA: Association for Supervision and Curriculum Development.

Walsh, Jackie Acree, and Beth Dankert Sattes. 2015a. "A New Rhythm for Responding." *Educational Leadership* 73 (September): 46–52.

———. 2015b. *Questioning for Classroom Discussion: Purposeful Speaking, Engaged Listening, Deep Thinking*. Alexandria, VA: Association for Supervision and Curriculum Development.

Williamson, Peter. 2013. "Enacting High Leverage Practices in English Methods: The Case of Discussion." *English Education* 46 (October): 34–67.

Woolf, Virginia. 1927. *To the Lighthouse*. New York: Harcourt, Brace & World.

10 | TEACHING TODAY
Ethics, Social Justice, and the Challenges of the Times

---

*What makes teaching a moral endeavor is that it is, quite centrally, human action
undertaken in regard to other human beings. Thus, matters of what is fair, right, just,
and virtuous are always present.*

    —Gary Fenstermacher, *Moral Dimensions of Teaching*

*Schools have always been sites of ideological struggle as competing interests struggle to
define the purpose and function of schools, and time and again, what emerges from
such struggles are initiatives and so-called "reforms" that make schools function even
more insidiously than before as sorting mechanisms that maintain economic, racial,
and other divisions.*

    —Kevin K. Kumashiro, *Against Common Sense: Teaching and Learning Toward Social Justice*

The consideration of social justice and ethics, of right and wrong, is not confined to
churches, mosques, and synagogues; it exists outside religious frameworks, too, notably
in schools and in teaching. "The implications for education have had to do with . . . the
resolution of moral dilemmas" (1988, 119), writes educational theorist Maxine Greene,
and those issues of social justice relate to us as teachers, as historian Joel Spring notes:

> Whose moral and social values will permeate the American school? [Nineteenth-century
> American educator] Horace Mann argued that there were certain moral values that all
> religious groups could agree upon and that these shared values would become the back-
> bone of the moral teachings of the school. A variety of religious groups have disagreed
> with this idea from the time of Mann up to the present. (1985, 13)

Yet, despite ongoing tensions in American public schools about whose ethics, whose morals, whose definition of social justice (as Kumashiro notes in one of the opening chapter quotations) will be directly taught or even discussed, issues remain. English teachers in particular confront not only the question of ethics in our content, exemplified by literary characters who confront serious dilemmas and make moral choices, but also in the act of teaching itself. Gary D. Fenstermacher makes this observation in a book on teaching and ethics:

> Whenever a teacher asks a student to share something with another student, decides between combatants in a . . . dispute, sets procedures for who will go first, second, third, and so on, or discusses the welfare of a student with another teacher, moral considerations are present. The teacher's conduct, at all times and in all ways, is a moral matter. For that reason alone, teaching is a profoundly moral activity. (1990, 133)

We must, as teachers, be fair in our dealings with students and have classrooms where, literally, social justice prevails. Further, much of what we consider in language and literature and writing also touches on issues of morality and ethics, and our classrooms should be places not only where individuals demonstrate fair behavior but also where issues of right and wrong can be discussed.

English Class as Ethics Arena

So is English class an ethics arena? A place to debate social justice? Beyond issues of the ethics of teachers and teaching itself, is there something about the subject matter that we need to also address? It seems very problematic to answer these questions definitively, especially in a pluralistic society where, first, not everyone agrees on what is right and what is wrong, and second, the schools are secular and public in nature. Disagreement among our students and the nonreligious nature of the public school are not, however, reasons for us to avoid ethical and social justice questions. As Kumashiro reminds us, "Yes, teaching is impossible, but only if we believe that teaching is successful when students learn exactly what we said beforehand that they were supposed to learn. . . . [Teaching is] a process that not only gives students the knowledge and skills that matter in society, but also asks students to examine the political implications of that knowledge and skills" (2015, 41). Although we need to be aware of prevailing community standards, we would be shortsighted as English teachers to sidestep the important issues that permeate language arts.

Thus, Brutus' choices, the actions of Huck, and the decisions of Celie are all issues of ethics and morals. In *Julius Caesar*, *Huckleberry Finn*, and *The Color Purple*, what were the characters' options, the considerations? What do you think was right, was wrong, and why? What political, economic, and racial issues affected their circumstances? For sure, you and your students will not always agree, but it is a seriously lost opportunity if we do not consider, discuss, and weigh these questions. Our classrooms are not just for the consideration of the art of literature or the craft of language—the way dialogue reveals, imagery enhances, sentences balance—but also of content, characters who confront life and make decisions that affect themselves and those around them. These considerations fall well within our discussion of content, so how then do you approach literature or language using an ethical lens?

For instance, Jonathan Swift's "A Modest Proposal" makes little sense unless the reader understands the absolute indifference of wealthy English absentee landlords toward their starving Irish tenants. Only then does Swift's savage satire, with which he advocates the eating of children, have the weight it surely deserves. George Orwell's essay "Politics and the English Language" is not about word origins and sentence structure but about the power of language to distort and even corrupt the perception of reality; its critique of totalitarian regimes and language is pertinent today and can be effectively used in discussions of social justice. The civil disobedience both Thoreau and King advocate in their writings are worth serious discussion; to what extent are their arguments pertinent to the defense of those today who break the nation's laws in the name of morality? We may feel great sympathy for the tormented Othello, manipulated and deceived by his evil lieutenant Iago, but does that excuse his murder of his innocent wife Desdemona? It is unfair that Rochester is duped into marrying a woman who had insanity in her family and who actually is now insane (and whom he cannot divorce), but is his response in *Jane Eyre*, confining her indefinitely to a locked attic room, justifiable? All these questions are worth asking, and although we most likely cannot—should not—enforce one group or class answer, they are important to explore and important to discuss.

Even as apparently dry a topic as technical communication can be rife with questions of ethics. Drawing on a stunning lesson from Professor Stephen B. Katz, tech writing theorist James E. Porter describes why a "technical communicator should be, first and foremost, a public advocate."

> Katz (1992) opens with a memo written to a supervisor in 1942 by a technical writer named "Just." The memo precisely and directly described technical "innovations" that Just recommended for vans to enable them to better transport their cargo. (Just recommended the vans' load space be reduced, the lighting be better protected, and a sealed drain be added to the vehicles to make cleaning easier.) (2005, 254)

The memo is a model of a "concise, well organized, and logically argued" (254) document. The problem, which is actually an ethical problem, is what the memo fails to pinpoint. The "cargo" discussed in the memo is Jews being transported to Nazi concentration camps, and the memo's intended audience is a Nazi officer. As Porter suggests, even for technical writers, it is no less than "dangerous . . . to assume that information is neutral" (254). As this example well underscores, to ignore or avoid what literature or informational texts often address—the world of ethics, social justice, and human beings' subsequent choices—is to eviscerate the English class and divorce what we read and what we discuss from reality.

Ethical Issues for the Classroom Teacher

Beyond English language arts content are ethical issues for us as professionals and teachers, as the opening quotation for this chapter implies. The discussions in this section may seem preachy to you, and if so, we apologize. We want, however, to call your attention to some topics rarely discussed in books about teaching that will affect—and possibly tempt—you as a teacher. We have great power to do good in the classroom. But we can also do great harm. The school-to-prison pipeline, student privacy, protection of students who are vulnerable, being friends with your students, and sexual ethics are some of the issues we need to consider.

A later section of this chapter, Breaking the Rules, addresses the scary but inevitable time when you find you must make a decision that is outside the official regulations. It might surprise you to think that such decisions may be part of your beginning life in the classroom, but they most likely will. If your career parallels that of most conscientious teachers, it is likely that very soon in your teaching career you will confront such a time when you must break the rules. Finally, we review a few of the challenges we see about teaching today.

TECH TALK: *Playing Games to Support Social Justice*

Check out engaging, online games to help young people learn about important social and political issues. Two sites of interest are Purposeful Games (sponsored by the MIT Games Lab) (http://purposefulgames.info/) and Games for Change (www.gamesforchange.org/). Both list many games that are available for free, online play.

In *Activate*, you play a middle school student who faces gamelike challenges, choosing quests (such as pamphleting, holding a bake sale, conducting a letter writing campaign) while learning facts about bullying and bullying prevention. *A Decision of Paramount Importance* teaches about the dangers of dating violence, and *Long Story: A Dating Game for the Real World* is a "queer-positive" game about relationships. *Against All Odds* enables players to live through the experience of becoming a political refugee, and *Admongo* helps young people understand the ways their spending habits are influenced by the billion-dollar advertising industry.

Warning: These games can be interesting components in your teaching, but be sure to play them yourself first—the content in some games can be quite mature.

School-to-Prison Pipeline

Schools can clearly be a place for students to succeed and excel, but they can also be places where students who do not "fit"—students of color, for instance, or those who have been placed in special education classes—can be punished unfairly and excluded. Using published statistics provided by school districts across the nation, some educational critics have become so alarmed at the disproportionate suspension and expulsion rates of some groups of students that they are calling educational institutions a "pipeline" to prison. The phrase may strike you as overly dramatic and even offensive, but the statistics are indeed troublesome. For instance, a 2015 National Council of Teachers of English (NCTE) resolution, "Dismantling the School-to-Prison Pipeline," notes the following:

> According to a nationwide study by the US Department of Education Office for Civil Rights, African American students are 3.5 times more likely than their White classmates to be suspended or expelled. Black children constitute 18 percent of students, but they account for 46 percent of those suspended more than once. For students with atypical abilities, . . . [o]ne report found that while 8.6 percent of public school children have been identified as atypical, these students make up 32 percent of youth in juvenile centers. . . . A 2014 landmark study tracked nearly one million Texas students for at least six years. The study controlled for more than 80 variables, such as socioeconomic class. The study found that African Americans were disproportionally punished compared with otherwise similar White and Latino students [as were] children with emotional differences. (NCTE 2015b) http://www.ncte.org/positions/statements/school-to-prison

The concern is that students "who are cognitively atypical or have endured histories of poverty, abuse, neglect, and/or trauma" (NCTE 2015b) are not welcome in school. They are students who drop out—or, as some critics argue, are pushed out—of school. Social and cultural differences, in this case, make school an unwelcome place, and, once out of school, many students become enmeshed in poverty and crime.

Scholar and activist Marc Lamont Hill guest edited a sobering issue of *English Journal* (*EJ*) on "Teaching English in the Age of Incarceration." He points out that over the past several decades the increase in zero-tolerance policies and shifting of discipline from school administrators to law enforcement has strengthened the school-to-prison pipeline. And, with increases in the prison population, "our English classrooms are increasingly filled with students whose parents, siblings, and loved ones are tethered to the prison system" (2013, 17). If we are to properly teach these students, we must acquaint ourselves with and understand our role in our nation's record-breaking incarceration rate, and you may find this *EJ* issue, filled with stunning statistics and compassionate, provocative lesson ideas, compelling reading.

As English teachers, we must continue to offer all our students instruction, support, and care. Schools and our classrooms should be places to strengthen skills and to encourage, not exclude. Thus, although none of us finds all of our students equally likeable, and we are kidding ourselves if we think we will be completely compatible with everyone who comes to class, we have an obligation not only to teach but to fairly evaluate everyone with whom we come into contact. We should not use assignments or grades—it is *wrong* to use assignments or grades—to punish or keep in line whomever we do not like or with whom we have a personality clash. That sort of punitive power is one of students' deepest fears—being failed or downgraded because of the teacher's personal tastes—and we should do nothing to further that fear. The inescapable conclusion is that we often cannot change our feelings about students, but we are *not allowed* to act on them. It may not be comfortable for us as teachers, but it is part of our obligation to treat our students fairly and to rise above petty behavior. If we don't, we may well become part of the school-to-prison pipeline.

For this reason, you once again need to be aware that you come from a culture and a background that espouses certain values. Further, you have a definite personality that expresses itself in certain traits. To ignore that background and your own personality, to assume that either you have no particular values or tastes or that those values and tastes are generally universal, is misleading. You will teach students with whom you have little in common, and ignorance of that fact is naive. "[W]hat we believe to be *normal* affects how we read the world" (Jones and Woglom 2013, 33), and that fact will color your teaching and your reaction to students.

You cannot, of course, adopt all of the values and background and personality traits of all of your students, nor should you jettison your own values. You do need, though, to acknowledge that you will at times react both negatively and positively to students on the basis of their class and race and gender, sexual orientation and identity, home language, and other individual characteristics. You will also have students with whom you share unresolvable tensions, and some of those tensions may be related to personality issues. Fair or unfair, your job as a teacher is to be just, to be professional, and to look at every student untinged by personal antipathy. We simply cannot reward and privilege only those who, without question or complaint, "read required texts, write grammatically correct papers in traditional academic English, leave their baggage at the door, practice creativity elsewhere, compete for grades and attention, and use polite discourse in the classroom" (27).

You are human, and you are certainly allowed to have negative feelings. You are, on the other hand, not only human but a human teacher, and the problem, the ethical dilemma, emerges when your feelings actively influence your evaluation of and your interactions with students. Do not indulge yourself in making favorites or making enemies. You are in the classroom to teach all and to teach all fairly. It may be hard, and it may take some conscious consideration on your part, but you must, as an ethical responsibility, deal evenhandedly with all who share the classroom.

Good teaching actually gets even more complicated than simply trying to eliminate our biases as teachers. We will be better teachers if we *like* our students. Liking our students will help us focus on their strengths, help us compassionately and honestly help them strengthen their weaknesses, and create a more rigorously productive classroom space. Peter Elbow, legendary composition teacher, even points out that liking student writing will make teachers better and more accurate respondents to student writing (1993, 200).

Student Privacy and Student Rights

Along with our teaching is the way we deal with our students and what they choose to share with us and with their peers. As English teachers, we are often in a position to hear revelations of sorts from our students—stories, embellished and true, of choices, decisions, triumphs, disasters. In journals, narratives, classroom discussions, and role plays, students often reveal large chunks of their lives. Some of those stories involve fairly intimate details, and the public revelation of such would be a personal invasion of privacy. Some of those stories further involve legal issues that have bearing outside the classroom.

Because laws differ from state to state as do school practices, you need to inform yourself about your obligations regarding certain student revelations. Issues involving threats of violence, suicide, drug use or sale, and physical or sexual abuse may come to your attention in your students' writing or conversation. When and how to inform the guidance staff, a building administrator, the school nurse, or school social worker of behavior that may be life-threatening or illegal is something you need to investigate. Ignorance of the law is not an excuse; ask what your school policies are and act accordingly.

As teachers, we also need to remember that students have a right not only to our respect but also to privacy. Beyond the very serious situation inadvertently shared, students may reveal other details of their lives and those of their family and friends. Tempting as it may be, we should not carry their revelations outside the school sessions for our friends' or relatives' edification or amusement. What we may consider atypical or informative or even entertaining stuff is our students' lives, and we need to honor the fact that often—and often with implicit confidence in our discretion—they share those lives with us.

As a last note, students also have a right to data privacy and security; a 2015 NCTE resolution affirms that right even in a "digital age" and urges that student test scores be treated in an "ethical, lawful, and responsible" manner (NCTE 2015a). It is not just what students choose to reveal in class; their grades and test scores are similarly issues of privacy.

Social Media

Many teachers find great value in using Twitter, Pinterest, Facebook, Edmodo, Todays-Meet, WordPress, Skype, Google Hangouts, and myriad other platforms in the seemingly infinite space of Internet communication. More and more students have access to electronic devices, and electronic discourse is becoming an ever-increasing part of and influence on human communication. New apps make everything a few clicks or taps away—from classroom record keeping to sharing complicated presentations with people around the world. These apps are enhancing classroom literacy in fascinating ways unimagined at the beginning of the century. One thing is clear: all students must learn how to communicate using social media if they are to be truly literate in the twenty-first century. That said, it remains tricky territory, especially for new teachers.

Should you allow your students to follow you on Twitter? If it's professional, sure. Should you friend them on Facebook? Almost certainly not. Should you allow them access to YouTube in your classroom? Look to your school's policy.

Free, wide-open access provided by an unencumbered Internet browser still makes many influential adults nervous, although we think that anxiety is waning. Many districts still enforce browser restrictions and block specific websites or search terms. Many have restrictive policies regarding social media communication in schools and between students and teachers. As a new teacher, it is crucial that you take the time to find out about your school's policies. And we encourage you to work with your school's technology coaches and administrators to learn the best ways to incorporate technology into your lessons.

You should also be aware of what's available online about *you*. Have you got some "spring break photos" that you didn't intend to be part of your professional portfolio floating around out there online? Have you posted a blog that, taken out of context, could cause you grief you're not ready for? Do you think your Facebook wall is really private? How much of your future do you want to bet on that? It's wise to do your best to scrub your posts, wherever possible, so nothing you don't want out there comes back to haunt you. On the other hand, we also have to get used to living in a world in which we cannot completely control what's online, including about ourselves.

To learn more about technology's value in English classes, consult these highly regarded resources:

- Sara Kadjer's (2010) *Adolescents and Digital Literacies: Learning Alongside Our Students*

- Troy Hicks' (2013) *Crafting Digital Writing: Composing Texts Across Media and Genres*

- Kristen Hawley Turner and Troy Hicks' (2015) *Connected Reading: Teaching Adolescent Readers in a Digital World.*

As you consider using social media in your classes, you should keep the following in mind:

- What is your school's policy for social media use? If it's restrictive, can you find influential school leaders who might help loosen it?

- Do all your students have access to technology at home? If not, can those students borrow devices from the school or the public library, or use them during after school hours?

- The Internet and Web 2.0 technologies are serious tools for research, presentations, communication, and more. Are you using the technologies to their fullest extent, or merely replacing pen-and-paper activities with an electronic screen?

- Technology can be fun and flashy, but are you engaging your students in appropriately rigorous and sophisticated activities that require higher-order critical thinking skills?

Protecting the Vulnerable

During middle school and high school, when apparent difference is especially unacceptable, students can participate in a number of negative and ultimately damaging activities that target others who appear vulnerable. No, you cannot police the entire school—sometimes you cannot police even much of the hallway outside your classroom. But you can enforce, in your own space, a code of respectful and kind behavior and language. This involves your active vigilance, and although you may be reluctant to intervene, it is your obligation to assert yourself in your classroom.

Any form of bullying and hazing, either physical or verbal, should be outlawed in your class. Whether a member of the majority or minority, *no student* has the right to harass those who are of a different race, religion, gender, sexual orientation, or appearance. Mocking someone's speech or accent is unacceptable; making fun of a student's clothes or hygiene practices is not to be allowed. Cliques and groups and gangs are inescapable in most school settings, and bullying through social media sites (see Conn [2005] for more information) is also a reality. Realistically, in school or out, there is little we can do to ensure all our students are socially comfortable and successful. But within our own classrooms, we can indeed rule and outlaw, immediately and precisely, the kind of harassment that some students will more than willingly inflict on others and that some students, in fear, will watch silently if not approvingly. Protecting the vulnerable is part of your ethical responsibility as a teacher, and although it may not always be comfortable or make you feel wonderful, creating an environment of respect and tolerance is part of your work in the English language arts classroom.

Note: The magazine *Teaching Tolerance*, published by the Southern Poverty Law Center, is a great resource for teachers who want to ensure just and equitable classrooms. For more information, write: 400 Washington Avenue, Montgomery, AL 36104 or call 334.956.8200 for subscriptions.

Leila's Story

When I returned to teaching high school, I so wanted everything to go smoothly, especially at that crucial beginning of the semester. In my very first week, though, during a large-group discussion, I was making a list on the board of comments students were calling out. It was going well, but after one student's contribution someone objected, "Oh, that's just so gay." The remark was not delivered lightly, and even writing on the board with my back to the room I knew that whoever said it meant it to silence, if not to wound. Turning around to face the class, I wished with all my heart that that comment had not been made because I knew that, right then and there, I had to call the language out of bounds and to say that I never wanted, in this class, to hear it again. And so I did. Many of the students' faces registered honest surprise, and the large-group discussion quickly sputtered. I sensed some students were shocked by the rebuke and resentful. For my part, the only good news—the only important news—was that I never heard the slur again.

Ken's Story

When I taught high school English, I also advised the school newspaper, and the student staff and I met in a classroom most days after school for a couple of hours. The time we spent after school working on the paper ended up becoming something more. These times and spaces became positive, relatively safe spaces for students who needed a place to be after school. I didn't do anything special, but the students knew this was an activity they could engage in where they would be treated well and not subjected to bullying or taunting (which, like Leila, I did not allow). Anyone could join us, even if they weren't strictly working on the paper—as long as they didn't distract from our work. Sometimes just by creating spaces like this we do our students a tremendous service. For further reading about preventing bullying, see these references:

In "Preventing Bullying Behaviors" from *English Journal*, you will find Nancy Mack's (2012) helpful essay as well as articles describing lessons that use young adult and classic literature to explore and prevent the reasons for bullying, using research-based letter writing to oppose cyberbullying, helping bystanders build their voice, and talking tough about bullying when it's called for.

The NCTE "Resolution on Confronting Bullying and Harassment" (NCTE 2011) includes specific suggestions and resources for addressing this problem.

Being Friends with Your Students

One of the hardest things for beginning teachers to do is to draw a line between their roles as professionals, teachers, and their understandable desire to be friendly, even friends, to students. If you are close in age to those you teach, if you come to know about their lives and care about them, it can be an even more difficult balance. For their part, students are often curious about teachers, especially young teachers, and if you are younger, your students may want to know a great deal about you and your personal life. It is understandable, certainly in the beginning of your career, that you may feel more of a peer to your students than a teacher. You need, however, to remember that you are now fulfilling a professional role and one that requires a necessary gulf between you and them. This is the nature of the business: friends do not give friends grades or credit for work; friends do not reprimand friends or impose sanctions for disciplinary infractions. Teachers, though, do all of these with and for their students, and it is part of your new professional life. Although being kind and supportive in class is important, you are there to teach, not to join your students' social circle. It is essential that you maintain a professional distance; students are not entitled to sensitive information about your private life, and you do not necessarily need to get involved in their private lives. You are not their mother or their father, an older sister or brother, but their teacher, and you must maintain a professional role.

In truth, students do not want their teachers to be their friends. Students want their teachers to like them and to value and respect them, but they want their teachers to do this from a professional, adult position. Students don't want teachers to use foul language or tell them inappropriate jokes or to talk about other students in catty or insensitive ways. They *have* friends. What they want are teachers who are mentors, trustworthy adult guides.

There may be times when students will test you, however. And this leads us to a more serious ethical issue, that of sex and our students.

Sexual Ethics and Your Students

When you walk down the halls of your middle school or high school as a beginning teacher and you see young people who are relatively immature, even awkward, some clearly with one foot still in childhood, you may wonder if we have lost our minds to even suggest that you could ever think of having an intimate relationship with one of your students. Even when you consider the more socially sophisticated, physically mature students you deal with, it may, early in your career, seem totally impossible that you would ever think of any of them in a romantic or sexual fashion.

You may never fall in love with one of your students, but experience teaches that many of the ingredients for strong mutual attraction exist in a school. Working closely with students over a period of time, getting to know and like and trust them—and they you—your feelings about their availability and their attractiveness may undergo a marked shift.

In a culture that deifies—and sexualizes—the young, it may become hard to re-member that the attractive and often appealing students you teach are not your peers and are not available for socializing and/or romance. When you spend the bulk of your time interacting with young people, you may well find yourself in a position, mutual or not, of being strongly attracted to one of your students. This happens to male and female teachers of almost all ages, to those married and unmarried, straight and gay and otherwise, and it is a serious ethical issue in our field.

The heart has a mind of its own, and at some point in your career you may convince yourself that a relationship with one of your students is eminently justifiable. You may find yourself in a vulnerable time of your own life; the student in question may be troubled or confused or lonely or just really infatuated with you. As the daily news tells us, there are numerous cases of students and teachers falling in love, having sexual re-lations, even having children with each other and marrying. Some of these cases result in scandal and ruined careers and criminal charges; some of them go on to happier and even permanently happy endings. We doubt there is a school system in this country where intimate teacher–student relationships have not occurred.

The entire issue, nevertheless, is poisoned by the sheer inequality of the players. A student is never in an equal power relationship with a teacher, the latter of whom holds authority, standing, and the weight of the grade. Further, in high school and mid-dle school, students are almost always younger than their teachers, even their young teachers, and regardless of the number of years between the two groups, teachers are generally viewed as parental or older sibling figures.

Using your power as a teacher, consciously or not, to further a sexual or romantic relationship with a student is wrong. It preys on students' vulnerability and trust; it makes school just another place where a young person can be used or exploited. Further—and very practically—states have laws prohibiting sexual relations with minors, and almost all your students will fall into that legal category. In most states, the legal penalties can be severe; in most states, teaching contracts and even certification can be terminated for such behavior, generally lumped under the term "moral turpitude."

In specific, touching and physical proximity are areas of concern. Often our students, male and female, will attempt close physical contact. Sometimes this is done from a sense of affection and care; sometimes it is done from a sense of curiosity and adventure. Certainly, also, some student-initiated physical contact is nothing more than an expression of veiled aggression. Regardless, you as a teacher must insist on maintaining appropriate physical space between yourself and any student. In addition, although any and all individual conferences with our students can be conducted out of earshot of others, they should never be conducted out of eyesight. Thus, meeting with a student in quiet corner of a public space—such as the media center, the school courtyard, or the cafeteria—is acceptable as is, of course, meeting with a student in a classroom with an open door. Conferencing alone with a student of any gender behind a closed door is asking for misinterpretation. Additionally, in a school that has a culture in which closed-door conversations between teacher and student are rare (or nonexistent), possible exploitive or predatory situations between teachers and students are easier to identify and stop.

If this talk of professional distance seems abstract, there are a few specific behaviors you can practice in the classroom that may help to ensure a healthy distance between yourself and your students:

- Minimize touching students and, when in conference, meet with them in public spaces and in view of others.

- Decline to share with students details of your own past or present personal life, including dating, sexual practices, or romantic involvement.

- Avoid extensive personal conversations in the classroom.

- Avoid in class what could be seen as flirtatious behavior and do not participate in sexually provocative conversations or jokes.

- Adopt a dress that is more like the teaching staff than like the students.

- Exhibit characteristics that are professional and adult.

Despite all of the cautionary nature of this discussion, however, this is not a plea for a return to some sort of puritanical past. All of us as human beings are endowed with a sexual identity. It is unrealistic to insist that you not appreciate the attractiveness of your students, that you be immune to their appealing natures. Our students are working on their sexual identities and even experimenting with those identities. They are also practicing their personal charm, often in our classrooms and with us and their peers. We would be less than human if we did not respond, if we failed to appreciate in a very real sense their emergence as accomplished young men and women. But beyond that appreciation we must not go. Young people need to find romantic and sexual partners outside the school teaching staff, and you as a teacher need to draw a line over which no one crosses. You are in a trusted position as a teacher, and violating that trust while the student is in your charge is serious and regrettable. Admiration from a certain distance is the honorable path. Taking care not to give students the wrong signals about your relationship with them is essential.

For Your Journal

Ethics and social justice are broad fields, and the topics listed in this section probably touch on only some of the issues. Identify an issue that you think affects the English classroom and that is not discussed here. What is the issue? Why, in your opinion, is it important to teachers and students? What do you feel are possible guidelines for teacher–student behavior with regard to this issue?

Breaking the Rules

The idea of going against the established order of school is a tough topic, but it's one that we think is important for you to think about early in your career. If that institution called school always operated in our students' best interests, we as teachers would never have to consider breaking—or bending—school rules. Those rules can be in the areas of curriculum, discipline, or just procedure, and as part of your ethical code you may, at some time for some good reasons or cause, have to move outside the regulations. To what extent and when and how you do this is no mild issue: breaking too many rules too blatantly will get you fired. And, of course, there are some rules, especially those regarding ethical teacher conduct, which should never be breached. Yet, you will face times in your teaching career when breaking the rules is just about the only thing to do. There are clearly risks to this, but it is an area that you will need to contemplate.

Leila's Story: Breaking the Rules and My Student, Ray

I had just finished writing the first edition of this book when I was named editor of *EJ*. I knew that my first issue would be a crucial one, and as I planned that issue I kept coming back to a student whose story I had not included in the book. For some time I thought about what Ray meant to me as a teacher and why I couldn't get him out of my mind. One day it came to me that Ray's story was central to an idea I wanted to discuss, breaking the rules in school, and that idea became the theme of my first issue as editor of *EJ* (Christenbury 1994).

In my high school teaching, I bent many rules to reward students and to keep them encouraged *about* school, a place that to some of them was more than occasionally inhospitable. Much of this rule bending was minor stuff and not terribly remarkable. In the case of Ray, though, I put my teaching career on the line. From the perspective of the years, I am not sure I would have the courage to do it again, but it made a significant difference for one young man, and I am glad I did it.

To this day I can see Ray vividly: he was a very small, sharp-featured, blue-eyed fifteen-year-old with pale skin and hair and eyebrows so blond they were almost white. He came from a single-parent home and lived with his mother and a four-year-old sister. Ray's mother was struggling to keep the little family together and was not, frankly, doing well at it. She was prone to deep depressions and had a hard time maintaining her life, her hourly wage job, and her two children. As with many such situations, Ray, at fifteen, operated more as a peer to his mother than as a child and took increasing responsibility in the home.

How did I know any of this? I knew this because Ray was in my class and because, particularly in response to home pressures and his mother's periodic breakdowns, he would cyclically drop out of school only, when things got calmer at home, to return, hopeful that he could salvage the year and salvage his grades. He knew that his academic career was imperiled by his family issues but, like many kids in similar situations, when the issue arose about sacrificing himself or turning his back on the family, there was no question as to what he should do.

I wish I could tell you that those of us who knew why Ray came late to school, didn't come to school, dropped out of school only to return again and again were sympathetic and knowledgeable and helpful. But such was not the case at all. Ray was a ghostlike boy, pale and unassuming; he did not share much with anyone, and many of his teachers and counselors were unaware.

Accordingly, the administration, particularly the vice principal responsible for Ray's numerous changes of status, became increasingly impatient with his pattern of attendance and dropping out. Because Ray was reticent, silent about this issue, his dropping out seemed as much about indecision as anything else. Few even suspected home responsibilities.

One memorable day, there was a climax of sorts. Ray, having dropped out twice that year, was reentering school once again. As Ray was exiting the vice principal's office after completing the latest set of forms, the vice principal followed him out into the hall. It was obvious that the vice principal had had it with Ray's most recent return to school and took the opportunity to vent his frustration. It was during a change of class, and the vice principal raised his voice at Ray's departing back and shouted at him over the noise of students *You aren't even worth the trouble you're causing.*

I was on hall duty at that change of class and saw the incident and heard it. I watched as Ray stood frozen outside the vice principal's office, both furious and humiliated. I knew Ray, watched his reaction, watched him whirl and move toward the vice principal. I immediately intervened: as small as he was physically and as calm as he usually was, it seemed clear to me that Ray was ready to assault the administrator at that very moment. I stood in front of Ray and moved him out of the hall. In the relative quiet of my classroom, Ray and I briefly discussed the incident. I, who had often silently observed that the vice principal was neither one of the most tactful nor even one of the kindest of human beings, told Ray in forceful terms that the administrator was *wrong*. It was a risky thing to tell a kid, but, at the same time, what I said was true, and both Ray and I knew it.

That was when Ray and I connected. Ray, thankfully, never quoted me. So Ray and I had a relationship and when, some months later, things got bad at home again, I was called to do something more serious than intervene in a potential assault and criticize a vice principal behind his back.

Ray's mother had collapsed again, and it seemed that the only solution was, one more time, for Ray to drop out of school and to be there, in the apartment, to take care of her and his sister. It would have, once again, put him behind, and as he was getting near the end of his junior year, it seemed hopeless that he would ever complete high school.

I talked to Ray after school; he saw no compromise. I was concerned. But what would happen, I asked him, if he went to school only part of the day and left early? Then, he would have the afternoon and night with his family. We released students after sixth period, at 2:20 P.M., but not all students had all six periods of classes. Ray had my English class fifth period. If he left right at lunch, fourth period, he could have the whole afternoon to take care of things at home and still keep his morning classes. Ray thought that those hours might be enough—but what to do with my class? We had a strict, mandated attendance policy, and if Ray missed more days, there was an automatic F with no chance of appeal. Ray needed to be marked present.

Looking back, I think I was at a crossroads in my life as a teacher. I knew that I would have to be the person to break the rules for Ray: the system, in my judgment, would just not accommodate Ray any more.

So every day for a matter of months I marked Ray present in my class although he was at home with his mother and his baby sister. The deal was that Ray would do independent written work for the class and turn it in. I would accept it and grade it as if he were present and working along with the other students. Only he and I would know that he was not *in* class at all; the other students, preoccupied with their own lives and hardly interested in the colorless Ray, were not likely to notice and not likely to turn either of us in.

And so we went for almost two months. If, indeed, the scheme had been discovered, I would have been in very serious trouble as I was deliberately lying, marking Ray present, day after day. It was not lost on me that attendance records are, in my state, virtually legal documents. I just lived on the promise and hope that Ray was a trustworthy kid who needed a break that not the school but I could provide. I also trusted that Ray would indeed turn in his written work and get a grade and credit from me.

Would I ever risk this again? Most likely not; it could have ruined my career as I was clearly lying. Also, if Ray had been in an accident or discovered off school premises at a time when his teacher vowed that he was present in her class, the school—and I, his teacher—would have been liable. In my case, I think it would have been just cause for dismissal. But I did it then because I knew the school would not bend, and because, I hoped and prayed, I knew Ray. I certainly knew that he was worth the risk of breaking the rules.

And, in the end, I did know Ray. He was not a stellar student, and I cannot tell you that he went on to be a brain surgeon or that his time at home cured his mother and that everyone lived happily ever after. But Ray did return to my class, did his work, and turned it in. I recall the afternoon when he handed me an inch-high sheaf of paper, done in careful handwriting and painstakingly correct and thorough. Where he had found the time to do this writing and reading, I'll never know. But Ray had fulfilled his part of the bargain, and I could tell from the expression on his face when he gave me his work folder, he felt a certain sense of accomplishment. For my part, I was incredibly relieved. Ray passed my class, and my consistent subterfuge was never discovered. He finished the year, and he finished English 11.

Ken's Story: A Case for Breaking the Rules of Grading

My favorite story of breaking the rules is not mine. A good friend who was a career English teacher tells a story of her early days as a teacher in which she learned from a guidance counselor that one of the students in her middle school class, Michael, a shy, sullen boy with very little interest in school, was routinely beaten by his father for grades below A. At that point, very early in the school year, she decided that this young man would get nothing but As from her regardless of the quality of his work—and it was far from A-level work. Was this a violation of grading rules? Absolutely. Yet this teacher felt it was the right thing to do. Here's the amazing part—and this still gives me goose bumps when I think about it. After several months of nothing but As and positive comments, this shy, young man began slowly to come out of his shell and show genuine interest in improving his work. By the end of the year, this boy who never seemed to have much potential was truly earning the As he was receiving.

My own stories are far less dramatic than this, but still instructive. As a high school teacher, I was a big fan of cooperative learning, a specific method for group work that requires all students to complete their own assignments (with help from the entire group). Though only one assignment from each group is chosen at random for grading, all the students in that group get the grade from that assignment. As you can imagine, this method generally obligates students to ensure each other's work is up to snuff. However, sometimes a group's dynamic simply does not work. More than once I've had students who were so ambitious that they would complete four versions of an assignment, one for each group member, so that no matter whose work was chosen, they would receive an A. Or, the ambitious student would be so grade focused, she or he would badger other students until they just gave up out of frustration and anger. Rather than simply give up on cooperative learning, in cases like this I would make a private deal with the overeager student. I would guarantee them an A on the assignment as long as they didn't tell any of the other students and they agreed to put in only an appropriate amount of work without badgering anyone. Most times this solved the issue, but there was one time the ambitious student, Sandra, could not help herself and she still badgered her fellow group members. Sandra revealed our private deal to the entire class and eventually I was summoned for a discussion with the principal about it. He didn't agree that my approach was best, but I was lucky to have a supportive administration to work under, and he defended my right to this unorthodox but ultimately acceptable method of evaluation. This was before the era of the "helicopter parent" and the "tiger mom." In some districts today with very ambitious and even aggressive parents, I'm not sure I'd choose to make a private deal again. I don't think I'd fare nearly as well in those cases.

Why are we sharing these stories? Are we encouraging you to lie and to tell falsehoods? To make deals with kids and mark them present in your class when they are not even on school property? To give students grades that they may not have earned or to manipulative evaluation schemes? No, we are not encouraging you to do that at all, but these are teachers' stories about students and compromises that teachers can make and no one else can, compromises that the school will often not allow. In both our cases, we broke the rules, took a risk, and it worked. In larger ways and in small ways, you, too, will find yourself bending the rules and moving the regulations because you, a teacher, have a student like Ray or Michael or Sandra and a need to make a bureaucratic system of rules more flexible, more responsive, more humane.

For Your Journal

Despite the previous stories, the very idea of a teacher breaking rules may strike you as unnecessary or even unethical. What is your feeling about teachers and school and curricular regulations? To what extent can you imagine a time when a teacher would be tempted to break a rule? From your perspective, what kinds of guidelines would dictate when or when not to break the rules?

Being and Becoming an Ethical Teacher

Our time in the classroom can be transformative in profound ways. For some, this issue becomes more than dealing with content and students in an ethical way. It expands into a broader realm, that of social justice, as described by Sonia Nieto:

> Teachers enter the profession for any number of reasons, but neither fame nor money nor the promise of lavish working conditions is at the top of that list. Instead . . . for many of them, social justice figures prominently among the motivating factors underlying their choice to teach. The urge to live a life of service that entails a commitment to the ideals of democracy, fair play, and equality is strong among many of those who begin teaching. (2003, 91)

Nieto continues, though, to remind us that "teachers are not miracle workers. Nor are they social workers or missionaries." Instead, "teachers need to understand their roles as involving more than simply attending to the minds of students; it also entails nurturing their hearts and souls . . . to do this without taking on the world of injustice is tricky business . . . an equilibrium that is difficult at best" (105).

Finding this equilibrium is one of the many challenges you face on the journey, and one of the most important. And remembering this aspect of our teaching, being true to it in a way, can be hard at times. Although policy makers and politicians often want us to educate only for test scores and efficiency, we are—inescapably—about bigger things. Educator Marilyn Cochran-Smith makes the point:

> From a social justice perspective, the purpose of education needs to be understood not simply as constructing a system where pupils' test scores and wise monetary investments are the bottom lines. Rather, the purpose of education must also be understood as preparing students to engage in satisfying work, function as lifelong learners who can cope with the challenges of a rapidly changing global society, recognize inequities in their everyday contexts, and join with others to challenge them. (2005, 416)

This is our challenge on the journey. It is personal, it is social. It also has profound consequences for ourselves and for our students.

The Challenges of the Times

Things Have Changed and Things Have Stayed the Same

And now to some of today's challenges you will face in your teaching future. As the French note, *Plus ça change, plus c'est la même chose* (The more things change, the more things stay the same). It is a truism of the age that times have "changed," that little of what we experience as adults today would be familiar to previous generations because our twenty-first-century society has been utterly transformed by modern life.

Changes are undeniable, advances in science and technology are startling, and what most of us take for granted in communication, medical care, transportation, and standard of life was hardly imaginable thirty years ago.

In education, however, change is not quite so clear-cut: things have changed, but things have also stayed the same. In our schools, although the specifics vary, the broad outline of teaching today is not vastly different from what it was decades ago. For some, this fact is comforting, giving school a familiarity and dependability that is occasionally lacking in other parts of our society. For others, however, the reality that school has not changed so very much is an indictment, a demonstration of the institution's inability to respond effectively to societal change.

The future and predictions of change in the future are not, as one wag noted, what they used to be. It seems that many of the predictions for sweeping revolution in school have just not come to pass. As an institution, school appears to be remarkably resilient to being reformed and transformed—however frequent the calls for restructuring, detailed the state standards, generous the funding from civic-minded billionaires, or dire the reports of student scores on high-stakes tests. Certainly, when Leila returned to high school teaching almost thirty years after she began her career, she was not overwhelmed by the changes in her students or in school. Some aspects were different, but she found her semester in Trailer 11 remarkably like the very first classes she taught in the beginning of her teaching career. And if that experience is typical, in some ways that is not very good news for you.

What *does* this mean for you? It means that although in your career you may see aspects of school change, you need to know that that change will probably not be overnight or even all that obvious to the outside observer. And if you are coming into teaching with the sure belief that schools as we know them will be transformed in the next few years and really reflect these calls for reform, you will need to adjust your expectations.

School has changed. School has stayed the same.

In high schools and middle schools all over the country, as in years before, classes meet, bells ring, lockers slam, buses arrive and leave. Sounds of band practice float through the halls; announcements are made over the loudspeakers for club meetings and sports and dances. There are cheerleaders, football players, brains, geeks, jocks, Goths, freaks, heads, and all the other attendant groups. Some students study; some never take home a book.

But there have been changes: the library is now the media center, and the labs hold not just beakers and microscopes but rows of computers linked to the Internet. Most students bring laptops and smartphones to class, and Internet connections are wireless. The school nurse tends to many more serious complaints than headaches, and the guidance counselors deal with problems far beyond deciding which college to attend. Metal detectors guard many school entrances, but deadly violence periodically erupts on school grounds or in the community, and students by the score use—and occasionally sell—drugs and alcohol. In American middle and high schools, myriad languages other than English can be heard in cafeterias, and the student body is a mix of races and ethnic backgrounds.

There are still proms and field trips and romances and schoolwide testing days and pep rallies and bake sales; there also are antibullying programs, security guards in the halls, classes for new mothers, police sweeps of student lockers, and information on teen obesity, AIDS, binge drinking, heroin overdoses, and date rape.

It's school; it's stayed the same in outline, but it has also changed as our society has changed. And it may be frustrating or it may be heartening, but there are virtually no arguments or issues or controversies in education that have not surfaced in some form in previous years and been discussed and debated in previous years. The issues are of course never identical, but perennial concerns abound in education. Let's look at a few such issues that today and in the future will shape—and challenge—your professional life.

Standards and Testing

Remember in Chapter 1, where we talked about the "sea of mediocrity" and the standards and testing movements? If not, recall that in 1983 the United States Department of Education issued *A Nation at Risk*, a report that contended that education was currently drowning in "a sea of mediocrity." Widely read and widely quoted, this report jump-started a movement to establish standards and tests related to those standards in every state in the country, a movement that has influenced classrooms to this day.

The English teachers' major professional organization, NCTE, has crafted twelve standards (NCTE and IRA 1996), and almost all fifty states have similarly agreed-upon standards in English and other subject areas, many of them taken from or adapted from the Common Core. These standards guide not only the curriculum but also testing. You need to be familiar with these standards and knowledgeable about how to implement them in your planning and classroom activities.

In addition, standardized testing, though perhaps the emphasis on the results is currently less fierce than previously, is still for some the only true "accountability" of the public schools to the public. Surely you can recall many tests in your school life; it has been contended that the current generation is the most tested group of students ever. What will ultimately happen to this huge emphasis on testing may not be completely clear, but it does seem that, for the foreseeable future, the influence of standardized tests will do little but expand.

The issue for you, the English language arts teacher, is that much of what you do in class will not always relate to the standardized test, which traditionally relies on multiple-choice questions with single right answers. In addition, the standardized test is largely based on knowledge retention, not judgment or speculation or argument. Finally, because many states feel the pressure to have all students score consistently well on these tests (after all, most states publish these scores by district and even by school, and perhaps soon by teacher), you will likely find yourself pressured to teach only what is noted in your state standards and which, therefore, appears on your state standardized test. You might even, as has happened in some schools, be told to test only in multiple-choice format so students are completely familiar with that kind of test question. If either of these is the case, it could well change your sense of freedom and individualization.

For the present and near future, issues of high-stakes testing and reporting will continue, at least for the thinking teacher, to be a source of tension and contradiction. The balance between authentic teaching of English language arts and the test will remain uneasy.

English Language Learners

As emphasized throughout this book, the public schools are for the public, and that public comes in different colors and from different ethnic and religious and cultural backgrounds. The presence of *multi*cultures in school is surely not new. But what is new, what you will face more squarely in your career than your predecessors in the classroom, is the proportion of students from many cultures and backgrounds and for whom English is a second language. As of this writing, the Latino population in the United States has, in some school districts, outstripped the Anglo population. Immigrants from the Pacific Rim and Asian countries are also growing in influence and number, as are those from Africa and Europe.

The result is an increased awareness in the schools, and in the nation, of differing populations that require, appropriately, representation in the curriculum and in school staff and school culture. Like every one of the issues cited in this section, this is not a passing fad but an issue that is here to stay and that you will face in the classroom.

As the English language arts teacher, your responsibility is to be aware of the variety of your students and, if the material from which you teach is not representative of that variety, to amend or supplement it. Latino writer Rudolfo Anaya demanded this in a speech at an NCTE conference, later reprinted in *English Journal*:

> Our community stretches from California to Texas, and into the Northwest and the Midwest. But not one iota of our social reality, much less our aesthetic reality, is represented in the literature read in the schools. . . . If you are teaching in a Mexican American community, it is your social responsibility to refuse to use the textbook which doesn't contain stories by Mexican American authors. If you teach Asian American children, refuse the textbook which doesn't portray their history and social reality. . . . But you don't have to be teaching in a Mexican American barrio to insist that the stories and social reality of that group be represented in your textbook. You shortchange your students and you misrepresent the true nature of their country if you don't introduce them to all the communities who have composed the history of this country. To deny your students a view into these different worlds is to deny them tools for the future. (1992, 19–20)

The presence of multiple languages and multiple cultures has serious implications for our classroom, our materials, and our interactions with our students. It is our obligation to provide English language learners with support and appropriate instruction.

Today the literal complexion of school is being transformed, and you, as a new teacher, need to be aware of, receptive to, and prepared for students from varying walks of life and for whom English is not their first language. You will also need to ensure that your classroom materials are balanced and inclusive.

Students' Right to Their Own Language

One of the most controversial—and difficult—issues for English teachers is their responsibility to students who speak not English as a second language but English that is considered "nonstandard," English that violates the usage rules we often mistakenly call "grammar." For traditionalists, the role of the English teacher is that of corrector and keeper of the standards; in this scenario, English teachers need to stop their students from speaking or writing in a nonstandard way. The question involves the definition of dialect and also whether it is prestigious or nonprestigious. Linguistics tells us that meaning or intelligibility is rarely the issue; to the contrary, social attitude and cultural norms are more powerful determiners of the value and prestige of a dialect. We know that nonstandard English does not affect the ability to read or think or write and rarely interferes with meaning. It is therefore hard to defend logically the traditional English-teacher-as-corrector role. When we advocate the eradication of nonstandard English in our classroom, we are more in the business of linguistic etiquette than in the business of better communication.

And, for some, the eradication of nonstandard English also means that we are more in the business of racial discrimination than language learning. When some years ago the Oakland, California, school board made public statements regarding Black English Vernacular (BEV), or Ebonics, a firestorm erupted across the United States. Spurred by weak test scores and concerned about Oakland students' ability to perform on such measures, the Oakland school board sought extra funding for their schools. Specifically, the Oakland school board argued that BEV constituted a separate language and, therefore, the Oakland public schools, populated primarily by Ebonics speakers, were eligible for federal funds.

One of the surprising results of the ensuing debate was the revelation that many educators were unfamiliar with much of the research and extensive literature regarding BEV. Some educators, with only a sketchy knowledge of the field, concluded that the Oakland school board and its defenders were, essentially, bringing a new issue to the table—possibly for political and financial reasons. Linguists and knowledgeable language arts teachers know that BEV has been studied, documented, and discussed in the education world for some sixty years or more and, as the noted linguist William Labov (1968) convincingly demonstrated, BEV is, like any dialect, entirely rule governed.

The controversy subsided, however, when it was made clear that the motivation of the Oakland school board was students' acquisition of Standard English. On the other hand, the political volatility of this issue cannot be overemphasized. When Anglo/Caucasian teachers are the prime transmitters of Standard English to Latino and African American students, there is often a real concern about equity and racism. You, as a beginning English teacher, need to be aware that, for many parents and members of the school community, how we talk and how we teach that talk in the classroom are sensitive and controversial matters.

What, though, should an English language arts teacher do? People outside and inside the school expect us to address the issue of standard and nonstandard language in our classes. After debate and discussion and even some soul searching, the National Council of Teachers of English issued *Students' Right to Their Own Language*, a position statement, which, among other things, maintains the following:

> The history of language indicates that change is one of its constant conditions and, furthermore, that attempts at regulation and the slowing of change have been unsuccessful. . . . Dialect is merely a symptom of change. . . . Diversity of dialects will not degrade language nor hasten deleterious changes. Common sense tells us that if people want to understand one another, they will do so. Experience tells us that we can understand any dialect of English after a reasonably brief exposure to it. And humanity tells us that we should allow . . . [all] the dignity of . . . [their] own way of talking. (NCTE 1974, 18)

What does this mean? It means, practically, that when students perceive a need to adopt a different dialect, they will do so—as they do when they leave your class and enter the lunchroom or their cars or their homes. As discussed in Chapter 7, telling or teaching students that their language is *wrong* or *bad* is not only damaging but also *false*. Reminding students, however, that different choices of language are appropriate for different contexts—for example, that their language may influence whether they get a job or a loan, that their language could be a barrier to some people—may be more accurate. If students perceive the need to change, they will do so.

Thus teachers need to offer students a choice of expanding their language rather than wholly rejecting their "home" language. Teachers must offer students instruction but also be sensitive to the fact that students who do not consistently or firmly conform to Standard English or what they perceive as "school talk" may be doing this deliberately. And, we firmly believe, *they have that right*.

Teacher Mark Larson addresses this very issue. Invited to a luncheon honoring a writer, he found that he was dressed too informally and was, to confound his feelings of being out of place, confronted at the meal with "a table spread with, among other things, three forks, two spoons, a stack of plates in graded sizes, and several glasses, one of which contained a napkin folded like a swan" (1996, 92). This is simple etiquette stuff, and Larson, an adult and a professional, was attending the luncheon voluntarily. He found, however, that the event not only made him feel uneasy and resentful—which rule was he going to break next?—but he also connected the event to his students:

> Not knowing the rules of so complex a meal, I knew I ran the risk of making my next ignorant blunder at any moment. . . . I felt conspicuous, as if every move I made revealed my status as an outsider. As my uncertainty increased, so did my resentment. . . . I wanted to grab the wrong damn fork, use it as conspicuously as possible and holler, *I don't want to be one of you anyway!*

How often have we heard variations of *I don't want to be one of you anyway!* in our classrooms? When we listen, we can hear it in our students' anger, in their withdrawal, in their refusal to do "our" work, in their defiant rejection of the prescribed rules of "proper" grammar. Every year, students will proclaim what they think is a fail-safe rule of thumb for taking grammar tests: "If it sounds weird, it's right." I believe they are saying, What you are teaching feels wrong. It isn't me. It's you. I'll play along, but I won't incorporate it into my real life. (92)

Although Larson is not, in this anecdote, offering us a way to teach grammar and usage more effectively, we would be wise to listen to what he is saying about our students who often will resist the teaching of standard usage. For many, and it is not a small issue, *I don't want to be one of you* may be at the heart of their resistance to incorporating "correct grammar" in their writing and their speech. We are not sure that any of us can do a great deal about this by ourselves, but it puts some student behavior in context. Teaching is, as you know, also a political act, and there is little that is more political than correcting and trying to change another's language.

That said, certainly we need to be in a position to offer students language choices and options. African American educator Lisa Delpit writes about this in "The Silenced Dialogue":

To imply to children or adults . . . that it doesn't matter how you talk or how you write is to ensure their ultimate failure. I prefer to be honest with my students. Tell them that their language and cultural style is unique and wonderful but that there is a political power game that is also being played, and if they want to be in on that game there are certain games that they too must play. . . . [S]tudents must be taught the codes needed to participate fully in the mainstream of American life. (1988, 96, 100)

We would hope, as Geneva Smitherman has advanced, that every student will know three languages: first, the "standard" dialect of English or what she terms "the language of wider communication" (1993, 170); a second, "home" dialect of English; and third, one foreign language. With this "tripartite language policy" (Smitherman-Donaldson 1988, 170), students might be more equipped to thrive in the world. It is not outlandish to give students exercises in which they speak or write in first one and then a second dialect. Certainly the Shakespeare-summary exercise in Chapter 5 asks students to write using different forms of language, and its language-play aspect is a large part of the exercise's appeal to students.

Students who want to be taken seriously will choose different language from that chosen by people who are trying to make their audience laugh; their purpose will guide their language. All students know—and instinctively adjust to—the different demands of context, shifting language choices depending on where they are—school, home, work. Students also know that language choices are often made in response to the listener; for example, there are certain phrases and words they would not use with grandparents that would pass unnoticed by their peers. Knowing when to adjust and how to use language to communicate successfully is a more powerful skill than is any monolithic list of (to steal from a title of a language book) *dos*, *don'ts*, and *maybes* of usage.

Teachers as Activist Professionals

Most of us who enter English language arts teaching are not fully prepared for its intimate connection to politics. Whether we like it or not, though, our classrooms and our content are often queried and even controlled by outside forces. We need to be responsive to a community, and, at the same time, assert ourselves as the professionals we are. We need to be activists, to reclaim our classroom in the face of Democrats and Republicans, in the face of liberals and conservatives, in the face of religious and nonreligious alike, in the face of anyone who would dictate to us, use legislation and funding, loss of accreditation, and other punitive measures or threats. We must shape our classrooms and our discourse with our students.

Although these people are often well meaning, sometimes they are not. And most importantly, they are so distant from our schools and our students that their policies have far more to do with partisan ideology than with the reality of teaching and learning. Accordingly, it is often hard to determine who is our friend and who is not in this business; we must look critically at what others outside the classroom advocate for the good of our students and our schools. Then we must make our professional choices, choices that are based on our earned authority, our teaching experience, and choices that are based on sound research and what we know of best practice. And we have that right.

We have always believed in the primacy of the teacher, in the fact that the teacher, who logs more time in the classroom than any local or national politician, than any administrator or school superintendent, is the expert and the professional. He or she knows English language arts, knows students, and knows the institution in which he or she works. We don't accept stories about the widespread presence in our schools of lazy and incompetent and uncaring teachers: the teachers we know are thoughtful, conscientious, hardworking people. They are the members of our communities, and we are proud to be one of them. As teachers, then, we must reclaim our authority in the classroom: the classroom is ours, our province, our field of endeavor, and for us that work, that reclaiming, is wholly in service not of our egos or of our professional advancement but in the service of our common treasure, our students.

And this is something we need to make a concerted effort to tell our parents and the public. Although it is simply not possible for many of us to directly refuse school district or state mandates, to resign from our teaching positions, to put, as it were, our lives and careers and finances at stake, if what we are told to do in our classrooms contradicts what we know is best for students, we must take action. We need to remember that we have a civic, yes, a moral responsibility, to inquire, to question, and, at times, to challenge what is going on around us in the name of education and educational reform. This means asserting ourselves in department, school, and PTA meetings, and becoming active with our professional organizations. There is strength in numbers, but no one will listen to us if we don't first speak.

What is essential is not the national directive, the local curriculum guide, the standards, state or national; it is not the expertise of the administration, the funding of the school district, or even parental support. The foundation, the bedrock, the basis of any change or improvement in education in this country is the individual teacher in the individual classroom, working in service of our students' learning. Teacher Todd DeStigter expresses this in *Reflections of a Citizen Teacher: Literacy, Democracy, and the Forgotten Students of Addison High*:

> In my view, this sense of urgency, this keenly felt desire to do some good in this world, may serve as a prompt for citizen teachers to adopt an expanded notion of their work, especially when that work takes place in contexts where students represent a diversity of cultures and languages. That is, teachers must cultivate an identity not just as instructors of academic content or even as activists dedicated to promoting democracy. Rather, citizen teachers must also think of themselves as social scientists striving to be more attuned to how their students view the world and how their culturally situated values shape the ways they think and live. . . . For I have come to believe that in order to change the world for the better, our actions should begin and end face-to-face, cara-a-cara, with others. In communities such as these, people could no longer be forgotten. (2001, 301–302, 324)

As you begin your life in the classroom, remember that you are a professional, and asserting your authority is not just an option, it is an obligation. As an activist professional, you will ensure that your students and those in your teaching community are not forgotten.

For Your Journal

The four issues cited may be very different from the ones you assume will be the unresolved tensions/perennial problems you will face in your first years as a teacher. If so, what other issues do you think you will have to confront and solve? How will you deal with them? If, on the other hand, the four issues discussed approximately cover what you expect to confront in the classroom, choose *one* and discuss what you feel is an approach to that dilemma, if not a total solution to it. What can a classroom teacher do with this issue?

Staying in the Classroom

The strain of teaching is acknowledged, if not understood, by the popular and educational press. *Burnout*, the accumulation of stress to a critical breaking point, is frequently cited as a reason experienced teachers leave the classroom temporarily or even permanently. And according to the National Commission on Teaching, the number of beginning teachers (those in their first three years) who do not return to their classrooms hovers anywhere between 40 and 30 percent. As exciting as teaching can be, as rewarding as students are, teaching is a high-intensity profession. It is marked by consistent, almost unyielding expectations from a large number of people, students, parents, and administrators alike. In addition, life in a classroom always entails a certain amount of isolation from other professionals; teachers can spend most of their day without any sustained contact with other adults. The pressure, the isolation, and the frequent feeling of being overwhelmed by the demands of the classroom can seem insurmountable after even a few years teaching in school. One of Leila's students, Lauren Dean, wrote about her feelings in the middle of her student teaching:

> I have realized something that I do not like about my new life as a teacher. I am completely oppressed by my workload. What I mean is that I feel as if I am always playing catch-up. The very minute I finally finish grading sixth period's essays, I then have another set of quizzes to grade, or journals to read, or journals to write, or lessons to write . . . right now I do not have a single moment's peace where there is not some type of schoolwork that I could be doing.

Kara Elder, also writing during her student teaching, echoes this, but she has come to what she sees as a partial solution:

> I have spent at least three nights a week at home working, one day a week at school late and every weekend working on school matters. The pace has stressed me to the point of affecting my health. . . . One thing has become clear to me, after my first year as a teacher, the only work I will do for school (except for the occasional task) will be done at the school. My home has to be my sanctuary, and I am even beginning to take that to heart and lessen my loads home as I student teach.

In *Supporting Beginning English Teachers: Research and Implications of Teacher Induction*, authors McCann, Johannessen, and Ricca note the kind of comments beginning teachers make and what those comments might imply. According to *Supporting Beginning English Teachers*, teacher talk is different for those who are likely to leave the classroom after a short period of time. Such teachers will:

- talk about how the workload is unreasonable and hopeless
- talk about the futility of any efforts to correct the problems they see as inherent to teaching
- talk more about their needs than the needs of the students
- talk about their plans to "escape" from teaching
- talk about their limited career choices and their view of teaching as a career compromise.

To the contrary, teachers who are likely to stay in teaching talk about the issues in very different ways. They:

- talk about a sense of duty to help the young people who can benefit from the teacher's instruction
- talk about an interest in developing their teaching skills
- talk about their growth as teachers and can account for factors that have influenced their growth
- talk about strategic plans to make bad situations better
- talk about bad experiences in the school as evidence of the need for good teachers
- talk about disturbing episodes in the school year as shared experiences between students and faculty and not as personal obstacles, aggravations, or attacks. (Mc-Cann, Johannessen, and Ricca, 2005, 35)

Staying in the classroom will, actually, require continuing work on your part. Donald Graves (2001), a teacher for many years, urges teachers to consider the classroom as a source not of stress but of energy and to energize from a number of areas: what we do well ourselves, what our colleagues and students offer, and even the curriculum itself. Leila's student, Lauren Dean, finally concluded that she would need to accept that "teaching is a way of life" and that she could "find some way to celebrate minor accomplishments and minor freedoms" so that she did not continue to feel overwhelmed. And that is where professional organizations may offer you real help and encouragement.

The Personal Nature of Professional Organizations

Some years ago, on the occasion of the seventy-fifth anniversary of her state English-teaching organization, Leila wrote about how that association helped save her fledgling and troubled teaching career. In "Growing Up in VATE" (Christenbury 1989), she named names and told stories; without the organization and its members, other teachers, she doubts she would still be in the classroom today. For Leila, VATE (the Virginia Association of Teachers of English) and NCTE have been professional homes, providing conferences and workshops, books and journals, and more important, teacher friends who continue to stimulate, challenge, and inspire. Ken has been an active member of NCTE since 1989, and he's also been active in the New York State English Council, the Illinois Association of English Teachers, and the Long Island Language Arts Council, in addition to several other national NCTE organizations. These professional groups help us stay in touch with other hardworking, like-minded colleagues who have lots of excellent experience and insight to share. Ken has also recently found a number of Twitter chats, which are fun, informal ways to get information and make connections with colleagues all over the world.

We recommend that if you plan to stay in teaching, you join your local *and* national English-teaching organization. This is, in our opinion, not a luxury but a necessity: those organizations will give you access to thoughtful and tested teaching ideas and provide conferences and workshops where you can share with other teachers. Those people are your colleagues and may, in time, even become your friends—there is, in fact, a highly personal aspect to professional organizations. Regardless, they will influence your own teaching and also give you important companionship in this journey.

TECH TALK: *Professional Communities on the Web*

The Internet has spawned various electronic venues for staying in touch with a wide variety of colleagues, both inside your building and across your state and even nation. These folks can inspire you on your tough days and share your successes on those great days. Here are some things to try:

Twitter: Twitter chats are great ways to engage in real time. You can also read the old chats after they happen. Tweets are by nature short, but they often contain links to longer, very useful sites. Try #edchat, #edtechchat, #tlap, #aplitchat, #ptchat, #engchat, and #nctechat.

Facebook: You already know Facebook, but you may not know you can create a private group based on a shared interest and that many such groups already exist. Do some digging and see what you find.

Voxer: Use this app (on smartphone or laptop/desktop) that easily records oral discussions among a group and create your own professional learning network. It's like a walkie-talkie that saves recordings for when others have time for them. No typing messages or ringing phones. You can speed up the playback, so if you've got a slow-talking colleague, no problem.

TodaysMeet: This site lets you create an invitation-only chatroom that functions like a private Twitter site. It's especially good for synchronous meetings or for establishing backchannel communication during a class or meeting. Then use **Storify** to save the chat for future reading.

Your Own Reading

Under the pressure of writing papers and reports and preparing for class, it may be very tempting to begin—and to continue—to dispense with time for your own reading. Certainly many conscientious teachers take that route, taking time only to glance quickly at the daily news feed or to skim professional magazines and articles. With their long hours and very time-consuming work, gone are any and all afternoons engrossed in a novel or Sunday evenings with the latest best seller.

If you wish to stay in the classroom, we strongly recommend that you not neglect your own personal reading—whatever that reading may be. Whether it be poetry or science fiction, history or romance, gardening or sailing, accounts of Inuit tribes or Italian countesses or hunting in the African veldt, fine literature or popular schlock, we encourage you to keep reading. It's one of the reasons that you got into this business; it feeds you mentally and emotionally. Without time for your own reading interests, your life can become devoid of the special joy that reading gives us. Ken's a fan of historical fiction; Steven Saylor's (1991) well-researched mysteries set in ancient Rome are a favorite—start with *Roman Blood*. Wilbur Smith's (1994) ancient Egyptian adventure novels, are fun, too, such as *River God*. Leila continues to explore memoir, and every year new writers emerge, from photographer Sally Mann's (2015) *Picture This* to Kim Barnes' (2011) *Hungry for the World* to writer Jeanette Walls' (2005) *The Glass Castle*.

Unfortunately, there are many English language arts teachers who have stopped reading; most all of them regret it, and most all of them, citing time pressures, can justify it. If you suspend your own reading, however, we think it will show in your teaching, and it may contribute to some professional unhappiness. On the other hand, if you continue to read you will find that your tastes change and grow, deepening unexpectedly in an area or perhaps shifting into new areas. And make sure that your students see that you read for pleasure. You will be able to share with your students what *you* are reading; you will be doing something for *you*; and your own reading will reinforce, once again, the power and magic of this business of reading and learning.

Becoming a Teacher Researcher

You do not have to be taking a graduate course to do research in your own classroom. As a teacher you may have questions about how or why something did not or did "work" in your classroom. You may want to try out a new technique of instruction or evaluation or organization. Doing your own research with your own students can keep you interested in what is before your eyes and can revitalize your teaching. Although it may seem intimidating or terribly complicated, setting up research in your classroom is not impossible and actually not that difficult; the books cited at the end of this chapter can be a real help to your work and are written by classroom teachers for classroom teachers. Being a student of your own teaching can be illuminating and rewarding. And, as we point out in Chapter 3, being a reflective practitioner is an important way to ensure your teaching is achieving what you think it's achieving for your students.

There are a number of good books on teacher research, but two names you will want to remember are Ruth Shagoury Hubbard and Brenda Miller Power (1999): in *Living the Questions* they offer solid, practical advice about looking at your own teaching and coming to useful conclusions.

For Your Journal

Imagine that you are entering your fifth year of teaching with many more years ahead of you and with a mild case of burnout. What are two challenges that you are confronting, two sources of concern, which might lead to burnout? How do you think you will handle those two problems and renew yourself? Be practical; be specific.

Making the Journey

Most teachers know that of all the figurative language we "explain" to our students, metaphor actually comes easiest. Almost all of us use metaphor regularly in everyday language and, possibly, many of us think in terms of metaphors. In literature, fairy stories, legends, myths, epics, folktales, not to mention poetry, novels, and plays, metaphor is a central element. The metaphors that seem to linger in our minds, the ones that appear and reappear in varying sources, are more likely than not the more central, the more elemental, the more archetypal. And for us, there is a metaphor in life and literature that at least partially represents what we feel this business of teaching is all about.

The metaphor is that of making the journey, a concept so prevalent in literature, in religion, in philosophy, in music, in everyday speech and aphorism that it requires virtually no elaboration. Some describe human existence as a journey from birth to death, and certainly our literature, from across the world and the centuries, is replete with heroes, both male and female, who journey out to discover, rediscover, and confirm. First steps, length, destination, and merit are all part of the lore of the journey metaphor. These heroes go on long and arduous journeys; the more humble travel not so far but with as great an effect. From classic literature to the more contemporary, the metaphor of the journey is widely used.

Who we are when we begin the journey is not, of course, who we are when we end. The journey, of and by itself, shapes and forms us, and often we arrive at a destination a bit differently from the way we had anticipated. And that is the stuff of literature and, of course, of life. The Native Americans who started the Trail of Tears, the African Americans who endured the Middle Passage, the surviving pioneers in the Donner party, and the hopeful immigrants who came to Ellis Island were all different at the end of their journey. Across the Atlantic and Pacific Oceans, the borders of Mexico and Canada, immigrants have made the journey into this country, and that journey has shaped them.

As a teacher, you too make a journey, and you too will change. Your reading, your life in the classroom, and inevitably, the lives of those people with whom you will have such extensive and consistent contact, your students, will alter if not transform you.

What we hope for you as you make your journey is what we hope for ourselves: that we remain open as teachers not only to the wonder of the literature and the language but also to our students' minds and hearts. On our journey, which continues as our teaching lives continue, the twists and turns of the path challenge and provoke and inform, and, we hope, help make us better teachers and better human beings. We hope the same for you.

We have written in this book of the tough times of teaching, and we do not think we have exaggerated. But there is also magic and passion and joy in the classroom; we hope we have written convincingly of that, too. You, also, will see many sides of the teaching life as you make your journey and continue to be and become a teacher of English language arts.

For us—and that is a large part of the authority we claim in this business, our experience—what is contained in English language arts has shaped our lives. The characters in books, the lines from poems, the language we use, the conversations we have, the writing we do, have all formed us as people. Teaching is, for us, utterly central: for both Ken and Leila, we are never more ourselves than when we are in the classroom, and we often think that within the four walls of the classroom is a universe in itself.

Tomorrow we will teach again. Our journey continues. Although we don't make everyone's blood run quicker in every class, every day, we try, and what we teach, the great and glorious English language arts, makes it easier. And the students, for their part, are all the reason to keep trying, are all the reason to make and to continue the journey.

For Your Journal

The metaphor of the journey is just one possible description for teaching. We have changed our own personal metaphors for teaching numerous times—and expect to change them again and again. If at this point in your career you were to pick a metaphor for what you think your teaching life will be or currently is, what would it be? Draw the metaphor or describe it (or both); choose a central image that means something to you and that illustrates your current thinking about the profession of teaching.

References

Anaya, Rudolfo. 1992. "The Censorship of Neglect." *English Journal* 81 (8): 18–20.

Barnes, Kim. 2011. *Hungry for the World*. New York: Anchor.

Brontë, Charlotte. 1994. *Jane Eyre*. Oxford, UK: Oxford University Press.

Christenbury, Leila. 1989. "Growing Up in VATE." *Virginia English Bulletin* 32 (Fall): 77–80.

Christenbury, Leila, ed. 1994. Breaking the Rules Focus. *English Journal* 83 (5).

Cochran-Smith, Marilyn. 2005. "Teacher Education and the Outcomes Trap." *Journal of Teacher Education* 56 (November/December): 411–17.

Conn, Kathleen. 2005. *Bullying and Harassment: A Legal Guide for Educators*. Alexandria, VA: Association for Supervision and Curriculum Development.

Delpit, Lisa. 1988. "The Silenced Dialogue: Power and Pedagogy in Educating Other People's Children." *Harvard Educational Review* 58 (August): 280–98.

DeStigter, Todd. 2001. *Reflections of a Citizen Teacher: Literacy, Democracy, and the Forgotten Students of Addison High*. Urbana, IL: NCTE.

Elbow, Peter. 1993. "Ranking, Evaluating, and Liking: Sorting Out Three Forms of Judgment." *College English* 55 (2): 187–206.

Fenstermacher, Gary D. 1990. "Some Moral Considerations on Teaching as a Profession." In *The Moral Dimensions of Teaching*, edited by John I. Goodlad, Roger Soder, and Kenneth A. Sirontnik. San Francisco: Jossey-Bass.

Graves, Donald H. 2001. *The Energy to Teach*. Portsmouth, NH: Heinemann.

Greene, Maxine. 1988. *The Dialectic of Freedom*. New York: Teachers College Press.

Hicks, Troy. 2013. *Crafting Digital Writing: Composing Texts across Media and Genres*. Portsmouth, NH: Heinemann.

Hill, Marc Lamont. 2013. "*EJ* in Focus: Teaching English in the Age of Incarceration." *English Journal* 102 (4): 16–18.

Hubbard, Ruth Shagoury, and Brenda Miller Power. 1999. *Living the Questions: A Guide for Teacher-Researchers*. York, ME: Stenhouse.

Jones, Stephanie, and James F. Woglom. 2013. "Overcoming Nomos." In *Cultivating Social Justice Teachers*, edited by Paul C. Gorski, Kristien Zenkov, Nana Osei-Kofi, and Jeff Sapp, 27–48. Sterling, VA: Stylus.

Kadjer, Sara. 2010. *Adolescents and Digital Literacies: Learning Alongside Our Students*. Urbana, IL: NCTE.

Katz, Stephen B. 1992. "The Ethics of Expediency: Classical Rhetoric, Technology, and the Holocaust." *College English* 54 (3): 255–75.

Kumashiro, Kevin K. 2015. *Against Common Sense: Teaching and Learning Toward Social Justice*. 3rd ed. New York: Routledge.

Labov, William P. 1968. *A Study of the Non-Standard English of Negro and Puerto-Rican Speakers in New York City*. Final Report, U.S. Office of Education. Cooperative Research Project no. 3288.

Larson, Mark. 1996. "Watch Your Language: Teaching Standard Usage to Resistant and Reluctant Learners." *English Journal* 85 (7): 91–95.

Mack, Nancy. 2012. "*EJ* in Focus: Bullying Reconsidered: Educating for Emotional Literacy." *English Journal* 101 (6): 18–25.

Mann, Sally. 2015. *Picture This: A Memoir with Photographs*. New York: Little, Brown.

McCann, Tom, Larry R. Johannessen, and Bernard P. Ricca. 2005. *Supporting Beginning English Teachers: Research and Implications for Teacher Induction*. Urbana, IL: NCTE.

NCTE. 1974. *Students' Right to Their Own Language*. Urbana, IL: NCTE.

———. 2011. Resolution: Resolution on Confronting Bullying and Harassment. NCTE Annual Convention, Chicago, IL, Friday, November 18.

———. 2015a. Resolution 1: Resolution on Student Educational Data Privacy and Security. NCTE Annual Convention, Minneapolis, MN, Friday, November 20.

———. 2015b. Resolution 2: Resolution on Dismantling the School-to-Prison Pipeline. NCTE Annual Convention, Minneapolis, MN, Friday, November 20.

NCTE and IRA. 1996. *Standards for the English Language Arts*. Urbana, IL: NCTE/IRA.

Nieto, Sonia. 2003. *What Keeps Teachers Going?* New York: Teachers College Press.

Orwell, George. 1980. "Politics and the English Language." In *Eight Modern Essayists*, 3rd ed., edited by William Smart. New York: St. Martin's Press.

Porter, James E. 2005. "The Chilling of Digital Information: Technical Communicators as Public Advocates." In *Technical Communication and the World Wide Web*, edited by Carol Lipson and Michael Day, 243–62. Mahwah, NJ: Lawrence Erlbaum.

Saylor, Steven. 1991. *Roman Blood*. New York: Minotaur Books.

Shakespeare, William. 1942. "Julius Caesar." In *Complete Plays and Poems of William Shakespeare*, edited by William Allan Neilson and Charles Jarvis Hill. Boston: Houghton Mifflin.

Smith, Wilbur. 1994. *River God*. New York: St. Martin's.

Smitherman, Geneva. 1993. "'Students' Right to Their Own Language': A Retrospective." *English Journal* 84 (1): 21–27.

Smitherman-Donaldson, Geneva. 1988. "Discriminatory Discourse on African-American Speech." In *Discourse and Discrimination*, edited by Geneva Smitherman-Donaldson and Tuen A. van Dijk. Detroit: Wayne State University Press.

Spring, Joel. 1985. *American Education: An Introduction to Social and Political Aspects*. 3rd ed. New York: Longman.

Swift, Jonathan. 1984. "A Modest Proposal." In *Jonathan Swift*, edited by Angus Ross and David Woolley. New York: Oxford University Press.

Turner, Kristen Hawley, and Troy Hicks. 2015. *Connected Reading: Teaching Adolescent Readers in a Digital World*. Urbana, IL: NCTE.

Twain, Mark. 1985. *Adventures of Huckleberry Finn*. Berkeley: University of California Press.

United States Department of Education. 1983. *A Nation at Risk*. Washington, DC: U.S. Government Printing Office.

Walker, Alice. 1982. *The Color Purple*. New York: Harcourt Brace Jovanovich.

Walls, Jeanette. 2005. *The Glass Castle*. New York: Charles Scribners.

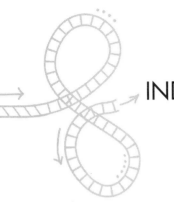

INDEX

Barnett, Ann Byrd, 89
Batman, 207
Beats, Rhymes, and Classroom Life, 281
"The Beauty of Data Visualization," 243
Beckelhimer, Lisa, 247
Beloved, 191
Benson, Jeffrey, 145
Beowulf, 219
Berchini, Christina, 294
The Best American Essays 2015, 232
The Best American Science and Nature Writing, 232
The Best Essays of the Century, 232
Beyond Discipline, 137, 159
"Beyond Grammar: The Richness of English Language," 270
Beyond the Bard, 197
big data, 243
Black English Vernacular (BEV), 379
"Black Walnuts," 179
blaming the students, 78
Blending Genre, Altering Style, 303
block scheduling, 40
Blockbuster Video, 230
blogs, 324
Bloom, Benjamin, 337
Bloom, Harold, 92, 244
body language, 74–75, 350
Bone series, 206
Booklist, 204
Books and the Teenage Reader, 204
Booth, John Wilkes, 232
Bootstraps: From an American Academic of Color, 274
Borrowed Finery, 233
Both Art and Craft, 217
Bowers, Neal, 179
Boys and Literacy, 142–43
Bracey, Gerald W., 42
Bradstreet, Anne, 212
Brandt, Deborah, 1, 9, 29, 33
"Breakings," 178, 179–83
Brief Intervals of Horrible Sanity, 89
Brooks, Gwendolyn, 193
Brown Girl Dreaming, 203
Bruner, Jerome, 30
Bryson, Bill, 262, 263
Buffalo Springfield, 238
Built to Last, 234
bulletin boards, in classroom, 64
Bullough, Robert V. Jr., 89

bullying, 25, 366
 addressing, 61–62
 cyberbullying, 26
bumper stickers, 276
Burke, Jim, 246, 343
burnout, 383–85
Bush, George W., 40
Butterworth, Jan, 17

Campbell, Joseph, 238
Campbell, Melissa, 14, 17, 44
"Can Good Composition Teaching Be Done Under Present Conditions?," 308
Capote, Truman, 232
Cardenas, Rafael Velazquez, 146
Cardinal Principles of Secondary Education, 29
career readiness, 121–23
Careless Love, 233
Carillo, Ellen C., 174
Carlsen, G. Robert, 204
Carlson, James R., 238
Carnegie, Andrew, 263
Cash, Johnny, 238
"Cask of Amontillado," 189, 190
Cassar, Erin McCrossan, 280
The Catcher in the Rye, 12, 25, 202
Catron, Carol Smith, 144–45
censorship, 208–10
Center Stage, 197
central claim, determining, 304
Chadwick, Jocelyn A., 237
change, disruptive nature of, 375–77
Chanteleau, Connie, 331
Charlotte's Web, 203
Chasing Lincoln's Killer, 232
Chaucer, Geoffrey, 171
Chernow, Ron, 233
The Chicago Manual of Style, 258, 261
Chopin, Kate, 189, 190
Christiansen, Mark A., 288
Cirelli, Michael, 216
Cisneros, Sandra, 107, 120, 246
"Citizen's Request for the Reconsideration of a Work of Literature," 208
City, Elizabeth A., 348
Claggett, Fran, 302
class journal, 325
Classcraft website, 159
classics, 204–205
 graphic novels based on, 206–207
 young adult literature as, 203

classroom
 arrangement of, 66–67, 71, 348
 avoiding burnout in, 383–85
 discipline in, 59–63
 environment, 63–69
 games in, 159
 information about, 73
 library, 64, 65
 life in the, 57–58
 observation in, 52
 rules in, 70, 71
 running, 70
 supplies for, 68
 underlife of, 54
Cleopatra, 233
Coates, Ta-Nehisi, 307
Cochran-Smith, Marilyn, 375
code-meshing, 280, 281, 284
Code-Meshing as World English, 281
code-switching, 279–80, 284
Code-Switching: Teaching Standard English in Urban Classrooms, 280
Code-Switching Lessons, 279
Codell, Esmé Raji, 89
Colbert, Stephen, 242
"Cold Snap," 342–43
Coleridge, Samuel Taylor, 175
college, preparing for, 121–23
Collier, Virginia P., 282
Collins, Billy, 193
The Color Purple, 359
Commission on the Reorganization of Secondary Education, 29
Common Core CPR, 124
Common Core State Standards (CCSS), 31, 32, 89, 205, 213, 235
 and college and career readiness, 121–23
 controversies about, 17, 119
 as guides, 123–24
 role of, 118–21
 shortcomings of, 136–37
 and Standardized English, 257, 259
 standards and skills in, 259–60
 on vocabulary, 266–88
community action, informational texts and, 246
community of meaning, 180
Conan Doyle, Arthur, 24
concrete operational thought, 21
Connected Reading, 365